THE COMPLETE BOOK OF CHURCH GROWTH

CORE
Group

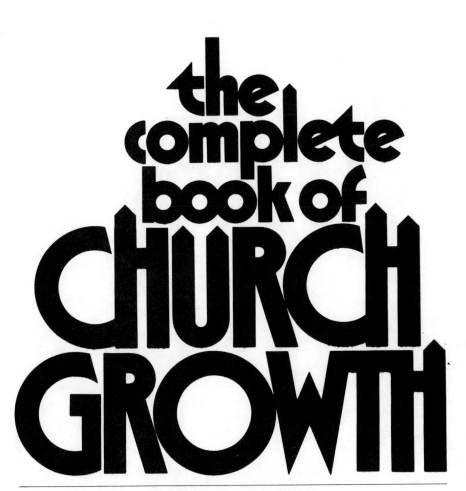

the complete book of CHURCH GROWTH

ELMER L. TOWNS
John N. Vaughan
David J. Seifert

Tyndale House Publishers, Inc.   Wheaton, Illinois

With gratitude
and loving affection
to our families,
especially our wives,
Ruth, Joanne, and Susan.

Library of Congress Catalog Card Number 80-54490. ISBN 0-8423-0408-8. Copyright © 1981 by Elmer L. Towns, John N. Vaughan, and David J. Seifert. All rights reserved. First printing, May 1981. Printed in the United States of America.

CONTENTS

PREFACE

Church growth is a modern phenomenon that crosses denominational and theological lines. You can find it in every part of this country and other nations. It knows no ethnic or regional barrier.

Because of these facts, everyone and everything having to do with the making of this book—authors, contributors, data, research, case studies—have come from diverse perspectives. The aim of the authors has been to examine growing churches, wherever those churches may be, and to acknowledge all possible reasons for that growth. This book includes some examples of growing churches that embrace doctrines and life-styles with which the authors disagree. Also, the contributors to this volume by no means concur on the issues of church growth. It might be said as well that the three authors come from various church backgrounds and differ on certain church matters, which, however, do not affect the fundamentals of the faith.

In short, *The Complete Book of Church Growth* is not married to denominationalism or sectionalism. There is strength in diversity. The reader can be assured that this book is committed not to the advancement of a particular church's view, but to the principle of growing churches.

The Complete Book of Church Growth is the most comprehensive book on church growth in print. It combines statistical research with biblical exegesis and informed opinion to provide student and layman with a complete, accurate, and contemporary view of church growth. It is hoped that this book will succeed both as a research tool and as a practical guide for churches, a map charting the good roads and the bad, the safe avenues to growth as well as the treacherous ones.

Dr. Elmer Towns is known for his research among large Sunday schools and is on the staff of Thomas Road Baptist Church, an independent Baptist church that has grown through aggressive evangelism.

Rev. John Vaughan, a graduate of Southwestern Baptist Theological Seminary (Ft. Worth, Texas), has also studied at the Institute for American Church Growth in Pasadena, California. For this study he has visited many growing churches. Vaughan is assistant pastor of the East Park Baptist Church in Memphis, Tennessee, a Southern Baptist church identified by the Home Mission Board of the Southern Baptist Convention as the twenty-fourth fastest growing among the 35,000 Southern Baptist churches in the United States during the past decade. Vaughan has worked in churches with memberships ranging from fifty to 5,000 members and brings this perspective to the book. (Towns and Vaughan may disagree on the application of the traditional laws of Sunday school growth, but they agree upon the basic strength of these laws.)

Dr. Dave Seifert is pastor of Big Valley Grace Community Church in Modesto, California, a Grace Brethren church that is growing through a balanced outreach. The strength of his ministry is preaching and discipling. While he has one of the outstanding Sunday schools in America, his church has grown through his pulpit ministry. When Dr. Seifert went to Modesto, the church was considered small by America's standards, but under his ministry, it has moved into the mid-size category. Dr. Seifert, then, has been involved with both small and mid-size church congregations in a small city.

And so, the experience and background brought to this book are considerable, the authors well-informed of that which they write. Indeed, the personal experience with actual church problems and dilemmas may be one of the most significant features of *The Complete Book of Church Growth*.

It is hoped that this project will prove valuable in the further discussion of church growth and that some of the ideas provided here will prod churches into new stages of numerical and spiritual development.

INTRODUCTION

Church growth is a subject that rushed to prominence in the United States during the 1970s. Certainly churches were growing before then; churches have been growing since Pentecost. But in past ages churchmen have been concerned about doctrine and spiritual life. Little was said about practical theology as manifested in the methods of ministry. Only in the last decade has church growth become a matter of public and academic fascination.

Why now? Well, ours is an age in which the American church has not been paid much respect. Gallup Polls have shown that Americans are losing confidence in their churches. Statistics have declined across the board: membership, attendance, offerings, recruitment of new clergy, and construction of church buildings. The religious life of the seventies has been characterized as despondent and deteriorating. However, some churches have grown phenomenally. These rare cases command people's attention. News that some churches have grown and grown large has encouraged smaller churches in the U.S. and abroad. As a result, renewed attention has been focused on the church growth movement.

The church growth phenomenon is a reaction to several trends in our society. First, America has given itself over to the measurement of institutions and the statistical evaluation of education. We have developed standardized tests, percentiles, and median scores. It is perhaps only natural that Americans would attempt to measure and analyze the church. Second, more attention has been paid to the efficiency of organizations. It follows that the church too should be studied in the light of improving its outreach and ministry. Third, there has been a communication explosion in America. The time is right for journalism and media to focus on church decline and growth. The question is being asked: "Why are some churches growing and others declining?"

The Complete Book of Church Growth begins with an analysis of church growth in the 70s, continuing with a research survey that investigates church growth trends for the 80s. Along with these chapters is a series of tables, located in Part VII at the back of the book, which measures church growth in five areas: church membership, total church giving, attendance at Sunday morning preaching services, Sunday school enrollment, and Sunday school attendance.

Perhaps one of the most practical helps to the church worker or the church growth advocate is to see churches in action. Part II, "Success Stories in

Church Growth," profiles twelve churches. These are churches of various sizes and different purposes, but each in its own way is growing and maturing.

Part III of the book, "Church Growth in Church Groups," examines church growth as it occurs among fundamentalists, charismatics, Southern Baptists, and mainline denominations, among others. Part IV, "Church Growth Methods," explains how church growth is achieved. This chapter includes explorations of soul-winning evangelism, research and scientific analysis, aggressive leadership, and faith and goal-setting. You may recognize some of these methods from their use in your own church.

What does the Bible say about how churches grow? What pictures or images of the church do we find in Scripture? Then, how can these "church portraits" be translated into practical, contemporary church methods? These questions are answered in "Church Growth and the Bible," Part V of the book, in chapters on the pictures, purposes, and priorities of the church as represented in the Word of God.

Frankly, *The Complete Book of Church Growth* is not the only book on the subject. Actually, there have been several outstanding books on church growth in the past few years. By reprinting some of these writings, the authors of *The Complete Book of Church Growth* hope to make an exhaustive contribution to the discussion of church growth. Consequently, this book includes both original and reprinted articles from these leading authorities in the field: E. S. Anderson, Win Arn and Charles Arn, Gene A. Getz, D. James Kennedy, Leon Kilbreth, Donald A. McGavran, C. Peter Wagner, and Tetsunao Yamamori. This makes up Part VI.

It is hoped that *The Complete Book of Church Growth* will be a valuable resource in the study of church growth, that its parts, just described, have been arranged logically and efficiently, and that its thoughts and ideas amply reflect the illumination of the Holy Spirit.

Church Growth
in the Seventies and Eighties

1. Sunday School and Church Growth in the Seventies

The stage must be set by reviewing the past decade. In the seventies the church/Sunday school experienced rapid and uneven, yet segmented, periods of growth.[1] While some churches were exploding in attendance, others in the same neighborhood were deteriorating in several areas of measurement.[2] Then, as though several decades were compressed into a few years, some of the rapid-growing Sunday schools of the seventies declined as they approached the eighties.

The Sunday schools that grew seemed happy, yet often they were unaware of the causes of their exploding growth. At the same time other Sunday schools worked hard for growth and even emulated growing churches but were frustrated or discouraged because they could not grow.

Sunday school growth could be characterized as elusive and confusing. A few schools experienced explosive growth, others marginal growth, but only a few seemed to understand the factors that produced it: culture, theology, mobility, revivalism/emotionalism, leadership, advertising, national temperament, and sociological factors in church families or denominations.[3] Therefore, a look at the factors of Sunday school growth in the seventies is necessary to lay a foundation for understanding Sunday school growth in the eighties.

The big-church/Sunday school phenomenon is the first thing that must be analyzed.[4] At the beginning of the seventies there was only one Sunday school averaging over 5,000 in attendance. Today there are five Sunday schools that size.[5] Research has shown that only twelve Sunday schools averaged more than 2,000 in attendance in 1968.[6] Today there are forty-nine that large. The largest Sunday school in America is First Baptist Church, Hammond, Indiana, with a reported average attendance of over 15,101.

The cause of these large Sunday school multimillion-dollar budgets has been analyzed. Some credit their appearance to American affluence, mobility, advertisement, or the influence of newly discovered ecclesiastical leadership by the pastor. Some have attributed their growth in the last decade to the annual listing of the "100 Largest Sunday Schools" in *Christian Life* magazine or the book *The Ten Largest Sunday Schools*. They note that the attraction of the listing's snob appeal motivated others to duplicate the same effort and build their church to the same size.

Others have said that America's failure in Vietnam was spiritual in nature, that the nation was motivated to demonstrate its spiritual success, and that large churches were the best avenue of such achievement. However, the large-church phenomenon of the seventies had worldwide manifestations, and none of the causal factors associated with American churches was evident in the large churches/Sunday schools around the world.

During the early seventies the mainline denominations experienced a downward trend in statistical indicators. Toward the end of that decade, they bottomed out, but the indicators have not yet pointed upward. Yet, some individual mainline denominational churches did grow in certain areas during the 1970s.

What mainline denominational churches are doing wrong may give us a clue as to what other churches are doing right. The cause of decline could be theological,[7] bureaucratic,[8] lack of excitement/commitment, lack of church planting, old facilities and/or location,[9] or lack of adaptation of new techniques to reach and evangelize.[10]

As America entered the seventies, she was embroiled in a war in Vietnam with severe repercussions at home. The mood of the country was anti-institutional, which included an anti-church feeling. A speaker told the Greater Chicago Sunday School Convention, "By 1980 the Sunday school will be functionally inoperative."[11]

The influence of the "group dynamic" movement in the church was almost cultic in its claims, though it had its positive results. However, its anti-institutional mood reflected the times. As a result, some people advocated abandoning the traditional church and assembling in small groups. People seemed to withdraw from churches of social success and power, especially those which could be measured quantitatively. There was a retreat to the inner/personal expressions of Christianity reflected in the Body Life and the living-room church.

In this milieu, a new breed of rugged individualists known as "fundamentalists" rose to prominence. The pastor did not take his marching orders from society or denominational headquarters. He tried to win as many people to Christ as possible. He felt the evidence of God's blessing upon his life was manifested by a growing church, and he used every means possible to obtain that goal. He bought a printing press and mailed a church newspaper to those in his neighborhood. He advertised extensively and purchased large plots of land for church campuses. He built buildings for the crowds. They sang enthusiastically and he preached evangelistically. Sunday school busing became a characteristic of this type of church growth.

The middle of the seventies marked a leveling off of fundamentalist growth.[12] The Arab oil embargo curtailed busing. Inflation eroded churches' extra money for advertising, employing staff members, and general expansion. The investigation by the Securities and Exchange Commission dried up the easy access these churches had to bond money. Hence, the building of new facilities slowed down.

Strong "negative" preaching by fundamentalists contributed to their growth. Americans perceived that the nation's morals were slipping, and the public responded to the authoritative message of the fundamentalists. However, the success of their pulpit became counterproductive by such tangential issues as the morality of pantsuits and long hair.

Also, fundamentalists seemed to de-emphasize organization and administration as a valid means to a growing church. To them, the causes of growth are the pastor, soul-winners, Sunday school teachers, and paid staff members. Another reason for the mid-seventies slowdown was that fundamentalist churches did not consolidate their gains by involving their people in the work of the church, thus minimizing their efficiency.

Church growth experienced by independent Baptists in the first part of the 1970s shifted to many other conservative/evangelical groups in the last part of the decade. These other groups were Southern Baptists, Nazarenes, Churches of God, Assemblies of God, and other church groups perceived as moderate in theology and posture. Many leaders in these groups confessed that they learned about church growth from independent Baptists. However, an observation is in order. These groups acquired the positive aspects of church growth without picking up its liabilities. The moderate groups had a commitment to discipleship, organization and administration, quality education, financial stability, and meeting the needs of their people in the total local assembly. When these groups studied the independent Baptists, they learned enthusiasm, warm preaching, innovative techniques of outreach, and pastoral leadership.

At the beginning of the seventies Sunday school attendance was usually larger than Sunday morning church attendance. However, at the end of the decade, the reverse was true; church attendance was almost universally larger than Sunday School attendance.[13]

At the beginning of the 1970s Sunday school busing was introduced to the Christian education world as a technique of growth used by the independent Baptist churches. Quickly, most conservative denominations adapted busing as an outreach technique. But the Arab oil embargo was the main influence to reverse the trend. Also, those Sunday schools that had gotten into busing for the wrong reasons found that busing was expensive, involved hard work, demanded extra teaching staff, additional facilities, and usually introduced to the Sunday school children from lower-class areas who brought discipline problems. Some Sunday schools found that the philosophy of busing evangelism was inconsistent with their established philosophy of nurturing.[14]

Busing will continue as a viable force among conservative churches that are committed to evangelistic outreach, especially within the transient areas of their society. It will not be an effective tool for the larger and established churches and Sunday schools but will be employed by "first generation" churches with age-graded and departmentally graded Sunday schools.

The energy problems of America could work to the advantage of the busing churches in the eighties because busing will conserve gas, especially in light of possible rationing.[15]

The growing Sunday schools of the eighties will be those perceived by the public as conservative/religious in nature, reflecting historic Christianity. This means they will be accepted by the stable sections of society and will be visible, accessible, and dominant.

2. Sunday School and Church Growth in the Eighties

Part VII of this book is a listing of the 100 largest churches and Sunday schools in America, the result of research done to form a portrait of the church in the eighties.

Originally, this research aimed to find the 400 largest churches in each of five areas (church membership, total church giving, attendance at Sunday morning preaching services, Sunday school enrollment, and Sunday school attendance). However, the researchers found that in four of the five categories there weren't enough large churches to fill the listing. (Large churches were arbitrarily identified by the figure 1200 or more.) Only in the category of church membership could 400 large churches be listed.

This idiosyncrasy led the researchers to four conclusions:

1. Churches regard membership as the most important measurement of church work.

2. Americans do not transfer their membership from churches after they move from an area, and many churches do not prune their membership lists.

3. Church membership is a status symbol, thus producing more membership than involvement.

4. Some Americans join churches simply because of a social pressure "to do the religious thing."

Consequently, we can determine the number of large churches by measuring their memberships, but that does not often match up with the measurement of a church according to its attendance, giving, involvement, or the more elusive figure of persons' loyalty to their church.

The goal to list the 400 largest churches in each of the five categories had to be dropped. Instead 100 largest churches have been identified, all of which fall within the large church category of 1200 or more.

This research enables us to summarize seventeen facts about the church/Sunday school as it stands today and to generate some predictions about what is likely to happen to the church/Sunday school in the 1980s.

1. There are relatively few large churches. The lack of large churches in America (in all categories) can be established as an identifiable fact. Whereas many might have thought there were more large churches because church attendance tends to be greater than Sunday school attendance, the fact is there are not that many more.

Ten years ago, the prediction was made in *The Ten Largest Sunday Schools* that by 1980 there would be 100 churches in America which averaged over

2000 in attendance. Some might have forecast an even higher figure. In fact, by 1980 there were only ninety-four churches in America with over 2000 in attendance.

2. There has been a decline in Sunday school enrollment figures. In attempting to gather material for this study, three facts became evident concerning Sunday school enrollment. First, enrollment in individual Sunday schools was not nearly as high as might be anticipated. This is because many Sunday schools are not placing as great an emphasis on enrolling children as in former days. Among Southern Baptists the stress on enrollment almost doubles the number of pupils in attendance. (Among other denominations the formula is not as reliable.) The lack of attention given to enrollment by individual Sunday schools indicates that fewer accurate predictions concerning Sunday schools can be made from enrollment statistics.

Today, many Sunday schools do not even keep enrollment figures. A careful examination of the charts will indicate many Sunday schools are listed on the chart of the 100 largest in attendance, but do not appear on the 100 largest in enrollment. Many of these Sunday schools use their mailing lists as the enrollment list. When this is done, we can question if those Sunday schools are adequately following up their pupils, if they are adequately measuring the growth of their pupils, and if they are giving adequate attention to meeting the needs of the pupils.

The third observation concerning Sunday school enrollment involves the denominations which no longer keep it. When research was done for the book, *The Ten Largest Sunday Schools* (1969), it was almost impossible to compile the figures of average weekly Sunday school attendance because most denominations did not keep the figures. At that time, it was easy to secure the figures for Sunday school enrollment because most Sunday schools and denominations kept that enrollment. However, the tables are now reversed. Today most denominations keep attendance and not enrollment. What has happened is that over the past ten years Sunday school attendance has become paramount in the attention of statisticians. Each year, denominational officials have been requested to supply statistics for the fastest growing Sunday school in each state and the 100 largest Sunday schools, which were printed in *Christian Life* magazine. At the same time, denominational officials have indicated that very few people have requested enrollment figures. As a result they have begun keeping attendance figures rather than enrollment figures.

Whereas it's difficult to draw conclusions from today's Sunday school enrollment figures, still we wonder if a deterioration process has not set in. Dean Kelly in *Why Conservative Churches Are Growing* indicates what has generally been known, i.e., that when Sunday school enrollment figures decline, eventually church membership follows the same pattern and also declines.

3. The Sunday school is no longer a single-purpose organization. During the early seventies, Sunday schools were characterized for their dynamic strength in one area, such as busing, auditorium Bible classes, contests, or other forms of aggressive outreach into the community. These Sunday schools could be characterized as being single-purpose institutions. However, recent statistics have shown that Sunday schools which grew because of a single purpose could also plateau or decline because of a limited foundation. The busing Sunday school was crippled by the Arab oil embargo and the rapid rise in fuel cost. The Sunday school built on contests was handicapped with short-term growth because it put emphasis on the results it sought rather than on the conditions that would bring about the results. The Sunday schools that continued growing throughout the seventies were those that were: (a) based on the Word of God, (b) based on meeting the needs of individuals, (c) had a solid New Testament concept of evangelism and follow-up, and (d) were led by individuals who personified the goals of the church and had the ability to promote, persuade, and finance.

4. The largest attendance has switched from Sunday school to the preaching service. Whereas in the early seventies most churches were growing because of their Sunday schools, this is seldom the case today. Actually, approximately 90 percent of most churches have larger morning services than Sunday school attendance. During the early seventies, the Sunday school was the main outreach into the community. However, this is no longer the case. There are several reasons for this subtle shift in emphasis. First, the average American thinks that Sunday school is for kids; they do not identify it with the total family. Second, the average American is looking for a metaphysical religion. They want a church that talks about the existence of God, sin, salvation, and the demands of a holy life upon their daily living. Most people find this in the conservative, evangelical, fundamental churches. As a result, they have been attending the preaching service because they were the most visible in the community. Now, the Sunday school can no longer be the steeple which attracts people; it must be the foundation upon which the superstructure is built.

5. Growth is built upon Bible study. The Sunday schools which have experienced continual growth during the seventies have been those which have been built upon a systematic, comprehensive teaching of Scripture and doctrine. It is possible for a Sunday school to mushroom overnight, but many of those that did not have quality teaching soon topped out. Some reversed the trend. The Sunday school of the future should not have to sacrifice growth for Bible teaching; both can operate together. Those church builders who feel they must substitute growth for quality education are just as wrong as those who are so committed to quality education that they do not grow.

6. A church member's attitude toward Bible study reflects the Church's attitude toward studying the Bible in Sunday school. Fast-growing Sunday schools that have neglected quality education have not been able to sustain their growth nor keep their gains. Ultimately, a fast-growing Sunday school without solid Bible teaching will plateau or decline in attendance. However, some have deceived themselves by making evangelism so important that they have minimized Bible study. They justify their imbalance by stating, "At least we won some to Christ." One can ask if those who claimed to be converted but who dropped out of the church were in fact converted. And, did the church have such a deep commitment to the Bible after all, since it allowed those who made decisions to drop out?

As a result of this study, the researchers conclude that those Sunday schools with sloppy Bible teaching could not be characterized as New Testament churches, no matter what numerical gains they have exhibited. Second, Sunday schools with high standards for quality education reflect a church where people are desirous of the Word and probably studying the Scriptures at home.

7. *Curriculum is absolutely essential for growth.* When the book *The Ten Largest Sunday Schools* was written, only three of the churches used a prepared curriculum in the Sunday school. The other seven wrote their own curriculum ("writing one's curriculum" is another phrase for *indigenous curriculum*, i.e., that which is prepared by the local church for its own use). However, nine of the ten churches used a prepared curriculum in 1980.

The benefits of a Sunday school curriculum are apparent. It offers a systematic, comprehensive, complete coverage of doctrine, Bible knowledge, and Christian living. While the researchers could find no cause and effect relationship between a good curriculum and growth, certainly there is a correlation. However, not all Sunday schools that experienced growth are properly using a Sunday school curriculum. As a matter of fact, the opposite is true. There are many Sunday schools that use an effective curriculum but are not experiencing growth. This is another way of saying that one may build a foundation (curriculum) without building a house (Sunday school growth). Not all of those who build a foundation go on to complete the house.

Curriculum content will have a significant effect on Sunday school growth in the eighties. The liberal drift of theology has produced humanism and secularism. The commitment that a person makes to become involved in Sunday school is a significant one. If the message of the Sunday school is not significantly different from the message of public schools, media, or society in general, the public will not make a commitment to attend Sunday school.[1] The public wants to hear an authoritative message of redemption, it wants God's direction for its culture, and it wants eternal answers to the problems it faces.[2]

8. *Doctrine and growth.* If the doctrine of the church was the issue of the seventies, the eighties will likewise be concerned with doctrine. For many

reasons, those who come to Sunday school will have questions and needs. Just as preaching must speak to modern issues with answers from doctrine, so teaching must be adapted to individual needs with answers from the Word of God. But beyond this, people who are searching for structure in their lives will demand a structure in their faith. As a result, the lay public will increasingly be interested in systematic theology that is authoritative and relevant.

9. *Methods of teaching and growth.* Teaching techniques also have a limited influence on Sunday school attendance. Tied to the content of curriculum is the method of instruction — techniques cannot be divorced from curriculum. The psychology of learning must produce a tie between divine revelation and life experience.[3] Not only must Sunday school hold to an authoritative revelation, it must be communicated with authority.[4] Also, since the teacher cannot be disassociated from his content and his method, the teacher must be an authoritative person.[5] The degree of growth in the future will be tied to the credibility of the Sunday school's message, method, and teachers.

10. *Sunday school leadership and growth.* The Sunday school growth of the eighties will be tied to leadership. We cannot assume that the program will grow indigenously.[6] The function of a prophet/seer is mandatory for Sunday school expansions, because out of this will emerge goals, priorities, and response to divine mandates.[7] The Sunday school leader interprets the questions of whom shall we educate, what shall we teach, when . . ., where . . ., and how. It is said, "A church is the length and shadow of its leader," and Sunday school is no different. But leadership does not imply dictatorship or even dominance. As the United States has a growing concern for individual rights, the growing Sunday school must be responsible to its people, must involve its people, and must build up its people.

This means the pastor must be involved in Sunday school, for this is one of the best areas through which he can pastor his people. He must assume a greater responsibility for Sunday school growth. Also, the job description of the Sunday school superintendent must undergo a thorough revision to include responsibility for growth. This must also extend to the professional minister of Christian Education, although often he has not assumed responsibility for growth and outreach. Finally, the Sunday school teacher must assume his responsibility for growth. Not only must these leadership positions include outreach as part of their job description, each person must internalize this responsibility and become an outreach agent.

11. *The impact of children upon Sunday school.* In former years, approximately 40 percent of the Sunday school attendance has been adults. However, the percentage of adult population in the United States will be growing more rapidly in the eighties than the population of children. The children's population will decline. This is because of abortion-on-demand, more couples choosing not to have children, plus the longevity of life; in short, there will be more adults, which means we should have a larger percentage of adults in

Sunday school. An examination of the statistics of Sunday school growth revealed that currently very few schools are growing in childhood population. Whereas in the early seventies many of the Sunday schools grew because of the bus ministry (which was mostly children), this is not the truth today. The number of children in the Sunday school will follow the national population trend. As a result, we can expect the children's division to go down in attendance. This means several things for Sunday school. First, the impact of busing will diminish somewhat. Second, growth will have to come from an age group besides children. Third, since children are the fruit of marriage, the church must teach its young families the biblical position on having children.

12. The greatest growth is now found among ages twenty to thirty-five. Historically there has been a dropout period in the Sunday school during the teenage years, but the pupils returned to church after they were married. This trend will continue in the future, but what percentage of the young people will return is yet to be seen. At the present the greatest growth in Sunday schools is found among young adults, ages twenty to thirty-five.

The Arab oil embargo that forced many churches out of the bus ministry may have been a blessing rather than a hindrance. Many churches have now turned their efforts to reaching families who can drive to church. After several years of ministry, those churches that have allowed their bus attendance to drift downward, while at the same time reaching more couples, will have a longer and more fruitful ministry in the future.

Approximately 75 percent of the churches that are presently experiencing growth are doing so among the young adults. Therefore, those churches which want to grow will have to: (a) start more classes for the young adults, (b) create programs and topics that will minister to the needs of young adults, (c) help young adults apply Christianity to contemporary problems, and (d) provide strong Bible teaching and doctrine on which to build young lives (especially since public education is so pervaded by humanistic philosophy).

13. The three elements of building an effective young adult class. Young adults are not choosing churches just because they are doctrinally correct, nor do they seek out churches that have special names for their young adult Sunday school classes. A program must be adapted to meet the needs and desires of the young adults. The three characteristics of effective young adult classes are (a) the coffee pot, (b) the overhead projector, and (c) the question. Not that these three items automatically guarantee success, but they are reflective of attitudes that must be adopted to minister to the needs of the young single adults.

Many young adult church programs begin their classes with informal fellowship and a cup of coffee. The key is not coffee, but the fellowship that the coffee pot symbolizes and effects. Bible study that is effective must be conducted in an atmosphere of fellowship. Young adults must get to know one another and be able to internalize the Word of God in a warm, accepting atmosphere.

Second, certainly an electronic visual aid such as the overhead projector is not any guarantee of a successful Bible class. However, when an overhead projector is used, it makes it possible for the teacher to reflect his teaching outline on the wall for the pupils to see. This forces the teacher to explain and illustrate rather than lecture. Young adults will not naturally go to hear lectures about the authorship of Exodus or the geography of Palestine. They want to be exposed to Bible principles that will help them live the Christian life.

Finally, the question is an essential element of successful young adults classes. Young people want to become involved in the teaching-learning process. The teacher must ask questions which create needs. Then young adults will want to ask questions that will meet their needs. And remember, teaching *is* meeting needs.

14. The auditorium Bible class. During the early seventies the auditorium Bible class (ABC), also called the Pastor's Bible Class, was one of the key techniques in building a growing Sunday school. At that time many Americans sat in small Sunday school classes which were drab and uninteresting. But excitement was generated when adults were moved into the large auditorium and exposed to an exciting master teacher. Many adults who were well-trained in their small discussion classes got caught up in the excitement of the large class. They became involved in reaching other adults, and the whole auditorium Bible class grew. But now, after ten years of emphasis on the auditorium Bible class, apathy has set in. Teachers have found it is easier to lecture than to prepare discussions and use the overhead projector. As a result, many of the large auditorium Bible classes are declining in attendance. To offset this trend, many Sunday schools are dividing the large class into smaller adult classes designed to meet their needs. However, the concept of the auditorium Bible class should not be completely eliminated.

Many Americans do not want to become involved in small groups. They want to visit a church and hear the message, but they do not want to become involved. The auditorium Bible Class is the place where visitors can make a first contact with Bible study. As such, the ABC can become the handshake with the Sunday school. After visitors become involved with a master teacher in the auditorium setting, they can become involved in the smaller classes that meet their needs.

The auditorium Bible Class, as well as all classes, should include a maximum use of visuals, including the overhead projector, charts, blackboards, tackboards, and other means of visual aids. America has become a visual society and young adults have grown up learning many of their attitudes toward life from television. It is said that over 75 percent of all their learning endeavors come through the visual channels. As a result, the church cannot resort to the audio channel exclusively and expect young people to learn and grow in Christ.

15. The preaching service is the tool for building churches. It has become apparent that the major tool in building church attendance is the Sunday morning preaching service. Obviously, it must be supported by Sunday school, counseling, evangelistic outreach, and other services of the church. Since the preaching service is the major tool in building the service, pastors will have to give more attention than ever before to the preparation and delivery of their messages. Musicians will need to give more attention to excellence in preparation and communication of both music and message.

16. Church growth and the electronic church. The influence of the electronic church on local church/Sunday school growth must be discussed, and the question must be raised, "Should there be an electronic Sunday school?" It was only natural that an electronic age would produce an electronic church. Since Americans are conditioned to receive news, commentary, information, and inspiration from electronic sources, it was only natural that the church should communicate to individuals through electronic sources.

The church seems unable to continue supplying society with competent pastors and churches which can adequately minister to growing masses and their increasingly unique needs. As a result, the electronic church will receive a growing reception by the masses. Therefore, the Sunday school of the eighties will be effective to the extent that it is supported and reinforced by the electronic church.

Also, as the energy crisis confronts society, many will be unwilling to travel to local churches, but will turn to television for religious stimulation, worship, and information. Denominations will have to begin national television programs of worship and education to accomplish their aims.

17. Christian schools and growth. The causes were analyzed in the *Journal Champion* as to why many churches stop growing when they begin Christian day schools as part of their ministry.[8] First, it was noted that money was usually diverted from buses, advertisement, and salary for personnel in evangelism. It went to the Christian school. Second, it was observed that the pastor became a leader of the school, which took his time from outreach and pastoring the flock. He became involved in administration and handling discipline problems. Third, promotion became essential. A person can ride only one bicycle at a time and most pastors can promote only one major project at a time. They promoted the Christian school, not the Sunday school.

The fourth reason had to do with the quality of Bible teaching. Sunday school teaching by laymen was usually inferior to the professional teaching during the week; the resulting loss of enthusiasm hurt Sunday school outreach. Fifth, the pupils got tired of coming to church five days a week plus Sunday. Also, they often had no unsaved friends to evangelize. All of these factors cause church growth to top out, simply because a church switches from outreach to inreach.

But conclusions must not be reached too quickly. Businesses do not measure success by gross income but by net profits. Maybe fast-growing churches are not ultimately growing as fast as slow-growing churches, at least when measured by eternity's standards.

In many churches the number of baptisms per year has gone down, but the number of people who continue with Christ after baptism has gone up. One reason is the quality education that comes from the Christian school.

Also, church growth is measured when total offerings go up as well as by increases in the giving ratio per person.

Perhaps the weekly crowd, often a crowd of irregular, uncommitted attenders, *is* lower because some churches have not spent money on advertising and buses. But at the same time the number of *steady* attenders may grow. As a result, a church's net growth may actually be larger compared with similar statistics in some fast-growing churches.

There is a second hidden factor in the growth of churches with Christian schools. More of their young people are going to Christian colleges to study for full-time service. This means that a particular church may not show rapid growth in its Sunday schools, but will reap fruit in the churches that its "Timothys" plant.

Also, the emphasis upon character training in Christian schools cannot be discounted. When a church has a pupil for five days a week, flaws in his character eventually show up. The Christian school can deal with the specific problems. Then the pupil can be trained in his total development for Jesus Christ.

A high school boy was captain of a Sunday school bus and through hard work averaged one hundred riders each week. He went to a Christian school and was disciplined for cheating. He went to another and was expelled for a worse offense. He tried a third and flunked out because of the standards. He could fill a bus with riders, but he could not become a disciple for Christ.

The embryonic problems of the high school boy are reflective of some fast-growing churches. They have the crowds on Sunday morning, but are they changing lives? The altars are lined on Sunday morning, but the pews are empty on Sunday evening. A church may be the fastest growing in one area, but is it ultimately and spiritually a growing church?

It is a shame that there is tension between explosive growth and dedicated discipleship, since one would not exist without the other. Balance is still the key word to make everything run smoothly.

The church that once was growing but now has a solid Christian school should not be criticized. Neither should churches that emphasize upward growth but have no roots in the Word of God be magnified.

A set of rules entitled "The Laws of Sunday School Growth" appeared in several forms in Southern Baptist literature.[9] Many attributed the source of Southern Baptist Sunday school growth to these laws. These laws of growth were basically organizational and administrative in nature. The author tried to demonstrate that these laws were never the cause of Southern Baptist growth. He tried to demonstrate this from case study, showing that many Sunday schools which broke these laws continued to grow.[10] These laws were used to organize people as they became involved in growing churches. The growth of Southern Baptists is attributed to the evangelistic fervor of their pastors, the commitment of their Sunday school teachers, and to the fact that their churches reflect New Testament aims and standards.

Yet we can draw certain conclusions concerning Sunday school growth for the eighties from the laws of organization and administration. Sunday school organization and administration will not guarantee growth, but a Sunday school will not grow without organization and adminstration. There must be a proper relationship of teacher, pupil, curriculum, facilities, equipment, and purpose. When this comes about, the Sunday school will grow.

Success Stories
in Church Growth

3. Theater-in-the-Round: Center Stage for the Gospel

Melodyland Christian Center
Anaheim, California
Ralph Wilkerson, Pastor

When is a church not a church?

When it's Melodyland Christian Center, an improbable conglomerate of fundamental believers set in the midst of one of Southern California's largest concentrations of hotels, bars, and amusement and sports facilities.

Its avowed purpose is to spread the gospel, of course, but Melodyland also is a healthy financial success with an income of more than $7.2 million (1977) and a goal of $20 million.

Its organization includes more than 150 "ministries" or projects, headquartered in a twenty-seven acre complex across Harbor Boulevard from Disneyland and valued at more than $13 million.

Its phenomenal success can be traced back to an idea—a vision from God, some say—that took root and sprouted in a soil rich in hostility, financial obstacles, and faith.

Some called it a miracle; others said it was the real estate deal of the century. Few can deny, however, that Melodyland Christian Center, housed in what was once a successful Orange County theater-in-the round, is most of all the result of the personal vision of its pastor and founder, Ralph A. Wilkerson.

More than anything else, Melodyland is a monument to the charisma and drive of the fifty-year-old Wilkerson, who draws capacity crowds to the central area to hear him talk of life and God.

He paces the circular center stage, booming out his message with a deep rich voice, coloring his sermon with homespun wit and anecdotes from his travels and work.

He told one audience recently of sharing a cab in another city with a lonely old woman, who welcomed his company and guidance. "Wasn't it nice of God to let me sit next to someone who was lonely?" he asked humbly, at the conclusion of his tale.

He "cures" the sick on stage—whether it's a medical malady or merely a troubled marriage—taking the opportunity to testify to the power of the Lord.

Despite the low-key, mellow atmosphere of the services, televised by a system of strategically placed cameras, the scene between services is frantic. Subordinates rush to and fro with questions and information.

Wilkerson slipped into a small waiting room during the break for a hurried interview recently, suddenly relaxed and calm as the door shut behind him.

He talked quietly about the early days with a candid confidence of someone who is sure he is right.

Today Wilkerson is nationally known—a television personality, a colorful evangelist, an author. His latest book, *Beyond and Back*, is the basis for a well-publicized movie that played on local screens and throughout the rest of the United States. He is not related, however, to another religious writer, Dave Wilkerson, a former social worker who wrote *The Cross and the Switchblade*. Some tend to confuse the two and they are friends. David Wilkerson has from time to time held or appeared at rallies on the Melodyland stage.

But there is no question which Wilkerson is in charge at Melodyland. Whether it's the spiritual or business end of the operation, Ralph Wilkerson is the boss. "God never intended for churches to be democratic," he states flatly. "They should be theocratic. If you get 10,000 voices involved, you get nothing."

Wilkerson is the president of all ten corporations which make up the Melodyland complex, even though members of the board vary from corporation to corporation.

"I'm the president of the corporation and the chairman of the board," he says. "I am involved in the business end of it. Every church ought to be that way. The business end is part of the load you have to carry and the pastor should be the leader. It's his vision."

Wilkerson claims he does not have any "hatchet men." If an unpleasant or nasty task has to be done—such as firing somebody—he says he does it himself, after praying over the matter.

The story of Wilkerson and his church is told so often by eager staff members and followers at Melodyland that what emerges takes on almost legendary proportions. Wilkerson came to Orange County in 1960 with twenty-seven followers, and he set up church each Sunday morning in the Anaheim Assistance League building, 1341 W. La Palma Avenue.

Those were humble days for Wilkerson, who had already put in more than ten years as a traveling evangelist and resident pastor at other churches. Each Sunday morning he and his wife, Allene, would arrive early before the service to clean up the leftover mess from the Saturday night dance held only hours before by another organization.

Despite such humble beginnings, the new Christian Center Church of Anaheim, as he called it, prospered and Wilkerson soon was able to move it into a new A-frame building on East Street, near the Riverside Freeway. By 1969, even that 900-seat building was so hard-pressed to meet the needs of a growing congregation that six services had to be held each Sunday. Plans were made to build a new and larger church building in east Anaheim.

Plans were drawn up for the new church when Wilkerson had what he calls "an inner witness," a vision that told him to buy Melodyland—then a popular theater spot owned by developer Leo Freedman.

Though the theater was a financial success, Freedman himself was going bankrupt because of other investments in the area. In the subsequent bankruptcy auction held on the Melodyland property, Wilkerson's church was the only bidder, buying it for the amazingly low price of $1.125 million.

"The acquisition of the property was a miracle to us," Wilkerson says. "The day after we acquired it in an open bid, three men came in with cash to buy it, but they were too late. They had gotten mixed up on the dates, even though there was a half-page ad in the Los Angeles Times announcing the date of the auction."

Even at the bargain basement price the church paid for its new headquarters, its financial reserves were stretched to the limit. And there were other immediate obstacles to be faced.

Members of the city council in Anaheim, where much of the city's prosperity depended on the Disneyland-Convention Center entertainment complex, were reluctant to allow a major religious facility to move in. The council consistently had voted not to allow bars or liquor stores to open near churches. Why, council members argued, should a church be allowed to open in the center of an area thickly populated with bars and nightspots? In fact, the Melodyland building itself was the site of the Celebrity Lounge, the largest bar in Orange County. The lounge operators still had twenty-five years to run. For months after the church group took over the theater, the Celebrity Lounge would open for a few hours each day, earning Melodyland the dubious distinction of being the only "church-with-a-bar-inside."

The council members' theory was that if the church were allowed to open in the area, it soon would be protesting the establishment of new bars in the area. Wilkerson pledged that his church would not be interested in getting the bars to shut down.

"My conviction is that you can close all the bars, but it's the people you should be going after," Wilkerson explained recently. "If you close the bars, those people will just go someplace else. It's not my job to try and close bars."

Though there was some talk about legal action against the church, that opposition faded with time. And the church—officially known as the Melodyland Christian Center—did not erect any crosses or religious monuments.

It lists its services and sermon topics on the same Harbor Boulevard-facing theater marquee once used to herald the coming of variety shows and big-name entertainers. Even today, the altars used in certain ceremonies are referred to as props and the theatrical facilities available are integrated skillfully into a slick Sunday service.

Numerous religious gatherings and productions are scheduled at the giant hall, generating business for the surrounding hotels and restaurants. "I don't know any of the hotels that aren't happy about the arrangement now," Wilkerson says. "We've upgraded the community."

The Celebrity Lounge, whose lease was finally bought by the church, is now the church's "fellowship hall." The popcorn and concession stand has become the bookstore, which claims to do more business per square foot than any other religious bookstore in the world.

There also is a Melodyland School of Theology for training new clergy, a Melodyland high school with 200 students, and Melodyland hot line and counseling services. A new $9 million, fifteen-story high-rise building is planned on the property for an ecumenical research academy. A multipurpose building is under construction, and a parking structure is planned for the near future. Capacity in the main hall of the theater-church is expected to more than double from its present 3,800 to 8,500 with the addition of a balcony above the present seating.

Statistics quoted by staff members can be impressive. Melodyland employs approximately 340 staff members — some part time. Though the church has about 12,000 "signed members" it is estimated that 17,000 to 18,000 attend services under the circular roof each week. More than 200 couples per year are married at the church and 5,000 of the faithful are baptized.

But, if the statistics are impressive, the surroundings are for the most part utilitarian. The complex, despite its size, is unpretentious — cinder block walls, small offices, plain but tasteful decor. Even Wilkerson's office itself presents an interior that is plush without being extremely expensive.

One side is dominated by stained-glass windows, salvaged from storage in a Santa Barbara church. The windows are the only stained glass in the entire complex. On the opposite wall is the re-creation of Jerusalem's wailing wall in real stone. A third wall is covered by a mural of the present-day Holy City, painted by a twenty-two-year-old art student who re-created the scene from a postcard.

The church's annual report for 1977 shows the Melodyland general fund receiving $4.7 million in contributions and $74,000 from the sale of books; the drug prevention and hot line center received $422,000 from contributions. The Melodyland School of Theology received $1.1 million from contributions and tuition and the high school took in $352,000 from contributions and tuition.

Of the total $7.2 million collected, the church spent $6.9 million on expenses. The remaining $391,000 was earmarked for capital improvements.

The report shows the real estate and improvements on the Melodyland property valued at a total $11.7 million, with total assets, including cash, inventory, and investments, of $14 million. Liabilities, including accounts payable and mortgage, total $6.6 million. Subtracting the liabilities from the assets shows the total net worth of the Melodyland organization at $7.4 million.

Of the $4.8 million in the church's general fund, the annual report shows 49.6 percent going toward the organization's 150 "missions," with the rest going toward such operating expenses as mortgages, salaries, supplies, and insurance.

Written by George Cunningham, *Register* staff writer.
Reprinted from *The Register*, Orange County, California, 12 March 1978. Used by permission.

4. Calvary Assembly—
Fastest-Growing Sunday School in the U.S.

Calvary Assembly
Winter Park, Florida
Roy A. Harthern, Pastor

Each year millions of people visit Central Florida, "the vacation capital of the world." Among them thousands are flocking to a place you won't find on the Chamber of Commerce tourist guide, but a place that is attracting national attention—Calvary Assembly in Winter Park, Florida, pastored by Roy A. Harthern.

Calvary Assembly has experienced such phenomenal growth that it was named "Fastest-Growing Sunday School" in the nation in 1977 by *Christian Life* magazine. It is one of the most exciting congregations in the world. Pastors from around America and vacationers who have heard of the church come to see what is going on.

What they find is impressive. Four Sunday services are required to pack in the 5,000 who attend each Sunday. There are identical morning services at 8:00, 9:45, and 11:30, and another service at five in the evening.

Services are exciting and informal. They begin promptly three minutes early and always end on time (in order to clear the parking lot for the next influx). The music is rousing, led by a 150-voice choir. The congregation frequently breaks into applause as praise to the Lord. Hands are lifted in worship, and frequently there is singing in tongues.

Visitors attend every service, and Pastor Harthern likes to mention that visitors who don't understand the exuberant praise might say that "this doesn't happen in our church." Pause. "Well, that's why we're not at your church." Everyone laughs.

The beautiful new sanctuary, which seats 1,400 and was completed in 1974, was too small the first Sunday the congregation moved in. Calvary Assembly has begun a program to raise $5 million to build a new auditorium which will be the largest in this part of the country. Two new educational additions have just been completed. A fifteen-story high rise for the elderly next to the church has just recently been completed.

The church serves the community, providing a full range of programs from nursery to Golden Agers. The church's youth ministry—the Rock House, which draws hundreds of youth each week, is also drawing national attention because of its dynamic program.

The County Commission in Orange County, Florida, declared July 2, 1978, as "Roy Harthern Day" in recognition of his eighth anniversary at

Calvary Assembly, as well as the 25th anniversary of the church. The Florida cities of Winter Park, Orlando, and Maitland, also proclaimed "Roy Harthern Day."

But statistics and recognition don't tell the true story of Calvary Assembly. That story is one of the transformation in the thinking of Roy A. Harthern, pastor for the past eight years.

Pastor Harthern says that for years he thought he was "God's superstar." He believed the more dynamic his personality could be, the more people would rally around him and the more his church would grow. But he began to see that his approach of organization, administration, and promotion wouldn't work.

He began to tire of moving people in the church from position to position when program after program died. Each time he had to come up with a new program more ingenious than the first. For example, he had one promotion of giving away goldfish in water-filled bags: "Be fishers of men." A problem arose one Sunday when several hundred goldfish died before Sunday school was over.

He says God began to show him that his pastor-centered church program would fail if his personality was the only thing holding it together. "I began to see that if I am building the church, it needs to fail," he says. "But if God is building the church, it cannot fail."

Once Pastor Harthern was willing to turn things over to the Lord, he was able to believe God to build the church. At first, he believed for 1,000; then for 2,000; and now he doesn't put a ceiling on what God can do.

But Pastor Harthern admits that a few years ago he could not have mentally handled a big church. He couldn't think of himself as pastor of a church like that.

"This is the trouble with most pastors," he says. "They limit God. They go to seminars to learn methods on how to fill up their empty churches; but if the crowds came, they would be scared. They couldn't minister to the people and would ultimately lose them." Too many pastors define success as having a church of 100, he says. The church grows to that level and stops because the leadership doesn't believe God for more. Leadership is important because as the leaders go, so goes the church.

Pastor Harthern has ministered this year in church growth seminars in various parts of the United States as well as in Korea, Australia, England, and Sweden. In the seminars he shares seven spiritual principles needed for church growth.

1. The Lord, not the pastor, must build the church.
2. What is born of the Spirit is Spirit, but what is born of flesh is flesh. God's answer to the flesh is crucifixion. If the pastor has to push and push to keep a program alive, Pastor Harthern believes he should let it die. Period.

3. People come where they get fed. It's like a restaurant. People will drive past many eating establishments to find the one where the atmosphere is right and the food is good.

4. Pastors should quit praying, "God bless what I'm doing." Instead, they should pray, "God help me to do what you are blessing."

5. Develop your faith. "You can have what you believe for," Pastor Harthern preaches. "If you don't believe God to do anything in your church, he won't."

6. Church growth comes from a willingness to rely totally on the Holy Spirit, Pastor Harthern teaches. Sometimes this is difficult, especially if it means creating new wineskins to hold the "new wine" of the Holy Spirit.

7. Objectives are important. Pastor Harthern's primary objective is training leaders. He tries to impart his own exciting, dynamic faith that God can do the impossible.

Another important principle is unity. Like the oil on Aaron's head that flowed down to his beard and finally his garments (Ps. 133), there must be a flow of the Holy Spirit downward from the leaders to the people. This can only come if there is unity among the leaders.

To this end Pastor Harthern has committed himself to help bring unity to the Body of Christ. "For too long we've tried to strive for doctrinal unity," he says. "That's not the way to go. We must learn to love the brethren first, then talk about doctrine."

He tells his congregation, "I have a love for and a loyalty to the Assemblies of God, but I am also committed to tear down the walls that have divided God's people and to build bridges of relationships with all members of the Body of Christ."

The philosophy of unity is also emphasized within the local fellowship of Calvary Assembly. Pastor Harthern has developed a close relationship with fifteen other "elders"—all full-time ministers who help him pastor the growing congregation.

When the church grew to more than 1,000 people several years ago, he began to see that he could not adequately oversee that many people. He began to draw around him men in the church to help him pastor the growing congregation in small groups.

Pastor Harthern saw New Testament Christians coming together in large gatherings and also in home groups. So he began to train leaders of the home groups. Today there are more than 300 of these groups meeting weekly in homes throughout Central Florida.

For the past several years, "fellowship groups," as they are called, have been the direction of Calvary Assembly. The fellowship group ministry is growing so rapidly that statistics are constantly outdated. But in early 1981, there were more than 1,000 people meeting in these small groups each Sunday night, as well as several thousand more meeting in groups every other night of the week.

Written by Stephen Strang, editor of *Charisma* magazine and member of Calvary Assembly since 1973.
Adapted from an article in the *Pentecostal Evangel*, 30 July 1978. Used by permission.

CALVARY ASSEMBLY GROWTH CHART

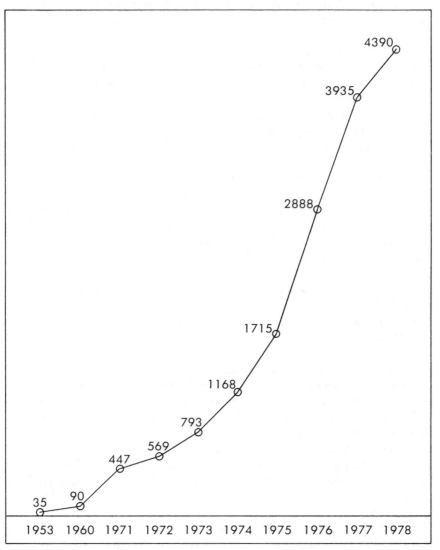

5. Pastor Parlays Drive-In Sermon into National Fame

Garden Grove Community Church
Garden Grove, California
Robert H. Schuller, Pastor

He could easily have been dubbed the "passion pit preacher" and vanished into anonymity—just another local pastor among the vast flocks of average American ministers.

He conducted his first religious service in California in 1955 atop the snack-bar roof at the Orange Drive-In Theater. Other ministers scoffed at making the "passion pit" into a house of God. "How can something turn out good when it starts off bad?" That was one of their questions to the young minister, a question he still remembers vividly. But Dr. Robert H. Schuller had the answer, so it turns out.

Within the next twenty-two years he parlayed $500, his refreshment stand pulpit, and his prayers among the whitewalls into a multimillion-dollar corporation, not to mention a nationwide ministry that attracts celebrities by the dozens and rank-and-file followers by the millions. Today, at fifty-one, the ivory-haired former Iowa farm boy is the dean of Orange County evangelist celebrities and rated among the top twenty most influential religious figures in the nation by a *Christian Century* magazine poll.

His walk-in, drive-in Garden Grove Community Church, affiliated with The Reformed Church in America, boasts more than 8,000 members while his "electronic church" congregation—viewers of his weekly "Hour of Power" television program—number an estimated 1.5 million.

Beyond being a successful minister, Schuller is a smart businessman. His ministries add up to an $11.4 million-per-year operation and are growing by as much as $2 million each year. The Schuller ministries own $6.2 million worth of land and buildings in Orange County, including the Garden Grove Church's fourteen-story "Tower of Hope" topped by a ninety-foot neon cross, as familiar a landmark to county residents as Disneyland's Matterhorn.

Work recently finished on a new Schuller dream, the Crystal Cathedral, an all-glass sanctuary costing nearly $15 million. The 10,000-pane building is a high water mark in the life of Schuller.

After attending Western Theological Seminary in Michigan and ministering to a small church in suburban Chicago, Schuller was called by local church leaders to California where he was to set up a church in booming Orange County.

With $500 "seed money" in hand, Schuller and his wife, Arvella, made the trek to California, but found no place to rent for church services. As a last resort, Schuller set up shop at the Orange Drive-In, bought an organ, borrowed a choir, built a wooden cross, and placed ads in newspapers urging people to "worship as you are . . . in the family car." On March 27, 1955, he started his new ministry. There were fifty cars at the drive-in. The first offering totaled eighty-three dollars.

Schuller pumped the offerings and his time into the new venture. When not perched on top of the outdoor theater snack bar, he rang neighborhood doorbells asking people why they didn't come to Sunday services and what programs they wanted. The grass-roots door-knocking apparently helped build a solid base for the new church.

The drive-in ministry also received a shot in the arm when Schuller was able to talk a fellow Reformed Church pastor, Dr. Norman Vincent Peale, into visiting and lecturing on his popular "positive thinking" theories. The visit proved to be a turning point in two ways — it helped attract more people and publicity to the new church and it also strengthened development of Schuller's own brand of positive thought philosophy, which he dubbed "possibility thinking."

It was several years before Schuller moved his burgeoning church into a Garden Grove chapel, and then in 1961 the Garden Grove Community Church took up residence on twenty-two acres of grassy, tree-lined land at 12141 Lewis Street. The "Tower of Hope" chapel-administration building was added in 1968, and a new $1.3 million "Hour of Power" communications center was established across the street several years ago.

Schuller is a study in motion, and appointments with him have to be made several weeks in advance. His staff carefully screens visitors and often tries to squeeze one-hour appointments into thirty minutes.

Schuller's family also is involved in church affairs. Arvella, his wife, serves as a full-time volunteer program director for "The Hour of Power." Sheila, his oldest daughter, is an assistant program director.

Schuller's only son, Bob Schuller, Jr., is a student at Fuller Theological Seminary and is interning at the church, regularly helping on "Hour of Power" telecasts.

In addition to the church, the Schuller ministries have two other major financial arms — The Robert Schuller Televangelism group, which runs "Hour of Power," and the Institute for Successful Church Leadership, which operates a church training seminar.

The main base of operations is still the Garden Grove Community Church, which had a 1977 budget of $1.8 million, raised through the collection plate, pledges, and other donations. The bulk of that budget, $855,120, went to pay salaries of the 190 full-time church employees, including the organization's ten ministers. Church office expenses were $160,995, fund-raising costs were $57,099, and maintenance costs of the buildings and grounds $149,188.

The rest of the money paid for such regular church programs as choirs, the

New Hope hot line, a singles group, a women's ministry, a day-care center, the Crystal Cathedral Academy private school, the athletic hall and "helping hand," a project which distributes groceries and clothing to destitute families.

On any given Sunday as many as 10,000 people will attend the five scheduled church services, two of which include worship from cars in the 1,000-space "drive-in sanctuary." Schuller decided to keep the auto aspect of his church because he has said he believes many people feel more secure in church behind the steering wheel due to handicaps, tattered clothes, or other social problems.

Today's drive-in lot faces the glass-lined walk-in sanctuary. While drivers tune in the service on their radios, fountains squirt and a glass door opens to a balcony pulpit where ministers can wave and talk to the in-car crowd.

During many services, especially the ones where Schuller preaches, the walk-in crowd overflows the sit-down church and fills folding chairs on the lawn near the automotive congregation.

The overflow is one of several reasons Schuller says the Crystal Cathedral is needed. The Crystal Cathedral, a huge glass building, seats 4,100 worshipers, has a choir loft which can accommodate 700, and an altar big enough for 500 people to kneel at one time.

The smallest of three major financial arms of the Schuller ministries is the Robert H. Schuller Institute for Successful Church Leadership. It has an annual budget of $235,000. Run by sixty-two-year-old Wilbert Eichenberger, the institute provides four-day seminars four times a year where church people can come to learn Schuller's techniques for building a viable ministry.

The event is held at the Garden Grove Community Church and generally draws about 300 people. The seminar costs $165 per person and fifty dollars extra for a spouse to attend. Money to run the institute comes from the fees and any special pledges or donations, according to Eichenberger. Included in the budget is $60,000 for salaries for Eichenberger and his staff of four, $60,000 for overhead expenses, and about $20,000 to promote the institute.

Promotion takes the form of advertising in Christian periodicals, setting up information tables at national religious conferences, and mailings to potential students on a direct mailing list of 26,000 names. Most of the mailing list names come from clergymen attending the institute who are asked to list ten people who might also benefit from the seminars. Eichenberger said the institute also occasionally purchases mailing lists from professional firms.

The program also includes several scholarships which are given to those with a desire to come, but who cannot afford the trip. Eichenberger estimated that more than 5,300 persons from all over the world have attended the institute since it set up shop in 1970.

One of the key lectures during the institute is the first at the Orange Drive-In where Schuller returns to the snack bar roof where it all began for him. There, he tells clergymen it's God's will for churches to grow. Using hand gestures patented on the "Hour of Power," Schuller weaves the tale of how he started at the drive-in twenty-three years ago with only $500. "Any church can grow as long as there are unchurched people around who have problems," the famous minister booms.

He then tells the assembled multitudes in Cadillacs and Toyotas that the information he obtained from ringing neighborhood doorbells in 1955 formed the basis for his current church-building programs for singles, teenagers, alcoholics, women, and others. Schuller concludes the lecture by urging his audience to have a plan for growth. "If you fail to plan, you are planning to fail," he snaps with a sweep of his arm. "Have a plan and live the gospel. And by living the gospel, I mean loving people where they are."

Probably nothing helped catapult Schuller into national prominence more than his "Hour of Power" televised program, which beams the smiling "possibility" preacher to an estimated 1.5 million persons each week. The idea for the show originated in 1969 when Schuller was a member of the executive committee for Billy Graham's fall crusade in Anaheim. Some of Graham's directors pointed out that there was no televised church service in Southern California and that Schuller's church would make an excellent spot for one because it had lots of visual movement—fountains, doors, trees, cars, and other things that would make a service exciting.

Although Schuller had never had any theatrical classes, he liked the idea and soon raised the $200,000 to buy time on KTLA (Channel 5) in Los Angeles. Today, seven years later, the weekly "Hour of Power" appears on 146 U.S. stations and twelve foreign channels.

The show reportedly is the highest rated religious program in most U.S. metropolitan areas and is said to be a favorite among such celebrities as Frank Sinatra, Glenn Ford, and the late Senator Hubert Humphrey, at whose funeral Dr. Schuller was invited to speak.

Schuller aides are quick to note that unlike other religious broadcasts which are dramatizations, "Hour of Power" is a televised Sunday service and thus can serve the church needs of hundreds of shut-ins across the nation.

However, a look at the show's format reveals little in common with traditional religious services other than a reading of the Psalms, the Lord's Prayer, or other well-loved Scriptures. Instead, Schuller prefers to get his message across through guests, humor, and animated stories about people who are positive thinkers and wind up happy. There are no hell-fire lectures on sin, Satan, or damnation, but rather smiling success stories laced with television shots of flowers, trees, and the mountains.

"God's biggest problem," the handsomely robed minister says with a sweeping gesture, "is not performing miracles, but getting you to think something beautiful is possible when by all odds it looks impossible." Whether or not other church leaders agree with his rosy religious philosophy, and many don't, they can't deny that Schuller packs 'em in.

On a recent Sunday morning, Schuller and his special guest, evangelist Oral Roberts, shared the pulpit before an overflowing crowd that braved driving rain to stand three deep in the church's lobby.

As one visitor put it, "It's the only place around where you can see a church service and the production of a television program at the same time." The show, coordinated under the auspices of the Robert H. Schuller Televangelism group, is the third and largest business component of the Schuller ministries. Its current annual budget is about $9.4 million, spent primarily on packaging, promoting and buying TV time for the taped Sunday service.

According to a 1976 budget breakdown, $2.5 million went to buy air time; $840,425 to pay the salaries of the 220 full-time staff members; $2.3 million to pay for religious items (giveaways) used to spark donations; $328,008 for advertising; $55,473 for travel; $56,870 for consulting fees; and about $400,000 for the forty-nine-dollar "Robert H. Schuller Correspondence Center for Possibility Thinkers," a newly developed course-by-mail.

Also located in the "Hour of Power" communications center at 4201 W. Chapman Avenue, Orange, is the "Possibility Thinkers Bookstore" which sells everything from Schuller message cassette tapes to Frisbees with religious symbols on top. The bookstore's annual budget is $260,000 and both its costs and income are divided among the three Schuller ministry financial organizations—the church, the "Hour of Power," and the institute.

"Hour of Power" gets its operating money primarily through contributions derived from a direct mailing list of more than one million people. Donations are indirectly solicited through religious messages, books, medals, key chains and other items offered "free" during the television program. People writing in are sent the items free and soon after receive a letter asking them to join the "Possibility Thinkers Club"—an implied request for a donation. Schuller aides are quick to point out that a person is placed on the mailing list and receives any items he wants regardless of whether he contributes.

Nevertheless, it is estimated that nearly three-fourths of the average of 40,000 letters sent to the "Hour of Power" building each week contain money. All of the letters immediately are processed through a security room where the money is removed and a receipt is written before it is passed to a bank of "readers."

If a person is seeking only the religious item of the week, the reader places the letter in a pile to wait for a pre-stuffed envelope containing the item and a computer-written thank-you letter. If a person is seeking guidance for a special problem, the letter passes to a staff of eight counselors who provide advice and answers. Some letter writers seek prayers for their problems or family, and the "Hour of Power" staff has special prayer sessions each week to answer those requests.

Not only is the "Hour of Power" the most successful Schuller venture financially, it is also the most sophisticated. The organization is run by a young and energetic staff using modern business and marketing techniques. The building itself sports colorful carpet, antique-style clocks, modern foil wallpaper, videotape machines, and other amenities commonly found in new business buildings.

"We are trying to communicate a great realtionship between people and Jesus Christ. Why shouldn't we do the best we can?" says Mike Nason, executive assistant to Schuller. "People criticize us for being too slick and professional," he adds, "but why should churches use ditto machines and staples when they can use color, sound, and motion to deliver their message?"

Does it need to be said that Nason is a "possibility thinker" in the best tradition of the Schuller ministries?

Written by Ron Kirkpatrick, *Register* staff writer.
Reprinted from *The Register*, Orange County, California, 5 March 1978, by permission.

6. Los Gatos Christian Church

Los Gatos Christian Church
Los Gatos, California
Marvin G. Rickard, Pastor

The Los Gatos Christian Church is a testimony to God's abilities when people are willing to respond to change. This church, south of San Jose, has grown from eighty-three, twenty years ago, to over 4,200 in morning services.

When Marvin G. Rickard came as pastor in 1959, he envisioned a ministry with 1,000 members. It was with patience and determination that he cultivated the hearts and spirits of the people for the Lord's leading. An emphasis was placed on ministering to hearts through faith, rather than building an organization through programs. A commitment was made to ministering to all those the Lord brought to this nondenominational fellowship.

The church outgrew its facilities by 1971 and began using off-site locations. Soon it saw over half its Sunday school, averaging 950, meeting in the YMCA, Elk's Lodge, and Carpenter's Union Hall. It was at this time that the Lord made available the vacant facilities built by an electronics firm.

Services began in the new location in September 1973 with 1,941 in church and 1,467 in Sunday school. By the fall of 1978 attendance had grown to 4,250 and 3,665 respectively.

The growth of the church is cited by its leaders as one of the measurements of the Spirit at work in people's lives. These are people attending because of a personal desire to attend, not because of buses, contests, or seasonal promotions.

A key emphasis of the church is the "quality of ministry." This is seen in the staff of ministers. Each of the twelve full-time men is a specialist in his field, whether it be music, education, youth, membership care, missions, or business. Meeting people's needs is more important than the efficiency of the program. Concern from this perspective has developed special ministries for singles, missionary families, family needs, and more. A spirit of love and caring can even be sensed among the congregation on a Sunday. It was such a spirit that motivated the church to open its doors to the care of 154 Vietnamese refugees for a week. Sixteen of the refugees accepted Christ as Savior through the example and love of the members who cared for them.

The ministry to the Vietnamese in 1975 was simply an extension of the church's missionary vision. Its commitment to missions has grown from $6,000 in 1966 to the present Faith Promise giving of over $600,000. The church's general budget has also grown, now totaling $2,245,900.

Opposition has always sparked the church of God. This has been especially true of the Los Gatos congregation. Much of the struggle has come from neighbors not wanting to be inconvenienced by the traffic generated by 4,000 people. A group representing less than twenty homes organized itself aggressively against the church. The stated purpose of the group was to stop the church from any further expansion. In self-arrogance it called itself AMEN, (Against Massive Environmental Nuisance)! In answer to AMEN's criticism of traffic, the church now rents six city buses and owns eight of their own that they use each Sunday. These now bring about 1,900 to church from three shopping center parking lots, and one school parking lot, two to three miles away. Nearly 800 to 900 cars are parked away from the church through this "Park-N-Ride" approach.

No one factor seems to characterize the scope of the church's impact. Some come because of the warmth of the services and the choir's music. Others find the impact on their young people and children vital. Whatever the reasons, it is evident that hundreds of people are excited about Jesus and find their center of fellowship in the Los Gatos Christian Church.

Written by Milton Davis.
Article reprinted from a small copyrighted magazine for church staff.

7. A Warm Church in a Cold Land

Anchorage Baptist Temple
Anchorage, Alaska
Jerry Prevo, Pastor

Much is heard about the superchurches in America — but can a large, aggressive church be built on the mission field? Especially on a cold, barren mission field located barely on the edge of comfortable living?

Four years ago Pastor Jerry Prevo went to Anchorage, Alaska, and took over a work that had 125 adults and 175 riders on Sunday school buses, meeting in a refurbished army barracks. Today the Anchorage Baptist Temple averages over 1,500 in attendance, receives $12,000 a week in offerings, has property and buildings valued over $1.5 million, and operates a Christian day school from kindergarten to grade 12.

Prevo was born in Oak Ridge, Tennessee, in 1945. His father worked at the atomic energy plant. During his sophomore year in high school he moved next door to his future wife. She became his high school sweetheart and ultimately his co-worker in the Lord. Prevo was ten when he accepted Jesus as his Lord and Savior at the Mount Pisgah Baptist Church, a block from his home. A beer parlor stood at the other end of the block.

"I could have gone either way except that God spoke to me through an accident," says Prevo.

As a ten-year-old he watched as three teenagers were pulled from a car. They were all dead. The reality of mangled bodies and broken glass frightened young Prevo. Every time he climbed into a car, he took a blanket to put over his head. Three weeks after the accident Prevo went to Vacation Bible School. When the invitation to accept Christ as Savior was given, Prevo asked the boy next to him to join him.

"No," was the response.

Each boy whispered the request down the pew until the word got to the teacher.

"I'll go with you," she responded.

When Prevo returned home, he wanted to take a ride in the car to see if he needed to put the blanket over his head. He didn't, so he decided that God had really made a difference in his life.

Prevo spent one year at the University of Tennessee studying industrial engineering. He took the usual battery of tests, including a vocational preference test. The counselor told him that the results indicated a lack of aptitude for the ministry. But in the back of his mind Prevo knew God was calling him to preach. He finished on the dean's list and that summer felt the burden to prepare for the ministry. He applied at Bob Jones University and became engaged to the girl next door. At youth camp he had heard about Baptist Bible College in Springfield where there was no tuition fee.

"I don't have enough money to go to Bob Jones University and get married, but if I go to the Bible College, I can get married immediately," Prevo rationalized. He left for Springfield on August 19 a married man.

After graduation, Prevo worked at the Beacon Baptist Church in Nashville and then was called to pastor the Pinecrest Baptist Church in Signal Mountain near Chattanooga, Tennessee.

At a missions conference in Signal Mountain in April 1971, God spoke to Jerry Prevo. "I knew God wanted me to go a great distance," Jerry says. "At first I thought it was New England."

His wife said no. A couple of months later, missionary Don White from Anchorage called and asked him to come and preach there. He did. A month later White resigned from the Bible Baptist Church in Anchorage, recommending that the congregation call Prevo. Jerry accepted.

Prevo appeared before the missionary board of the Baptist Bible Fellowship, asking for approval, but there was no response. Then John Bonds, pastor of Bethlehem Baptist Church in Arlington, Virginia, volunteered to send out a letter to raise support. It brought pledges totaling $225 a month for six months. The church in Signal Mountain gave him a 1969 Dodge van and an $800 offering. They also gave him a credit for gas and motel expenses on his way to Alaska.

The church in Anchorage had been started by Don White in the winter of 1955 in a home outside the city. A year after White began the work, the congregation erected their first building, a twenty-by-forty-foot structure, covered with tar paper. An unspectacular beginning, yet a base for a handful of people who wanted to reach souls for Christ. The work grew, a wing was built the following year, and in 1959 they purchased a barracks on a nearby army installation. The work was organized into the Bible Baptist Church of Anchorage, and on Easter Sunday, 1958, they had a high attendance of 142.

In that first building the congregation needed water and had only $500 for the well. The people got on their knees and asked God to guide the well diggers to the right spot. When the rig backed onto the property the next morning, White told the workman to dig $500 worth and then stop.

The workman told White it was foolish to start. "That's not enough money to get to water." But he asked where he should dig. White told him to get as close to the building as possible. Then the people remembered that if they spent $500 to drill the well, there would be no money for the pump and tank. So they added to the prayer request, asking God to give them an artesian well that was free-flowing.

White expected the operation to last a couple of days, but by noon that day, the rig pulled out of the drive. The workmen had hit water that morning—with money to spare. The well was free-flowing. God had answered their prayer.

Grace Mitchell, now church secretary, remembers praying in 1958 for a bus.

"It was too cold for the children to walk to Sunday school," she says.

In response, God provided the little church with twelve city buses! A private line had brought twelve white buses to Anchorage, but the city bus line secured an injunction and would not let them go into operation. White offered $5,000 for the twelve buses and, to everyone's amazement, he got them. Some of the buses were sold, others were kept for parts, and the church used five or six.

Between 1960 and 1970 church attendance had averaged between 100 and 250. "We couldn't hit 300," says Mitchell. White had to go to the lower forty-eight states for support and missionary conferences.

Every time White left the church, however, attendance went down. In addition to the Anchorage work, White had to spend time in the bush and attend to other duties throughout Alaska. The congregation wanted a full-time pastor.

When Prevo arrived in Anchorage in 1971, he found the renovated barracks on four lots. A basement had been dug under it for classrooms. The church had six buses bringing in approximately 175 a week. Attendance averaged 300 with a high of 500. Some called it a military church because servicemen came from the nearby Army and Air Force bases. Offerings averaged $900 a week.

The Sunday school was a unified service with only six classes and an auditorium filled with adults.

Prevo saw that there was little spirit or excitement in the church. He split the service into the traditional Sunday school and morning church format, and assured the people that he was there to build a large local church. He learned who had the largest Sunday school in Anchorage and set a goal to pass them, "not for numbers, but to motivate our folks to win souls."

Prevo had a strategy. He noted that "half of Alaska lived within a ten-mile radius of our church, and the other half lived in a state twice as large as Texas." He told the people he would let the missionaries go out into the bush, but he was there to build the largest church in Alaska and through that platform, ultimately to reach all of Alaska.

Because the church had no budget, Prevo met with the deacons and told them there had to be a 50 percent increase in the offerings. Next, Prevo started a Sunday school teachers meeting on Wednesday night, and insisted that each one be there, faithful to his task.

Then he started Saturday visitation. The buses would not only be used for transportation but for soul winning. The bus workers began to go out and win people to the Lord, then bring them to Sunday school.

Prevo assured the church that they would support the work of missions in Alaska. Within two months of the Prevo's arriving, the church planned a missionary conference and brought in missionaries from the bush, who were assured of the church's continued financial support.

The church planned its first big day and reached 1,364 in Sunday school the following spring. A circus had come to town in June and Prevo got the use of the tent to have church services.

Since Jack Baskin had launched a successful mission conference and faith promise in Signal Mountain, Tennessee, he was invited to spearhead the program in Anchorage. They did the unbelievable. Sixty-four people raised $143,000 for expansion. Prevo had been looking around for property. The present location was saturated and property immediately to the west was tied up in a court lawsuit. People had been asked to give by faith to the building fund. The pastor announced, "If we show God we mean business, he'll open the door." Within a year after his coming to the church, the people were giving $800 a week to the building fund, plus the regular church offerings. In response to their sincerity, God opened up ten acres four months later. The property cost $300,000 and the owner financed it interest free for eight years, giving them an option on five more acres. At this time they raised the $143,000 from sixty-four people. The bank filled out the notes and brought them to the church. The people signed them and the bank honored their signatures.

In March 1973 the church broke ground for a one-million-dollar building. The problem was that they could not get financing. But the deacons felt that they had to go ahead by faith. They had enough money to put in the foundation. Some thought that the people would laugh if they began a project that they could not finish. Jerry Prevo went to the Alaskan Mutual Bank and applied for a one-and-a-half-million-dollar loan, but the committee turned him down. Not to be discouraged, he went back with a different package and asked for three million dollars. This time they loaned him $500,000. The men did the volunteer labor, the pastor acted as general contractor, and they erected a large two-story steel building with an auditorium that seats 1,200 and school facilities for a thousand in Sunday school. During the year 1973-74, the men finished a 35,000-square-feet building, with the exception of the electrical and mechanical work, which was done by a contractor.

The congregation was eager to get into the building. They swept away the sawdust, and between the raw stud walls they had their New Year's service. Prevo preached that night on "Be Like a Nail . . . Hold Things Together." The message had its impact. The people continued to work hard. Then on July 4, 1974, they had their patriotic service. A candidate for the U. S. Senate spoke, and they moved into their new facilities.

A year later Prevo realized that no church in Alaska had ever had 2,000 in

Sunday school. So on May 18, 1975, they had a campaign, "Be one of 2,000" and invited people to come and "help us make history." They promoted the campaign for eight weeks and had 2,210 in attendance.

Today the church averages over $12,000 each week in income from tithes and offerings, another $3,000 comes in from the Christian school tuition. But prices are high in Alaska. However, Prevo is not discouraged by the high prices; when people make more, they tithe more. Ten percent is still in proportion, whether it comes from a large or small salary.

Immediately after arriving in Anchorage, Prevo realized there were a lot of working parents who wanted a Christian environment for their kids. Anchorage had a drug problem, and so that first year he started a preschool nursery for children of working mothers. The next year he began with eighty students, grades 1-6. All of the teachers were Alaskans; they came out of his church. He didn't have to employ any from the lower states. The next year he added classes through grade 12 with a hundred and fifty students. This year they had 315 students in a Christian school that asks $800 tuition per pupil. Dr. Delbert Brock is the principal. The church has five assistant pastors, eight on the paid staff and thirty-one on the staff in the school. These count full- and part-time employees.

One of the big problems in pastoring a church in Anchorage is the turnover in personnel. Because of the long winters, severe weather, and isolation in the wilderness, people want to go back to the lower forty-eight states. According to Prevo, they lose about twenty percent of the tithing families each year who must be replaced through an aggressive visitation program.

At present the church is building nine new classrooms. They are bulldozing land to add a new gym and classroom building that will cost a half a million dollars, yet the gym will seat 1,000 people in the stands and 1,000 on the floor. Prevo plans for a thousand in his day school when the new facilities allow for expansion. And then, up on the hill overlooking the property, they plan a new auditorium that will seat 3,000. In Alaska where the average age is twenty-eight, there is a youthful vitality with an optimistic view of the future. Prevo thinks there will be no difficulty in building a church of 5,000. Today Anchorage has a population of 180,000 and within the next five years there will be 250,000 people in the city. The fruitfulness of the past four years predicts a bright future for Prevo, who is under thirty years of age. Last year Hyles Anderson College awarded the Doctor of Divinity to Jerry Prevo. In awarding the degree, Dr. Jack Hyles said, "This is the equivalent to an earned degree; Jerry Prevo has built a large work in a difficult place. He is one of the most deserving young men in America of our recognition."

Written by Elmer L. Towns.
Reprinted from *Christian Life* magazine, 1975, "Humility Helped Them Grow," by permission.

8. Chile's Superchurch

Jotabeche Methodist Pentecostal Church
Santiago, Chile
Javier Vasquez, Pastor

The services are simply overwhelming in the huge church located on Alameda Avenue in downtown Santiago, Chile. For the midweek prayer meeting, the "cathedral" is jammed with thousands of worshipers (depending on the observer, the "general services" attract anywhere from 7,000 to 18,000 persons with people standing three deep in the aisles). The probable attendance is in the neighborhood of 15,000 persons.

On one side is a balcony which holds the *coro* of some 2,000 persons. About one-half play instruments made up mainly of guitars, violins, and mandolins—the other half sing. On the opposite side is the *coro polifonico*, made up of 150 trained singers who render the more formal hymns of the church.

The service begins with the traditional *tres glorias a Dios* (three glories to God—in honor of the Trinity) and proceeds with hymns of the church sung by the massive congregation as if they constituted one huge voice. Later in the service, the pastor, Javier Vasquez, mounts the pulpit and, to the shouts of the joyful crowd, delivers a simple message about salvation and the fullness of life in the Holy Spirit.

At the conclusion of the message, prayers for salvation and healing are offered for the thousands who indicate their needs by kneeling at their bench-like pews. There is no invitation for seekers to come forward for the simple reason that there is no space anywhere in the church for a traditional altar call. As the singing and rejoicing continues after the prayer, many begin to shout their praises to God or "dance in the Spirit" as the church fervently sings the closing hymns.

Such is a typical service at the Jotabeche Methodist Pentecostal Church, pastored by Javier Vasquez. It is in every respect a superchurch which, more than any other congregation, has inspired the church growth movement around the world in recent years. No one seems to know how many members belong to the congregation. The pastor estimates his flock members at around 80,000, counting only those twelve and over as full members. Some outsiders would estimate the total community served by the church at over 100,000.

On a typical night only one fourth of the congregation attends at the *Templo Matriz* (mother church). The others await their turn to attend once a month. Otherwise, they attend one of the many "classes" connected with the church. The smallest class numbers over 800, with the largest—*Valledor*

Sur—numbering some 3,000. Each class in turn has many *annexos* in its area of the city. Since 1964, fifteen *templos* have been built for the classes by the mother church. Leaders of the classes are assistants to Vasquez who carry the title *Predicador* (preacher).

The congregation was founded by Manual Umana a few years after the Pentecostal Methodist Church was begun in the port city of Valparaiso in 1909 by American Methodist missionary Dr. William C. Hoover. In 1918 a small prayer group led by Umana rented a storefront building on Jotabeche Street and used this location as a center for street preaching. The movement swept Santiago like a prairie fire, despite persecution from the police and the Catholic church.

In 1925 a large sanctuary, which would hold 5,000 persons, was built on the same block. Since this building soon overflowed, a system of classes and annexes was instituted to provide pastoral care for the burgeoning congregation. From his base in Santiago, Umana was elected as Bishop of the entire Methodist Pentecostal Church of Chile, which at the time of his death in 1964 claimed over one-third of all the evangelicals in Chile. Other Pentecostal groups split off from Jotabeche in the years after 1918. By 1980 Pentecostals constituted about 90 percent of the 2,000,000 evangelicals in Chile, a nation with a population of over 10,000,000.

In 1967 the Methodist Pentecostal Church of Chile signed an affiliation with the Pentecostal Holiness Church of the U.S. in which both churches entered into full communion. (Both groups had origins in Methodism.) In May of 1980 Bishop J. Floyd Williams and Rev. Bernard Underwood, World Missions director of the Pentecostal Holiness Church, visited Mancilla and Vasquez. The purpose of the visit was to strengthen relations between the two sister churches.

The Jotabeche Church continues to be one of the most spectacular of the world's superchurches. Both Mancilla and Vasquez speak confidently of the day *"Chile sera para Cristo"* (Chile will be for Christ).

Written by Vinson Synan.
Reprinted from the *Advocate*, 13 July 1980, by permission.

9. Elkhart's First Baptist Grows

First Baptist Church
Elkhart, Indiana
Dan Gelatt, Pastor

God can build a powerful church in a small town. First Baptist Church of Elkhart, Indiana, is a testimony to that fact. Elkhart is surrounded by Indiana cornfields and has a reputation for building the most recreational vehicles in the nation. Yet, in this small town the First Baptist Church averages over 1,300 in attendance and has an annual income of almost $1 million. It has over 500 Christian school students in kindergarten through high school, forty-five full-time employees and each year gives $200,000 to missions around the world.

The First Baptist Church is powerful because it is a balanced church. The congregation, like the center of a seesaw, has a great leverage in that it reaches from Bible teaching to soul-winning, from foreign missions to home missions, from pastoral leadership to congregational authority, and from beautiful buildings to those that are practical and well-utilized.

If all churches had the balance of First Baptist Church and if every town were receiving a testimony like Elkhart, America would feel the impact of the Great Commission as it should be felt, because the Great Commission is not completed until a powerful church is attempting to reach its town for Christ.

The church was begun in 1860 and has been true to Christ over the years. There is a member in the congregation who remembers the hard days of depression. He walked the railroad tracks with a bucket to gather coal so that the church could be warm for the preaching of the gospel.

During the 1930s the church withdrew from the American Baptist Convention because of liberalism. In the 1940s it joined the General Association of Regular Baptist Churches and remains in good fellowship with them to this day. The previous pastor, Dr. Hugh Hall, is credited with building a congregation of well-taught, well-trained believers, who also have vision. When the church was averaging 500 in attendance, they built an auditorium that would seat 1,200.

Dr. Hall left and in 1968 the church was searching for a pastor. They heard about the work of Rev. Dan Gelatt in Horseheads, New York. The pulpit committee decided to phone him.

Dan Gelatt was having dinner at home with a pastor friend. Gelatt said to his friend across the dinner table, "I know Horseheads is the place God wants me to minister." He went on to emphasize, "If God wants me to move, he will have to write in the sky."

The phone rang and interrupted him. The voice introduced himself, "I am

Don Metzler, chairman of the Pulpit Committee . . ." After explaining the situation in Elkhart, Gelatt was invited to go there for an interview.

"No," was Gelatt's reply. Metzler was insistent, so Pastor Gelatt relented, "You can send a delegate to talk with me in New York."

They came and liked what they saw. After several conversations, Gelatt flew to Elkhart. He met with the representatives from the church and noted, "They were a congregation with faith and vision and they needed a leader." His heart was stirred. He walked into the auditorium and looked at the 1,200 seats, then knelt by the communion table and prayed, "Lord, I don't want to move. But if you will help me fill this building to your glory . . . I'll come."

Gelatt became pastor of First Baptist Church in April 1968. The first item of business that he brought to the board was the hiring of a staff member for evangelism and outreach. Dick Etner, an insurance salesman from Gelatt's church in New York, was hired and is still with the church. Because of Etner's quiet approach to soul winning, he is not known around the country. But because of the numerous families he has reached for Christ and the number on the buses, he is well known in heaven.

The church began to grow. According to Gelatt, the reason for the growth was that "the people had a mind to work." He felt that there was great need among independent, fundamental Baptists for a balanced ministry. More than fifteen years ago, he began preaching through the books of the Bible consecutively — Sunday morning, Sunday evening, and Wednesday evening. He has proven that a church can grow numerically by strong expository preaching. As a result, he built his church on the Word of God, which means that the church has numerical growth and its Christians have grown to maturity.

When Gelatt came to Elkhart, the church had two buses in operation; today they have ten. Even though the church averages between 200-300 riders, the buses have not been a dominant factor in the growth of the church. Gelatt noted, "We did not want large crowds to disrupt the teaching of the Word of God, we wanted children we could discipline and love."

Originally, the church owned eight acres in the city and as it grew, it added Christian education facilities. As a result, they could no longer expand on eight acres. In 1971 pastor Gelatt and a businessman were flying to Grand Rapids, Michigan. The layman asked, "What would it take to start a Christian school in Elkhart, Indiana?"

Gelatt thought about it and gave his answer, "About $1 million to have the right kind of school and facilities to provide a quality education." The church began praying for the $1 million, and within six months God provided it.

Everyone realized that they could not expand on their present property. The church began praying for a solution. One of the staff members came back from visiting and suggested, "What about the Cook property?" He had visited Mrs. Cook in the hospital; she was a member of the church. Gelatt went to the home and talked with Mr. Cook, but did not talk to him about the property. Mr. Cook was not a Christian. He carefully explained the plan of salvation and Mr. Cook knelt by the couch, praying for Jesus Christ to come into his heart.

Later, Mr. Cook agreed to sell forty acres at $1,000 per acre, and he even gave a gift toward the purchase price. After he had made the agreement, he went to the window and looked out over the acreage. "Do you suppose I will ever see the day when anything will happen there?"

God was beginning a miracle and would see it through. Gelatt indicated that the greatest miracle in the life of the church had come after they had an option for the property, but discovered that there was no way to dispose of sewage. It was too expensive to connect to the city sewage disposal system. But they needed a place for the clean water to drain. A gentleman owning the property through which the drainage ditch ran refused to grant them an easement. Someone told Gelatt, "He will never let you use the ditch."

On many evenings Gelatt went out and knelt in the ditch, asking God for a solution. He went and saw the man on several occasions. When he became a friend, he gave the church the right of way and even shared in the cost of the ditch.

Today the church owns forty acres, one-and-a-half miles south of its present property, with three softball fields, one baseball field, a gymnasium and a Christian high school building. It is worth $1 million and is all paid for. Plans are now under way for a half-a-million-dollar expansion program to provide for an additional 350 in both school and church.

When Gelatt was in Horseheads, New York, he had always sponsored soul-winning conferences, bringing in Dr. Lee Roberson, Dr. Jack Hyles, and other great fundamentalists to challenge his congregation to evangelism. That was the great need in New York. However, in Indiana the emphasis on soul winning was close by. Gelatt stated, "We wanted to minister to the whole body of Christ, not just our assembly." Therefore, he began a Sunday school conference eight years ago that has increased in influence each year. They have workshops on every topic and bring in the great fundamentalist speakers. This past January they registered over 800 delegates from other churches in addition to the members of the First Baptist Church.

The church reached its highest attendance last fall when there were 1,706 in the church service during a promotion called "Everyone Bring One."

Last Christmas the church sponsored a one-hour television special that was shown three times over the local station. They are still reaping the results of that exposure and plan to do more televison work in the future.

Also at Christmas time, the church took up a special offering of $22,000 for the purpose of sending ten couples to the mission field. The tradition of the Christmas offering began sixteen years ago when Gelatt realized that many Christians gave small trinkets to other Christians. At that time he asked the church to adopt a policy that Christians do not give presents to one another, but rather, that they give an offering to the church for missions. Gelatt realized that when he made this policy, he would be giving up the traditional Christmas bonus that was given to the pastor by the church. However, over the years, God has honored that commitment. The children were asked to keep their money in a decorated tin can during December. One kid marked his "To Jesus, From Joe." Gelatt pointed out to the congregation that "wise men still bring their gifts." The teen department set a goal of $1,000 and raised $2,000.

The church has beautiful facilities, but more than elegance, there is meaning to the architecture. When they began to design the sanctuary, the architect asked, "What is the center of a Baptist church?" The people told him that it was the pulpit, the preaching of God's Word. The architect wanted the building to be different, but he could not put the pulpit in the center of the church. Therefore, he created a round auditorium and at the very center is a baptistry. The pulpit is near the center, showing that a church of people must come together.

Also, the architect allowed the laminated beams to show because he said, "The church ought to show its strength." Then he requested that they not be painted nor varnished, because the church should not be artificial, it ought to be itself.

Around the outside of the building, the architect called for four feet of cobblestone. When Gelatt came to the church, he wondered why the different sizes of rocks. The architect explained, "These show the different sizes of Christians who surround the church." Someone wanted to put in crushed stones instead of the cobblestones and the architect said, "Why? All Christians are not the same size!" Then he picked up a deformed rock and noted, "That's symbolic of the cripple who needs the help of the church."

The church has a unique baptistry. The changing rooms are below the main auditorium and the baptistry is situated on a large elevator hoist. The pastor and several candidates enter the baptistry and it is hoisted up for the baptismal service.

The church owns nine parsonages and is presently building two missionary homes for missionaries on furlough. The missionary homes are called "Fair Haven."

A recent program has been inaugurated to invite interested pastors and their wives to involve themselves in the church for one week. The church has a burden to train men in balanced evangelism and education. A full-time pastor will head up this internship. The visiting pastor will involve himself in every aspect of the church's program from hospital visitation to board meetings.

The church's present indebtedness is $250,000, but its total worth is over $3 million, a very stable approach to debt.

The church has an active intramural sports program, including volleyball, softball, and basketball, with nearly 200 participants. It is age-graded so that the young boys as well as the men may participate. The uniqueness of the program is that a father and son may become involved in the program together, hence building a family spirit.

First Baptist Church is a strong, influential church because it is balanced. They are strong because they are not overextended; they are influential because they are far extended. Whether it is Bible teaching or soul winning, buses or baseball, First Baptist Church is a dynamic testimony in Elkhart, Indiana.

Written by Elmer L. Towns.
Reprinted from the *Journal-Champion*, 9 February 1979, by permission.

10. People's Church Runneth Over

People's Church
Fresno, California
G. L. Johnson, Pastor

You might not visualize the dapper G. L. Johnson as a bible-totin', arm-wavin' preacher, but after talking to him you wouldn't be a bit surprised.

Johnson has been shepherding the Fresno-based People's Church, one of the largest and fastest growing flocks in California, since 1963.

He preaches with the fervor and charisma that mark great politicians and "boy wonder" entrepreneurs. His sermons have boosted membership in the People's Church more than 1000 percent and moved the church, once forced to meet in converted turkey houses, into a brand-new $4 million religious center on Cedar and Herndon Avenues.

The new People's Church—the "Complex," they call it—is huge. So huge that maps have been strategically placed on outside walls, pointing out "You are here" to unwary visitors.

Pastor Johnson's office is located way in the back. It is wood paneled and comfortably furnished. A large bowl of red, green, and yellow fruit jellies sits invitingly on the coffee table. On the wall behind Johnson's desk are diplomas, pictures of his family and a small blue sign that reads, "Shalom, Y'all."

To reach Johnson by telephone, you must go through the switchboard operator and the pastor's secretary. Johnson realizes this might intimidate some. "But of course," he says, "when you have this many people you have to have a switchboard.

"I just hope it seems like the smallest large church in town. I want them to be impressed not with the size of the church, but with the love of the church.

"Then," says Johnson, "they'll forget the size."

Many obviously have. Admirers point to Johnson as the reason behind the church's phenomenal growth. In fact, bankers financing the new buildings required a much-publicized insurance policy on Johnson's life for "a little more than a half a million," says Johnson. "I don't know that it was necessary except that there is a debt here.

"I suppose any time a church loses its pastor you hope you're going to get somebody that can keep it going. But you don't have any guarantee that you will." The insurance money, Johnson says, would be used to reduce the mortgage debt in the event of his death.

Johnson's supporters are quick to point out a marked drop in attendance at the services conducted by assistant pastors in Johnson's absence. At this, Johnson shrugs, then laughs.

"Well, I guess they know me and they feel comfortable with me," he says.

"And maybe they've been waiting for a chance to get away anyway, so they say 'Well, the pastor's not preaching; this is my chance.' "

Johnson feels that the key to church growth is lively preaching with strong convictions. "You have to say very strongly what you are in order for people to believe in you and come.

"I don't think people are interested in a church or religion that's just dead," Johnson says. "I think they want life. They've gotta have a little fire and zip. We are a church that emphasizes the preaching of the Bible, the warmth of God's spirit, and I mean a lot of spirit."

And Johnson has "spirit." His eyes begin to water as he speaks of a woman whose son is going blind. His voice quavers meltingly at the words "poor little widow woman."

"There are some churches," says Johnson, "that do that and still aren't growing, because they do it in a dead way. You know—a monotonous, drawling sermon. If you've heard me preach, well, some people make fun of me, but I get loud, I laugh, I cry, I wave my arms, I stomp. It has spirit to it and life and I think people want this."

Johnson believes in tailoring his sermons to the congregation's needs. "When a family goes to church," he says, "and if they've got a daughter that's run away from home, or a son that's hung up on dope, or the man's lost his job, the woman's just learned she has breast cancer or home is like hell, they're not interested in busing in Los Angeles or Cesar Chavez in Delano or the Middle East.

"They want to know, 'What does God have to say to my problem? What's the answer?' We do get involved in social outreaches. But first you've got to deal with a man's heart, his home, his problems—where he's hurting."

Johnson scoffs at the notion that his church attracts people mostly from the upper-middle income brackets. "We can't pay any attention to that. We figure that in Christ we're all on the same level.

"This church was built because a lot of people gave a little bit. Large gifts to this church probably amounted to five percent of its total cost.

"You really can't build a church, in my opinion, out of upper-class people," says Johnson. "In the first place, there's not that many of them.

"In the second place, usually those people that back the church, attend the church, support the church are poorly—your middle and lower. They give more money because they give consistently.

"The rich?" sighs Johnson. "They'll drop one big check—boom—that's it. A lot of times that's the way it is, but not all of them."

Two months ago People's Church decided to reach a wider audience through televised Sunday sermons. Johnson has no patience with detractors, many of whom say televised preaching is too commercialized.

"You know," he says, "when the Bulldogs play I've found that the guy that gets tackled is the one that's carrying the ball . . . I think it just tells more about them than it does about us. We use all means possible to bring people to Christ.

"If there is a God," muses Johnson, "then he allows things in this world to happen. Then television is here because he allowed it. Right?

"Why did he allow it? For Budweiser? For 'plop-plop-fizz-fizz'? I believe that God allowed television and radio because that was a way by which his message could get to every person on earth."

Johnson pointed to two video cassette tapes on his desk. "I could put that on television and get a lot of people I'd never get inside this building. But I can get inside their homes. It costs plenty, but with everybody giving a little bit, why, we'll get it on the air."

Pastor Johnson is a very busy man. He is already late for his next meeting and can't spend any more time explaining his church's growth. His secretary rushes to hurry him onward. But at the door she pauses and smiles. "If you've talked with our pastor," she says, "you know why this church is growing."

Written by Cyndi Morgan.
Reprinted from *Insight*, California State University, Fresno, 4 October 1978, Volume 11, No. 4, by permission.

11. Biggest Little Church in the World

Yoido Island Full Gospel Central Church
Seoul, Korea
Paul Yonggi Cho, Pastor

On a sandy island in the middle of the Han River in Seoul, Korea, stands a remarkable edifice that almost any major city in the world would be proud to call its civic auditorium. Incredibly, it is not a national cultural center, fine arts building, or museum, though any of these would appear at home in the setting.

Rather, it is a Christian church, designed, constructed, and paid for by thousands of humble Koreans in the past few years. And, more incredibly, the vast structure is filled six to seven times each Sunday by these same vibrant, zealous Koreans who call this Yoido Island Full Gospel Central Church their spiritual home.

Just how large is the congregation? That depends on how one looks at this church that could well be characterized as the "biggest little church in the world."

"This building is only the hull," says Dr. Yonggi Cho, the thirty-eight-year-old pastor who has shepherded its flock since the church was just a tent that covered a floor of grass mats in 1958. "The real church is out there," he says with a sweep of his arm that seems to indicate the whole city of 6 million people.

And by "out there" he might have in mind a particular paper-walled house on a noisy street where six to ten families gather for their church service every Tuesday night—or any other night of their choice. The pastor of this congregation is a busy housewife who has only a high school education and has never received a cent for her work. She leads a friendly and informal service. Newcomers are introduced and welcomed. Singing is lively and sharing is personal and welcomed. One may tell of a recent answer to prayer or report victory over a bad habit. Another will ask for prayer for a specific need which might result in the whole group praying audibly and simultaneously for it. Before finishing up with refreshments amid cheerful fellowship, this housewife/pastor leads her flock in a carefully prepared Bible study especially developed and printed for folks just like the ones in her living room.

That's how big Central Church is. It is fifteen to twenty-five people worshiping, learning, and evangelizing in the convivial atmosphere of a cozy home. But from another viewpoint, this Assembly of God church is a mammoth Christian family of some 30,000 who jam the 8:00 A.M., 10:00 A.M., 12:00 noon, and 2:00 P.M. Sunday services 8,000 at a time. It is a church of almost sixty full-time ministers and an annual budget of well over $1 million. A million American dollars! In Korea!

And, to tie the "bigness" and "littleness" of this remarkable congregation together, it is a church with (at last count) 1,311 house churches and 1,311 unpaid pastors or "shepherds." It is in the development of these house churches that we find the story behind the story of this incredible church growth.

In 1964 Dr. Yonggi Cho was a dynamic twenty-six-year-old pastor on the way up. Starting with just a handful in 1958, Dr. Cho, with an almost unbelievable amount of zeal and hard work through days that began with 4:30 A.M. prayer services and finished past midnight, saw his congregation swell to about 3,000 members. "I was young and puffed up and trying to do everything in my own strength," he said recently. "I carried the whole load of preaching, visiting, praying for the sick, counseling, writing books and articles, launching a radio ministry, and administering everything from the janitorial service to the Sunday school and youth groups."

But one Sunday evening while preaching for the sixth time that day—and after personally baptizing 300 converts that afternoon—he collapsed in the pulpit and was carried out on a stretcher. "The doctor told me that I had the worst kind of nervous breakdown and that if I wanted to live I would have to leave the ministry," he said.

During his long convalescence he struggled with the question of how he could change his approach so that he would not have to give up his growing ministry. As he studied the book of Acts and the Pauline epistles, the Holy Spirit repeatedly hammered into his mind the phrase, "church in the home." A new and daring plan began to form in his mind. He would turn the work of the ministry over to faithful "shepherds" who would establish home groups (churches) in their neighborhoods. They would do the teaching, administering, counseling, praying for the sick, and visiting.

"But how can I get the ministers for this?" he questioned. The answer also came from the book of Acts. He read that such evangelists as Phillip were just deacons. This appeared to be against the Korean tradition—as well as his theological training—but he thought he might as well try. He was a dying man. What did he have to lose?

Calling his deacons together, he said, "I must choose one of two things: Either I leave this church or we reorganize the whole system and divide the church and give it to the lay people."

With their approval of the new plan, Dr. Cho enlisted the help of his mother-in-law—a gifted Christian leader in her own right. She surveyed the congregation and on a map divided the city up into districts. Then she gathered about sixty of the most suitable and trustworthy candidates for the role of church-in-the-home shepherds.

"Folks, you see that I am a sick man and you are the ministers now," Pastor

Cho said to them. "As Christ is depending on me, I am now depending on you to win and train converts. I am a co-worker with the Lord, and in this new plan you also are co-workers with the Lord of the harvest. As the Lord called me and sent me to be a shepherd, so he is now sending you as shepherds into your neighborhoods." Many of these humble folk wept at the words of their pastor. "No one has ever trusted us like this," they said. "We are just lay people."

They were not even the elite of the Central Church which included a two-star general, a congressman, and the vice-mayor of Seoul. Rather, they were housewives, school teachers, office workers, shop owners, small businessmen, and laborers. Two thirds of them were women. None of them would ever be paid for their ministry.

But with amazing allegiance in this crisis, they began to share the ministry and to experience its joys and heartaches. And as they grew in the Lord, so did the church grow. Before that same year of 1964 was out, eighty-five home groups with as many shepherds were in full operation, and membership in the mother church grew to 3,857, an increase of nearly 1,000 after the collapse of the pastor. A thousand more were added in each of the two following years and 2,000 more in 1967. By this time, 8,000 were attending the morning worship, and a fourth service had to be added.

The growth chart for the next six years shows that members were added only by the hundreds. But this is deceptive. The facilities had become so jammed that Pastor Cho actually begged his stronger Christians to stay home on Sunday so that newer Christians could attend! His carefully kept records, therefore, indicate "only" 12,556 members by the end of 1973. But Pastor Cho estimates there were actually about 16,000 in all the house churches put together. This seems reasonable since membership took a leap of over 7,000 in 1974, the first full year that their new structure, seating 8,000, was in use.

Air-conditioned, acoustically perfect, and sporting a suspended dome that reaches about five stories above the main sanctuary, this building almost seems to be a contradiction to the house church concept. Many people— including some in the Assemblies headquarters in Springfield, Missouri— predicted that the church would be a failure when the new site was selected. It was a choice piece of land next to the House of Parliament in an as yet undeveloped area of Seoul—an area slated to be the showplace of all Korea, with the strictest building code in the country. But it was a long way from where the people lived. "Cho, you are moving out in the sand dunes," warned a mission executive. "No one will come way out there. There isn't even good transportation to the island."

True to his New Testament vision, Cho replied, "I am not building a church to bring all the people out here. God told me one thing: the church is to be a training center. I will train all who come over here and send them out to saturate the whole city with cells."

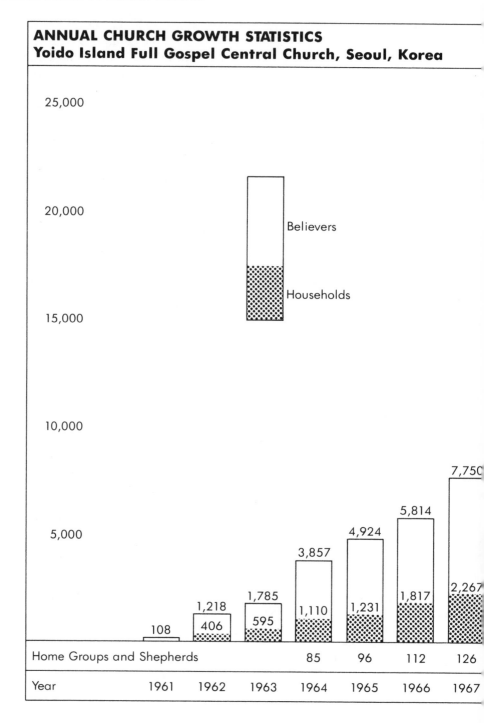

ANNUAL CHURCH GROWTH STATISTICS
Yoido Island Full Gospel Central Church, Seoul, Korea

Year	1961	1962	1963	1964	1965	1966	1967
Believers	108	1,218	1,785	3,857	4,924	5,814	7,750
Households		406	595	1,110	1,231	1,817	2,267
Home Groups and Shepherds				85	96	112	126

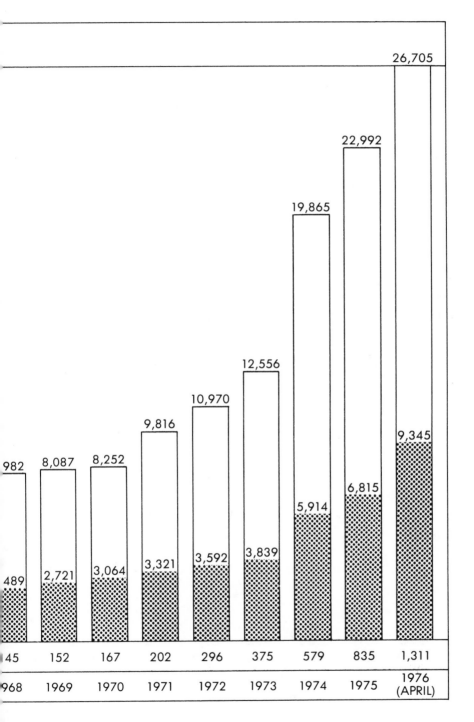

	982	8,087	8,252	9,816	10,970	12,556	19,865	22,992	26,705
	489	2,721	3,064	3,321	3,592	3,839	5,914	6,815	9,345
	45	152	167	202	296	375	579	835	1,311
	1968	1969	1970	1971	1972	1973	1974	1975	1976 (APRIL)

And train them he did. In spite of the informality of these house-church services, they were always carefully planned and prepared. At first there were no printed materials; Pastor Cho began with just simple Bible training for his people. Eventually, carefully designed materials were developed for the Bible lessons to be taught in the house churches. Now, all 1,311 shepherds attend the mother church each Wednesday to receive careful instruction on how to present the Bible passage for the week as well as on other pastoral duties. It is a thrill for guests to visit on a Wednesday and see 800 in one chapel, 300 in another, 150 in a small hall and fifty in an even smaller room—all receiving their training through pre-taped, closed-circuit television.

Twice each year Pastor Cho conducts week-long seminars at the mother church for all the shepherds. They commute daily at their own expense, though Central Church provides lunch. The seminars are on the order of church growth workshops where shepherds are inspired, motivated, and trained to go out and win their neighbors for Christ and then build them up in the Lord.

To fully appreciate what has happened, one would have to understand the great organization and leadership abilities the Lord has given Dr. Cho. Dr. Donald McGavran observes that it is probably the best organized church he has seen anywhere in the world.

ANNUAL ADDITIONS TO THE CHURCH

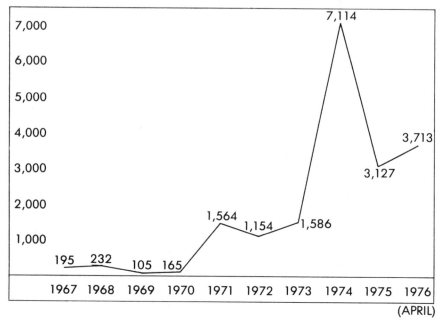

The organizational plan developed for this massive church actually results in close, personal fellowship, training, and supervision for virtually every member and staff person. Each member has a direct relationship to the shepherd of the house church (cell) he attends. Then there is one full-time, paid minister to supervise each twenty-five or so of the shepherds. In turn, each ten of these ministers is guided by a district supervisor. And the six supervisors in turn are the personal responsibility of Pastor Cho himself. In this situation, no one is ever very far away from a helping, guiding hand!

Six large offices are provided (one for each district) in the Central Church where careful planning takes place. In each office, each house church is located exactly on a huge wall map, and careful records are kept of the attendance, offerings and names of newcomers for every cell.

All districts are given a lot of autonomy. They plan and hold their own picnics and summer camps. They occasionally rent large auditoriums for their own training programs, consecration meetings, revivals, or evangelistic campaigns.

With this careful organization and with the new building dedicated near the end of 1973, the membership grew by more than 7,000 in 1974. But the graph shows growth of just a little over 3,000 in 1975, the year that Pastor Cho spent more than six months overseas on a preaching tour. Does this indicate that the whole structure might collapse when and if Dr. Cho passes out of the picture? Probably not. For the church *did* grow by more than 3,000 in the year when he was gone. This is remarkable growth by any standard!

Pastor Cho further minimizes his importance when he considers what will happen when the communists come. "When they came during the Korean War," he says, "they destroyed some 2,000 churches and killed 500 ministers. When they come back they can take me, but that's all. The church can never disappear. This building is just the hull, the superstructure. The church is out there. It is all over town with more than a thousand ministers. It will survive and expand."

But under the present conditions—with peace and with Pastor Cho— there is no question but that they are on the way to saturate all of Seoul with house churches. Beyond that is the whole nation and the whole world. For this they have already reached an annual mission budget of $100,000!

But the key to this growth, Dr. Cho reminds visitors, is always the layman leading the little neighborhood churches in homes. It is in this setting that new converts with their many friends in the world and their new enthusiasm and power in Christ become potent transmitters of the faith. It is in the security and familiar surroundings of a home—instead of the grand cathedral—that Koreans like to accept Christ. With this continued emphasis there is every reason to believe that Dr. Yonggi Cho will continue to lead forth in great victory the biggest little church in the world for many years to come.

In January of 1978—two years ahead of schedule—the Full Gospel Central Church in Seoul, South Korea, surpassed the goal of 50,000 members that had been set for the end of 1980.

In reporting that its membership had tripled in the past three years, Dr. Paul Yonggi Cho, pastor, commented that ". . . the church's primary growth comes through the channel of our home cell units."

The accompanying chart shows a three-year increase of 437 percent in the number of home cell units and a 200 percent increase in membership. In 1977 alone, FGCC's membership increased by 13,181 with 85 percent of them coming by conversion.

CATEGORIES →	HOUSE UNITS	FAMILIES	MEMBERS
November '74	542	4,922	16,309
November '75	755	6,815	22,992
November '76	1,584	13,712	35,704
December '77	2,910	18,392	48,975

Reprint from **Church Growth Bulletin,** May 1978, Volume XIV, No. 5. Used by permission.

Written by John Stetz with the editors.
Reprinted from *Church Growth Bulletin*, September 1976, Volumn XIII, No. 1, by permission.

12. The Church of the Future
Thomas Road Baptist Church
Lynchburg, Virginia
Jerry Falwell, Pastor

During 1979 more than 20,000 people visited the well-known Thomas Road Baptist Church in Lynchburg, Virginia. This independent Baptist church, which was begun by Jerry Falwell, its only pastor, with thirty-five adults and their children in 1956, now records a membership of more than 16,000 persons, and is the hub of multiple ministries which extend worldwide.

Dr. Jerry Falwell is senior pastor of Thomas Road Baptist Church, and Dr. Jim Moon is copastor. They are assisted by more than forty associate pastors and more than 900 full-time employees in the operation of the many-faceted ministries of which the Thomas Road Baptist Church is the fulcrum.

The national and international scope of the ministry of Thomas Road Baptist Church is generated from syndicated television and radio programs, from Dr. Falwell's speaking engagements across the United States, Canada, and in many foreign countries, and from numerous mission teams which canvass the globe ministering and representing Thomas Road Baptist Church and the Liberty Baptist Schools. The Liberty Baptist Schools, of which Dr. Falwell is founder and chancellor, presently (September 1979) boast an enrollment exceeding 4,000 students.

The related ministries of the Thomas Road Baptist Church include:

The Old-Time Gospel Hour. A weekly, one-hour syndicated television program. The program is videotaped each Sunday morning from the auditorium of the Thomas Road Baptist Church for distribution to 327 television stations throughout the United States and Canada. The program is edited on site at the Thomas Road Baptist Church and sent to Pittsburgh, Pennsylvania, where the final, edited version is duplicated and syndicated for national distribution. A one-half-hour daily radio program is heard on 279 stations throughout the United States and Canada.

Teaching ministries of the local church. The Thomas Road Baptist Church is the center for an extensive teaching program, for nursery age through senior citizens. Besides the five preaching services conducted in the auditorium of the Thomas Road Baptist Church each Sunday, scores of individual classes are designed to relate to all age groups. Attendance at Thomas Road Baptist Church Sunday school averages 10,000 people weekly. There are more than 700 workers in the Sunday school departments, many of whom are volunteers. Children and adults are provided the opportunity of riding church buses to the services. Many hundreds are provided transportation to the church in this way.

The Children's Ministry specializes in providing spiritually sound programs and activities for all children. When just eighteen months old, children are taught Bible lessons.

In addition to the regular Sunday programs, youth are ministered to through activities, athletics, Bible clubs, camps, evangelism, visitation, and AWANA Clubs. Thomas Road Baptist Church has one of the most extensive local church youth ministries in the world. "Youth Aflame" is involved in hundreds of activities and programs, including singing groups that travel to high schools to conduct assemblies and to foreign countries to engage in short-term missionary work.

Annual conferences. Throughout the year, special conferences, workshops, seminars, and religious crusades conducted by the church attract thousands of people from across the United States. Preachers and speakers include those on the staff of the Thomas Road Baptist Church and key religious leaders from across the nation.

Counseling Department. The Counseling Department of the Thomas Road Baptist Church is staffed with highly qualified personnel. The department offers, through conferences and written and taped material, a family seminar series, besides personally counseling more than 2,000 people in its offices each week.

Elim Home for alcoholics. The oldest of the outreach ministries of Thomas Road Baptist Church, Elim Home has been operating for almost twenty years. Located on six acres of land, Elim Home serves as a residential/rehabilitation facility for those men with alcoholic problems. Each man served by Elim Home voluntarily agrees to participate in the disciplined sixty-day program. He is personally counseled and given spiritual direction. His physical needs are also ministered to, particularly through the encouragement of vocational rehabilitation.

Hands of Liberty Deaf Department. The Old-Time Gospel Hour television program is interpreted for the deaf, as is every service, class, and activity of Thomas Road Baptist Church and the Liberty Baptist Schools. Deaf people are provided activities and are visited consistently. The Thomas Road Baptist Church provides regular correspondence to deaf people across America.

Senior citizens. The "Senior Saints" ministry of the Thomas Road Baptist Church is organized into five major areas, including: (1) the Jolly Sixties Club, a local ministry, (2) the chaplain program, which sends teams to local nursing homes and retirement villages, (3) evangelistic teams which minister in churches, rest homes, and other meetings, (4) visitation to senior citizens who are not able to leave their homes, (5) the national Senior Saints ministry to churches across the United States, including an annual Senior Saints weekend retreat held at Thomas Road Baptist Church.

Treasure Island Children's Camp. Treasure Island Children's Camp operates eight weeks each summer and accommodates 300 children each week. This dynamic camping experience is offered free to all children on a well-equipped thirty-four-acre island.

Publications. Printed material is sent to thousands of homes from Thomas Road Baptist Church. A bimonthly magazine, *Faith Aflame,* and a biweekly newspaper, the *Journal Champion,* are mailed to thousands of supporters of the Jerry Falwell Ministries. Other printed material which is distributed by the church includes Sunday school curricula, tracts, youth literature, resource material, etc.

Ministry to "special people." The Thomas Road Baptist Church buses in more than 200 mentally retarded and physically handicapped people each week. These people are provided special Sunday school classes and activities. Weekly Bible studies are conducted at a local institution.

Liberty Baptist schools. Students from all fifty states and many foreign countries attend the Liberty Baptist Schools, all of which were founded by Dr. Jerry Falwell.

Lynchburg Christian Academy, begun in 1967, is a private, fully accredited school for grades Kindergarten through 12.

Liberty Bible Institute, founded in 1972, is a two-year Bible college program offering a diploma. It offers a concentrated study of the Bible and is conducted through an evening school as well as a day school.

Liberty Baptist Seminary, founded in 1973, is a graduate school offering programs leading to the degrees of Master of Divinity in Pastoral Studies and Master of Arts in Christian Education, Christian Day School Administration, Christian Counseling, and Christian Business Administration. Liberty Baptist Seminary was granted state approval in May 1977, and is actively pursuing candidate status toward accreditation with the Southern Association of Colleges and Schools.

Liberty Home Bible Institute, begun in 1976, is the mobile counterpart of the Liberty Bible Institute. Through correspondence, the Institute diploma can be earned. Over 8,800 students are now enrolled in this in-depth correspondence course.

Liberty Baptist College, founded in 1971, is a four-year liberal arts college, offering programs leading to the Bachelor of Science degree in eight major areas: business administration, religion, communications, education and psychology, music, natural science and mathematics, social sciences, and television-radio-film. In its ninth year of operation, it has received state accreditation and candidate status toward accreditation with the Southern Association of Colleges and Schools.

The acquisition and development of Liberty Mountain can only be described as phenomenal. During the first six years of the college's existence, students met for classes at the Thomas Road Baptist Church and dilapidated, rented buildings all over the city of Lynchburg. In February 1977 it was imperative to begin consolidating the campus on what was then 3,500 acres of brush and trees on Liberty Mountain. The student body had been denied rental of the largest of their rental buildings for the next school year. Dr. Falwell called his students and faculty together for a prayer meeting in the snow on Liberty Mountain. By September of that year more than 2,000 students attended classes in buildings on Liberty Mountain. The building program continues to progress at a highly accelerated rate, and Liberty Mountain boasts a multimillion-dollar campus. Today there are two classrooms buildings, a gymnasium, a Fine Arts Center, and sixteen dormitories on the mountain campus of Liberty Baptist College. Other buildings are under construction.

Liberty Baptist Schools offer the opportunity to their students to participate in traveling singing teams. The college alone has twelve different singing groups. Some students take a year out of their education to tour the United States and minister in local churches. Other groups minister to the elderly, to high school students, or to numerous others. A mission group travels overseas and conducts its concerts in the foreign languages of the countries it visits. This past summer (1979) SMITE (Student Missionary Intern Training for Evangelism) teams traveled and ministered in Korea, Japan, Africa, Australia, Europe, and Latin America. In 1979 the "Youth Aflame" singing teams sang in four hundred high schools, three hundred churches, and two hundred detention homes.

Because of the LBC music ministry, enthusiastic young people have sung for U.S. presidents, senators, congressmen, Supreme Court justices, governors, generals, members of state legislatures, and other dignitaries from every strata of society. They have sung in prisons, in juvenile courts, on skid rows, and in missions, shopping malls, service clubs, hotels, parks, sports stadiums, as well as at colleges and universities.

It is the goal of Dr. Jerry Falwell to build the college to university status, with the ability to train 50,000 students. It is his goal to soon have all the Liberty Baptist Schools on Liberty Mountain.

Mission board. Strategic Baptist Missions, the newly organized mission board of Thomas Road Baptist Church, has already placed missionaries around the globe.

Liberty Mountain. Plans have been made for Liberty Mountain to one day be the home of not only all the Liberty Baptist Schools but of the Thomas Road Baptist Church, a retirement village for senior citizens, and the base of hundreds of other ministries.

Dr. Falwell's travels. Jerry Falwell travels more than 200,000 miles annually, speaking and ministering in churches, conferences, rallies, and in colleges and universities. He is a frequent guest on television talk shows. Major magazines and newspapers across the country regularly carry features about him, the Thomas Road Baptist Church, and the "Miracle of Liberty Mountain." The

Jerry Falwell Ministries have been reviewed by the major news networks and by CBS's "60 Minutes."

"I Love America" rallies. Due to what Dr. Falwell calls "a rapid degradation of our free society" he has for the past two years been actively involved in a massive "Clean Up America" campaign to "bring this nation back to God and to a stance of biblical morality." He has for the past two years conducted national surveys regarding the issues of known practicing homosexuals teaching in public schools, laws legalizing abortion-on-demand, and laws permitting the display of pornographic materials on newstands, on TV, and in movies. The findings of these surveys have been and continue to be brought to the attention of congressmen, judiciary members, educators, and business leaders. On April 27 a rally held by Dr. Falwell and his "I Love America" team attracted thousands of students and their principals from Christian schools from New York to Florida. Many congressmen, government officials, and senators, including Senators Byrd and Warner of Virginia were present at the rally which attracted 12,000 people.

Today, Dr. Falwell and his "I Love America" team are traveling to the steps of individual state capitols to rally support for pro-family, pro-Bible morality, and pro-American ideas.

Written by Ruth Tomczak, editor for *Faith Aflame* magazine, the devotional magazine of the Old Time Gospel Hour. Used by permission.

13. Eleven Decisions That Produced Growth
Big Valley Grace Community Church
Modesto, California
David Seifert, Pastor

Ten years ago it was unusual for a church to grow without Sunday school buses, contests, or promotion. But that is not the rule today. Many churches are growing by following the simple methods of preaching, teaching, and winning souls to Christ.

Big Valley Grace Community Church has reflected these principles by growing from an average attendance of sixty-eight persons in 1976 to over 850 in the spring of 1980.

Recently Dr. David Seifert, pastor, met with the deacons and elders of the church in a restaurant to discuss why the church had grown so rapidly. The group did not intend to come up with a list, but out of the conversation, they wrote on a napkin eleven decisions that were the reasons why the church has grown so rapidly.

1. The church decided to study the growth potential of the area. Dave Seifert had been in the Long Beach area when the church in Modesto called him to come as pastor. Before accepting the call, Seifert told them he had one more thing he wanted them to do—to make a growth study of the area. Seifert indicated, "I want to know the area, the people, and the potential of growth." The study was a step of faith for the church because it cost $1,200. The church did not have it and agreed to pay two six-hundred-dollar payments stretched over six months.

They found that California has the third lowest percentage of church membership in the nation. Only 35 percent of the people in Modesto were members of a church, which meant that 65 percent were unchurched and candidates for the gospel. But the study covered more than just greater Modesto. First, it looked at the potential in the nearby neighborhood and found there were 65,000 unchurched people within a fifteen-minute drive of the church. Because there was a potential for growth, Seifert made a commitment to Modesto.

Then someone told Seifert that there was already a large church in the city. The person went on to say that Seifert could not build a large work because of the other church.

Seifert answered, "When I was back in Ohio, I learned that corn grew as high on one side of a road as on the other." Then he laughed and continued, "If you are fishing, you catch fish on both sides of the boat, and I believe both congregations can build a great church in Modesto, California." Finally Seifert indicated that the other large church indicated Modesto had a climate for growth because it reflected that the community had a consciousness of God and a hunger for the gospel.

2. *A decision to develop male lay leadership.* When Seifert came to Modesto, there were six deacons in the church. He challenged them to meet him every week for a 5:30 A.M. morning Bible study. Shortly thereafter another man was added, and Seifert called them the "magnificent seven." By meeting at that hour, he determined their commitment. They studied the Word of God, prayed, and planned to become the church that God wanted. Their minds were welded together and they agreed on the goals of the church. They learned to love one another and made future decisions for the growth of a church.

One day they went through the qualifications of I Timothy 3, determining what were the qualifications of an elder. Seifert asked three questions:

    a. Do you believe your life-style fits the qualifications of a New Testament elder?

    b. Would you like the responsibility of being a New Testament elder?

    c. Is there an area in your life that does not match the standards of the Word of God to become an elder?

Out of those early morning meetings have come ten elders and forty-two deacons. These have become a team of lay leadership to build a church.

Recently the church began a woman's discipleship program, and now approximately 150 are involved in a program of study and praying.

3. *A decision to change the church's name to impart vision and remove barriers.* When Seifert first walked into the building he saw the name, Greenwood Grace Brethren Church. He asked, "What is Greenwood?"

The men answered him that it was a small subdivision. He asked them, "Is that the extent of your vision?"

Seifert feels the name of a church should not communicate limitation or smallness of a vision. When traveling through Ohio with his son they saw a church named, "Little Washington Congregational Church."

"What's wrong with that name?" Seifert asked his son.

"The first word—little?" was the boy's answer.

Seifert agreed. He often exhorts his congregation that there is no little church in God's sight. Any church where God is working is a big work.

Recently a pastor came to Seifert indicating he pastored a small church in Pennsylvania. "Wait a minute!" Seifert said to the pastor. "When you say a small church you limit your vision. The church is the greatest work God has on this earth because it is the living organism—the body of Jesus Christ on this earth."

Seifert prayed for a new name for the church in Modesto. As he drove a nearby Interstate highway he saw the acres of grape vines. He saw a stake in the form of a cross on which the vine was stretched out. He wanted the church to reflect the Scripture, "I am the vine, ye are the branches." And there he got his name, Big Valley; a church right in the heart of a big valley, And the logo of the church is a vine and branches stretched out on a cross. With that insight, the church agreed to change the name to impart vision and eliminate barriers.

With this decision, the church decided upon a low-key denominationalism. Seifert goes on to say, "I love the Grace Brethren Church denomination, and there is no other group of which I would want to be a part. The imperative thing in life is to fellowship with people who love Jesus Christ and want to know his Word."

4. A decision to saturate the community with the gospel. As Seifert read the New Testament he found that the early Christians were saturating the city of Jerusalem, going from house to house and street to street, attempting to win people to Jesus Christ. The church decided to saturate Modesto. First they secured a mailing list of 200 people in the city so they could take out a permit to mail to them. They began a newspaper, *The Big Valley Vine,* to advertise the church. Recently the newspaper was sent out to 15,000 homes, communicating the gospel through pictures, articles, and stories.

5. A decision to move outside of the four walls of the church building. The four walls of a church building can become barriers to keep the gospel inside. The New Testament church was not kept within the walls of a building; the people went out into the streets carrying the gospel to their friends.

When Seifert first came to the church, only about thirty or forty people attended prayer meeting. He actually thought about doing away with prayer meeting. At the same time the church wanted to inaugurate an AWANA program for children, but there was no space. The church members loved their children, but how could they minister to them? The pastor went before the deacons and said, "Let's give the church to our children on Wednesday night."

Because of the early-morning discipleship program, men were willing to become Bible study leaders in homes on Wednesday night. Instead of having one prayer meeting, the church had four. Children came into the church for the AWANA program. Within a few short weeks, prayer meeting had tripled in attendance because they got the church outside of the four walls of the building.

Later, the church took its Sunday school into surrounding homes, clubhouses, and elementary schools. They were able to expand because of the principle of going outside of the walls of a building.

6. A decision to surround the pastor with complementing staff. The first prerequisite to be a staff member at the Big Valley Grace Community Church is to be godly. Seifert feels he has the greatest team of church secretaries. He did not necessarily attempt to find someone who could type or fulfill the office skills, although they do that well. He was looking for someone to be a fellow worker in the ministry of Jesus Christ.

One day Pastor Seifert had lunch with a young pastor named Darrell who shared his philosophy of ministry through music. The young pastor said, "I do not primarily want to be a musician but a man who will minister to people through music as an avenue to reach people for Christ and build them up in the gospel."

Darrell worked without a salary for six months, actually purchasing choir music with his own money, and built the choir as a ministry. Today Darrell is a minister of music on the full-time staff of the church.

7. *A decision to launch out and develop a Christian school.* The church only had a nursery school and had added a kindergarten. The people came to their pastor and told him their children needed to be in a Christian school when they finished kindergarten. The people wanted a place where their children could grow in Christian grace Monday through Friday, and not just on Sunday. The desire for a Christian school came out of a deep need from the people.

Seifert knew that a Christian school would cost the congregation and at times he feels it would be easier not to have a Christian school. Seifert knew he had to do what God told him. They began a Christian school that has expanded their ministry and added to their influence.

8. *The church decided to conduct a definite stewardship campaign.* A consultant met with Seifert when the church needed space to grow. As a result, the pastor challenged the people with a financial plan. According to Seifert, "This way we found the people who were really committed to the church." The church launched the "Together We Build" campaign, and the people were challenged to give over and above their regular giving for 156 weeks — this meant they gave sacrificially. The theme was not "equal gifts" but "equal sacrifice." As a result, the church's expansion is being paid for in three years.

9. *A decision to expand the early childhood and nursery facilities.* The nursery was located in a small room in the original building. When Seifert first came, he walked in and counted only two cribs. He realized it was too small for his vision. He envisioned twelve screaming babies in that small room, then he realized they would interrupt the church service. A decision to provide space for a nursery was critical because young couples would not attend church if they did not have a place for their babies.

The church bought a modular building for expansion. Some of the members did not like the building because of it's inferior construction. It was a critical decision. Seifert reminded the people that ministry was more important than a building. As soon as a building was provided for more children, it was filled. Then they provided another building for early childhood education, and that building was filled. Then the kindergarten class had to use the overflow area of the auditorium for its classroom.

10. *A decision to move forward only in unity.* Seifert remembers on one occasion a man voting "no" in an elders meeting. This was a shattering experience for a church that had experienced such harmony.

"Hold it . . . we are not unified. Let's wait," Seifert said. He explained to the elders that they were not moving ahead until they could move ahead in unity. The man responded, "Pastor, I am not against the program. I just have some questions that were not answered."

"Do you mean that?" Seifert asked.

They soon voted 100 percent and moved forward in unity.

Seifert says that when ten elders vote yes and forty-two deacons agree, it is the mind of the Lord. Recently someone came into the church and commented, "Don't you ever vote against anything?"

11. They decided to carry out the Great Commission in their area. Seifert's greatest desire is not to be comfortable, nor to please himself, nor to have a nice little church that pleases the congregation. His greatest desire is to reach out into the community. The pastor feels that the church has a responsibility to God to carry out the Great Commission in their community. He feels they can grow to become the church God has designed for them.

Churches grow for a number of reasons, and there are many contributing reasons why Big Valley Grace Community Church is growing. Being decisive is one of the reasons, and the eleven decisions in this church reflect a church that could determine the plan of God and follow it.

BIG VALLEY GRACE COMMUNITY CHURCH
YEARLY ATTENDANCE AVERAGES

	1975	1976	1977	1978	1979	1980
A.M.	59	68	169	349	546	860
P.M.	37	42	109	183	308	
S.S.	60	60	128	218	363	

OFFERINGS

1975	$ 49,235.39
1976	32,306.18
1977	108,761.80
1978	211,014.30
1979	389,650.49

14. Grace Community Church: A Profile of Ministry

Grace Community Church
Panorama City, California
John MacArthur, Pastor

Grace Community Church, located in Panorama City, California (Sun Valley), a suburb of Los Angeles, began in 1956 in a medium-sized home with about twenty-five people, and today more than 7,000 gather each Sunday.

Since its first public service on July 1, 1956, the congregation has served as "a non-denominational community church," but it's not anti-denominational. Dr. John MacArthur, the church's current pastor-teacher, has served since February 1969 and is the third pastor of the congregation. Dr. Don Householder, Grace's founding pastor, was a Methodist and was followed by a Baptist, Dr. Richard Elvee, who has succeeded Billy Graham as president of Northwestern College in Minneapolis. The Church has a great heritage.

The Sunday morning worship attendance has increased tenfold, from 700 members in 1969 to over 7,000 each Sunday in 1979. Yearly first-time visitors have grown from less than 2,000 in 1969 to nearly 5,500 in 1979, according to the sixty-five-page 1979 Annual Report of the congregation. While baptizing almost 100 in 1969, nearly 400 were baptized in 1979. During the decade of John MacArthur's leadership as pastor, membership in the church has increased dramatically from 670 to 3,115.

Pastor John MacArthur routinely reports receiving an estimated fifteen telephone calls and twenty to forty letters daily. A graduate of Pacific College (B.A.) and Talbot Seminary (M. Div.) he has received due honors from Western Graduate School of Theology (Litt. D.) and Talbot Seminary (D.D.). Books written by the pastor-teacher include: *The Church: The Body of Christ, The Charismatics, Why Believe the Bible?, Take God's Word For It, Kindgom Living: Here and Now,* and others.

Grace Community Church is administered and ruled by a forty-five-member board of elders. During 1979 the board consisted of twenty-three laymen and twenty-two pastors. That same year a council/committee system was implemented by dividing the board of elders into seven groups whose separate responsibilities include: outreach, trustees, personnel, communication, training, youth, and worship coordination. Each Sunday morning they gather for prayer before the morning worship service, and they meet monthly to conduct the business of the church. All decisions made by them must be unanimous.

Each age-graded adult group also has its own deacons and deaconesses, and all leaders are required to meet biblical qualifications for their offices. Leadership development is a priority in all ministries.

Ministries of Grace Community Church include radio, tapes, books, thrift stores, cross-cultural and community evangelism, jail and prison ministries, a premarital program, an extensive camping ministry to families, couples, and single adults, and conferences to equip members in meeting needs of the mentally retarded, spastic children and the deaf. The church serves as a seminary extension center, has a Bible institute (one-year program), and provides both lay and professional counseling to Grace members and the surrounding community.

Among the fastest-growing areas of ministry at Grace Church are cassette tapes and radio. The original 100 tapes produced each week back in 1970 have mushroomed to sales of over 10,000 each week currently. This represents an increase of 10,000 percent during the past decade. The radio broadcast, known as *Grace to You*, originated in 1977 and was received by eleven stations the following year. That base soon increased to thirty-six stations in 1979 and the goal projected for 1980 is seventy-six stations. The thirty-minute program is currently receiving about 3,000 letters per month and church leaders expect this to increase when the new stations boost the listening audience from 11,000 to 1.7 million. "All of the radio station air-time costs have been met through gifts from the listening audience. Over 17,000 listeners have written to express gratitude for this ministry."

Outreach ministries of Grace Community Church are overseen by eleven elders. The three areas of recognized outreach responsibility are: (1) cross-cultural ministries, (2) community evangelism ministries, and (3) local church work ministries. Mission fields and missionaries visited by members last year include: Seoul, Tokyo, Brazil, India, Havana, Moscow, Yucatan, Argentina, and Columbia. The congregation has supported missionaries in Burundi (Africa), Bangladesh, Sao Paulo, Rio de Janeiro, and Osaka.

The report of the church also states, "Exciting things were also occurring closer to home. From February (1979) to April, two Brazilian pastors associated with Overseas Crusades, Paulo Moreira and Osmar DaSilva, interned at Grace Church." Approximately twenty homeless Indochinese refugees have been "adopted" by the church and over $19,000 was collected to assist in the needs of this tragedy. Also, fifty of the young people from the church went to Urbana '79 at the University of Illinois.

Community evangelism centers around "Evangelism Explosion," evangelism seminars, missionary support, and juvenile hall ministry. The church reports, "The Spring 1979 Evangelism Explosion program had 260 participants and expanded in the Fall to 325 people with seventeen area leaders." More than 3,000 people were visited during 1979. Missionary groups supported by Grace Church include Navigators, Missionary Gospel Fellowship, and Friends of Israel. These resources aid in training seminars like those offered by the church in Jewish evangelism (five-day) and Catholic evangelism (one-day). Tom Brown coordinates seventy people involved in the juvenile hall ministry.

The Widow's Mite thrift and gift stores are also a ministry peculiar to Grace Church. The stores are all operated by seminary students of the church and supply quality second-chance clothing and household items at reasonable prices. Store locations include Sepulveda, Reseda, and Sunland/Tujunga. Recently, a panel truck was purchased to further assist families and the increased donations of items by Grace members and others. Income from the stores is used to assist in paying student salaries and scholarship assistance.

Jail and prison ministries are a vital part of the church ministries. At present nine teams of part-time workers visit the jails of the Los Angeles County area to teach and preach. Four facilities are being visited thirteen to fifteen times each month. Included in this ministry of the congregation are the full- and part-time chaplains. Rich Hines serves as full-time chaplain of the maximum security facility while Ned Whitman and Bill Heinz minister to those confined to the minimum security.

During the past year, the Spanish work led by Daniel Lozano and Duane Rea has grown from seventy-three to 200 in attendance with 104 first-time visitors. An estimated 250,000 Spanish-speaking people live in the San Fernando Valley area.

Camping and retreats at Forest Home registered 3500 participants for the fourth annual all-Grace family weekend in June and the three Grace Couples Conferences offered during September, January, and February. The couples conferences include couples between ages of twenty and sixty.

Grace Church is a teaching church first and foremost, committed to the Bible and a firm belief in its inerrancy. The Logos Bible Study Center is offered to both members and community residents to improve lay and full-time ministry staff skills. Both daytime and evening college level classes are offered. As a new and unique experiment, Grace Church is now the location of an extension of Talbot Theological Seminary in La Mirada, California (a municipality located in the southern sector of the Los Angeles metro area).

The resident faculty and Grace pastors work together to integrate theology and practice. Begun in 1971, the library now includes 7,500 volumes and the Center has registered over 1,237 students for forty-six evening classes and seventy day students.

Over 1,000 counseling sessions are reported by the two major counseling ministries of the church: the Lay Counseling Ministry and the Grace Counseling Service. The latter is centered in counseling referrals from Christian lawyers. Fifty committed and trained counselors serve the Prayer Room.

The ministries mentioned above represent most but not all of the ministries of

Grace Community Church. These are shared with the hope that others may catch a new vision of possibilities for church growth through evangelism and finding needs where people hurt, then reaching out to meet those needs in the name of Jesus Christ.

Church Growth in Church Groups

15. Fundamentalism

"A new movement," reports a recent article in *The Nation*, "reminiscent of the fundamentalist surge associated with the Rev. Billy Sunday and William Jennings Bryan, which culminated in the famous Scopes trial of July 1925, is emerging in the Sunbelt States."[1] The writer further credits the leadership of the movement as being "considerably more sophisticated than those of the 1920s. . . ."

Academic leaders representing virtually every major scientific discipline have adopted "scientific creationism" as the foremost model for their specialties.

University of Texas political scientist Steve Hendricks writes, "We are seeing a tremendous change in the composition of fundamentalist churches. . . . They are becoming massively middle class."[2] He also cited "many highly technically trained individuals in fundamentalism." The *Psychology Today* article accents statistics compiled by the University of Michigan Survey Research Center and Chicago's National Opinion Research Center and concludes that "successful young fundamentalists are attracting others at their economic level who were raised in other denominations."

Interestingly, the revival of fundamentalism in American church growth has appeared noticeably among Baptist congregations. The rise and growth of these churches have been recorded in the annual listing, "The 100 Largest Sunday Schools," written by Dr. Elmer Towns in the *Christian Life* magazine. While the churches listed are the superchurch variety, it is important to remember that these churches have been frequently copied by the myriad of smaller fundamentalist churches.

Dr. Jerry Falwell, pastor of Lynchburg, Virginia's militant Thomas Road Baptist Church, and Dr. Elmer Towns write in the book *Church Aflame:*

> The authors believe the large church is a strategy that God has raised up in this decade to reach the metropolitan-dwelling American. Historians will probably look back on the decade of the 70's as the beginning of the large church movement. They believe that over 300 churches will be raised up in this country that will be averaging over 2,000 in attendance in this decade. This amounts to one large church for each of the 300 major metropolitan areas of America.[3]

*This chapter was prepared by John Vaughan. Even though Elmer Towns is an author of this book, Vaughan quotes from him and uses the designation "Towns" in this chapter because of his contribution to fundamentalism.

Critics of fundamentalist church growth persist both within and outside the movement. Elmer Towns, the leading literary spokesman of fundamentalist church growth, focuses on one frequent objection from non-Baptist members of fundamentalism by specifying, "Some denominational churches are growing, but usually, more Baptist churches are growing and more Baptist churches are large."[4] (Seventy-four of the largest Sunday schools in *Christian Life's* 1976 listing were in Baptist churches).

Garry Wills, adjunct professor of humanities at Johns Hopkins University, presents added insight into the predominance of Baptists:

> The theologian Robert McAfee Brown recently told me, "We main-line religions are just recognizing that the Baptists are the main line in terms of numbers."
>
> . . . Baptists have been the leading sect in American Protestantism for all of modern history. They constitute 20 percent of the population . . .[5]

Secondly, others question the ministry capabilities of the large church. Dan Bauman, pastor of Central Baptist Church in St. Louis, asked, "How can a pastor give personal care to more than 300 people?"[6]

But Dr. Jackson W. Carroll, coordinator of research in the Church and Ministry Program for Hartford Seminary Foundation (Hartford, Connecticut), states in his book, *Small Churches Are Beautiful:*

> We don't expect to see the preoccupation with bigness and the admiration of the large church disappear overnight . . . Across evangelical America, the dream of creating the largest and fastest-growing church is still very much alive and will remain so.[7]

While fundamentalism tends to be both opposed and ignored by its opponents, there appears an occasional voice outside the ranks with encouraging affirmations for the superchurch concept. Almost four decades ago an article appeared in a Southern Baptist publication entitled, *God Is for Numbers.* Dr. Warren Wiersbe, formerly pastor of Chicago's Moody Memorial Church and of Calvary Baptist Church, Covington, Kentucky, is quoted as saying, "We want numbers . . . not so we can count people but because people count."[8] Thirty of the 100 largest Sunday schools listed in *Christian Life* (1976) were Southern Baptist churches.[9]

In Hollis L. Green's *Why Churches Die* we read, "Generally, slow growth indicates that something is wrong with the quality of life in the church. . . . There is abundant evidence around the world in Brazil, in Chile, in Indonesia, and in Latin America that rapid growth continues to be the norm for New Testament congregations."[10] So growing churches are not just an isolated episode in American church growth.

Dr. Thomas R. McFaul, assistant professor of sociology at the University of Houston, concludes, "Moreover, the conservative churches are excellent image-makers. And they are uninhibited in their use of the mass media to market charismatic personalities. In brief . . . the fundamentalist groups have simply 'outhustled' the mainline Protestant denominations."[11]

Just as Body Life congregations tend to focus on discovery of spiritual gifts and the local church as a family unit, the fundamentalist churches noticeably view the church as an army of soul winners.

Commenting on the trends in Sunday school growth, one observer wrote, "Who cares about the 100 largest? There are one-third of a million other Sunday schools that need a transfusion." Unknowingly, the critic answered his own question all too well. If for no other reason than the widespread need for "a transfusion," the rapidly growing fundamentalist churches have much to offer as models of growth. While all fundamentalist churches are neither large nor growing, the fact cannot be ignored that many of the superchurches began as infant churches themselves within the past two decades. Most have demonstrated a strong desire and ability to overcome many of the same barriers that face multitudes of non-growing churches across America.

Dr. Elmer Towns's reply to the above inquirer is highly appropriate for our study here:

> Like waves in the pond, the innovations among the 100 largest are predictions of trends in the Sunday school world. What they do in 1976 will filter down to other Sunday schools in two or three years. Their emphasis on quality will affect thousands of other schools.[12]

You can be certain that fundamentalist church growth is opposed to the view expressed in the article "God's Arithmetic" by Dr. Hans-Ruedi Weber, director of the portfolio for biblical studies in the World Council of Churches. Weber writes:

> Numbers and growth are important in God's arithmetic: not necessarily large and increasing numbers, but representative numbers and growth in grace. The representative few stand for all. . . . The key question is not how churches can grow numerically, but how they can grow in grace and so become God's representative number.[13]

The two most frequently identifiable groups of fundamentalists in American church growth are those churches identified as "independent Baptist" and those who collectively constitute the "Baptist Bible Fellowship." The 1976 listing of the 100 largest Sunday schools in *Christian Life* magazine indicated seventeen as being affiliated with the Baptist Bible Fellowship, twenty-one as being independent Baptists, and thirty as Southern Baptists.[14] The former two groups are commonly identified as "independent" Baptists. Collectively, the five Baptist groups in the listing compose 70 percent of the 100 largest Sunday schools in the United States.

The Sword of the Lord, perhaps the most influential fundamentalist publication in the country, quoted a source from the Southern Baptist Home Mission Board as saying that "between 750 and 800 churches have gone independent between 1963 and 1972. . . ." Earlier the same article concluded, "Probably about two or three churches may be leaving the Southern Baptist Convention each week to become independent."[15] This article merely accents that fundamentalist churches are able to extend their ranks both through evangelistic and transfer growth methods.

PIONEERS AND PRINCIPLES

" 'Fundamentalism' is still a fighting word. Many use it primarily as a derogatory term to pin on any Christian more conservative than themselves," states George Marsden in *Christian Scholar's Review*.[16] He then lists four general qualities found among fundamentalists which more liberal groups tend to modify: (1) mass evangelism, (2) stress on personal evangelism and individual religious experience, (3) world missions, and (4) personal ethics that magnify purity and separation of the church from carnal influences.

Historically, fundamentalism's leaders in America were members of the large established denominations. Many were pastors of influential churches and seminary professors representing several denominations. Groups and their leaders included: Presbyterians (J. G. Machen, W. J. Erdman, R. D. Wilson, William J. Bryan), Congregationalists (R. A. Torrey), Methodists (Shuler), Reformed Episcopal (Gray), and Baptists (W. B. Riley, T. T. Shields, J. Frank Norris). This diversity of groups allowed fundamentalism to develop into a widespread movement instead of an isolated sect.

Dr. Harold Lindsell, editor-emeritus of *Christianity Today* and author of *The Battle for the Bible*, writes, "The charge that they are 'wooden-headed literalists' shows the bias of those who make the charge."[17]

The three periods when fundamentalism has blossomed in the last two centuries were the 1880s, 1910-30s and the 1970s. These have also been times of intense controversy and criticism for fundamentalists. The first period centered around giants like Warfield, Hodge, Briggs, and Smith. The second period (1910-30s) marks the events of J. G. Machen and the 1929 division of Princeton Seminary. Two other events the same era include Cornelius Van Til's role in the founding of Westminster Seminary (1929) and the 1942 formation of the National Association of Evangelicals. The 1970s have proven to be a time of explosive church growth rather than theological confrontation.

During those early days, fundamentalism was a movement within the membership and leadership of several major denominations to reestablish the scriptural basis of five essential doctrinal truths: (1) the inerrancy of the Bible, (2) the virgin birth, (3) the physical resurrection of Jesus Christ, (4) substitutionary atonement, and (5) the imminent, physical, and visible return of Christ. Publications like *The Sunday School Times* and *Moody Monthly* served as forums for communicating the views of fundamentalists. "The second generation of fundamentalists," remarks Daniel B. Stevick in *Beyond Fun-*

damentalism, "were less revolutionary and tended to prefer to voice themselves through more 'evangelical' magazines like *Christian Life* and *Christianity Today.*"[18]

The term "fundamentalism" was born when the "fundamental" doctrines and others were printed in twelve paperbound volumes between 1909-1915 under the title, *The Fundamentals: A Testimony to the Truth.* These booklets contained sixty-five articles and were circulated freely to church leaders throughout the English-speaking world. Eventually over 3 million copies were circulated. Stevick reminds us:

> While a premillenial eschatology was not shared by all of the groups related to Fundamentalism, it did characterize the movement. . . . The Niagara Prophecy Conferences, dating back into the late 1800's, were among the first organized movements that led into Fundamentalism. And the . . . Schofield Bible of 1909 . . . became almost everywhere a distinctive mark of the movement.[19]

Various interpreters of the movement classify it into various "subspecies" or "camps." These classifications are essential to understanding why only a segment within fundamentalism has been visibly touched by the revival of church growth in North America.

Daniel B. Stevick suggests the following strains and their resulting elements: (1) evangelicalism, (2) puritanism, (3) revivalism, and (4) Plymouth Brethren.[20] He later reduces their roots into two abbreviated forms: (1) popular fundamentalism, and (2) scholarly fundamentalism.[21]

Elmer Towns, meanwhile, distinguishes between (1) "withdrawing fundamentalists" (represented by the Northern Bible Church Movement), and (2) the "aggressive fundamentalists" (the aggressive soul-winning churches). "The two camps among fundamentalists," writes Towns, "have fellowship with each other and are more similar to each other than either is to the evangelical camp."[22]

Now let's examine the implications of fundamentalism's history for church growth. Basically, the two major forces to emerge from the fundamentalist past were largely baptistic (aggressive soul winners) and presbyterial or reformed (academic apologists). When the battle for the Bible led to the actual separation and exodus of many fundamentalists from major denominations (i.e., separatists), many others chose to remain to correct error from within the denominational ranks (i.e., puritans). The models were thereby formed that would have a definite effect on present church growth patterns and philosophies.

Numerical church growth is directly affected by the view of the "fundamentals" and "separation" held by churches. Few churches that reject the fundamentals ever grow to be either large or Bible-centered congregations. Numerical growth usually centers around their leaders' personalities or culture-related issues.

EVANGELICAL-FUNDAMENTALIST

The diagram illustrates the probable direction that a person will go when moving from a denominational church, and vice versa. While there are "puritans" within fundamentalism, there are also churches, groups, and individuals who are at various levels of being both separatists and puritans among denominational evangelicals. Some fundamentalist-presbyterian-type churches consider themselves as evangelicals, but fundamentalists (independent Baptist) do not.

EVANGELICALS

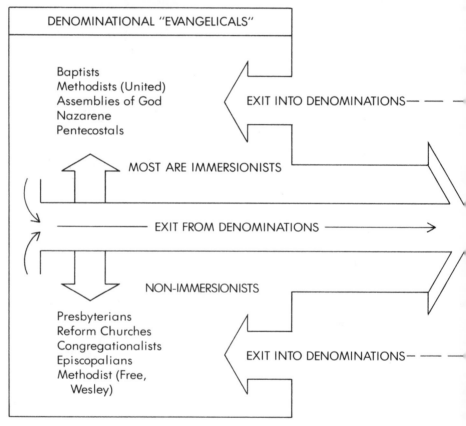

DENOMINATIONAL "EVANGELICALS"

Baptists
Methodists (United)
Assemblies of God
Nazarene
Pentecostals

EXIT INTO DENOMINATIONS— — —

MOST ARE IMMERSIONISTS

EXIT FROM DENOMINATIONS

NON-IMMERSIONISTS

Presbyterians
Reform Churches
Congregationalists
Episcopalians
Methodist (Free,
    Wesley)

EXIT INTO DENOMINATIONS— — —

Note: Three major articles giving correct sociological research information on religious mobility in the U.S. are:

1. Christopher Kirk Hadaway, "Denominational Switching and Membership Growth: In Search of a Relationship,"**Sociological Analysis,** vol. 39 (Winter), pp. 321-337.

2. Frank Newport, "Religious Switchers in the United States," **American Sociological Review,** vol. 44, no. 4, pp. 528-552.

3. Wade Clark Roof and Christopher Hadaway, "Denominational Switching in the Seventies: Going Beyond Stark and Glock," **Journal for the Scientific Study of Religion,** 1979: vol. 18, no. 4, pp. 363-379.

EMBERSHIP FLOW CHART:

FUNDAMENTALISTS

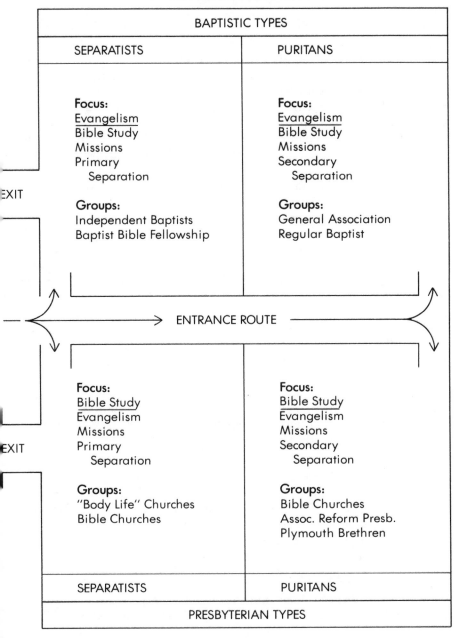

BAPTISTIC TYPES	
SEPARATISTS	PURITANS

Focus:
Evangelism
Bible Study
Missions
Primary
  Separation
 	
Groups:
Independent Baptists
Baptist Bible Fellowship
	Focus:
	Evangelism
	Bible Study
	Missions
	Secondary
	  Separation
	
	Groups:
	General Association
	Regular Baptist

EXIT

⟶ ENTRANCE ROUTE ⟶

Focus:
Bible Study
Evangelism
Missions
Primary
  Separation
 	
Groups:
"Body Life" Churches
Bible Churches
	Focus:
	Bible Study
	Evangelism
	Missions
	Secondary
	  Separation
	
	Groups:
	Bible Churches
	Assoc. Reform Presb.
	Plymouth Brethren

SEPARATISTS	PURITANS
PRESBYTERIAN TYPES	

EXIT

Two types of "separation" need to be defined: *primary* and *secondary* separation. Separation is the measurable social scale whereby the degree of mutual cooperation between two groups or individuals can be determined. The separatist fundamentalist's personal life-style is the one most affected by his view of separation.

Primary separation allows a separatist fundamentalist to cooperate and fellowship with any born-again believer who believes the biblical fundamentals. It does not, however, allow the fundamentalist to cooperate or "give Christian recognition to those who are unconverted or who deny any of the basic essentials of the Christian faith. . . ," according to a resolution adopted by fundamentalist evangelists, pastor-evangelists, and educators assembled in Chicago during December 26 and 27, 1958.[23]

This form of separation drew leadership from among the following individuals and groups: Dr. John R. Rice and independent Baptists, Dr. Bob Jones, Jr., Associated Gospel Churches, Conservative Baptist Association, Southern Baptist Fellowship, the National Association of Free Will Baptists, and others.

Secondary separation, however, is a view practiced by groups and individuals who do not fellowship or cooperate with any other group or individual who has known ties or sympathies with the unconverted and who deny any of the fundamentals of the faith. Examples of groups adopting this view include: Regular Baptists, churches whose ancestry is the Northern Bible Church movement, and Independent Fundamental Churches of America.

It is this writer's observation that when considering fundamentalist numerical church growth, Baptist-type congregations usually surpass Presbyterian-type churches; separatist-type churches outgrow the puritanist variety; and primary separatist groups repeatedly surpass secondary separatist groups. Dr. Jack Hyles, pastor of the largest Sunday school in America (which averages more than 14,000 attendance each Sunday) voiced the mood and method of leaders in rapidly growing churches when he said, "I don't believe in growth; I practice it."[24]

Many pioneers have influenced the building of great fundamentalist churches in America. Four men, two publications and one institution have been selected for our study: Dr. Louis Entzminger, Dr. Elmer Towns, Dr. Jack Hyles, Dr. Jerry Falwell, *Christian Life* magazine, *The Sword of the Lord*, and Baptist Bible College of Springfield, Missouri.

DR. LOUIS ENTZMINGER (1876-1958)

A converted lumberjack, Louis Entzminger served as pastor of First Baptist Church in New Orleans. In 1913 he became full-time Sunday school superintendent for J. Frank Norris (First Baptist Church, Fort Worth, Texas). Just two years earlier in 1911 an estimated 600 of the 1,200 members had left the church.

Entzminger organized the Sunday school into groups, classes, and departments. The visitation efforts under his leadership with his pastor frequently reported 1,000 calls weekly.[25] By 1928 First Baptist Church had developed the world's largest Sunday school with 12,000 members and an average attendance of 5,200.

When he moved to Fort Worth, Texas, Entzminger was instrumental in the formative years of planning and developing the Fundamentalist Baptist Bible Institute, later known as Bible Baptist Seminary.

Dr. W. B. Riley, for forty-five years (1897-1942) former pastor of First Baptist Church of Minneapolis, Minnesota, and called "the greatest statesman in the American pulpit" by William Jennings Bryan, said, "Dr. Louis Entzminger I regard as the greatest Sunday school man on the American continent."[26]

The following summary from Dr. Entzminger in his own words describes his contribution to church growth among fundamentalists:

Some years ago, after considerable research and investigation, I was able to make a list of the twenty-five largest Sunday schools on the North American continent.

I discovered that I had conducted enlargement campaigns, graded and reorganized, installed my system of records . . . in twenty-three of them.

I do not claim credit for building these twenty-three largest Sunday schools; but I claim that my work, plans, and methods doubled, and in some instances, immediately tripled the attendance of these Sunday schools. . . .[27]

Dr. Entzminger thereby became one of the first recorded researchers and compilers of America's largest churches.

The twenty-three largest Sunday schools listed by Dr. Entzminger in 1949 included:

First Baptist Church—Ft. Worth, Texas
Temple Baptist Church—Detroit, Michigan
First Baptist Church—Birmingham, Alabama
Dauphin Way Baptist Church—Mobile, Alabama
First Baptist Church—New Orleans, Louisiana
First Baptist Church—Shreveport, Louisiana
First Baptist Church—Minneapolis, Minnesota
Jarvis Street Baptist Church—Toronto, Canada
First Baptist Church—Houston, Texas
Broadway Baptist Church—Knoxville, Tennessee
First Baptist Church of Maywood (Los Angeles), California

First Baptist Church — San Diego, California
First Baptist Church — Charlotte, North Carolina
First Baptist Church of Lockland — Cincinnati, Ohio

Interestingly, this list of churches illustrates the problem of succession and transfer of leadership from one generation to another. From the 1969 *Christian Life* listing of the 50 largest Sunday schools in America, only one church, Temple Baptist Church of Detroit, retained its rank and momentum numerically. The 1971 listing in *Christian Life* indicated that Dauphin Way Baptist Church in Mobile, Alabama, ranked as having the fiftieth largest Sunday school in America. Today, First Baptist Church of Fort Worth, Texas, averages approximately 500 instead of 5,000 in its weekly attendance.

Some critics question the validity of building large Sunday schools that diminish noticeably with leadership changes. While it is true that decline is a real part of the growth cycle, many denominations cannot claim the almost 8,000 new converts baptized as reported in the 1976 *Christian Life* listing for First Baptist Church of Hammond, Indiana. These churches appear for a season, as do great periods of revival, to restore biblical purity and result in multitudes of souls being claimed for the kingdom of God. Even with the decrease in weekly Sunday school attendance from 5,000 to 500, First Baptist Church of Fort Worth still ranks in the top ten percentile of churches by size in the United States.

DR. ELMER TOWNS

Recognized as one of ten Sunday School Newsmakers of the Decade by *Christian Life* magazine, Dr. Towns is the acknowledged authority on both the largest and fastest-growing churches in America. He has spoken in over seventy of the 100 churches with the largest Sunday schools.

Author of twenty-seven books with nine publishers, Dr. Towns has had three about Sunday school listed among the best-sellers list in *Christian Bookseller* magazine. He has served as Sunday school editor of *Christian Life* magazine for twelve years and has written over 1,000 articles in popular and professional publications. The October 1977 issue of *Christian Life* says of him:

> His *Christian Life* reports on the largest Sunday schools rocked the nation in the late 60's because most people thought the Sunday school was dying. Many credit his "crusading typewriter" as one of the factors in the up-swing in Sunday school attendance.[28]

Dr. Towns is dean of Liberty Baptist Seminary for Thomas Road Baptist Church in Lynchburg, Virginia (third largest Sunday school in America). Prior to his move to Lynchburg in 1978 he served as: executive vice-president and co-founder of Baptist University of America (Decatur, Georgia); executive vice-president and co-founder of Liberty Baptist College (Lynchburg, Virginia); professor of Christian Education at Trinity Evangelical Divinity School (Deerfield, Illinois); president of Winnipeg Bible College (Winnipeg,

Manitoba); and past president, Canadian Conference of Christian Educators.

Dr. C. Peter Wagner, associate professor of Church Growth in the School of World Mission, Fuller Theological Seminary (Pasadena, California), says, ". . . probably the most prolific writer on growing churches in America is Elmer Towns."[29]

"Elmer Towns, in his book *America's Fastest Growing Churches*," concludes Dr. J. Robertson McQuilken, president of Columbia Bible College (Columbia, South Carolina), ". . . shows clearly in the churches he examines, growth is almost wholly dependent on the abilities of the leader."[30]

DR. JACK HYLES

As pastor of the First Baptist Church in Hammond, Indiana, he has seen his people grow from an average weekly attendance of 3,000 to over 14,000 from 1968 to 1977.

First Baptist Church is the largest church in America and gathered more than 101,000 for bible study in May 1976. The church registered nearly 6,000 pastors from all fifty states and several foreign countries for its 1978 annual Pastor's School. The school describes in great detail how the church is organized and operates.

Hyles-Anderson College, founded in 1972, is training 678 student preachers among its 1400 enrollment. First Baptist Church of Hammond is the most copied church in the world. The church in 1976 reported a Sunday school teaching staff of 800 teachers, 7,733 baptisms and a financial income of nearly $4 million.[31] Approximately 7,000 riders came to church regularly on the fleet of over 200 buses. Both of Dr. Hyles' basic books, *The Hyles Sunday School Manual* and *The Hyles Church Manual*, have each sold more than 35,000 copies.

DR. JERRY FALWELL

The Thomas Road Baptist Church of Lynchburg, Virginia, has the third largest Sunday school in America. The church began in June 1956, with only thirty-five adults and Jerry Falwell as their new pastor. The pastor led his people to literally claim the challenge of Acts 5:28 and fill Lynchburg with their doctrine.

"Known as the 'Television Pastor of America' because he preaches on more than 320 television stations," reports *Christian Life* magazine, "Falwell cofounded the 2,000 student Liberty Baptist College." The article continues, "And his concept of saturation evangelism, 'preaching the Gospel by every available means, to every available person, at every available time,' has influenced thousands of other pastors."[32]

Falwell is co-author of two books, *Church Aflame* and *Capturing a Town for Christ*, with Dr. Elmer Towns.

95

CHRISTIAN LIFE MAGAZINE

Founded almost forty years ago, this publication has become the major voice for church growth during the decade 1968-78 under Robert Walker, editor. Walker enlisted Dr. Elmer Towns who served as professor of Christian Education at nearby Trinity Evangelical Divinity School to serve as Sunday school editor of *Christian Life*.

Exclusive reports of the twenty largest Sunday schools appeared in the September 1968 issue of *Christian Life* and in the following year the list was expanded to fifty churches. Thereafter an annual listing of the 100 largest Sunday schools began to appear.

Then in November 1974 the first annual list of the fifty fastest growing Sunday schools in America began to be printed. "These 50 growing churches should motivate all Christians because small, mid-size, and large congregations are involved," reported the publication.[33] The magazine subtitle read, "The staggering total of 15,827 new Sunday School pupils was chalked up by the fastest growing Sunday Schools in the U.S. this year—a testimony not only to hard-working pastors, but to committed laymen."

Number of Churches in U.S. with Average Attendance		
Year	1,500-2,000 Pupils	over 4,500 Pupils
1968	15	2
1978	100	10

Source: "Sunday Schools of the Decade," **Christian Life,** October 1977, p. 65.

"Churches were founded because of the '100 Largest' listing. *Christian Life* has on file more than 200 pastors who wrote of the inspiration they received to build a church. . . . The '100 Largest' list also motivated Sunday Schools to become number-conscious and to set goals to reach unchurched multitudes."[34]

THE SWORD OF THE LORD

Founded in September 1934 by Dr. John R. Rice, this weekly Christian newspaper made its home in Dallas, Texas (six years), Wheaton, Illinois (twenty-three years), and Murfreesboro, Tennessee (fourteen years). Dr. Rice in those early days was pastor of the Galilean Baptist Church of Garland, Texas, and was "used of God to build a church of 1,700 members, with over 7,000 professions of faith, in the midst of the bitter depression times— 1923-40."[35]

Before his death in 1980, Dr. Rice spoke with other fundamentalist pastors and leaders at twenty-five *Sword of the Lord* conferences each year. He wrote over 185 books and pamphlets with 52 million copies circulated in thirty-eight languages. *The Sword of the Lord* also sponsors a radio network of fifty independent stations, nine of these being 50,000-watt stations. *The Sword* is a major tool for evangelism and is also instrumental in updating denominational evangelicals and others about historic and biblical fundamentalism.

Reporting in the April 21, 1978, issue of *The Sword*, Dr. Rice wrote, "We have already had this year 197 letters from people saved through our literature. Such letters come every day. We have had about 19,000 such letters from those saved through sermons in *The Sword of the Lord* and the literature which we promote . . . What other magazine in the world has done as much to stir churches to put soul-winning first, to build new churches?"[36]

BAPTIST BIBLE COLLEGE (Springfield, Missouri)

Few colleges in America have had as much influence on church growth as this school. Founded under the leadership of Dr. G. Beauchamp Vick, associate of J. Frank Norris at the Temple Baptist Church in Detroit and later Norris's successor in that same congregation, this has been for decades the officially recognized college for Baptist Bible Fellowship students.

Christian Life, in listing Dr. Vick as one of the Sunday School Newsmakers of the Decade, says that more important than serving the church that in 1955 "housed 'America's Largest Sunday School' . . . he was founder and president of Baptist Bible College. . . . America's largest Bible college which stresses Sunday School." In 1973, twenty-three graduates of the college were serving as pastors of the nation's 100 largest Sunday schools.[37]

Often, fundamentalists are criticized for their focus on "bigness" to the exclusion of small churches. This claim, however, is ill-founded, since all of the large fundamentalist churches began as small churches. Dr. Towns and *Christian Life* have for several years expanded the fastest-growing churches in each state to ensure inclusion of the small churches. Their interest is to encourage growth, not to downplay the smaller congregations. No critic, to this writer's awareness, has ever given credit to the following quote by Dr. Towns:

> I heard the phrase "10 smallest" so often that an attempt was made in *Christian Life* magazine to write a series on 10 small, but outstanding, Sunday Schools. The articles failed to gain reader interest, and the series was aborted. People are not interested in small Sunday Schools, but they are interested in growing Sunday Schools because growth reflects life.[38]

An analysis was made of six texts written by five well-known fundamentalists. The goal was to determine the frequency of occurrence of specific church growth concepts presented by each source. These concepts or principles are tested and proven effective for two kinds of churches: (1) infant congregations, and (2) churches that have leveled off in numerical growth patterns. The selected texts include:

Dr. Louis Entzminger, *How to Organize and Administer a Great Sunday School* (1949). See Chapter 6.

Dr. Elmer Towns, *The Successful Sunday School and Teachers Guidebook* (Carol Stream: Creation House, 1976). See Chapter 27.

Dr. Jerry Falwell and Dr. Elmer Towns, *Church Aflame* (Nashville: Impact Books, 1970).

Dr. Jack Hyles, *The Hyles Church Manual* (Murfreesboro: Sword of the Lord Publishers, 1968).

Dr. Jack Hyles, *The Hyles Sunday School Manual* (Murfreesboro: Sword of the Lord Publishers, 1969).

Dr. Tom Malone, *The Sunday School Reaching Multitudes* (Murfreesboro: Sword of the Lord Publishers, 1973).

A total of 141 concepts were listed from the above sources. Nonfundamentalists will be surprised to learn that evangelism was not the principle mentioned most frequently. This is probably because evangelism is naturally assumed by fundamentalists to be the basic presupposition for effective ministry in any New Testament church.

Listed below are the results of the survey. The numerical percentages indicate the topics mentioned most frequently by these men:

	CATEGORIES OF PRINCIPLES:	ENTZMINGER %	TOWNS %	FALWELL %	HYLES %	MALONE %
1.	Corporate Life		24*	11	8	
2.	Admin/Leadership	43*	18	33*	25	19
3.	Facilities		8	6	4	3
4.	Finance		2	11	4	
5.	Ministry		10	6		
6.	Christian Education	29	25*	22	55*	55*
7.	Ecumenism					
8.	Evangelism	28	13	11	4	23

(*) Categories of principles mentioned most frequently.   Note: Each column totals 100%

The categories of principles occurring most often are ranked as follows based on this writer's evaluation:

1. Christian Education
2. Administration-Leadership
3. Evangelism
4. Corporate (Body) Life
5. Facilities
6. Ministry
7. Finance
8. Ecumenism

ORGANIZER OF PRINCIPLES	NUMBER OF PRINCIPLES
Louis Entzminger	7
Elmer Towns	61
Jerry Falwell	18
Jack Hyles	24
Tom Malone	31

NOTE: All of the principles indicated above have several secondary principles.

Seven principles listed a decade ago to describe fundamentalist church growth are still amazingly current:

1. Emphasis on numbers
2. Evangelism
3. Emphasis on the Bible
4. Caution against over-organization
5. Shepherds lead sheep; sheep don't lead the shepherd
6. Paid Christian education staff
7. High teacher-pupil ratios in the classroom[39]

16. The Fuller Factor

Evangelicals from all points on the ecclesiastical continuum agree: the Church Growth Movement is "hot," the debate it has stirred is getting hotter, and evangelicals around the world—not just those in the U.S.—are going to have to deal with it.[1]

The identity of several varieties of American church growth can be distinguished as making unique contributions to the movement today. Three elements of the broader movement are (1) church renewal, (2) growing churches, and (3) the Church Growth movement.

Renewal's focus is on the existing heterogeneous and sometimes fragmented relationships within a church. Sociological principles, group dynamics, and personal discipline activities are used to create stronger individuals, families, and churches. The method of the renewal movement is to begin with a heterogeneous Christian group and lead it to become more homogeneous as a body. The Yokefellow Institute in Richmond, Indiana, and the writings of Dr. Lyle E. Schaller are representatives of renewal growth.

The second sector of American church growth is best observed in the army of fundamentalist superchurches. This type growth is usually unified around a capable leader and a mobilized laity committed to a well-defined code of spiritual and social disciplines directed toward capturing entire cities for Jesus Christ. The method used here is to mobilize an already homogeneous body to multiply itself in a heterogeneous population. Evangelization is the force used to transform an alien world into a recognizable and homogeneous body of born-again saints. Superchurches often reproduce themselves as smaller churches adopt them as models. Dr. Jack Hyles, Dr. Jerry Falwell, and the writings of Dr. Elmer Towns are among the best known leaders of the "growing churches" variety of growth. They are viewed by some as growth practitioners rather than Church Growth scientists.

Third, the term "Church Growth" is a technical term adopted by Dr. Donald McGavran, founder of the School of World Mission and Institute of Church Growth at Fuller Theological Seminary in Pasadena, California. This movement has its roots in principles of church growth observed from growing churches in many countries outside the United States. The principles were transplanted from foreign to American churches in 1972, though McGavran had written about growth since 1936. This chapter will focus on the principles formulated by the founder, faculty, and disciples of the center of world church growth at Pasadena during the past four decades.

The method of the Church Growth movement is to locate and evangelize winnable populations or "peoples" already established as homogeneous units. This means the conversion of groups within populations rather than attempting to merely evangelize isolated individuals. Since social science techniques are employed in locating and measuring the winnability of groups, the Church Growth movement considers itself to be unapologetically scientific in its methods of accessing and formulating church growth principles. Church Growth is considered a science, and Church Growth scientists tend to consider others as practitioners and chroniclers of growing churches.

Dr. C. Peter Wagner, another Pasadena strategist, recognizes five methods used by most growth movements to publicize widespread awareness of American church growth principles. The five channels include (1) books, (2) how-we-do-it conferences by superchurches, (3) consultant services, (4) national and regional seminars, and (5) research institutes.[2]

Basic motivations of the Church Growth movement include (1) obedience to Jesus Christ as expressed in the Great Commission, (2) an optimism in God's willingness and provision in reaching hosts of reachable populations with the gospel, and (3) the urgent need to direct all available resources to reaching the unreached peoples of earth. Multitudes die daily without the good news of Jesus Christ.

According to Peter Wagner, the problem is more serious than many realize:

> The unreached peoples of the world now total almost three billion, with over 150,000 new ones being added daily. Fewer than 100,000 missionaries are actively spreading the good news, but 100,000 will not be able to accomplish the task.[3]

Dr. Ralph Winter, professor of Historical Development of the Christian Movement at Fuller Seminary, further lists "5,390 languages and 16,750 subgroups" that can technically be classified as "unreached."[4] Though language is hardly the only barrier to reception of the gospel message, the number of estimated human languages needing a translation of the Bible has increased from 2,000 in 1960 to 5,000-10,000 in 1970.[5]

Cultural barriers exist in addition to language barriers, as is illustrated by Winter in his booklet, *The Grounds for a New Thrust in World Missions*. He warns that while the 600 existing mission agencies in North America have the task of reaching the "nominal" Christian populations of the world, 84 percent of all non-Christian populations are culturally unreachable by English-speaking mission agencies. The only hope of reaching 84 percent is by cross-cultural mission strategies involving Christian populations in other cultures sending their own people as missionaries to their neighbors.[6]

Since the publication of McGavran's *The Bridges of God*, which launched the Church Growth movement in 1955, dramatic alterations in the world's Christian population have occurred. David B. Barrett's article, "AD 2000: 350 Million Christians in Africa," encapsules the intensity of such change:

. . . our analysis is that by AD 2000 the centre of gravity of the Christian world will have shifted markedly southwards, from Europe and North America to the developing continents of Africa and South America. . . . Whereas during the twentieth century the Western (or "older") churches will have *doubled* in size . . . the Third-World (or "younger") churches will have multiplied seventeen times . . . the churches in the developed world.[7]

Missiologist Ralph Winter, commenting on the rapid birth rate of new churches and denominations outside the Western world, calls the phenomenon "already astronomical, especially in Africa." He estimates a rate of "at least one a day."[8] Another analyst calculates that with the world population increasing at its current 2 percent annually and with the Christian population growing at much higher rate, conservatively an estimated 55,000 new Christians are added each day. He also computes at least 1,400 new churches per week around the world.[9]

World church growth has advanced rapidly in some countries while making little or no visible progress in other locations. For years much attention centered on China. However, though Catholics had served on Chinese soil since 1587 and Protestants since 1807, Alan R. Tippett writing in *Missiology,* a major missions publication, concludes: "When the Communists came into power in 1949, the Christian population is said to have numbered about 4 million . . . two-thirds of one percent of the people."[10]

China is not an isolated illustration. Populations that have been unusually resistant to Christian evangelistic efforts are presented below from 1955 statistics given by Dr. McGavran[11] and 1973 figures by Dr. Arthur F. Glasser, dean of the School of World Mission at Fuller Seminary.[12]

PERCENT CHRISTIAN POPULATION AFTER 150 YEARS

POPULATION	1955	1973
Chinese	less than 1%	—
Japanese	less than .5%	1%
India	2%	2.85%
Muslim World	less than .1%	—

World Vision International's executive vice president, Dr. Ted W. Engstrom, in the book *What in the World Is God Doing?* refers to statistics given by Dr. Edward C. Pentecost for responsive populations:

. . . the projects for Africa and Asia stagger us. . . . It is estimated that the number of people yet to be won in those countries has more than doubled since 1900 and will triple in the next twenty years [i.e. —by A.D. 2000]. . . . Today there are thirteen times more Christians in Africa and parts of Asia than there were in 1900, and we are told by knowledgeable authorities that by the year 2000, at the present rate of growth of the church, the Christian population will be more than thirty times as large.[13]

The philosophy of Church Growth, continuing to be formulated by Dr. McGavran and his colleagues in Pasadena, also accounts for the mass migration to urban centers during the past two centuries. Estimates have been published by Ted Engstrom[14] and Roger S. Greenway, Latin America secretary, Board of Foreign Missions, Christian Reformed Church.[15] (See chart, next page.)

Interestingly, through the research efforts of the Fuller strategists and others, it is now known that the world's largest churches are outside the continental United States. Most are also located in major urban centers.

CHURCH	LOCATION	MEMBERS/ ATTENDANCE	SEATING CAPACITY
Yoido Island Full[16] Gospel Central Church	Seoul, Korea	50,000*	8,000+
Yung Nak[17] Presbyterian Church	Seoul, Korea	12,000	3,000
Brazil for Christ	Sao Paulo, Brazil	8,000[18]	25,000[19]
The Congregacgo Christa[20]	Sao Paulo, Brazil	—	7,000
Jotabeche Church[22] (Methodist Pentecostal)	Santiago, Chile	80,000	16,000
Madureira Church[23] (Assemblies of God of Brazil)	Rio de Janeiro	40,000	—

(*) Source: (Church Growth Bulletin, Vol. XIV, No. 5 (May, 1978), p. 195.
    Note: More recent reports place this figure above 100,000.
(+) Adjacent to the 8,000-capacity auditorium are the closed-circuit overflow auditoriums capable of seating another 4,000 worshipers.

Meanwhile, the Church Growth planners have turned their skills toward needs relating to American church growth. Dr. Lyle Schaller estimates that of the 330,000 churches in America, *95 percent* of them average 350 in weekly attendance; *50 percent* attract seventy-five worshipers each Sunday; and only *5 percent* of all American churches average above 350 during the eleven o'clock hour.

Dr. Peter Wagner reports that "most churches plateau at about 200 members, give or take fifty."[24] At this point a congregation makes the vital decision of extending its growth to the equivalent of two congregations under one roof or to establish a zero-population level. Most choose the latter. He indicates that their own calculations estimate 106 million Americans over age eighteen who still need to be evangelized (i.e., three out of four Americans in the category). Imagine such an evangelistic assignment in a land that boasts one church for every 700 citizens.

Statistics provided by McGavran and Arn in *Ten Steps for Church Growth* graphically illustrate that nearly 30 percent of the U.S. population is actively Christian, 49 percent is nominally Christian and 21 percent is non-Christian.[25] Of equal concern to Fuller missiologists is the fact that 40-48 percent of our population is isolated from receiving the gospel because of ethnic or cultural barriers.

McGavran postulates that the most effective tool for reaching the unreached is through planting new churches at the density of slightly less than one new church for each one hundred unchurched members of the population.[26] With approximately 151 million souls in this category in America, assuming that all could be reached and that none of these unchurched held membership in existing churches, 1.5 million *new* churches are needed to reach them in this generation.

The exact contribution of the Church Growth movement is more vividly magnified in the caution of C. Peter Wagner, who reminds us that ". . . only a small percentage of these would even fit into our present evangelical churches."[27]

PERCENT OF WORLD'S POPULATION IN CITIES

YEAR	% URBAN POPULATION
1800 A.D.	3%
1900 A.D.	13%
1950 A.D.	21%
1978 A.D.	40%
2000 A.D.	60-87%

NOTE: The twentieth century began with 13 percent of the world population living in the cities and will conclude with 13 percent living outside the cities.

PIONEERS AND PRINCIPLES

Since its beginning in 1955, the Church Growth movement has grown to include a larger sphere of influence than the movement which Dr. McGavran originally founded. Other publications now echo the pages of the *Church Growth Bulletin*, the movement's official publication. Publishers like Moody Press, Wm. B. Eerdmans, Gospel Light Publications, and the William Carey Library of Pasadena have each unveiled series of books on Church Growth concepts. Fuller Seminary has generated interest and influence for Church Growth principles to campuses far beyond the borders of Pasadena and North America. Other Church Growth magazines are now published in Canada, the Philippines, Taiwan, Korea, Malaysia, and Singapore.

The scope of teamwork required to launch a movement of this magnitude is graphically presented by Dr. McGavran himself in a message he delivered to the Association of Professors of Mission:

> The Church Growth School of thought is a joint production. I have, in fact, played a rather small part in it. The men of our faculty have played a large part. Alan Tippett, Arthur Glasser, Ralph Winter, Charles Kraft, Peter Wagner, Edwin Orr, and Roy Shearer have all added significantly to the complex. So have men not citizens of the United States — like Dr. Peter Coterell of the great Sudan Interior Mission and David Barrett of the Anglican Church Missionary Society. Church Growth is much bigger than Pasadena.[28]

Interestingly, each faculty member of the Fuller School of World Missions is an experienced former missionary and has received basic theological training, while holding graduate degrees in nontheological fields which stress scientific methodology.

Dr. McGavran isolates five key events that have contributed immeasurably to the expansion of the movement. The five episodes include: (1) in 1961 establishing the Institute of Church Growth on the campus of Northwest Christian College (Eugene, Oregon) to develop students knowledgeable in growth concepts; (2) publication of *Church Growth Bulletin* since 1964 by Overseas Crusades, Inc.; (3) relocating the Institute of Church Growth from the campus in Eugene (1961) to Fuller Seminary at Pasadena (1965); (4) establishing the William Carey Library (1969) for the mass publication and circulation of church growth books; and (5) creation of the Institute for American Church Growth in 1973 by Dr. and Mrs. Win Arn. Dr. McGavran also includes the Fuller Evangelistic Association Department of Church Growth.[29]

As a third generation missionary, McGavran served with the United Christian Missionary Society (Disciples of Christ) in India from 1923-1955. This service followed completion of undergraduate training at Butler University (Ph.D., 1933). His doctoral dissertation was a statistical analysis of the influence of Christian schools on the religious beliefs of students from Hindu families.

A significantly new era unfolded for Dr. McGavran from 1934-35 through the influence of Bishop J. Waskom Pickett, a Methodist observer of "people movements" in India. Donald H. Gill gives this commentary in an article, "Apostle of Church Growth":

> This led McGavran to further research which indicated many of the reasons why the church in 136 districts had grown by 11 percent in 10 years while in 11 other districts it had grown by some 200 percent in the same period.[30]

Prior to his experience with Bishop Pickett, McGavran considered the individualistic "one-by-one" approach to evangelism as the most biblically based and pragmatically fruitful. He had heard of large groups of "peoples" claiming to have undergone Christian conversion and baptism but viewed them as suspect. In fact, his term for this was "half-baked mission work"! In an interview with John K. Branner for *Evangelical Mission Quarterly*, he confides:

> In 1934-35 I began to see that what we had heard was quite wrong. What we had deemed "unsound, half-baked work" was really one great way in which the church was growing quite effectively. God was blessing that way of growth. They were becoming better churches than ours. It was heresy to say that in 1935.[31]

In the same interview Dr. McGavran shares that these concepts germinated in his mind. Earlier, in 1930, he had written *How to Teach Religion in Mission Schools*, and now in 1936 he collaborated with Pickett and Singh in writing the early classic on people movements, *The Mass Movement Survey of Mid-India*. This title was revised in 1958 to *Church Growth and Group Conversion*.

Resigning his position as executive secretary in 1937, he spent three years as a researcher in Chattisgarh and served as principal of mission schools as well as superintendent of the leprosy home and hospital. According to Donald Hill, another cornerstone event occurred in 1953 when McGavran and his wife agreed that she would manage the mission while he absented himself for a month to a retreat site about twenty-five miles away to compile research notes and write *The Bridges of God*. Furlough time, scheduled to begin in 1954, allowed him to share his manuscript with Sir Kenneth Grubb in London. As a result, World Dominion Press published both this book and *How Churches Grow* (1959).

These were difficult days for what proved to be a message rejected by many mission leaders. Dr. McGavran writes, "In 1959, a profound discouragement seized me, and I was on the point of quitting. . . . What I had to say had not caught fire . . . and my efforts seemed futile."[32]

Opinions changed rapidly, however, when colonial empires began to take measures for self-government during the decade of the 1950s. Revolutionary movements destroyed or seized missionary properties, and McGavran says, "Missions wallowed in a twenty-year trough, which reached its lowest point around 1968." Pessimism then began to turn into optimism as mission leaders searched for new approaches to world evangelism. A wave of hyper-ecumenism followed and love as a theme displaced evangelism. These forces led to a moral relativism that strongly opposes Church Growth's priority of evangelism.

A major revival of obedience to the Great Commission occurred in 1966. The Congress on the Church's Worldwide Mission assembled at Wheaton, Illinois, in April. In late October 1,200 delegates assembled in Berlin for the two-week World Congress on Evangelism. McGavran and his team of missiologists had much influence on the Wheaton congress, but less in Berlin. Receptivity by evangelicals for Church Growth concepts was heightened by the 1970 publication of *Understanding Church Growth* by McGavran, *Church Growth and the Word of God* by Australian missiologist Dr. Alan Tippett, and Fuller missiologist Dr. Ralph Winter's *The 25 Unbelievable Years: 1945-1969*. Articles on the movement would soon follow in both *Eternity* and *Christianity Today* magazines (1972).

During this period of the 1960s four other events of magnitude occurred. First, almost obscured by the slopes of the Cascade Mountains, just a hundred miles south of Portland, Oregon, the Northwest Christian College (Disciples of Christ) employed Dr. Donald McGavran to begin the Institute of Church Growth in 1961. Second, the *Church Growth Bulletin* was published just three years later in 1964 under Dr. McGavran's leadership and Norman Cumming's initiative in offering Overseas Crusade's printing and mailing sponsorship.

Third, the dream of Dr. Charles Fuller became reality when Dr. McGavran accepted the invitation to establish the School of World Missions and Institute of Church Growth at Fuller Theological Seminary in Pasadena, California (1965). At that time the present faculty of missiologists began to be assembled.

Finally, North American interest in church growth was awakened to the abundance of superchurches in the land by Dr. Elmer Towns's best-seller, *The Ten Largest Sunday Schools* (1969), and the annual listing of the largest evangelical and fundamentalist churches in his articles for *Christian Life* magazine. Dr. Peter Wagner reminds us of Dr. McGavran's earlier plans in 1963 (i.e., six years prior to Towns) ". . . to add to the Institute of Church Growth at Eugene an American Division headed by an American minister of church growth convictions, but the plan did not mature."[33] He also notes that while McGavran's *How Churches Grow*, published in 1959, had "definite application to church growth in America, and though the reprinted chapter version, *Do Churches Grow?* sold several thousand copies, it ". . . failed to light any fires. The time was not yet ripe."[34]

Before leaving the 1960s, the one additional historic gathering of Church Growth leadership requires our attention. "The first annual Church Growth Colloquium—to consider church growth and evangelization in North America—was held at Emmanuel School of Religion, Milligan College, Tennessee, June 16-20, 1969," reports *Church Growth Bulletin*.[35] Dr. Medford H. Jones, president of Pacific Christian College (Fullerton, California) directed the meetings. Sixteen topic areas were considered during the four-day conference, including: "The Biblical Basis of Church Growth," "The Scientifically Measurable Factors of Church Growth," "Why Churches Stop Growing," "How to Activate 'Stopped' Churches," and others. The second colloquium was announced for 1970.

The decade of the 1970s built boldly on the achievements of previous accomplishments. A pivotal year for Fuller Seminary came in 1972 (i.e., three years after Elmer Towns) when the combined efforts of both Dr. Donald McGavran and Dr. Peter Wagner constituted the first pilot course to apply Church Growth philosophy to American churches. This became a historic event in the movement's history. The nationwide effort at ecumenical evangelism known as Key '73 appeared and quickly faded into obscurity. That same year, however, Win C. Arn established the Institute for American Church Growth in Pasadena, California. He was formerly one of the first students to participate in Fuller Seminary's church growth institute.

The Institute for American Church Growth (Pasadena, California) is the information and research center for North America church growth. Dr. Win Arn, besides having served as producer of twenty-seven films, being a pioneer in new concepts for religious films ("Charlie Churchman" series), and having served as director of Religious Education in Baptist and Congregational churches, has received two graduate degrees from Philadelphia's Eastern Baptist Seminary. His son, Dr. Charles Arn, has served as Instructional Development Coordinator.

Dr. Peter Wagner describes Dr. Win Arn as the best communicator in the field and compares him to Dr. Virgil Gerber, whose specialty is growth research in Asia, Africa, and Latin America. The elder Dr. Arn described the Institute's role as interpreting and applying Church Growth principles to congregations in North America. This is accomplished through color films, books, seminars, workshops, audio tapes, the *Let the Church Grow!* curriculum and media pac, and most extensively through the semimonthly magazine, *Church Growth: America*.

The Institute has established the Center for American Church Growth Studies, "the only training center exclusively devoted to American church growth study and application . . . to equip 'the saints for the work of the ministry.' "[37] The program, designed for laymen, consists of six elective courses to be taken at the center or at home by correspondence over a twelve-month period under Center staff supervision. The course leads to a certificate in American Church Growth.

In a recent interview with James H. Montgomery, Dr. Arn indicates that "seminars of the Institute for American Church Growth have reached nearly 20,000 key lay leaders and pastors representing over four thousand local congregations" in one recent year alone.[38] In the same interview, Dr. Peter Wagner reveals, "The problem is that America has 200,000 trained pastors, none of whom studied church growth in seminary or Bible school."[39]

Critics of the movement are tinted with a rainbow of motives in their assessments. Topics of criticism occurring most frequently include: mass baptisms, manipulation of growth by planting new churches, authority of Scripture vs. pragmatism, stress on numerical growth, stress on use of sciences and measurable goals, proselytism, primacy of the church, priority of evangelism or mission over ministry and evangelism without barriers.

Foremost among all concepts mentioned by adversaries is the principle of the homogeneous group. Most of these will be discussed in the following pages. Some critics were candid in their rejection of some Church Growth concepts and leaders while being openly favorable toward the other concepts and leaders. Two examples of critics who were both candid and favorable are J. Robertson McQuilkin in his *Measuring the Church Growth Movement: How Biblical Is It?* (Moody Press, 1973) and Pius Wakatama's *Independence for the Third World Church* (InterVarsity Press, 1976).

Fundamentalists, discussed in another chapter, would tend to oppose Church Growth concepts of ecumenism and compromise in doctrinal purity as viewed in cooperation with charismatics. Body Life churches would be favorable to McGavran, Wagner, and Arn's positive assessment of spiritual gifts and body life but critical of their concept of accountability through overt research resulting in measurable goals, statistical analysis, and comparison of churches. Charismatics would tend to be most favorable and least critical, with possible exception to the movement's focus on ecclesiology and research.

ORGANIZERS OF PRINCIPLES	NUMBER OF PRINCIPLES
Donald McGavran	67
C. Peter Wagner	51
Win Arn	28

Each of the three major representatives listed above offer abbreviated listings of Church Growth principles. Various reviewers have also encapsuled the essential ingredients of each leader. Dr. J. Robertson McQuilkin, president of Columbia Bible College, reduces the multitude of Church Growth concepts to five areas: (1) numerical growth, (2) focus on receptivity, (3) people movements, (4) use of science as a tool, and (5) right method guarantees large response.

In the book *Measuring the Church Growth Movement* each of the five principle categories are classified as either (1) biblical mandate, (2) biblical principle, or (3) extrabiblical. McQuilkin, speaking as a "friendly outsider" concludes, "The Church Growth Movement would change completely in character if any of the five basic presuppositions were omitted."[40]

CLASSIFICATION	PRINCIPLE
1. Biblical Mandate (Commanded in Scripture)	1. Importance of Numerical Growth
	2. Focus on Receptive Groups
2. Biblical Principle (Implied in Scripture)	3. People Movements
	4. Science, a Valid Tool
3. Extrabiblical	5. Right Method Guarantees Large Response

C. Peter Wagner in *"Church Growth": More Than a Man, a Magazine, a School, a Book,"* lists six elements as the irreducible minimum of the movement. Concerning them, he writes, ". . . these distinctives are not the exclusive property of church growth. . . . Evangelicals who disagree with the church-growth school of thought almost invariably do so on one or more of these six distinctives. . . ."[41]

The six factors include: (1) nongrowth displeases God, (2) numerical growth of the church is a priority with God and focuses on new disciples rather than decisions, (3) "disciples are tangible, identifiable, countable people" that increase the church numerically, (4) limited time, money, and resources require strategy based on results, (5) social and behavioral sciences are valid tools in measuring and encouraging church growth, (6) research is "essential" for maximum growth. A repeated premise of *Church Growth* is that nongrowth is a disease, is abnormal, is displeasing to God, and in most cases correctable.

The discovery of new growth principles is readily expected, no single formula is insisted upon, and there is general acceptance of McGavran's maxim, "Church growth in Africasia is different from that in Europe."[42] He further recognizes that "people" and the sovereignty of God constitute the major constants in worldwide growth among churches.

Terminology of the movement is sprinkled with unique McGavranistic labels, as is characteristic of Tielhard de Chardin and others. Such contractions as "Africasia" (Africa + Latin America + Asia) and "Eurica" (Europe + America) are trademarks of the Pasadena heritage. Even the term "Church Growth" is used to replace often overworked words like "evangelize" and "witness" among more liberal, World Council of Churches organizations who tend to redefine words commonly used by evangelical Christians. The adoption of the words "Church" and "Growth" and declaring them as the exclusive possession of the "Church Growth" school or movement has invited criticism, however, since they are not always used in the upper case letter with consistency within the strategists' own literature.

Dr. McGavran, who has given abbreviated versions of Church Growth's distinctive principles on many occasions, with occasional slight variation, is well represented in the following outline:[44]

1. Priority of evangelism over material support and education.
2. Multiplication of unpaid leaders who can communicate Christ to unsaved relatives, neighbors, and fellow laborers.
3. Apply the sciences as tools to help win the millions without Christ.
4. Evangelism's priority is to responsive populations.
5. Evangelism's priority places winning of groups over individuals.
6. Growth principles can be discovered by analyzing growing churches.

In October 1976 more than 400 church leaders assembled in Kansas City, Missouri, for the National Consultation on Evangelism and Church Growth. The opening and closing messages of the three-day convocation, sponsored by the American Lausanne Committee and others, was Dr. Donald A. McGavran. That opening message consisted of four major reasons for congregational growth and decline:

> Why do some Churches grow? They believe that God wants his lost children found. They pray ardently for church growth. They find out all they can about church growth. And they do what they know will, under their circumstances, bring about a mighty finding and folding of the lost. The church has one mission . . . to call men from death to life.[45]

The principles discussed in this chapter constitute only a fragment of the larger whole. Definite contrasts and similarities will become increasingly observable between the growth concepts of Body Life churches, fundamentalists and team members of the Fuller-related group.

The following graph categorically indicates the percentage and frequency of principles as they often appear in their literature. For example, when you list all Body Life principles together, approximately 21 percent relate to "Corporate Life" while only 13 percent of principles discussed by either fundamentalists or Church Growth writers examine the same topic.

PERCENTAGE OF GROWTH PRINCIPLE OCCURRENCE IN MAJOR PUBLICATIONS

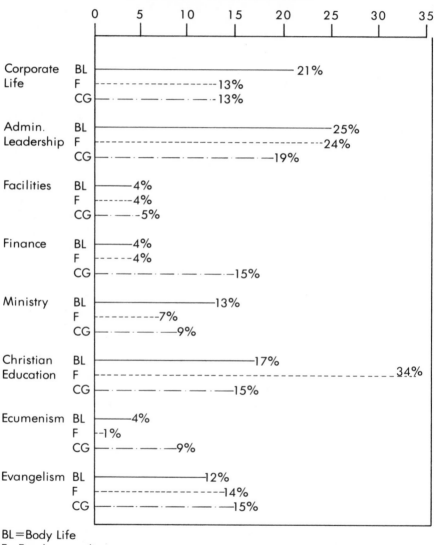

Corporate Life	BL	21%
	F	13%
	CG	13%
Admin. Leadership	BL	25%
	F	24%
	CG	19%
Facilities	BL	4%
	F	4%
	CG	5%
Finance	BL	4%
	F	4%
	CG	15%
Ministry	BL	13%
	F	7%
	CG	9%
Christian Education	BL	17%
	F	34%
	CG	15%
Ecumenism	BL	4%
	F	1%
	CG	9%
Evangelism	BL	12%
	F	14%
	CG	15%

BL = Body Life
F = Fundamentalists
CG = Church Growth (Fuller)

Now, before surveying collected principles of growth, we need to confirm (1) our understanding of how to recognize growth and nongrowth indicators and (2) our ability to recognize patterns of growth.

The possibility is very real that a group can enlist impressive hosts of new souls into its membership and still actually be losing members. Dr. C. Peter Wagner, in a *Church Growth Bulletin* article, "World Baptists: 3,176,954 New Members and Standing Still!" reminds the reader:

> If over the next decade, Baptists grow by only 7½ million new members, they will be standing still! Some of the most serious growth problems for Baptists are in Europe and North America where they are growing at minus 2.8 percent and 20 percent respectively. . . . Growth rates in Africa and Latin America are a healthy 76 percent and 72 percent respectively. . . .[46]

Did you notice that Dr. Wagner used the term "growth rate"? Rate of growth is a numerical measurement of the units of time at which a specified percentage of net growth (increase exceeds decrease in membership) occurs.

Can a "healthy" rate of growth be determined? Church Growth missiologists Donald McGavran and Peter Wagner have, by analyzing growing churches, determined a minimum rate of 50 percent per decade (i.e., 5 percent per year). Dr. McGavran estimates that research results reveal that this 50 percent is composed of (1) 15 percent due to biological births exceeding deaths within the church membership and (2) 35 percent due to winning and baptizing persons from the population of non-Christians in the unchurched community.[47] Dr. Wagner mentions that Dr. McGavran has previously calculated biological growth on the basis of 25 percent per decade.[48]

Fuller Evangelistic Association of Pasadena, California, publishes a growth analysis form suggesting six rates of growth. The scale measures from "poor growth" (25 percent) to "incredible growth" (500 percent). A popularized summary of that scale is given by Dr. Wagner, also an officer with the Fuller Association, in *Your Church Can Grow:*

> . . . if a church is growing at only 25 percent per decade it is barely growing at all.
>
> In the U.S.A. (other countries might differ), a decade growth rate of 50 percent is not too bad. Not really healthy perhaps, but not unhealthy either. A church growing at 100 percent per decade is in pretty good shape. If it shows 200 percent, the church is newsworthy, and when the figure gets up around 300 percent the pastor better prepare to hold seminars to share his methods with others.[49]

Just as growth occurs through biological, transfer, or conversion modes, there are also four types of church growth recognized by the Pasadena School. The four are *internal, expansion, extension,* and *bridging.* Each type is designed to reach a different target group. *Internal* growth's focus is on the children of existing believers and renewal of local members. *Expansion* is reaching the population of the immediate community (i.e., "our kind of people"). *Extension* growth is the creation of a new church group in another similar culture. Finally, *bridging* growth is beginning a new congregation in a radically different culture or community. These four types of growth are often identified as Type 1, Type 2, Type 3, and Type 4.

Several examples of growth rates over a ten-year period ("decadal growth rate") in American churches include:

DECADAL GROWTH RATES OF SAMPLE CHURCHES IN AMERICA
SOURCE: DR. PETER WAGNER

CHURCH	DECADAL RATE
Garden Grove Community Church—Calif.	500%+
First Baptist Church—Hammond, Ind.	400%+
Whittier Area Baptist Fellowship—Calif.	740%
North Ave. Alliance Church—Burlington, Vt.	644%
Church at Jerusalem	215,343%

PRINCIPLES OF GROWTH AND MINISTRY

PRINCIPLES OF CORPORATE (BODY) LIFE

(1) The principle of the Local Church. The Church Growth movement is unapologetic in its opposition to the contemporary "churchless ministry" referred to by Australian missiologist Dr. Alan Tippett. He criticizes their emphasis upon ". . . the adequacy of merely 'being a Christian out there in the world' without the need for a specific worshipping fellowship." He equates it as "plain rejection of Scripture."[50]

According to Dr. McGavran, the profession of faith of any believer is suspect if identification with a local church is ignored.[51] In his *Eye of the Storm* we hear him saying, "I am a 'gathered church' man. . . . I agree that the Church is ideally not a culture-church of any land. . . . Yet the hard fact of the matter is that, from the first days of the Church to date, a culture-church is all there has ever been."[52]

Dr. Win Arn, after serving as executive director of a nationally known parachurch organization, confides: "My search led me to the local church. The church is God's plan for making disciples and for winning a world."[53]

(2) The principle of shared goals. Effective goals must be "owned," reports

Win Arn, by members of the congregation. The key role of the pastor is to establish a growth-inviting climate. This climate thrives on an informed people who know why growth is needed and are acquainted with available resources and opportunities for growth.

(3) The principle of homogeneous groups. Simply stated in the words of the movement's founder, "all men like to become Christian in their own social groupings, without crossing barriers. . . . Every man should be able to become a Christian with his own kind of people."[54] McGavran is the first to recognize that in addition to social, cultural, economic, political, literacy, and linguistic barriers there are always the ultimate barriers of the gospel message, faith, and prayer for the nonbeliever. He insists that our primary concern must be to remove the rubble of unnecessary and nonbiblical barriers that hinder the gospel and conversion.

"World-wide research in church growth," insists C. Peter Wagner, "continues to confirm . . . that churches grow when they concentrate on only one homogeneous unit. . . . Show me a growing church, and I will show you a homogeneous-unit church. Sometimes it will take a while to detect."[55]

Both McGavran and Arn write that while all peoples are welcome to local Christian bodies, people tend to group themselves within churches composed of their own kind of people. "Others, of course, are cordially welcome, but the church made up of different kinds of people about equally distributed is generally a nongrowing church."[56]

The only recognized successful exception to the homogeneous principle exists in Urban Center Churches. In *Understanding Church Growth* McGavran suggests that factors in these cases include: (1) rapid rate of conversion growth, (2) worship in a standard language, (3) supratribal identity, and (4) disregard for class differences. He notes, however, that most churches gaining new members through transfer growth are heterogeneous and are not experiencing growth.[57]

The homogeneous principle is the most criticized of all Church Growth concepts. Some critics call it sub-Christian, racist, and others attack it as extrabiblical. Church Growth strategists simply state it as demonstrable worldwide fact and indicate that the test is the high percentage of converts and church stability that it produces repeatedly. God prospers homogeneous growth.

Critics of the principle include Jurgen Moltmann, Lawrence O. Richards, Francis M. DuBose, Rufus Jones, Luther Copeland, Jack Rogers of Fuller, editor Robert T. Coote, and Orlando E. Costas.

Dr. Charles H. Kraft, associate professor of Missionary Anthropology and African Affairs at Fuller Seminary, claims that the root source of homogeneous principle opposition is the American "myth of the infinite assimilability of foreign peoples into a single homogeneous 'American Way.' "[58] Other Church Growth leaders point to the regrettable guilt and overcompensation by Americans to a history of racial injustices. Interestingly, outside the United States in multiracial cultures the homogeneous principle is recognized and accepted as realistic and compatible with growth and Scripture.

Those who reject the principle without testing it invite continued church splits, the creation of new denominations, rejection of the local church by unbelievers, and cultural-racial suicide of ethnically rooted new believers. Church Growth insists that converted Jews, for example, should have Messianic Jews who are able to nurture them as new converts without requiring radical abandonment of dietary, social, and cultural life-styles. Such abandonment would immediately erect barriers to reaching other Jews with their newly discovered Messiah. This principle holds true for all other ethnic populations.

Finally, many oppose the concept while being totally uninformed of its meaning in Dr. McGavran's own experience:

> As one who has been a member of a Negro church in the United States for some years, I believe devotedly in integration. As one concerned that the gospel spread mightily in every land I want to leave the door wide open to people movements . . . which take in every member of a given people before becoming integrated. In New Testament terms, I do not want the pig-eating issue to prevent my brother Hebrews from seeing, desiring, and obeying the Lord. Till A.D. 50 I am on the side of Peter. After A.D. 50 I am on the side of Paul.[59]

(4) The principle of stability. The mortality rate of new converts isolated from the local church is three converts out of every four, or 75 percent.[60] Even with harvesting efforts like city-wide crusades, without rooting in a local church, converts tend to become "decisions" rather than "disciples."

Dr. Win Arn quotes one denominational home missions secretary as calling this an "obedience gap" resulting from a failure to accept the Great Commission as rooted in the local church—God's nurture center.

(5) The principle of expectancy. "A common denominator of growing churches," according to McGavran and Arn, "is fervent faith."[61] C. Peter Wagner calls it "the indispensable condition." Churches lacking a desire to grow do not grow. Obedience to God is the primary motive for growth according to Church Growth authorities.

(6) The principle of spiritual gifts. Awareness and application of spiritual gifts is a recurring characteristic of growing churches. Mere activity in the church without the purposeful employment of these gifts is no guarantee of growth. Dr. McGavran positively states, "They are essential for church growth."

Research indicates, according to the dean emeritus, that the gift of evangelist is the key gift necessary for church growth. He adds "Church growth occurs when the gift of evangelist is being used, but it will not happen if the other gifts are not operating simultaneously. . . ."[63]

In *Missions in Crisis: Rethinking Missionary Strategy*, Eric S. Fife and Arthur F. Glasser conclude that the role of the believer's priesthood needs greater emphasis, and they insist, "It is not merely an expedient; it is a principle."[64]

(7) The principle of arrested growth. The corporate climate has much to do with growing a church successfully. Wagner indicates that at least three factors are common agents of arrested growth: (1) excessive feeling of "family" spirit within the church and feelings of irritation toward "outsiders," (2) spiritual "birth control" expressed through undue attention toward "Christian perfection" (i.e., "spiritual navel-gazers"), and (3) "bad air" generated by self-centered bickering within the congregation.[65]

Both *The Bridges of God* (chapters 2, 6, 8) and *Understanding Church Growth* (pp. 141, 142) by Donald McGavran offer over twenty reasons for arrested growth. These elements are also referred to as "fatigue" in advanced stages of arrested growth resulting from resources shortage and lack of a master plan during a period of maximum growth. Organizationally, the frustration of the congregation expresses itself as a "plateau."[66] Church Growth leaders diagnose arrested growth as a disease that can be corrected in most churches.

PRINCIPLES OF ADMINISTRATION AND LEADERSHIP

(1) The principle of pastoral leadership. A church can grow beyond one man's leadership, but its growth will always be limited if he builds it around his own resources alone. The pastor is the key agent of church growth outside that of the Holy Spirit himself.

Interestingly, Dr. Peter Wagner, after a period of personal unbelief in the crucial role of the pastor in growth, writes:

> I would personally rather believe differently, but I cannot escape the mounting evidence that the pastor heads the list of factors common to the growing churches in America . . . show me a rapidly growing church, and I will show you a dynamic leader whom God is using to make it happen . . .[67]

He notes that while pastoral authority appears to some as arrogance, it is in most cases the powerful manifestation of the gift of faith — an expectation of the future possessed now!

Wagner visualizes the task of the pastor as that of leading his people as witnesses and as skillful exercisers of their spiritual gifts. The pastor need not be a superevangelist himself. This should be encouraging to pastors who know that they can witness while not personally having the gift of evangelism.

Every pastor faces the need of knowing his people. Dr. Win Arn, founder and director of the American Institute of Church Growth, indicates that each founding pastor of a church tends to attract his own kind of people (homogeneous group). Pastors who go to established churches usually enter "a homogeneous group which is already formed and is usually fairly rigid in structure."[68] Happy is the pastor and church who meet and discover, in many instances, that they are both "the same kind of people."

(2) The principle of delegation. In asking the question, "What makes churches grow?" one missiologist's answer is delegation of leadership: "The only pastors who can possibly do all the work are pastors of small churches."[69]

Neil Braun, educational missionary to Japan, notes in *Laity Mobilized* this observation:

> Examination of rapidly growing churches . . . affords substantiation of the principle . . . a major secret of power and of church growth is the recruiting and training of large numbers of people for responsible places of leadership in the congregations.[70]

If a pastor has not learned to delegate leadership tasks by the time his church reaches 200 members, Dr. Wagner cautions that his church will probably never grow beyond that level.[71]

(3) The principle of misplaced priorities. Most churches design their use of time, manpower, and budgets for maintenance instead of growth. According to McGavran and Arn, churches grow when the hours spent in outreach equal those spent in ministry to members; when a church's most qualified leaders assume growth responsibilities centering on evangelism; and when at least 10 percent of the budget or more is used to saturate the immediate community with the gospel "in ways that really communicate."[72]

(4) The principle of church staff longevity. The secret to gathering and keeping a growth-minded staff is to select each on the basis of his or her spiritual gifts for the positions to be filled. This compensates for and compliments the gifts of the senior pastor. There is also less friction and jealousy within the staff and toward the senior pastor.

Also, research indicates that adding pastors and staff can actually arrest growth in some instances.

> . . .adding pastors and staff can decrease the church's growth when they take upon themselves responsibilities of the laity. If . . . staff see their roles as enablers to help the laity use their gifts, growth results can be expected.[73]

(5) The principle of graduated levels of leadership. Church growth requires levels of training and service mobility within a congregation. Numerical growth will not occur on a sustained basis without structuring for graduated leadership. This allows the creation of "meaningful roles with which people can identify."[74]

Donald McGavran early in his career established a recommended scale for determining the distribution of needed manpower in stabilized as well as rapidly growing church populations. For adaptation to American church growth, the term "missionary" might be substituted by the term "pastor" or "staff member."[75]

STAGE OF DEVELOPMENT	NO. MISSIONARIES/ CHRISTIANS
Young Vigorous People Movements: (500-5000 souls)—200%/Decade Growth Rate	1:200
People Movement (over 20,000 souls) 70%/Decade Growth Rate—No Trained Nationals	1:500
People Movement (over 20,000 souls) 70%/Decade Growth Rate—Trained Nationals Involved.	1:1000
Completed People Movement Churches— Involves Many Trained Nationals.	1:3000
Gathered Colony Church (Maintenance)— Involves Many Trained Nationals.	1:3000

NOTE: Dr. Win Arn discusses manpower ratios for U.S. churches in the January/February, 1979 issue of CHURCH GROWTH: AMERICA (p. 12).

PRINCIPLES OF FACILITIES

(1) The principle of mobility. While frequently mentioned by Church Growth leaders, this principle is best described by Dr. Ted W. Engstrom, executive vice president of World Vision International:

> . . . we must continue to face the truth that churches . . . fail when they become prisoners of their buildings and lose their mobility, confining their activities within the walls of the sanctuary, without evangelism goals and a world mission strategy.[76]

(2) The principle of house cell units. For the first 150 years in Christian church history the home was the church's center of evangelistic and nurture activities. According to Dr. McGavran, most groups experiencing growth throughout the world make abundant use of house-church strategy. Others remind us that one secret of Assembly of God growth in Latin America is the expectation of new converts to immediately begin witnessing and to organize a Sunday school class in the home.

Leaders may think this model is impossible in the twentieth century. In Seoul, Korea, with over 7.5 million people and almost 2,000 individual evangelical churches, many of them with wall-to-wall people, the Yoido Island Full Gospel Central Church thrives.[77] The church's pastor estimates more than 16,000 members with active house cell units scattered in almost 7,000 locations each week. The church is reported to have won 3,700 persons to Jesus Christ in the first quarter of 1976 and reached its faith goal of 50,000 members by 1980 in 1978. Currently, an estimated 12,000 persons assemble in each of six worship services on Sunday. This figure does not include children. As of January 1980 a total of 6,728 home cell units were active.[78]

House cell units liberate Christian groups in at least four ways states McGavran: (1) they eliminate the expense of buildings, (2) they put minimum focus on the church's name or brand, (3) each unit exposes a new segment of society and (4) they bypass the obstacle of limited leadership.[79]

PRINCIPLES OF FINANCE

(1) The principle of the disruptive dollar. Just as the dollar can benefit church growth, it can also retard and even destroy its progress. The combined opinions of E. LeRoy Lawson and Tetsunao Yamamori in *Church Growth: Everybody's Business* advise:

> The missionary dollar is bad when . . . it creates dependency . . . it builds institutions which cannot maintain themselves . . . it shows a disrespect for the nationals . . . it stops church growth.[80]

A common practice by some mission groups is to publicize their financial commitments as "missions" while in reality they function as service projects to persons who are already Christians. Integrity in this matter is essential.

(2) The principle of chronic accommodation. Chronic shortage in funding tends to strengthen mission and evangelistic activities by reinforcing indigenous concepts and practices of church growth. Carried to the extreme, however, severe casualties may result.

One regrettable aspect of chronic shortage is that those affected by the pinch through necessity accommodate or adapt their evangelistic life-styles and expectations equal the minimal funds being received. The result can be arrested growth as limited finances and resources generate limited faith.

(3) The principle of opposition. The amount of foreign feeling can nearly always be expected in exact proportion to the amount of foreign funds used. The more foreign funds used in the work, the more antiforeign sentiment you are likely to have.[81]

(4) The principle of receptivity. Church Growth leaders are easily recognized by the priority they almost always give for the people who are receptive to the gospel. Dr. McGavran declares: "Only after the hundreds of thousands have been discipled is the world church justified in spending treasure in witnessing to the million of gospel rejectors.[82]

This precept is so pronounced within the movement that recommendations have been made to eliminate subsidy funds whenever growth stablizes or stops.

(5) The principle of self-support. This premise was gathered by John K. Branner when he interviewed Donald McGavran about missiologist Roland Allen:

> There is no question at all that to the degree that self-support can be

achieved . . . to just exactly that degree a denomination, a cluster of churches, a new movement is free to grow.[83]

(6) The principle of flexibility. The chief roadblocks to church multiplication, according to Neil Braun in *Laity Mobilized* are: (1) the high cost of land and buildings and (2) the high cost of the pastor's salary for a new struggling church with limited income. Latin American believers have bypassed both barriers through lay preachers and house worship units.

> . . . there will never be enough foreign funds to construct church buildings in every village and town . . . This method of church multiplication is doomed the moment the limits of the mission budget are reached.[84]

PRINCIPLES OF MINISTRIES

(1) The principle of social obstacles to conversion. We have previously discussed under the homogeneous principle the premise that people prefer to cross as few barriers as possible when they become Christians. These two principles have observable similarities.

> . . . whenever becoming a Christian is considered a racial rather than a religious decision, there the growth of the Church will be exceedingly slow . . . the great obstacles to conversion are social, not theological.[85]

(2) The principle of social strength. McGavran, in *How Churches Grow,* uses the illustration of six volts of electric current as opposed to 110 volts to operate an incandescent light. In the same manner, the minute Christian population in Japan does not normally exert the magnitude of influence as does the Christian community in Brazil. He points to evangelism as a key to social reform:

> The sooner great populations follow in His steps, the more effective will social changes be. . . . If the world is to become Christ's and fully know the abundant and eternal life, churches must multiply enormously.[86]

Added commentary is provided by Dr. Peter Wagner, who also presses for social involvement. His observation, however, is that being saved does not in itself ensure that a convert will effect needed social change through social involvement.

(3) The principle of salvation substitutes. Church Growth leaders distinguish a crucial doctrinal difference between social action and social service. "Action" is understood to be politically rooted while "service" is ministry-motivated. Christian social service focuses on need and eternity. "To the degree that socially involved churches become engaged in social action, as distinguished from social service, they can expect church growth to diminish.[87]

Again McGavran reminds his readers, ". . . remember, meeting needs, by itself, is not evangelism. Social action must not be substituted for evangelism."[88]

According to Church Growth concepts, social needs are best met when those concerned are equipped with a knowledge of homogeneous units. These units have an innate ability to provide for needs within their own groups. By homogeneous design, these solutions are usually all social in nature.

PRINCIPLES OF CHRISTIAN EDUCATION

(1) The principle of inverted discipleship. Once a mission outpost is established, there exists the danger known as the syndrome of church development. The basis of the syndrome is the tendency to invest an increasing measure of time and resources toward the encampment as though it were a permanent settlement. When this is allowed to happen, energy, time, and resources are spent to develop maturity in those already converted at the expense of the unconverted.

This principle narrows the view of the missionary or evangelizer to see that "the goal of good missionary strategy is to make disciples. But . . . disciples cannot be made in the church—they are made only in the world."[89]

(2) The principle of syncretism. The enemies of Church Growth include: pessimism, the belief that everyone is already a Christian, religious relativism, and moral relativism. McGavran, like a dentist who just discovered a cavity, is uncompromising in his treatment of these enemies: "These are really stupid ideas; yet they became fairly common and they mitigated against the growth of the church. . . . They are substantially non-Christian."[90]

(3) The principle of communication. Dr. Arthur F. Glasser lists six reasons for failure of Western missionary penetration of China. His analysis reveals that the communists also were weak in the first four areas but were unquestionably successful in the final two points. Those two factors indicate that while the missionaries "taught," many of the pupils did not "learn."

The two deciding elements that result in failure for our missionaries and victory for the Communists, according to Glasser, are: "the ability to relate the social and religious dimensions of their message" and the ability to "utilize trained Chinese in the vanguard of all evangelistic advance."[91]

(4) The principle of the "tired" Christian. Who among us does not personally know of "tired" Christians who retire from Kingdom ranks before their time? Donald McGavran, pioneer Church Growth authority, summarizes the problem in this manner:

> . . . it is perfectly true that much of the load of each church is carried by a small number of people. Yet, when you analyze it, you will find it is *not really tiredness* but unsuccessfulness that brings fatigue.[92]

(5) The principle of spontaneous growth. Just as surely as biologists reject the theory of spontaneous generation of life (i.e., life comes from nonliving matter), so Church Growth specialists reject the idea of spontaneous growth

of churches. Dr. Peter Wagner writes: "Even growing churches which claim spontaneous growth, upon analysis, will usually reveal a significant degree of planning below the surface."[93]

(6) The principle of discipling and perfecting. A common mistake being made by multitudes of churches is their minoring on "discipling" and majoring on "perfecting." Church Growth spokesmen distinguish "discipling" as referring to the initial step of acknowledging and receiving Jesus Christ as Lord.

The second step is "perfecting" and has as its aim the development of baptized believers into biblical believers. Dr. McGavran issues this word of caution to American churches: "In America today many Christians are interested solely in perfecting existing Christians and not in finding the lost and discipling them. This is a mistake."[94]

(7) The principle of learning motivation. Bishop Waskom Pickett, the missionary to India whose influence on Dr. Donald McGavran has had measurable effect, is noted for research in motives and learning. This study is rooted in claims by some that converts coming to Christ in large group conversions (people movements) make poorer Christians and churchmen than those won as individuals.

Pickett interviewed 3,947 converts won through the group evangelism method to determine their motive for coming to Christ. He also measured their knowledge of the Bible and "attainments in the Christian faith." Research based on these interviews measured attainment in eleven areas and identified four types of motivation (spiritual, secular, social, and natal). Dr. McGavran evaluates the research results in this manner:

> The great surprise in his findings, however, was the small degree of differences between the Christian attainments of those who came from spiritual, secular, and social motives. Whether they had good postbaptismal training made more difference in their attainments than the motives from which they became Christian.[95]

The Bishop's studies indicated that, among the cases he reviewed, 70 percent of those not "spiritually" motivated at conversion were active church attendees, 90 percent of their homes were purged of idols, and 90 percent were financial contributors to the church.

McGavran indicates that a frequent problem for new converts is their ability to fluently verbalize great details of doctrine already familiar to veteran Christians. He stresses, however, their high receptivity to instruction after conversion and their willingness to sacrificially offer life for their newfound experience with Christ.

(8) The principle of redemption and lift. At conversion a series of events normally occurs almost automatically in the new Christian's life. Due to the high receptivity to Bible teaching following the redemptive transformation of a new convert, growth occurs rapidly when a new convert is nurtured. Redemption is the spiritual dynamic of this new growth.

The cultural dynamic of Christian growth is called "lift" by the Church Growth school. The convert is "lifted" into a new social pattern. Caution should be taken at this level, since lift can be diverted from Christian to purely secular expressions. An observable tendency of lift, when it becomes excessive in a church, is to divert the priority of the congregation from evangelism toward nurture, "deeper life," and even preoccupation with education.

Lift, if allowed to progress too rapidly, may also isolate the new convert from his non-Christian family and friends. The event of lift literally "lifts" a person to be more godlike and God-conscious as he matures. The process, according Dr. Peter Wagner and others, is evidenced in local church life by the numerical decrease of a convert's social contacts with former friends and acquaintances after only one year.

The period subsequent to this first year as a convert leads him toward Bible study and a high percentage of activities with other Christians. This occurs in a proportionate decrease in intimite contacts with non-Christians. Obviously, this has dangerous implications for world evangelism.

Arrested church growth results when lift is ignored, according to both McGavran and Glasser of the Fuller School. Dr. Glasser refers to these perpetually small and stagnant congregations as " 'islands' of arrested growth."[96]

(9) The principle of pragmatism. The ultimate test of both evangelistic and educational methods is their ability to lead nonbelievers to Christ, toward the goal of their becoming "responsible members of His church," and toward the multiplication of new churches capable of reproducing themselves. "If what we are doing does not produce these results, then we must either modify or discard our behaviour for activity that does."[97]

(10) The principle of Bible curriculum. Curriculum and curriculum design are seldom mentioned in Church Growth literature. The Church Growth movement does not oppose literature produced by independent and denominational publishing houses. This may be because these resources are associated with churches in the United States but used much more infrequently in other countries.

Often, however, stress is placed on the use of the Bible itself for instruction of the total man. Dr. McGavran suggests, "The open Bible should be made available as an essential part of redemption. . . ." He concludes, "Ordinary Christians should teach other ordinary Christians to read the Bible. The omission of this duty . . . is sin."[98]

(11) The principle of new units. The world's largest churches, as previously listed, are almost all located outside the United States. Most of these are also presented by Church Growth strategists as products of people movement evangelization. When compared to the myriads of smaller congregations, however, it becomes obvious that the large churches are in the minority,

though they influence nations and cities.

Church Growth recognizes the cutting edge of worldwide growth is the small unit of believers that grows, divides, and multiplies. The classic axiom, "New units grow faster and win more converts," is a working principle with the Church Growth team.

New converts, new Sunday school classes, new home Bible study groups, and new churches tend to be more productive in evangelism and growth than older established ones.

(12) The principle of celebration, congregation, and cell. As a church grows, the worship, educational, and fellowship climates take on more well-defined characteristics. These three climates are respectively called celebration, congregation, and cell. Each manifests itself by a definite organizational and accountability pattern. Accountability to the group is least with celebration, moderate in congregation, and highest in the cell.

Small churches have cell and congregational qualities but seldom achieve the celebration level due to the absence of a large enough attendance each week.

Celebration is best described as an atmosphere charged much like that of a championship game in an open-air stadium. A balance is needed between these three functions in a growing church if growth is to continue. Examine the chart below for details.

CHURCH FUNCTION	GROUP SIZE	CHARACTERISTICS
CELEBRATION	Over 400 (approx.)	1. Anonymity 2. Meet God, not new friends. 3. Worship Service (no grading)
CONGREGATION	Units of 100-200 each	1. Loss of Anonymity 2. Sunday school structure 3. Usually graded, structured 4. Task-oriented (choir, buses)
CELL	Units of 10-12 each	Commitment to close, spiritual, family-type relations.

Adapted from **Your Church Can Grow,** Peter Wagner (Regal Books, 1976).

Dr. C. Peter Wagner, in his discussion of this principle, observes: "Churches can grow for a time with just a great celebration. But such growth can be illusory. This is one reason for using composite membership figures whenever possible."[99]

(13) The principle of diagnostic research. The significant role of Christian education is to assess blind spots in the health of the church. Beyond this determination lies the responsibility to recommend remedy.

Diagnostic research methods assist those with "church growth eyes" to skillfully locate problems. In the article, "How To Diagnose the Health of Your Church," Dr. Wagner indicates that while the measurements don't cure the sick patient, they are definitely an invaluable tool in diagnosing the seriousness of the illness. He further evaluates the tragic view of those who prefer feelings and guesswork to research as being "hardly beyond the witch-doctor stage."[100]

The national goal of zero population, for example, is a declaration of death to a church committed largely to biological growth in upcoming decades. Dr. Foster H. Shannon calculated and reported in the Church Growth publication *Church Growth: America:*

> The single most significant factor to determine whether a church grows or does not grow is new members received as a percent of membership . . .
> Churches that are losing substantially more than four percent of their total membership by attrition should especially examine the way they handle new church members. . . .[101]

One of the most refreshing examples of Fuller's influence upon denominational agents for growth is seen in the book *Design for Church Growth.* Charles L. Chaney and Ron S. Lewis, both Southern Baptists, propose a seven-fold test of growth in a church. The criteria include: (1) the Numbers Test: has the church been growing?; (2) the Percentage Test: determine the rate of growth; (3) the Body Count Test (Addition): determine how new members are being added; (4) the Body Count Test (Subtraction): determine how members are lost; (5) the Geographical Test: where do new members come from?; (6) the Leadership Test: determine the kinds of leadership you have; and (7) the Time Test: determine how the church structures and uses its time.[102]

PRINCIPLES OF ECUMENISM

A critic of the Church Growth movement, Dr. Francis M. DuBose, writes in *How Churches Grow in an Urban World:*

> Interchurch and parachurch groups have much to share with each other. The Fuller School has led the way in providing training and producing studies which have benefited many church groups and missions.[103]

(1) The principle of ecumenical contact. The frequency or even the duration of time various church groups or cultural groups spend together is not necessarily an accurate indicator of genuine Christian faith.[104] Cooperative ventures do not necessarily indicate or generate spirituality.

(2) The principle of hyper-cooperativism. As one of the foremost Church Growth strategists, C. Peter Wagner claims to have observed few growing churches across America where growth can be correlated with cooperative efforts. In fact, his research indicates just the opposite: "I do not know of many which attribute their evangelistic success to cooperation with other local Churches."[105]

(3) The principle of mergers. Mergers can pose a dangerous threat to one or more of the contracting groups. Due to variation in their histories and rates of growth and decline, the mix of each component should be evaluated carefully. McGavran affirms that "if church growth is to be achieved and stagnation avoided, United Churches must keep in mind the homogeneous units which comprise them. . . ."[106]

United church leaders may desire and plan for union while forfeiting unity. Excessive member loss through transfer growth is symptomatic of this problem.

(4) The principle of parachurch specialists. Parachurch organizations are those groups formed to assist the churches as specialists in penetrating secular non-Christian subcultures. They evangelize through either proclamation or presence.

"Presence" evangelism assists in mercy ministries that aid in creating a climate for conversion. "Proclaimers" simultaneously and/or subsequently verbalize the gospel and actively invite public commitment from non-Christians.

Medical Assistance Program is an example of presence missions while Campus Crusade and Christian World Liberation Front represent proclaiming mission groups. Fuller Seminary's thrust through its School of World Missions constitutes characteristics common to parachurch organizations.

One noted missiologist categorically claims that "the best success in world evangelization" has resulted from the church's willingness to cooperate with parachurch mission organizations. These groups are much like the marines who penetrate resistant subcultures.[107]

According to one growth specialist, parachurch groups have been a familiar part of church and mission history landscape. Their assorted names include: the Jesus People, charismatics, Waldensians, Lollards, Pietists, Assemblies of God, and the Sudan Interior Mission.

Some, like Jurgen Moltmann and C. Peter Wagner, are confident that "parachurch voluntary associations of Christians for political goals are the most appropriate structures to implement Christian social action."[108]

PRINCIPLES OF EVANGELISM

Dr. Kenneth S. Latourette of Yale University wrote the introduction to Dr. Donald McGavran's *The Bridges of God* in 1955. McGavran also has roots in Yale. Interestingly, just two years earlier, today's classic, *A History of Christianity,* had been published.

In the 1953 series Latourette's theory of Christian expansion unfolds as he identifies the four major eras of global church growth. Each successive advance has grown progressively shorter in duration while also reaching a larger world population with each surge. The four historic cycles occurred as indicated below:

LATOURETTE'S 4 PERIODS OF GLOBAL CHURCH GROWTH

Period of Advance	Approximate Duration
A.D. 30-500	500 years
A.D. 950-1350	400 years
A.D. 1500-1750	250 years
A.D. 1815-1914	100 years

Others, like David B. Barrett, confidently conclude that we now live during the fifth great advance in Christian history. This is founded on the explosive growth this very hour throughout the Third World.

In a world where an estimated 50 percent have never heard the name Jesus or the gospel and where 75 percent have yet to receive Christ in any fashion, Donald McGavran issues this mandate: ". . . if a congregation is not reproducing, it is not a New Testament church, no matter what it calls itself!"[109]

Three streams of evangelism have been identified for American church growth during the past three decades by Dr. C. Peter Wagner: (1) 1950s — *Crusade Evangelism*, as with Harry Strachan in Latin America and Billy Graham; (2) 1960s — *Saturation Evangelism*, Kenneth Strachan in Latin America and the improvement of follow-up procedure of crusades through Key '73; and (3) 1970s — *Body Evangelism*, as represented by Dr. Virgil Gerber. Wagner sees a new strategy being generated every decade.[110]

The Church is perpetually only one generation from extinction. During the International Congress on World Evangelism at Lausanne (1974), Dr. McGavran reemphasized, *"Many kinds* of evangelisms are required. Each must be tailored to suit one particular piece of the mosaic."[111]

Fuller Seminary's Church Growth research team has developed a system of classifying six categories of evangelism. Their code letter "M" for missionary was modified to "E" at the Berlin World Congress on Evangelism (1966). We will adopt the evangelism model ("E") in a modified form for our consideration (E-1, winning your own kind of people; E-2, winning those of another cultural or ethnic background; E-3, winning those of another language and cultural base). The letter "G" is being designated for geography (G-1, your homeland; G-2 foreign territory for you). We may now specifically identify the type of evangelism (local) or mission (foreign) we are referring to:[112]

SIX TYPES OF EVANGELISM

	G-1	G-2
E-1	TYPE 1	TYPE 4
E-2	TYPE 2	TYPE 5
E-3	TYPE 3	TYPE 6

(1) *The principle of cross-cultural evangelism.* Dr. Ralph Winter, professor of the Historical Development of Christian Movement at Fuller Seminary, caught the attention of many at the Lausanne Congress by his statistics on cross-cultural evangelism needs.

Cross-cultural evangelism should have the very highest priority because at least 80 percent of the non-Christians in the world today are beyond the reach of ordinary evangelism.[113]

Some movement leaders suggest that every church might ask its members to learn another culture and/or language to improve witness skills.

(2) *The principle of decisions vs. disciples.* As mentioned earlier, Church Growth spokesmen minor on leading people to make public "decisions" in a church service for Christ, and major on making "disciples."

"Surveys among Christian people show that approximately half cannot recall a moment of definite 'decision' for Christ."[114] Movement leaders have, on occasion, questioned the valid use of public invitations at the conclusion of Church services and at crusades.

Dr. Win Arn has written: "The concept of *decision* has outlived its usefulness. The word is unbiblical and inadequate to describe the life commitment called for in Scripture."[115]

The January/February (1978) issue of *Church Growth: America* carried a cover story, "Mass Evangelism: The Bottom Line," that proved controversial in its conclusions about the effectiveness of crusade evangelism. Dr. Arn says, "A 'decision' is an inadequate concept; a truth recognized by the best evangelists themselves."[116] This has interesting implications when you consider the fact that *Decision* is the official publication of the Billy Graham Evangelistic Association.

In the same issue of *Church Growth: America* Dr. Arn refers to a study conducted by his organization and another by Fuller Evangelistic Association. These two studies reported that of the multitudes of decisions, hundreds of thousands made during Campus Crusade's Here's Life, America, "97 out of every 100 were never incorporated into a church."

(3) The principle of people movements. People movements, earlier called "mass movements," are viewed as different from "mass evangelism," since the former claims (1) to be more effective in rooting new converts to a New Testament church and (2) to have as its goal that of reaching total social units and families rather than winning individuals in isolation.

People movements have characteristics similar to those of mighty revival movements. The distinguishing difference is that revival awakens the saints to service and holy living, whereas people movements are the mighty movements of God to awaken souls to salvation.

A major aspect of this principle is its focus on those groups and individuals who indicate high receptivity to the gospel. J. Robertson McQuilkin, president of Columbia Bible College, comments that this principle was the first to "draw worldwide attention" for the Church Growth movement.[117]

In *The Bridges of God* McGavran considers people movements as gifts of God, the builder of stronger and healthier churches and individuals, the conserver of human resources, the quickest and best way to win the masses, and the method God is most likely to use when the Third World suddenly is moved toward God.

Research indicates, according to Dr. Alan Tippett, that people movements are not "faulty evangelism." Instead, he argues that the fault is most frequently related to poor post-conversion follow-up and care.

Early misunderstandings developed over the term "people." Some did not understand that these were multi-individual decisions made within and by social groups together. This is not to imply that all group members followed the decision of their social group to become Christians.

Church Growth leaders get excited about the ability of people movements to almost totally bypass social and cultural barriers to salvation. They also are able to avoid isolation from the convert's social ties which serve as bridges leading to convert possibilities. In conclusion, Dr. McGavran testifies:

> For every one out of a new people brought to Christian faith separate from his group, God has converted hundreds in chains of families. He has used the People Movement. That is the normal way in which the Christian churches have grown.[118]

The principle of reaching responsive peoples is thoroughly consistent with Scripture (Matthew 10:14; Acts 13:51; Luke 10).

(4) The principle of the harvest. Briefly stated, this principle acknowledges that the Lord's command was and is to win the winnable while they are winnable.

The harvest mentioned in Matthew 10 and Luke 10 is a ready harvest and requires laborers now or never.

Also, God ripens the field but he requires us to reap. Fields that were ripe yesterday are gone today; today's ripe fields will be gone tomorrow; and tomorrow's field requires no labor today.

Harvie M. Conn, critic and editor of *Theological Perspectives on Church Growth*, affirms:

> Church Growth writers have served us well by reminding us that while certain lights may be dimming and even going out in one part of the world, new lights are appearing and burning brightly in others. If we take the broad view, we cannot escape the conclusion that we live in the best century of all for the spread of the Gospel.[119]

Dr. McGavran cautions comfortable harvesters that church growth is not automatic just because we are busy and kind. God holds man personally responsible for gathering the sheaves. "The harvest is granted only to those who arrive sickle in hand, labour all day and have carts ready at noon to carry in the piled sheaves."[120]

The "noncultural" factor in church growth is none other than the Holy Spirit at work in the people and in the circumstances. God ripens . . . man harvests.

(5) The principle of scheduled evangelism. Who has not heard that "evangelism is everything we do"? Church Growth planners recognize that this is a misleading statement. McGavran and Arn write: ". . . until we are sure that evangelism is an essential part of every ministry of the church, not much evangelism will be done."[121]

(6) The principle of the ten percent. The spiritual gift of evangelism is the issue of this principle. First formulated by Dr. Peter Wagner in 1973, the concept states that each evangelical congregation has an average of approximately ten percent of its members who have the gift of evangelism. Few churches have more than ten percent. This precept is observed operating near maximum capacity in great soul-winning churches. For example, First Baptist Church of Hammond, Indiana, with the largest Sunday school in the United States, and Coral Ridge Presbyterian Church, the largest Presbyterian Church in the nation, both reflect the principle.

This principle grew out of Wagner's research as a missionary in Bolivia. As he observed defects in the "total mobilization" theory of evangelism proposed by Kenneth Strachan of the Latin American Mission, the Fuller professor began his search for a church able to mobilize its total membership in evangelism. He soon discovered that even the superaggressive soul-winning churches in America tend to mobilize approximately 10-15 percent regularly.

After three years of examining American and Third World mobilization practices, the pattern proved consistent. The biblical doctrine of spiritual gifts (Romans 12:3-9; 1 Corinthians 12:7-11; 12:27-31) seemed to offer the most reasonable answer for the phenomenon. Dr. Wagner concluded that while every Christian is commanded to be a witness (Matthew 28:19, 20), not every Christian has the scriptural gift of evangelism. This includes some pastors.

CHURCH	YEAR	MEMBERSHIP	SOUL-WINNERS	%
Jerusalem	30	120	12	10
1st Baptist, Hammond[122]	1974	18,000	1800-2000	10
Coral Ridge[123]	1971	2,500	250	10
	1976	3,000	450	15

The greatest obstacle to evangelism today, according to Wagner, is that of the ten percent, "only about one half of one percent are actively using [the gift]."[124]

The Fuller strategist further states that if a church mobilizes its total ten percent and each only won one person each year to Christ, "the church would triple every ten years . . . on a decadal rate of 200 percent."

This knowledge, coupled with the principle of redemption and lift, opens a totally new understanding of why conversion growth is so crucial to church growth.

(7) *The principle of divine selection.* An examination of Romans 1:18-20 and 2:14, 15 reminds us of God's mighty initiative and man's awesome responsibility in salvation. Dr. J. Robertson McQuilkin evaluates Scripture and Church Growth in this way:

> . . . Scripture does indicate at least one basis on which God is selective in His approach to men. God is responsive on the basis of men's response. To those who respond to the light they receive, more light is given. Those who are resistant have the light reduced or taken away.

(8) *The principle of "sheep stealing."* A frequent accusation of nongrowing churches against those experiencing growth is the issue of "sheep stealing." McGavran and Arn are boldly unapologetic in their answer to this charge:

> Millions of neglected "Christians" live around us. . . . Well-fed sheep cannot be stolen. Convinced Christians stay in their churches. . . . In fact, one may say that if sheep can be stolen, the practice is not sheep

stealing. Finding sheep running wild in the streets or hungry . . . and bringing them back to the fold is not sheep stealing.[126]

(9) The principle of secular mythology. The secret to winning the masses to Christ is in realizing that our evangelism must identify animism, not secularity, as its target. Dr. Alan Tippett postulates that the symptoms of this age (example: rise of astrology, witchcraft, and a myriad of other cults) are those of animism, not secularity.

Animism thrives on the supernatural, whereas the secular resists the supernatural. Tippett concludes:

> The animism of the modern city is reinforced by big business. . . . I press again the point that these are not signs of a resistant secular society. I believe we can say the fields are whitening unto harvest.[127]

17. Body Life

"In recent years," observes Dr. Lloyd John Ogilvie of Hollywood's First Presbyterian Church, "a term has been used extensively to describe the essence of the church. It is 'body life,' and refers to what Christians are and what they are to do as the called-out, called together people of God. . . . Institutionalism has built fine buildings, but have we built great people?"[1]

Dr. C. Peter Wagner writes:

> The idea of all members of the body working together has recently been called "body life." The term did not originate either in Latin America or in a Pentecostal church. It comes from Pastor Ray Stedman of the Peninsula Bible Church in Palo Alto, California. Stedman has popularized the phrase in a book by the same title, but the concept is still relatively new to many Christians. Not to Latin American Pentecostals, however, because they have been practicing body life for decades, even though they might not use the term as such.[2]

The publisher of *Body Life* says that since its publication in 1972 approximately 325,000 copies of the book have already been sold in all fifty states, England, New Zealand, Japan, South Africa, and other countries around the world.

What exactly is body life? Does it have identifiable principles and traits? Can a church like yours benefit from it and does it result in visible, numerical growth?

"Body life" is a term frequently associated with spiritual gifts and the priesthood of all believers. A survey of 1 Corinthians 12 reveals that the term "body" is used eighteen times to mean the church.

Dr. Ray Stedman, author of *Body Life*, describes the term this way:

> Perhaps the best term for it is commonality, the clustering of Christians together in a shared intimacy that, rather mysteriously, forms a clear channel for the moving of the Spirit of God in power . . . It is this shared intimacy with one another and the Lord which is the missing note in today's church life.[3]

An important clarification needs to be made. Three different usages of the term "body life" have already been made: (1) the scriptural reference, (2) the adaptation of the scriptural usage by churches and church bodies, and (3) a particular North American variety of body life centered around the Peninsula Bible Church and the book by the same title. (For the specialized use of

134

this term in this latter case, Body Life is capitalized.) All three examples can exist simultaneously and may be very much alike or noticeably different in the way they are expressed. Books have been written about all three forms.

The intent of this survey is to focus on that particular expression of Body Life that exists among the people of the Peninsula Bible Church of Palo Alto, California, and similar churches. The Sunday evening worship service at Palo Alto has become the model for American churches as they try to describe what Body Life is like. In fact, both the pattern and principles of Body Life tend to vary, as currently applied, among groups unfamiliar with the Peninsula model. Realize, however, that even among Pentecostal churches, many groups have adopted Peninsula characteristics due to the influence of the book *Body Life*, articles, sermons, seminaries, tapes, and word of mouth. The concept of Sunday evening has become an increasingly accepted pattern across North America.[4]

The Sunday evening service is known for its informality, no pulpit, free sharing of testimonies, needs, and prayer requests. It was this service that gained worldwide recognition when the public announcement was made allowing those in attendance to take up to ten dollars from the plate if they had a specific need.

Peninsula's auditorium seating capacity of nearly 1,200 scarcely sheltered more than 250 on Sunday nights until December of 1973. A church-wide prayer meeting initiated an event now known worldwide. Sunday morning

SELECTED BODY LIFE CHURCHES*

CHURCH	LOCATION	PASTOR**
Peninsula Bible Church	Palo Alto, Calif.	Ray Stedman
Fellowship Bible Church	Dallas, Tex.	Gene Getz
Mariners Church	Newport Beach, Calif.	Joe Aldrich
Trinity Church	Seattle, Wash.	Gib Martin
Our Heritage Church	Scottsdale, Ariz., Phoenix and Tempe	

(*) Some churches adopt selected Body Life principles while preferring not to use the name "Body Life."

(**) Most of these churches actually have several pastors.

attendance spurted from a modest 100 in 1950 to nearly 3,000 in 1977. Presently, the Sunday Body Life service reaches between 700 and 1,000.

"No matter how large or small the group . . . or for what purpose it gathers," if the four principles of (1) commitment, (2) openness, (3) reliance, and (4) enlargement are present, says Stedman, "the meeting becomes a *koinonia.*"[5] The Palo Alto service is noticeably made up of almost 80 percent youth under age twenty-five, 25 percent over age twenty-five, and about 10 percent of all attenders being visitors.[6]

Four new congregations have developed from outlying segments of Peninsula's membership through their network of home Bible study groups. One now has about seven hundred members and another about five hundred. Additionally, seven other churches similar to PBC have sprung up in more distant cities.[7]

Each of these congregations have common principles that identify them as Body Life churches and have also exercised their right to develop individual styles of ministry.

Many non-Body Life congregations have adopted methods that relate to the climate of their communities and churches. Five such churches include: First Church of the Nazarene, Pasadena, California; First Southern Baptist Church of Los Angeles; First Baptist Church of Tucson, Arizona; First Baptist Church of Houston, Texas; and Lake Avenue Congregational Church of Pasadena, California. So we see that Body Life methods and principles are also being adapted in some denominational churches.

The young adults of First Baptist Church, Houston, have begun over thirty "Discipleship Families." These groups are for all assortments of life-styles: couples, mixed, single women, all men, and all women. Additional ministries include a Body Life worship service, Agape meals, life-style outreach, a retreat ministry and classes on Body Life using the Ray Stedman book. "Disciple Families" are groups of approximately six to twenty that meet for discipleship training and friendship activities such as bowling, beach trips, expositional Bible book studies, special topical studies, quiet time, and Scripture memorization.

Dr. Gene Getz, associate professor of Christian education at Dallas Theological Seminary and pastor of the largest Body Life congregation in Texas, reminds us:

> What may work in one community may not work in another. Thus, it is dangerous to borrow programs. What we must do is search out and apply the supra-cultural principles of the Bible—those principles that will work in any culture and at any given moment in history.[8]

What are some of these principles that account for growth among Body Life churches? How does doctrine relate to growth? Body Life leaders tend to identify the two as being irrevocably interrelated.

PIONEERS AND PRINCIPLES

"The apostles initiated the growth process," claims Dr. Getz, "in the believers' lives in Jerusalem by exposing them to Bible doctrines."[9] Imagine, growth being initiated through your contact with the Word! (1 Pet. 2:2, KJV).

According to Lawrence O. Richards in *Three Churches in Renewal*, the growing time required to nurture Our Heritage Church in Scottsdale, Arizona, Mariners Church in Newport Beach, California, and Trinity Church of Seattle, Washington, was almost ten years for each.[10] Dr. Stedman accepted his call as pastor to Peninsula Bible Church in 1950, the growth peak came in 1970 (January-April), and therefore growing time required for significant increases in attendance to occur was about twenty years.

The basic principles and organizational implications for Body Life churches are considerably different from those taught by fundamentalists. ". . . What the Big Churches have accomplished seems impressive! And examination shows principles the renewal (Body Life) movement is most critical of."[11]

Principles come in assorted packages. Dr. Ray Stedman, while recognizing the existence of several principles, chose to focus on four primary ones in 1967. Each has already been listed elsewhere in this report.

Lawrence O. Richards lists six principles of "renewal" churches: (1) unified body, (2) love life-style, (3) servant leadership, (4) ministering laity, (5) growth emphasis (i.e., discipleship vs. initial conversion), and (6) scripture response, (i.e., willingness to obey learned doctrine).[12]

David Roper, associate pastor of campus ministries at Peninsula, lists twenty principles of ministry that relate to growth in the book *When All Else Fails . . . Read the Directions* by Bob Smith. The publishers indicate that sales on this book for the three years since it was first printed total 30,000, or 10,000 per year.[13]

In the book *Sharpening the Focus of the Church* Dr. Gene Getz gives a catalog of forty-one New Testament principles for growth and ministry. Seven relate to evangelism; eight to edification; seven to leadership; seven to administration; four to organization; and eight to communication.

Organizer of Principles	Number of Principles
Ray Stedman	4
Gene Getz	41
David Roper	20
Lawrence O. Richards	6

Our present study will now consider twenty-four principles of growth and ministry generally found among Body Life congregations. They are divided into eight major categories.

1. Corporate Life (5 principles)
2. Administration and Leadership (6 principles)
3. Physical Facilities (1 principle)
4. Finances (1 principle)
5. Ministries (3 principles)
6. Christian Education (4 principles)
7. Ecumenism (1 principle)
8. Evangelism (3 principles)

PRINCIPLES OF GROWTH AND MINISTRY

PRINCIPLES OF CORPORATE BODY LIFE

(1) Focus on a common service. This time of sharing, testimony, singing, Bible study, and encouragement is scheduled at different times by various churches. Peninsula Bible Church meets every Sunday night under the name "Body Life," while at Fellowship Bible Church in Dallas there are four identical services each weekend with the discussion coming at the final half of the two-hour period, following the sermon.

(2) Compatability with academic communities. Dr. Dan Baumann, in *All Originality Makes a Dull Church,* concludes his study of nine churches:

> While the "body life" service functions best in an academic community where high premium is placed on verbal communication, the concept of caring is universally applicable. . . . The application of this truth will differ from community to community.[14]

(3) Informality. Body Life churches tend not to have pulpits or choirs. Suits and ties are in the minority in most services. For the fellowship and sharing time following the Bible teaching, a stool is frequently used to maintain an informal climate.

(4) Meeting needs where people hurt—now! Several Body Life churches circulate detailed "prayer" and "need sheets" with a want-ad format: for example, "Missionary needs temporary living quarters from September 1—October 8"; "Two lovable, playful kittens with Siamese features. Free."; "Need occasional daytime babysitter"; "Job opportunities"; "Rides needed for an older lady to Body Life."

During Body Life meetings at Palo Alto, when a need is shared, a person with a similar need usually is asked to stand and pray with them.

(5) Body Life builds burden-bearers. Dr. Lloyd John Ogilvie writes, "Every time Barnabas is mentioned in Acts, he is bringing encouragement. . . . Body Life is the fellowship of the sons of encouragement."[15] Members learn to magnify the ministry of others.

PRINCIPLES OF ADMINISTRATION AND LEADERSHIP

(1) Statistics are minimized. Mariners Church, Our Heritage Church, Trinity Church, Fellowship Bible Church, and Peninsula tend to function more as a fellowship than as a traditional church.

One observer reports, "I tried to get exact numbers from the leaders of these three churches. It was difficult because they don't keep statistics . . ."[16]

Baptismal reports are almost nonexistent. Membership rolls are not kept at Peninsula. The same is true of records for most classes. Apparently nobody has an accurate count of the total number of home Bible study and prayer groups, since they are often viewed as ministries of individual members rather than of the church.

(2) Elders lead and pastors teach. Fellowship Bible Church in Dallas is administered by a board of thirty-five elders: approximately two-thirds are non-staff and one-third are staff elders. All are considered pastors.

Every vote during the past five years has been by consensus. Fellowship Church minimizes spiritual gifts whereas Peninsula magnifies gifts.

Both Trinity Church (Seattle, Washington) and Mariners Church (Newport Beach, California) are governed by a permanent board.[17]

Peninsula Bible Church is governed by fourteen life-appointed elders. They administer but do not "run the church." They have an unwritten law that on all votes the will and mind of God is to be decided by unanimous vote and not merely by majority.[18]

(3) Multiple pastoral leadership. Dr. Ray Stedman, in the article "Should a Pastor Play Pope?" says: ". . . no one man is the sole expression of the mind of the Spirit; no individual has authority from God to direct the affairs of the church. A plurality of elders safeguards against the all-too-human tendency to play God over the people."[19]

Among the seven principles of New Testament leadership listed by Dr. Gene Getz we read, "The 'one man' ministry is a violation of this important guideline. . . . No local church in the New Testament was ruled and managed by one person. Plurality of elders appears as the norm."[20]

(4) Avoidance of sensational publicity. James Hefley, writing of Peninsula Church, reports that newspaper advertising is never used and that the telephone directory only carries two lines for the church. Yet, Sunday attendance still exceeds 3,000 weekly.

Pastor Stedman insists, ". . . I think it is important that the church again imitate its Lord by approaching the world with an avoiding of all sensational publicity and without seeking to cultivate prestige. . . ."[21]

The communication bridges used most effectively in Body Life churches are the Bible, printed and taped Bible studies, and home Bible study groups. Literally tens of thousands of printed sermons have found their way as gospel tracts from the main hallway at Peninsula to friends and strangers through interested members.

The volumes of books written by Body Life pastors like Ray Stedman and Gene Getz have saturated Christian bookstores and churches across the country.

(5) Success is more than high attendance. As already mentioned, Dr. Stedman listed "enlistment" as the fourth principle needed for *koinonia* or body life. He defines "enlargement" as waiting on God to give the increase. He further comments:

> Perhaps this principle will be the most difficult to change because everywhere the church seems to be committed to the concept that it is some kind of a club whose task it is to build up its membership through drives, contests, visitation programs, etc. But these activities are entirely missing from the New Testament.[22]

David Roper, campus pastor at Peninsula, admonishes readers, ". . . Don't count noses. Operate on the basis of biblical principles and God will bring enlargement (Acts 2:47). When we feed our people, we won't need to waste time on promotional gimmicks."[23]

(6) Leadership is not lordship. The "leadership is not lordship" concept of pastoral ministry continually surfaces as a sensitive topic with Body Life leaders.

One observer, after interviewing pastors and non-staff leaders in Mariners Church, Trinity Church, and Our Heritage Church, was noticeably impressed with "servant leadership" as an area of common agreement among all three Body Life churches.[24]

Body Life congregations want strong leadership in their pastors, but both pastors and members tend to oppose an authoritarian style or model of ministry.

PRINCIPLE OF FINANCE

(1) Focus on ministry rather than maintenance. According to Roger C. Palms, writing for *Decision* magazine, "Only 7½ percent of the money received goes into building and maintenance; the rest is spent on people and ministry. The statement is heard at PBC, 'We major in people and minor on buildings.' "[25]

Even without a formal budget, expenses are usually met within one-tenth of one percent of receipts at Peninsula Bible Church, the report indicates. Approximately 90 percent of all funds received at Palo Alto go into the general fund with the remaining 10 percent going to specific ministry-related funds. The congregation receives an annual report of financial expenditures for the almost $500,000 received.

Another observer notes that members of the Palo Alto church are encouraged "to give directly to missionary organizations" as individuals rather than as a collective body. A monthly missions newsletter, *The World Outreach*, updates the Body on missionary activities abroad.[26]

Similarly, a recent survey of Our Heritage Church in Scottsdale, Arizona, indicates a giving pattern where 51 percent of the giving from the people goes through the church while 49 percent is given directly by members to people in need and for missionary support.[27] Our Heritage also elected a committee whose specific task is to pray about the financial needs of the group.

In contrast, Seattle's Trinity Church annually increases its budget to include support for one additional missionary. This church has increased the total number of missionaries being supported by more than one for each year since being organized as a church.

Fellowship Bible Church of Dallas recently paid $70,000 cash for their learning center facilities.

PRINCIPLE OF FACILITIES

(1) Priority of multiple services over new buildings. Most Body Life congregations are relatively small and medium-sized in their memberships. Several exceptions have been reviewed in this article. Except for Mariners Church in the Los Angeles area, Peninsula Bible Church in the San Francisco area, and Fellowship Bible Church in Dallas, most Body Life congregations are not yet bursting at the seams with wall-to-wall people.

Church	Auditorium Capacity (approximately)	Approximate Attendance	Number of A.M. Services
Peninsula	1,200 *	3,000	2
Fellowship	254	1,000	4 **
Mariners	700***	1,700	2
Trinity	400	200	1****
Our Heritage	—	75	3 locations

 * Includes opening of adjacent space for 400 seats.
 ** Fellowship Bible Church (Dallas) provides four identical services, and each family unit selects one (Friday P.M., Sunday A.M., Sunday afternoon, Sunday night).
 *** Mariners proposed new auditorium will seat 2,000. Upon completion of this facility, Mariners will have the largest seating capacity while Peninsula will probably still have the largest attendance.
 **** Trinity maintained two morning services until moving into a new facility two years ago.

PRINCIPLES OF MINISTRY

(1) Priority of exploring and employing gifts. Interestingly, one observer refers to Peninsula Bible Church as the "Saints Employment Agency."[28] The Body's pastor stresses, "It takes the whole church to do the work of the church. . . . The supreme task of every Christian's life is to discover his gift

and put it to work."[29] He further warns that if gifts are ignored or misused," "the whole body will suffer."

(2) Ministry functions belong to members, not pastors. Stedman recalls that when he came as pastor over twenty years ago, the one clear principle before him was ". . . my deep conviction . . . [was] that the work of the ministry belonged to the people and not to the pastor." His role is to ". . . leave to laymen the major responsibility for the visitation of the sick, presiding at and leading church services, and evangelizing the world."[30]

Dr. Gene Getz, while recognizing the validity of gifts, teaches his church families that Scripture places priority on maturity over gifts. "If having *obvious* spiritual gifts is a prerequisite for serving in the church—as some people say it is—it is very interesting that Paul himself did *not* make this stipulation for New Testament church leadership."[31] He concludes, ". . . 'body function' [i.e., Body Life] is not dependent upon the list of 'spiritual gifts' in the New Testament, but rather a love and concern for 'one another.' "[32]

(3) New ministries are initiated by members. This concept is actually two-fold. First, the usual procedure at Palo Alto is to encourage members with new ministry ideas to share them with the church's elders for direction in using them within the body.

Secondly, to quote James Hefley, "Another . . . policy adhered to through the years has been not to look outside for a man to start a new ministry but to recognize the energies of one in the congregation with the gifts for leadership in a needed area of work."[33]

Space literally prohibits any listing and consideration of the myriad of the ministries exercised through these congregations. At Palo Alto alone, at least twenty-nine various ministries function simultaneously. Viewed together, the ministries directed by the churches surveyed in this article alone touch the lives of tens of thousands each year.

PRINCIPLES OF CHRISTIAN EDUCATION

Body Life churches are noticeably different from fundamentalists in their basic views of the Sunday school. Body Life churches view the church as a local seminary designed for saved sinners, while fundamentalists teach that the church is a hospital for both saved and non-Christian sinners. This has vital implications for evangelistic strategy in the local church.

(1) Home: God's seminary. By far, this principle is best explained by Walter McCuistion, pastor and coordinator of children's ministries for grades 1-7 at Peninsula Bible Church:

> We ought to consider *parents, rather than children, the targets of Christian education.* We ought to consider parents, rather than teachers, as the prime educators. These two changes would revolutionize Christian education. . . . Actually, it is as old as Deuteronomy itself.[34]

One strategy he has begun to help apply·this concept has been the attachment of a "Message Supplement for Parents" to the printed sermons. Copies are available the week following the date of delivery. This tool is designed to help parents apply the sermon creatively in the home the following week.

(2) Reach families rather than children. Dr. Gene Getz makes a forceful statement that no doubt will be difficult for many non-Body Life members to accept. He declares:

> Nowhere in the New Testament are examples given of 'child evangelism' as we frequently practice it today; that is, to win children to Christ out in the community apart from the family setting. . . . This does not mean there is no emphasis on the importance of child life and child conversion. . . . The New Testament pattern is clear! The target for conversion was adults.[35]

Five specific advantages are then listed by Dr. Getz for reaching adults for Christ and consequently the whole family.

Due to the focus on adults in Body Life churches, you will observe, when visiting one of their worship services, that the younger children are receiving training elsewhere in the building.

(3) Sunday school: boot camp for believers. Basic to Body Life understanding is that the church is a training center for believers and not a stadium for evangelism. Sunday activities are for Christian education rather than evangelism.

Bill Dempster, pastor of the South Hill Community Church of San Jose, California says, "We felt that Sunday school should not be a tool for direct evangelism . . . but for training children to evangelize."[36] "Every church should be a seminary . . . a place where seeds are planted," is the conviction of Palo Alto's second ranking staff member.[37]

Dr. Gene Getz writes in *Sharpening the Focus of the Church* concerning life-style evangelism:

> Very little is said in the New Testament about evangelism *in* the church; that is, where believers gather to be edified. This is of course a New Testament norm. Generally speaking, unsaved people are to be reached *by* the church, not *in* the church."[38]

One characteristic that is almost universal with Body Life fellowships is the staggering number of Sunday and daily Bible study groups meeting away from the main worship facility. Peninsula Bible Church, for example, has Sunday classes meeting on the Stanford University campus and at scores of restaurants all over the Palo Alto metro area from junior high through adults.

Approximately half those attending return to the main facility for the larger gathering. If all returned at one time they would not even find standing room because of the packed pews.

(4) Body growth is more visible than personal growth. Someone has said that our vision must be as large as the world but as small as one. If you plan to saturate

a city with your doctrine, however, it will require a network of believers.

> Faith, when expressed through a "body" of Christians, has a power of expression and visibility that is nearly impossible to match by a Christian who is living out his faith in isolation.[39]

PRINCIPLE OF ECUMENISM

(1) Unity is stronger than union. Unity without union expresses itself on three levels: with ministerial unions in the same city, with parachurch organizations, and with other Body Life churches. Any basis for unity must be doctrinal and not organizational.

Dr. Stedman, for example, has declined membership in the ministerial union in Palo Alto; declines the use of the title "Reverend" in front of his name; feels that Christian parachurch groups and churches should magnify the name of Jesus above their own; and encourages no organizational ties with other Body Life congregations. "We don't have organizational ties with any of the churches that have spun off from us. Nor do we want to be tied to anything else."[40]

PRINCIPLES OF EVANGELISM

Evangelism among Body Life churches, as with Christian education, is definitely not a traditional approach to ministry. These congregations and their leaders, however, are confident that their principles and methods are scripturally based.

(1) Church meetings are designed for the converted, not the unbeliever. To adopt a quote from Dr. Howard Hendricks of Dallas Seminary, there is a marked difference between the church in A.D. 78 and the church of A.D. 1978. "The New Testament church was primarily called to be a school, a training ground, a place for the equipment of saints to do the work of the ministry. . . . Today we reverse those arrows. Instead of going out, we have constituted the church as a soul-winning station. . . ."[41]

Dr. Ray Stedman indicates in his book *Body Life* that at Palo Alto the worship services are for exhorting, equipping, and edifying the saints and are not designed to merely evangelize the evangelized.

> We determined from the start that we would do no direct evangelizing in the regular services of the church, or within the church building, but all evangelization would be done in homes, back yards, rented halls or other public places.[42]

Dr. Joe Aldrich, pastor of Mariners Church (Newport Beach, California), stresses priority of evangelism outside their worship services to the extent that much of the ". . . evangelism at Mariners . . . is done by men and women of the church without . . . the brand name 'Mariners' on it."[43]

Pastor Gib Martin of Seattle's Trinity Church explains: "I feel that the great commission says to disciple, and it does not say to evangelize. I think evangelism is an extension of a mature disciple."[44]

(2) Priority of body evangelism over pulpit evangelism. "Our services are not basically evangelistic in nature," reports Associate Pastor Walter McCuistion of Peninsula Bible Church. "We do not give people an open invitation to come and accept the Lord. We feel that the purpose of the church is to train the saints . . . and people are coming to know the Lord all during the week."[45]

Pastor Ray Stedman agrees and indicates that the regularly given public invitation "tends to weaken a church."[46]

In an exposition of 1 Corinthians 14:24, Dr. Gene Getz comments on the conversion of the unbelievers discussed in the text: "Note too that he does not come to Christ because of a special evangelistic message preached from the pulpit. . . ." He adds, ". . . generally, evangelism in the New Testament took place, not as the 'church gathered' but as the church was 'scattered' into the world. . . ."[47]

(3) Home Bible studies: model for evangelism. The informality of the home Bible study group has many similarities to the informal worship service in Body Life churches. One major difference, however, is that these home meetings are the evangelizing centers of the congregation.

Other Bible study groups focus on men or women only and attract attendance into the hundreds. One such group in Seattle is led by Mila, a member of Trinity Church, who with forty other group leaders leads 400 women.

"Mass evangelism campaigns are helpful," notes Stedman, "but the bread and butter of evangelism should be the neighborhood group."[48]

Each group is intentionally "nonchurchy." By some Body Life fellowships they are regarded as personal ministries of individual Christian family units. Others are sometimes considered as being specifically church-led ministries. While most sermons on Sunday are basically monologues, home groups present ". . . biblical concepts in everyday language and then invite no-holds-barred comments and questions."[49]

Home Bible study groups have an amazing ability to shatter "the huddle syndrome" among Christians, according to Dr. Stedman. Groups meeting in homes, report Body Life churches, restore confidence in the power of the gospel and help remove the fear of bold witnessing for Christ. "Most witnessing and evangelizing is done now on a personal basis through friendship and hospitality evangelism."[50]

Bob Smith, before joining the pastoral staff at Peninsula, was a professional steel fabricating engineer for thirteen years. He shares that the first home Bible study group grew from two families to thirty-two. Then their first convert to Christ brought nine friends and led his wife to Christ.

"A class was started in the couple's home. They invited a hundred friends and seventy came. Around twenty became Christians," reports James Hefley.[51]

On another occasion, in the same church, comes the report that "in one two-year Bible study in Romans, led by a young two-year-old Christian converted from drugs and his friend, the attendance among the youth grew from 45 to 165 kids."[52]

Some home Bible study groups are known to have grown as large as 300 and others as large as almost 200 in size. The recommended group size in most Body Life churches, however, averages between twelve and twenty.

Meetings in industrial plants like Lockheed Missile and Space, General Electric, and Pacific Telephone have also been conducted. One summer, through Moody Science films, in industries and homes over 7,000 viewers were reached with the gospel.

Almost all Body Life churches focus on home Bible study groups. They are for Body Life churches what the bus ministry, television-radio ministries, evangelistic revivals and crusades, and weekly public invitations are to tens of thousands of evangelical and fundamentalist churches.

BODY LIFE CHURCHES

STRENGTHS	WEAKNESSES
1. Avoidance of rigid formality in corporate worship services.	1. Exclusion of the public invitation as an opportunity for genuine conversion commitments.
2. Focus on reaching the total family for Christ as a single unit.	2. Neglect of conversion readiness among children and youth who can be reached though parents are not responsive to the gospel.
3. Teachings and involvement of members in a biblical understanding of spiritual gifts.	3. Tendency to isolate themselves from the larger Christian community of evangelicals due to doctrine of separation.
4. Priority on developing great Christians and not just great buildings.	4. Unwillingness to see how multiple use of buildings can edify the body and be tools for evangelism-discipleship.
5. Strategy to encourage and equip families for "hospitality evangelism" in their own neighborhoods.	5. "Hospitality evangelism," while effective is also highly "selective evangelism." Effective bus captains penetrate entire neighborhoods of families with less manpower per harvest of souls and homes. Both are needed.
6. Magnifying follow-up of new converts and reclaiming casualties of carnality through friendship discipleship.	6. Assumption that their results are superior qualitatively and scripturally without a demonstrated willingness to maintain accurate records to allow verification through statistical analysis.
7. Development of intimate social relationships through home (neighborhood) Bible study groups.	7. Allowing doctrinal introversion and stress on relationships to purposely or unintentionally solicit involvement of leaders in other churches through home study groups. This results in transfer growth whether so intended or not.
8. Caution against overemphasis on collecting and/or publicizing of statistical records about attendance, membership, conversions, finances.	8. Avoidance of collecting and/or publicizing of statistical records about attendance, membership, conversions, finance, etc., (cf. Luke 15:4; Acts).

147

18. Charismatic Renewal

Pentecostals are also showing rapid growth in North America as well as other parts of our world. According to Hollenweger, there are about two hundred Pentecostal denominations in the U.S., not all well known and not all showing healthy growth.[1] The Assemblies of God represent the largest Pentecostal organization in the U.S. and are the most organized and have exhibited excellent growth. According to the chart, their growth since 1965 has reflected a membership increase of 229,356. The number of Pentecostal churches in the United States as of the end of 1975 was 9,019. According to Wagner, the Assemblies of God denomination is showing explosive growth in Brazil and Latin America. Wagner says that the largest denomination in Brazil is the Assemblies of God and estimates their size at about 1,500,000.[2] He also notes that the largest denomination in Latin America is the Assemblies of God of Brazil.[3] This is not the first example of a denomination being planted in foreign soil which outgrows the size of its "mother." Why are the Pentecostals and especially the Assemblies of God growing, and what can be learned from them to the benefit of others?

CHURCH MEMBERSHIP IN USA 1925-1975

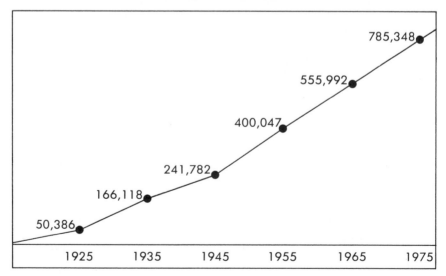

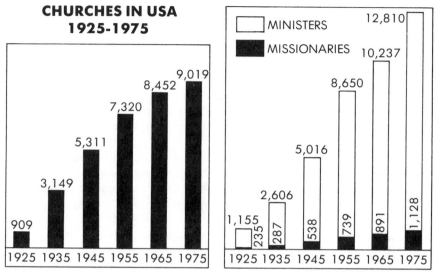

Reprinted from "Facts and Figures on the Assemblies of God" (Springfield, Mo.: Office of Information for the Assemblies of God, n.d.).

THE CHARISMATIC DISTINCTIVE

Donald Palmer, in his analysis of Pentecostal church growth in Colombia, submits:

> Most of the Pentecostals themselves would claim that the *main* reason for their superior growth lies neither in methodological nor sociological factors, but rather in their having more of the fullness and power of the Holy Spirit in their lives, ministries, and churches. For they believe that while we preach and practice only a partial gospel, they have the "full gospel," which places special emphasis on the supernatural power and charismatic gifts of the Holy Spirit.[4]

Melvin L. Hodges, secretary for Latin American and General Council of the Assemblies of God, West Indies, admits:

> Pentecostals themselves give the main credit for church growth in their midst to the moving of the Holy Spirit. They believe that only the Spirit can exalt the Lord Jesus Christ in the way that will bring the multitudes to Him.[5]

Dr. Rodman Williams, president of Melodyland School of Theology, in an interview concerning church growth emphasized that growth is a by-product, that it is inevitable when the Holy Spirit is not quenched. Williams mentioned that "you don't find charismatics very much interested in Church Growth seminars, but yet we are growing."[6] He further stated that the supernatural, the presence of God (miracles, healings, etc.), are those elements of the movement which attract people.[7]

149

What then is a charismatic? According to Hamilton,

> The term *charismatic* applies to those who have experienced a "baptism of the Holy Spirit" that involves receiving certain spiritual gifts. This event, sometimes as important as conversion, usually leads to a new style of living for the recipient, and public witness to the benefits of baptism in the Spirit become a central and joyous aspect of his life. Tongue-speaking, technically known as glossolalia, is the distinctive, though not necessarily the most important, gift received at this baptism of the Spirit.[8]

> The prime distinguishing mark of charismatic believers is their insistence that the baptism in the Holy Spirit, accompanied by external signs of confirmation, usually glossolalia, is necessary for empowerment to witness, and that the normative pattern for such is found in Scripture.[9]

In citing the difference between a Pentecostal and a charismatic, one Assemblies of God leader said:

> In a pure definition, there is no difference. In terms of function, a charismatic is a person who was involved in a denomination other than pentecostalism, who now believes in the full use of the gifts.[10]

When referring to the uniqueness of the A.O.G. (Assembly of God) denomination over others, VanStennis replied: "We are not that unique. Other than full use of all the gifts, enthusiasm, good music, infilling of the Holy Spirit, teaching the Word, and evangelism."[11]

Their distinctive has been and is obvious today, although there appears a definite feeling among some that this is not the "magic secret" for church growth. Successful pastor Mike Johnson of Calvary Temple in Springfield, Illinois, proposes:

> For far too long, charismatics and Pentecostals have thought only the blessings of God would bring increase of the Body. They have relied upon the Holy Spirit to "bring them in." Though no spiritual work can be done in the lives of men without the Holy Spirit, I know that we must work to attract people to our services, where we can then win them to Christ.[12]

In commenting on how Pentecostals differ from evangelicals in their doctrine of the Holy Spirit, Wagner cites two differences. One is *degree* and the other is *kind*. Concerning *degree* he notes that "Pentecostals emphasize the Holy Spirit in their preaching, their worship, their conversation, their singing and their writing more than other Evangelicals."[13] Concerning *kind*, Wagner confirms the most common understood difference involves the post-salvation experience called "baptism in the Spirit." Pentecostals are convinced "that this baptism in the Spirit with the sign of tongues releases a spiritual power for Christian life and witness that other Christians do not have."[14]

FAITH HEALING AND PRAYER

To speak of charismatics and Pentecostals without noting the accompanying emphasis on prayer and faith-healing would certainly present less than an accurate picture. Hollenweger summarizes when he states:

The attitude of individual Pentecostal groups to the healing of the sick by prayer in general, and to the healing evangelists in particular, varies a great deal. On the whole one can say that the more recent and more enthusiastic groups look with favour on the healing evangelists. On the other hand, the older Pentecostal groups have gone to some trouble to keep the healing evangelists at a distance, for until recently they held and taught the view of the healing evangelist which they now condemn as false; "Anyone who believes is healed: anyone who is not healed has not believed aright."[15]

Whereas all evangelicals believe that God can heal, and most would refer to James 5:14, 15 as the specific direction to the church today, the Pentecostals, believing that all the gifts are present today, also include the gift of healing.

Pastor Ralph Wilkerson of Melodyland, while stressing that people today are "searching for churches that are preaching Jesus in power," also stated that he thought "*the number one thing* that draws people to Melodyland is the supernatural. We have miracles of healing while we are preaching the Word of God."[16]

Wagner, referring to Latin American Pentecostals, cites:

Studies have shown that faith healing is a more universal characteristic of Latin American Pentecostals than other charismatic gifts, for example, speaking in tongues. . . .

The physical suffering that is so much a part of today's Latin America becomes a strong motivating force to bring men and women under the hearing of the message the Pentecostals preach.[17]

He goes on to support the good intentions of the Pentecostals by referring to illustrations to verify that divine healing is a means to an end—the end being eternal salvation of those whose needs have been met in this temporary way. Wagner states that divine healing

. . . is for the most part a manifestation of the power of God that will ultimately attract unbelievers to Jesus Christ as Savior and Lord. Healing is, thus, an effective evangelistic tool which only incidentally brings temporal blessings.[18]

After the divine healing crusades pass on out of the city, according to Wagner, the churches handle praying for the sick on a more regular daily basis in the sick rooms or wherever, constantly giving testimony to their belief in James 5:14, 15. He concludes, "I wouldn't be surprised if some Pentecostals pray for the sick as often as Presbyterians repeat the Lord's Prayer. And they continue to believe in it because they all have seen it work so frequently."[19]

This same cycle has been observed here in the United States with several leading healing evangelists. Rex Humbard, pastor of the Cathedral of Tomorrow in Akron, Ohio, built his ministry on the basis of healing prayer for the sick. It was phenomenal how the multitudes were attracted, and again it was the lower classes at first. As time went on, Rex Humbard and family stayed in Akron and developed a local church ministry. Prayer for the sick and healing continues to be an integral part of their services but hardly so ostentatious as it once was. Now Pastor Humbard reads James 5 and prays with those desiring God's healing.

OTHER FACTORS

While recognizing these two differences concerning the doctrine of the Holy Spirit, Wagner argues that "the evidence indicates that, whereas doctrine undoubtedly has *something to do* with Pentecostal growth, it by no means is the only factor. It probably is not even the principle factor."[20]

Wagner's positive Church Growth thesis is that non-Pentecostals can learn much about winning the lost from Pentecostals without agreeing with Pentecostal pneumatology. In proving his point, he argues cogently that the following principles and methods have greatly affected the growth records of Pentecostals in Latin America:

1. A proper understanding of the Great Commission.
2. Planning to plant new churches constantly.
3. Sowing the Word to receptive people (the masses versus the classes).
4. High degree of laity involvement in body life.
5. Effective training for pastors with great emphasis on practical experience.
6. Making the church celebration a fun experience for all.
7. Prayer for the sick and seeing them healed.
8. Staying with the priority of aggressive evangelism, not social action.[21]

McGavran, while admitting that Pentecostal growth in Latin America is complex, states concerning their specific activities:

> A missionary researcher after years of study voiced the opinion that the Pentecostals, by their marchings, witnessing, praying aloud, giving testimonies in church, telling what God has done for them, gathering in large numbers, speaking in tongues, pressing into buses by the hundreds, preaching on street corners, and defying the customs of the traditional Churches, are helping Christians of the "masses" to overcome their feelings of inferiority. These activities give them a taste of victory in the moral and spiritual realm. . . .
>
> No doubt these activities are a major factor in Pentecostal growth and would operate anywhere among victims of the social order. By contrast, quiet, respectable congregations of traditonal Protestant Churches, where the minister, a professional, does most of the speaking, praying

and witnessing, are much less able to dissipate the social inheritance of inferiority and the inborn conviction that "we are little people."[22]

Palmer, although again dealing with a society outside of the United States, confirms this by the results of a survey among pastors and leaders of non-Pentecostal churches when he reports:

All of them answered that there were some definite lessons to learn from them (Pentecostals) and gave what they considered to be the principle ones. These are listed according to the frequency with which they were mentioned, with the first being the most often mentioned: (1) meetings which are more alive, joyful, and enthusiastic; (2) the mobilization of a greater percentage of the believers in the churches; (3) the opportunity for more people to participate in the services and activities of the church; (4) more emphasis in the churches on the Holy Spirit and His gifts and power; (5) the self-support system in the churches; and (6) a greater emphasis on the apprenticeship system of training pastors and church leaders.[23]

When we draw our attention back to the Assembly of God in the United States, many of their nongrowing churches could also learn principles and methods for growth from their nearby comrades in Latin America, Brazil, Chile, and Colombia.

In reference to other reasons for growth in the United States, VanStennis cites four basic reasons for A.O.G. current increases:

1. Excitement about the gifts (healings, tongues, etc.), thereby drawing attention to the activity of the Holy Spirit.

2. Christ-centeredness, as seen by a renewed interest in teaching the gospels again and studying the life of Christ. This represents an attempt to set up principles of God's divine life for people to live by, using Christ as our example.

3. Applying the Scriptures in bite-sized practical segments as a brand new emphasis blending together exegesis and devotional treatment so that people aren't lost.

4. Renewed emphasis on evangelism of the grass roots type where everyone who is born again is expected to go out and win one.[24]

Assemblies of God statisticians are saying that the current widespread charismatic renewal has played an important role in the recent growth of the movement. Lebsack clarifies this matter: "While Calvary Temple (South Bend, Indiana) emphasizes Holy Spirit baptism, the main thrust remains in leading the lost to Christ."[25]

Tommy Barnett, pastor of the Westside Assembly of God in Davenport, Iowa, has led his church from seventy-seven to an average of 1,124 in Sunday school over a twenty-year period. When asked to what they attribute this phenomenal growth, Pastor Barnett replied:

It is soul winning. Our people are literally obsessed, a magnificent obsession, to win souls. All week people plan on who they can get to church and how many more they can reach. They come believing and knowing that an altar call will be given and that many people will come forward to accept Christ.[26]

In noting the common denominator among the "Top 10" churches, author Lebsack summarizes:

All the pastors heavily emphasize evangelism. They come from many backgrounds, with different approaches, but all seem to also possess a burning passion of care for their community. And, without question, they are leaders of dynamic ability who are able to motivate people for service.[27]

It's interesting, in reading Lebsack, to note the obvious lack of emphasis on the "charismatic distinctive" and the solid evangelical principles and methods which have been tried and proven by other groups. Lebsack affirms that "A common denominator of all these pastors in *Ten at the Top* is their strong work habits. They are not lazy men, but work hard. Their churches reflect their efforts."[28]

SUNDAY SCHOOL GROWTH

While at some Pentecostal churches (Calvary Chapel and Melodyland included) Sunday school is not a main emphasis, this is not true in the Assemblies of God denomination. Lee Lebsack, church growth activist and pastor at Ravenna, Ohio, states that "recent statistics indicate a surge in Sunday school growth in the Assemblies of God that has not been matched in the denomination's 60-year history."[29] He goes so far as to state that the long-held Baptist lead in Sunday school is now "being challenged by a growing group of Sunday School-minded pastors in the Assemblies of God."[30] Referring to a compilation of statistics from their 6,915 Sunday schools (as of 1973), he cites the following increases: "Enrollment climbed by nearly 78,000 during the last Sunday School year, compared to 21,000 the previous year. This is a 7 percent gain and brings the average enrollment per school to 126. Total enrollment is now projected to be 1,777,616."[31] In addition, he adds that "attendance grew by more than 54,000 during last year, making the average attendance per school figure climb from 85 to 90. The total average attendance is projected to be 839,812, representing a 6.9 percent increase."[32]

J. Don George, pastor of the Assemblies of God Calvary Temple in Irving, Texas, is committed to outreach as the key to growth and believes "evangelism must be the major emphasis of the Sunday School." He says, "Our Sunday School is a teaching arm, but more than that it is a soul-winning arm of our church."[33]

In reviewing Lebsack's work, it is interesting to note that three of the "Top 10" refer directly to Hyles and Falwell, and the impact that their influence, through pastor's schools, etc., have had on them. When reading of the philosophy of these successful Assembly of God churches, it sounds very familiar, almost as if Hyles and Falwell were speaking. Themes such as "sold on Sunday school," "building with buses," "aggressive evangelism," and "pastoral leadership" are seen again and again. Obviously, the world will never know the result that godly leaders of the church growth movement are having on other churches, but it certainly causes our hearts to rejoice when we see such direct evidence.

19. Evangelical Bible Churches

Admittedly, this segment or grouping of churches is the most difficult to place into a well-defined "camp." Although variations of methodology and emphasis exist in the other church growth schools of thought, more diversity is found here. Yet while there are differences, there are also some definite similarities. In order to define this grouping it is imperative to keep both "evangelical" and "Bible" together, which forms the outstanding characteristic of the churches which will be chosen as representatives. It is clearly the authoritative and relevant teaching of God's Word. While Towns in his comparison between "sect/fundamentalist" and "evangelical/institutionalist" describes the evangelical in a negative light, he does recognize this distinctive when he states:

> Evangelicals prefer to think of themselves as conservative in doctrine, yet *relevant* in methodology. One thing an evangelical knows for sure, he is not a fundamentalist. There are other names which might apply to evangelicals. The term *orthodox* and *conservative* is usually applied to both fundamentalists and evangelicals. However, the term *orthodox* and *conservative*, when applied, usually designates "that branch of Christendom which limits the ground of religious authority to the Bible."[1]

STRONG TEACHING EMPHASIS

Based squarely on the authority of the Bible, the preaching ministry of evangelical Bible churches is normally strong and long. While the watchword of the reformers was *sola scriptura*, "scripture alone," these churches believe that Luther did not go far enough in extending his radical commitment to Scripture to the doctrine of the church.[2]

Here are examples of those who preach forty-five minute to one-hour messages weekly: Charles Swindoll, pastor of the First Evangelical Church of Fullerton, California; David Hocking, pastor of the Grace Brethren Church of Long Beach, California; John MacArthur, pastor of the Grace Community Church of the Valley, Panorama City, California; and Gene Getz, pastor of the Fellowship Bible Church of Dallas, Texas. These and other pastor-teachers, such as Ray Stedman, Joe Aldrich, Michael Tucker, and Marvin Rickard, normally follow a plan of expository, book-by-book preaching. They are individually committed to the position that the Word of God alone can cause Christians to grow spiritually and non-Christians to be saved.

Michael R. Tucker, pastor of the Temple Baptist Church of Colorado Springs, Colorado, believes:

> The whole concept of spiritual growth lies here. We believe that Christians love and minister when they grow in Christ. *The only way to grow is through study of God's written Word.* . . . Christians who have sat for years under topical, surface preaching have "come alive" under exposition of the Scriptures.[3]

Tucker, a graduate of Conservative Baptist Seminary, cites the definition of Haddon Robinson, president of Denver Conservative Baptist Theological Seminary, to explain his understanding of expository preaching:

> The proclamation of a biblical concept derived from an historical-grammatical study of a passage in its context which the Holy Spirit has first made vital in the personality of the preacher and through him applies accurately in the experience of the congregation.[4]

He admits that his commitment to this style of ministering demands fifteen to twenty hours of personal preparation per message.[5]

Gary Inrig, pastor of Bethany Chapel in Calgary, Alberta, Canada, and a graduate of Dallas Seminary, agrees:

> The complete and consecutive teaching of Scripture must receive a very high priority in assembly life. Nothing is more beneficial than a ministry of expository preaching which covers the sweep of all the books of the Bible. Bible teachers can all too easily develop pet doctrines or ride hobby horses or carefully avoid very important, but touchy, matters. Expository preaching will keep solid food before believers and bring a balanced and nutritious diet.
>
> It is my conviction that nothing is more worthy of my best time and effort than the study and teaching of God's Word. Only God's Word quickened by His Spirit can establish believers and make them strong in Christ, and so all of our church services focus upon the teaching of Scripture.[6]

Referring to the First Evangelical Free Church of Fullerton, Baumann reports that Sunday morning attendance is averaging around 2,800 in three services with overflow rooms. He adds that "people do not mind coming early and walking two blocks, due to woefully inadequate church parking, because they know that their pastor is well prepared and will give them a thoughtful exposition of Scripture."[7]

While Swindoll may be more concerned about application than some, and Getz presents his teaching while sitting on a stool in a conversational manner, MacArthur will lace his hour-long message with humorous quips and illustrations. Differences are there, but the common denominator is clear. These men believe a church is built by the solid teaching and preaching of God's Word, and nothing less will do.

The pastor-teachers of these Bible churches may have more in common than meets the eye. Not only do each possess an unusual manifestation of the gift of teaching but most of these men are students of the church and have written articles and books concerning it. A result of their study and practice is God's obvious blessings upon their ministries. The churches they pastor are growing! (See chart.)

GROWTH STATISTICS
FOR REPRESENTATIVE BIBLE CHURCHES

According to interviews of April 1976, the following available information is included to cite the growth of Evangelical Bible Churches.

FIRST EVANGELICAL FREE CHURCH
of Fullerton, California
Pastored by Charles Swindoll since 1971

STATISTICS:	1970	1975	1979	NOTES OF INTEREST
Church membership	784	1526	2342	Poor parking and no facilities for additional Sunday school growth.
A.M. attendance	1200	3100	4000	
Sunday school	921	1381	No attendance taken	

LOS GATOS CHRISTIAN CHURCH
of Los Gatos, California
Pastored by Marvin Richard since 1961

STATISTICS:	1970	1975	1979	NOTES OF INTEREST
Church membership	NA (not available)	1698 (families)	4900	Well organized, good programs in every area. Excellent music program.
A.M. attendance	785	2899	5000	
Sunday school	785	2243	3900	

GRACE COMMUNITY CHURCH OF THE VALLEY
of Panorama City, California
Pastored by John MacArthur, Jr., since 1969

STATISTICS:	1970	1975	1979
Church membership	NA	1738	2342
A.M. attendance	NA	2626	4000
Sunday school	NA	2348	1600

GRACE BRETHREN CHURCH
of Long Beach, California
Pastored by David Hocking since 1968

STATISTICS:	1970	1975	1979	NOTES OF INTEREST
Church membership	1312	1946	2385	Operates one of the largest Christian Schools by a single congregation in U.S.—over 1000 students. Home of new Grace Graduate School and Grace Bible Institute.
A.M. attendance	1192	1898	2718	
Sunday school	1047	1403	1807	

PENINSULA BIBLE CHURCH
of Palo Alto, California
Pastored by Ray Stedman since 1951

NOTES OF INTEREST:

No membership and no records are available. An admission into fellowship form is given to those who desire to feel a part of the church. They average currently approximately 1,000 for each service (2 morning and 1 evening). They have approximately 50 new people each Sunday.

FELLOWSHIP BIBLE CHURCH
of Dallas, Texas
Pastored by Gene Getz since its beginning in 1972

NOTES OF INTEREST:

No records of services are kept. The church began 3 years ago with 140, including children. Currently there are approximately 600 family units or 1,000 in attendance at morning service. There is no Sunday School as such, but one meeting of 2½ hours. Their program includes studying the Word for the first hour, a fellowship coffee time with an emphasis on meeting the visitors and a Body Life program for the last part. Their children's learning center is one of the strongest drawing points.

MARINERS CHURCH
of Newport Beach, California
Pastored by Tim Timmons

NOTES OF INTEREST:	1979
No records of services are kept. This is not important to them. Current church membership is guessed at 300, but 1800 are in attendance, including approximately 800 families.	1900

TEMPLE BAPTIST CHURCH
of Colorado Springs, Colorado
Pastored by Michael R. Tucker since 1970

STATISTICS:	1970	1975	NOTES OF INTEREST
Church membership	135	638	They have three A.M. services and have started another on Saturday night 6:00 P.M. (same sermon)—150 in attendance.
A.M. attendance	140	675	
Sunday school	125	500	

EDIFICATION "IN," EVANGELISM "OUT"

Concerning the purpose of the church, Pastor John MacArthur, in his book *The Church, the Body of Christ*, believes:

> The local church essentially is a training place to equip Christians to carry out their own ministries. Unfortunately, for many Christians the church is a place to go to watch professionals perform and to pay the professionals to carry out the church program. In many quarters Christianity has deteriorated into professional "pulpitism," financed by lay spectators. The church hires a staff of ministers to do all the Christian service.
>
> This scheme is not only a violation of God's plan, but an absolute detriment to the growth of the church and the vitality of the members of the body. To limit the work of the ministry to a small, select class of full-time clergymen hinders the spiritual growth of God's people, stunts the development of the body, and hinders the evangelistic outreach of the church into the community.[8]

This concept of the church has several practical ramifications. Tucker believes that it is his personal commitment to the Word of God that leads him to stress edification during the church services. He admits that most evangelism takes place outside the building and that the services are primarily for maturing the saints.[9] While he is careful to include at least a "capsulized" gospel in each message, he states that "there are never any evangelistic meetings inside the church's walls. The whole concept is that as Christians are built up in the faith and equipped to do the work of the ministry, they will grow and respond to God's Word. In a natural overflow of the Christian life, they will share God's good news with others."[10]

Obviously not all Evangelical Bible Churches will agree on the application of the edification-evangelism issue. However, it is a major point of distinction between this group and the Bible Baptists. Ray Stedman, author of the pace-setting *Body Life* testified:

> I have had the privilege of pastoring one church for over twenty years. In all that time we have never held an evangelistic meeting in the church, but there has been a continual stream of new converts coming into the church for instruction and development of the Christian life. Evangelism has been occurring within the homes of members, and in public halls, backyards, school rooms, and wherever a hearing for the gospel could be obtained. But every meeting held in the church building has been aimed at the instruction, training, or worship of Christians together. Our entire Sunday school is set up to equip the saints, of all ages, to do the work of the ministry. The work of expounding and applying the Scriptures begins with the pulpit and is continued in every class, in every gathering and in many of the homes of Christians. Stress

is laid upon confronting life as it is really lived with the insights and viewpoints of Scripture and drawing upon the resurrection power of an ever-present Lord.[11]

Aldrich, pastor of the Mariners Chapel of Newport Beach, agrees with this view of Stedman, according to his recent message presented to the Southern California-Arizona Ministerium of Grace Brethren Churches.[12]

According to researcher Henry Lord, Grace Brethren Church of Long Beach, pastored by Dr. David Hocking, lists evangelism as its first objective. Of Hocking's three preaching goals, the first one is "to win people for Christ." However, according to Lord, it is most interesting to note that of the 200 who made public decisions during 1974, only ten percent (or twenty people) had *not* made a personal decision to receive Christ before the services. Ninety percent had in fact received Christ through the ministry of someone else prior to making the decision public.[13]

Baumann, pastor of the Whittier Area Baptist Fellowship Church of Whittier, California, in his analysis of this school of church growth, affirms that "by their definition, the church is *not* primarily a soul-winning station, a forum for contemporary issues, or a showcase for music and/or drama; it is a schoolhouse for the training of Christians."[14]

As seen in Stedman's earlier statement, it is certainly true that this group believes and is deeply committed to evangelism, although evangelism may be accomplished through many avenues outside the church buildings proper. Tucker agrees that the New Testament commands the church to evangelize, but sees "no hint" that it should take place in church meetings. He balances his statement with a list, similar to Stedman's, of a number of vehicles that their church uses for aggressive evangelism. This practical application of the edification "in" and the evangelism "out" "allows the church services to center on the teaching of God's Word for God's people."[15]

PASTOR'S ROLE IS EQUIPPING

MacArthur gives a classic illustration concerning what a pastor of a local church should do.

> I remember seeing, at a circus, a man spinning plates on eight sticks. He would just get all eight going and have to run back to keep Number One moving, and so on up the line. This seems to me an apt illustration of the role of the pastor, who has figured out the plates he wants to spin and looks through the congregation to find the right sticks. He gets it all going and discovers that the sticks don't keep the plates moving, so he is stuck with running up and down from plate to plate, operating programs which the sticks are not motivated to spin. How much better is it to concentrate all on "perfecting the sticks" so that as they grow they become motivated to begin certain ministries, services that are on their

hearts and interest them. Perfected, mature saints will develop ministries in the energy and excitement of their maturity.[16]

Getz, successful pastor and seminary professor, argues for balance. While agreeing that it is the Word of God which is basic to spiritual growth (1 Pet. 2:2), he submits another means of maturation, that being the "functioning body."[17] Thus as the Word is preached and the saints minister to one another, they are equipped to do the work of the ministry.

Hocking, seeing a plurality of elders in every New Testament church, states that "one of the main tasks of the elder is to 'equip' the believers in the body for the 'work of ministering' in order that the body might be built up or edified (Eph. 4:11, 12). The elders are not doing the building up in this text or the work of ministering, but rather their work is that of equipping."[18]

Understanding the proper role of pastor-teacher and layman has long been a difficult area. It seems in church life that there is a constant drift to "professional-pastor-ministers" as opposed to the total body ministering. Stedman affirms:

> Throughout the Christian centuries no principle of church life has proved more revolutionary (and therefore more bitterly fought) than the declaration of Ephesians 4 that the ultimate work of the church in the world is to be done by the saints — plain, ordinary Christians — and not by a professional clergy or a few select laymen. . . .
>
> The four offices of apostle, prophet, evangelist, and pastor-teacher exist for but one function: that of equipping the common Christians to do the tasks which are assigned to them.[19]

SPIRITUAL GIFTS ARE FOR TODAY

If the pastors and elders are to equip the body, with the chief means being the teaching of Scripture, and if the church responds properly, then each Christian should know, understand, and minister his spiritual gift to others. Although no one seems to be dogmatic as to what exact gifts and how many exist for today, there is a consistent teaching among this group of their importance to church life.

Pastor Gene Getz de-emphasizes the specific nature and usage of spiritual gifts listed in Scripture passages but emphasizes qualities of maturity. He sees the functioning body as absolutely essential for the qualitative growth of the church.

> It is no doubt true that every believer in the New Testament church was gifted by God in a special way to function in the body, but it was not always possible nor necessary to identify that gift by name or to be able to "pigeonhole" it by placing it in a "gift list."
>
> It is also true that though specific spiritual gifts are mentioned on several occasions in the New Testament, the use of all of them was not

essential for "body function," or for maturity to take place in the body.[20]

DISCIPLESHIP FOR SPIRITUAL LEADERS

Whenever spiritual gifts, body life, edification, and qualitative growth are stressed, discipleship becomes another key principle. Bob Smith, disciple and associate of Ray Stedman at Peninsula Bible Church, sees discipleship groups as a motivating factor. He encourages the enlisting and leading of men in a group situation to be disciples (disciplined learners) of Christ.[21] Dave Roper, another pastor-teacher at Palo Alto with Stedman, gives the following principles for implementing a discipleship program within the local church:

1. Select key men from the larger Christian body to which you are ministering (congregation, Sunday school class, Bible study group, etc.). Note these verses for the basis of your choice: 2 Tim. 2:2; Luke 6:12, 13; Mark 3:13.

2. Begin to spend time with this select group (John 3:22). Spend leisure time with them (Mark 6:31). Get them into your home and family life; involve them in your personal life and ministry (Mark 5:37).

3. Provide additional opportunities for teaching through Bible study and discussion, reading, Scripture memorization, tapes, etc.

4. Expose them to other teachers and leaders. It takes all the saints to know all the dimensions of the knowledge of God.

5. Encourage them to open up and share their lives with one another. Set the pace by your own openness and honesty.

6. Be sensitive to teachable moments (Mark 10:13-16).

7. Don't be afraid to be hard on these men; God's men will bounce [back] (Mark 8:18, 33; 9:1-8; 9:19).

8. Welcome adversity in their lives; these times are opportunities for advancement (Mark 4:35-41).

9. Encourage them into ministries on their own. Give them plenty of rope. You can trust the Holy Spirit in their lives. Provide counsel and encouragement. Evaluate periodically (Mark 6:7-13, 30). Move them out into positions with increasing responsibility. Gently push them out into situations beyond their depth so they have to trust the Lord.

10. Impart your vision to encourage them to disciple others and send them out (John 20:21).

11. Maintain a support base even when they are on their own. Provide help as they need it. Pray for them, write, be available for counsel.[22]

It's interesting to note that Getz formed the present leadership of Fellowship Bible Church with a commitment to similar principles. In his book *The Measure of a Man* he speaks of "his men" meeting together to study the qualifications of New Testament leaders and characteristics of maturity as found in 1 Timothy 3 and Titus 1.[23]

SHARING THE MINISTRY

Without exception, all the men who represent this "camp" adhere to some form of a shared ministry concept. Tucker summarizes the reason when he states:

> Already you recognize that the pastor who invests so much time in sermon preparation must be in a church where either (1) many parts of the ministry are neglected, or (2) many people share the ministry. For a pastor to devote time to studying, the congregation must understand that their lives are enriched through the results of his preparation. This concept implies that the pastor *cannot* be involved in many areas traditionally dumped into his lap.[24]

Getz, armed with New Testament teaching, affirms:

> . . . multiple leadership in the church is a New Testament principle. The "One Man" ministry is a violation of this important guideline. The Scriptures frequently stress the "mutuality of the ministry." No local church in the New Testament was ruled and managed by one person. Plurality of elders appears as the norm.[25]

Fellowship Bible Church of Dallas enjoys the ministry of thirty "lay" non-paid elders who have oversight of various ministries with their pastor. This severely indicts the "benevolent dictator" attitude of some who run their churches like businesses, hiring and firing and telling elders and deacons what to do. Getz recognizes the validity of the "top man" position but urges acceptance of more than one spiritual leader of a local church. He adds that "preaching" without giving the body members a chance to share their gifts with others is incorrect. Yet Getz hastens to emphasize the importance of "the preaching" when he says, "Nothing is more basic than teachiing the truth of Scripture."[26]

In Colorado Springs, pastor Michael Tucker has seen that sharing the ministry goes farther than just including other paid staff or lay elders. He believes that the platform is the place to prove the shared ministry concept to the people by encouraging others to read Scripture, pray, make announcements, etc. Baptizing at Temple Baptist can also be done by others. In studying the New Testament, Tucker discovered that any Christian can baptize another, and so they do. Fathers baptize children and campus workers baptize converts.[27]

Findley Edge attacks a fear of some about the shared ministry when he states:

> What we need to understand at this point is that this is not a devious plan which a group of scheming preachers worked up to try to trap the laity into doing work that preachers don't want to do. Neither is it a malicious program planned in some denominational headquarters to tap a vast untapped resource of manpower. This is God's design for the accomplishing of his redemptive mission in the world, and we have

missed it! It is God's plan and we have been trying some other way. Regardless of what our theology may be theoretically, in actual fact and practice we have been relying upon the wrong people as ministers for God.[28]

What are the principles of church growth to these churches? MacArthur, a spokesman for Bible churches, gave twelve marks of a successful, effective church at a recent minister's meeting. They are as follows:

1. Plurality of godly leaders.
2. Functional goals and objectives.
3. Strong emphasis on discipleship.
4. Strong emphasis on community penetration.
5. An aggressive, active, ministering people.
6. An intense "caring" spirit.
7. A genuine, high level devotion to the family.
8. Strong biblical teaching and preaching.
9. Willingness to change and innovate.
10. Constant effort to stretch the people's faith.
11. A spirit of sacrifice.
12. Primary thrust must be on worshiping God.[29]

Hocking enlarges these twelve with an additional eight principles for church growth.

1. A continual desire and challenge to reach as many people as possible with the gospel until Jesus comes again.
2. A constant dependency upon God's power and direction through much prayer and careful study of biblical principles.
3. Emphasis on the body of Christ and the unity and fellowship of God's people rather than denominational affiliation and distinctives.
4. A simplicity of organization and operation.
5. A dedication by pastors to do what God tells them to do and to refuse to do what the people should do and must be trained to do.
6. A desire to grow.
7. A continual learning spirit.
8. A resistance to and exposure of sin as the one thing hindering true growth.[30]

20. Southern Baptists

The Southern Baptist Convention is the largest of what is considered to be the evangelical denominations or groups in America today. According to the chart, Sunday school enrollment as of late 1978 totaled 7,317,960 and church membership was at an all-time high of 13,379,073.

PAST GROWTH

Donald McGavran, in illustrating the possibilities of church growth in the book *How to Grow a Church*, refers to the Southern Baptists' outstanding growth of the past when he states:

> Until 1937 California was regarded as the province of the Northern Baptists, who now call themselves the American Baptists. The Southern Baptists consequently were not actively planting churches there. In 1937, however, seeing the multitudes of unchurched, seeing that the Northern Baptists were not meeting the need, the Southern Baptists aggressively entered the state. At that time they had twelve Southern Baptist churches in California. Today they have Nine hundred Ninety-two! In the course of thirty-five years they have grown from twelve to nearly a thousand, perhaps over a thousand by this time.[1]

"The Southern Baptist Home Mission Board in Atlanta," reports Dr. Peter Wagner, "is to my knowledge, the most sophisticated agency for starting new churches in the United States. Currently organizing one new Baptist church per day . . . Southern Baptist churches are multiplying much more rapidly than others. . . ."[2]

Baptist Press, the national news release agency of the denomination, issued a report in early 1980 about a comprehensive five-year plan (1980-1985) to increase enrollment in Southern Baptist Sunday schools from the present 7.3 million to 8.5 million by 1985.

As director of the denomination's national Sunday school department, Dr. Harry Piland observes an obvious transition in current and past enrollment growth patterns. Between *1950-1958* a total enrollment increase of *2 million* was registered (growth from 5 to 7 million). *Since that time*, however, only *200,000* new persons (net) have been enrolled by the present 35,605 congregations (7.1 to 7.3 million enrolled). (See chart.)

To achieve the goal of 8.5 million in Sunday school by 1985, an additional 151,380 workers and 64,320 class units are needed, according to the Nashville leader.[3]

SOUTHERN BAPTIST CONVENTION STATISTICAL PROFILE (1968-78)

	TOTAL CHURCHES	NUMERICAL CHANGE	% CHANGE	S.S. ENROLLMENT	NUMERICAL CHANGE	% CHANGE	TOTAL MEMBERSHIP	NUMERICAL CHANGE	% CHANGE	NUMERICAL ADDITIONS PER CHURCH
1968	34,295	148	.43	7,545,513	− 33,690	− .44	11,332,229	189,503	1.70	5.53
1969	34,335	40	.12	7,418,067	−127,446	−1.69	11,489,613	157,384	1.39	4.58
1970	34,360	25	.07	7,290,447	−127,620	−1.72	11,629,880	140,267	1.22	4.08
1971	34,441	81	.24	7,141,453	−148,994	−2.04	11,826,463	196,583	1.69	5.71
1972	34,534	93	.27	7,177,651	36,198	.50	12,067,284	240,821	2.03	6.97
1973	34,665	131	.38	7,182,550	4,899	.07	12,297,346	230,062	1.90	6.64
1974	34,734	69	.20	7,190,829	8,279	.12	12,515,842	218,496	1.78	6.29
1975	34,902	168	.48	7,281,532	90,703	1.24	12,735,663	219,821	1.73	6.30
1976	35,073	171	.49	7,458,375	176,843	2.37	12,922,605	186,942	1.45	5.33
1977	35,255	152	.43	7,430,931	− 27,444	− .37	13,083,199	160,594	1.23	4.56
1978	35,605	350	.98	7,317,960	−112,971	−1.54	13,379,073	295,874	2.21	8.30
AVERAGE YEARLY INCREASE/DECREASE			.41			−5.87			1.83	5.85
10 YEAR CHANGE		1428			−261,243			2,236,347		64.29

ANNUAL, SOUTHERN BAPTIST CONVENTION (Nashville, Tennessee: Convention Press, 1969-1979)

According to the annual reports issued by Southern Baptists during the decade 1968-1978, the congregations removed from their Sunday school rolls 261,243 persons while gaining 2,236,347 new persons for church membership. This equals a Sunday school daily decrease in enrollment of about 65 persons and a daily increase in total church membership of about 557. This means that for every one person going out the back door of the church, eight are coming in the front door.

The decadal growth rate has averaged *18 percent* since 1968. Reflecting on these statistics of church membership increase over the decade, it is interesting to note current church growth thinking. Dr. McGavran, years ago, developed the guideline:

> . . . biological growth should be calculated on the basis of 25 percent per decade. Biological growth occurs when the children of believers are raised in a Christian way, taught about Jesus, converted and incorporated into church membership.[4]

Wagner argues that "if a church is growing at only 25 percent per decade, it is barely growing at all."[5] Until 1972, the decade was marked for Southern Baptists by declining enrollment. Then in 1972 a modest gain was recorded that culminated in 1976 in the highest net gain in enrollment—176,843. Both 1977 and 1978 were marked by decline in enrollment.

THE ENROLLMENT DEBATE

Throughout past decades of Sunday school and church growth, Southern Baptists have placed major attention on the importance of enrollment in growing a church.

Enrollment policy varies among denominations and church groups. Research often reveals wide variances of at least four types. *Some congregations*, both growing and nongrowing varieties, totally avoid recording either attendance or enrollment statistics. A *second* group of churches in their annual reports record enrollment to the exclusion of attendance. Most major denominations tend to be in this category. Departing from both of the previous views, a *third* cluster of churches publicize only attendance information and may even consider enrollment as camouflage for poor attendance. A *fourth* sector of churches, usually represented by Southern Baptists, report both enrollment and attendance information. Almost all records published on a county-wide area of Southern Baptist churches include both items.

Southern Baptists have formulated laws of growth by attendance and enrollment for decades. Skeptics have always questioned the precept, for example, that attendance will usually average about fifty percent of the number of people enrolled in Sunday school. Dr. E. S. (Andy) Anderson, growth consultant for the Sunday School Board of the Southern Baptist Convention, refers to the "laws of growth" when he cautions critics, "They operate in every church whether the pastor and his corps of workers and leaders recognize them or refuse to acknowledge them. They are working in your church now."[6] He further comments:

> The only denomination in the history of Christianity to enroll over 7,000,000 people and teach 3,500,000 of these each week in Sunday School is the Southern Baptist Convention. The methods and organizations used to accomplish this are fundamental. Some of these have been questioned by critics, but until someone reaches more people for Christ, for Bible study, and for salvation, I do not feel that there are any valid criticisms.[7]

Obviously, not everyone agrees with the above position. Towns argues that "some may attempt to determine size of Sunday school enrollment, but such a survey would reveal 'paper growth' of expanding rolls. But this does not reflect vitality or actual accomplishments."[8] Most Southern Baptists, however, disagree and insist that the final test is the turnout for Sunday school in the churches on Sunday morning.

"ACTION" ENROLLMENT

"Action" is a relatively recent Southern Baptist program designed to provide growth in Sunday school attendance through increased Sunday school enrollment. Andy Anderson, while pastor of the Riverside Baptist Church of Ft. Myers, Florida, came to the realization that even given his best efforts or the efforts of others, his church would always average about forty percent of its Sunday school enrollment. (Note: some church groups report somewhat higher percent of enrollment attending, but this is usually due to frequent removal of absentee members from the roll. Others drop members immediately as they become inactive or move out of the city. A third category includes those groups originating or currently existing as relatively closed ethnic or cultural communities.)

Deciding to honor a long standing principle of growth related to enrollment, Andy Anderson devised a simple formula to depict the relationship between attendance and enrollment: $E = P + A$ (E = enrollment; P = Present; A = Absent).[9]

Briefly summarized, the number of people present and the number absent will remain relatively constant in a ratio of 40 percent (attending) to 60 percent (absent). As enrollment rises, so does the proportion of those attending the classes.

Southern Baptists are taking the positive approach and moving with renewed zeal toward planting additional Sunday schools via the "Action" method. This approach, interestingly, has demonstrated that of all persons enrolled by door-to-door canvassing, approximately 20 percent will never attend, 40 percent will come at least once but will not become active, while the remaining 40 percent will become active attenders.

"Action" has been instrumental in leading Southern Baptists to "plant"

2,000 new churches in the north-central states of Wisconsin, Indiana, Illinois, Michigan, Ohio, Minnesota, and Iowa between 1949 and 1979. Beginning with 621 churches and 108,000 members in 1949, there are now 2,000 churches and 475,000 members. This represents an increase in membership of 340 percent while the population increased 30 percent. The future goal is to begin 780 new churches in 1980-81. That is a rate of one new church daily.[10]

CHURCH GROWTH THROUGH SUNDAY SCHOOLS

Though the term "church growth" is certainly a new concept to Southern Baptists, the term used most often as its equivalent within their ranks and literature is "enlargement." To them the use of "enlargement" usually signifies enlarging the church through the Sunday school. Two significant texts in this area are *A Guide to Sunday School Enlargement*, compiled by George W. Stuart, and the Magna Carta of SBC Sunday schools written by Arthur Flake in 1922, entitled, *Building a Standard Sunday School.*[11]

Dr. Paul B. Leath of Truett Memorial Southern Baptist Church and former president of the California Baptist Convention, said, "Although the terminology has somewhat changed, we haven't been able to improve on Flake's book."[12]

Concerning the Southern Baptist philosophy about enrollment, the proponents cite that it is often more difficult to enroll in the average non-Southern Baptist Sunday school than it is to join the church. As a result of these difficult enrollment procedures (for example, the requirement that a vistor attend three times before being eligible to enroll in a class), opportunities to reach and enroll people are lost. Dr. James Bryant, pastor of the Hoffmanton Baptist Church, Albuquerque, New Mexico, said "Enrollment is more important than attendance. If people are committed to Sunday school by enrollment, attendance will automatically rise."[13]

Dr. Andy Anderson offers classic advice to those who might desire to more fully understand this Southern Baptist concept of enrollment as it commands priority attention even over attendance:

> IMPORTANT: We need to get away from the idea of "cleaning the Sunday school roll." We should not remove people from the roll just because they do not attend. This is the reason to keep them! Why place them on a special list? Why not leave them on a list where they will receive maximum exposure to our efforts. *The church is in the people business, not the percentage business!* We need the names and addresses of as many people as possible. Names should be removed only when the person has moved away from the city, joined another Sunday school, or died.[14]

Flake's philosophy is established in his ten-point "Standard of Excellence." This includes the following: (1) church relationship (officers and reports), (2) enlargement (through visitation), (3) grading (age group classes), (4) Baptist literature (use of Baptist-published materials), (5) use of the Bible (as the main text), (6) preaching attendance (attending church as well as Sunday school), (7) evangelism (attempting to lead pupils to Christ), (8) meetings, equipment, and records, (9) training (ongoing education for teachers and leaders), (10) stewardship and missions (promotion of needs and projects for giving).[15]

So committed was Flake to these ten points that he was willing to offer the following conviction:

> Development in Sunday school growth is not confined to any particular locality or section of the country nor to any special types of Sunday schools. Rural churches, town churches, and city churches, both in "down-town" and residential sections, can experience a material increase in enrollment and in attendance when right methods of Sunday school building are employed.[16]

VISITATION IS VITAL

Maintaining an aggressive, growing Southern Baptist Sunday school depends heavily on an active visitation program. Among the SBC there has traditionally been an extremely strong commitment to this area of visitation. Although the method may differ somewhat from the continual calling of those involved in a bus ministry, it is in essence the same. If the SBC is doing it "according to Flake" then all organization, enlistment of workers, provision of adequate facilities, taking of neighborhood censuses, and combing the church roll is preparatory to the work of visiting prospects in their homes.[17] Flake verifies:

> If we stop here, all the work which has been done will be largely in vain, the organization will go to pieces and discouragement will result on every hand.
>
> The thing needed now to enlarge the Sunday School membership is that this organization should be led by the superintendent and pastor to visit every one of the prospective pupils during the coming week and urge them to come to the Sunday school, and then keep visiting them from week to week with the same urgent invitation until all of them join.[18]

Another SBC author confirms the importance of "visitation for Sunday School growth" when he adds:

> As the principles of growth are applied, all other steps may be taken, but without this step—continual visiting, going after new persons, following up on absentees—little or no growth can be expected. In Sunday School work, *nothing produces more growth* than making a crusade out of systematic, continual, and personal cultivation visitation by concerned Christians to the homes of persons not involved in regular Bible study.[19]

172

21. Mainline Denominations

In the United States today many churches are growing. Apart from cults or false religions, those churches experiencing the greatest degree of growth are those who hold to the evangelical conservative position concerning the Bible, i.e., that the Bible is God's Word, and the purpose and message of today's church is clearly taught within it. While these evangelical churches are growing, some churches are in a state of decline. For the most part, those churches declining in numbers are ones which do not hold to the evangelical position. Excluding the Southern Baptist denomination, the three largest bodies of Protestant members are the Lutheran Church in America, the United Presbyterian Church in the U.S.A., and the United Methodist Church. These three groups are showing rapid decline.

The most important book to be written in the last four years showing the decline of these three major denominations is Dean Kelley's *Why Conservative Churches Are Growing*. Wagner affirms that Kelley's book is "in some respects . . . the most important book for the church growth movement in America."[1] A United Methodist minister himself, Kelley points to the significant decline in these mainline denominations during the latter part of the 1960s. [2] He proves his point by revealing the statistics shown on three different graphs.

LUTHERANS IN AMERICA

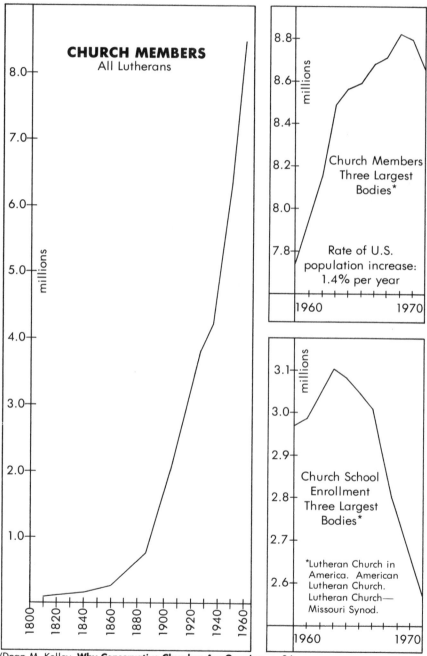

CHURCH MEMBERS
All Lutherans

millions

Church Members
Three Largest
Bodies*

Rate of U.S.
population increase:
1.4% per year

1960   1970

Church School
Enrollment
Three Largest
Bodies*

*Lutheran Church in
America. American
Lutheran Church.
Lutheran Church—
Missouri Synod.

1960   1970

(Dean M. Kelley, **Why Conservative Churches Are Growing,** p. 3.)

METHODISTS IN AMERICA

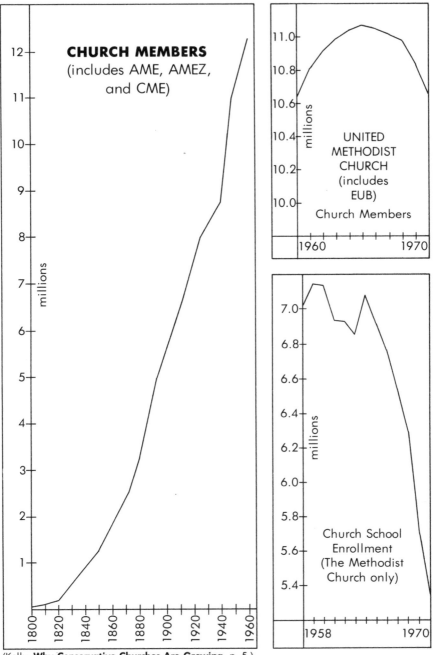

CHURCH MEMBERS
(includes AME, AMEZ, and CME)

millions

UNITED
METHODIST
CHURCH
(includes
EUB)
Church Members

millions

Church School
Enrollment
(The Methodist
Church only)

millions

(Kelly, **Why Conservative Churches Are Growing,** p. 5.)

PRESBYTERIANS IN AMERICA

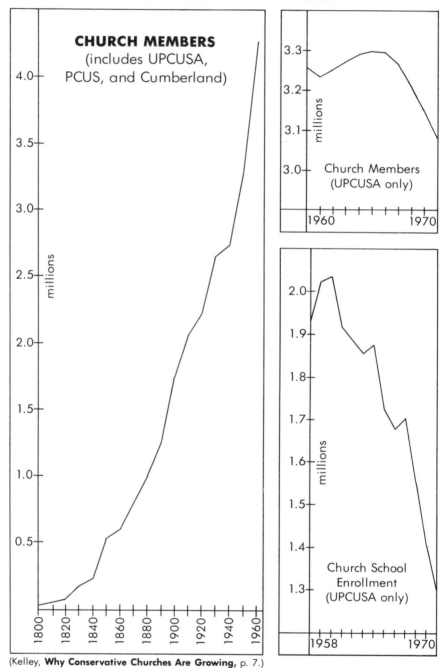

CHURCH MEMBERS
(includes UPCUSA,
PCUS, and Cumberland)

Church Members
(UPCUSA only)

Church School
Enrollment
(UPCUSA only)

(Kelley, **Why Conservative Churches Are Growing,** p. 7.)

Even more recent statistics from the *Yearbook of American and Canadian Churches* show this continual decline among these three denominations. (Kelley's book only shows the figures up to 1970.) By comparing the figures from the *Yearbook* between 1970 and 1979, the following information can be determined: (1) The Lutheran Church in America declined in numbers from 3,279,517 (1970) to 2,967,168 (1979)—a loss of 312,349 members; (2) The United Methodist Church declined in numbers from 10,990,720 (1970) to 9,785,534 (1979)—a loss of 1,205,186 members; and (3) The United Presbyterian Church in the U.S.A. declined from 3,222,663 (1970) to 2,561,234 (1979)—a loss of 661,429 members.[3]

In additional sources concerning two of these three major denominations, even *more* of a decline is evident. The United Methodist Church at present has 9.9 million members, which means a loss of one million members during the past seven years.[4] The United Presbyterian Church in the U.S.A. has declined by 15 percent over the years 1968 to 1974, showing a loss of nearly 500,000 members.[5] Due to much concern on the part of the United Methodist and The United Presbyterian Church in the U.S.A., study into their problems has made available additional information which is of value to the student of church growth.

UNITED METHODIST CHURCH

The loss of members in these denominations has caused the leadership at the national level to do some serious soul-searching. As early as 1968 the General Conference of the United Methodist Church (hereafter the UMC) asked for a study on membership loss and conservation which was to be presented to the 1972 General Conference by the General Board of Evangelism. (General Conferences are held every four years in the UMC.)

LACK OF EVANGELISM

The Rev. Lyle Schaller, in charge of the study, presented his findings to the 1972 General Conference. Of his fourteen reasons given for the statistical decrease of the UMC, only one touches the principles to which evangelicals are committed. After listing various factors for membership losses, such as mergers of local churches, the changing national climate, the increase in apartment construction, etc., Schaller offers this most important factor: "The vigorous and aggressive evangelistic approach of the holiness, adventist, Pentecostal groups, the independent churches and other sect bodies has meant that many people today are joining these or similar groups rather than joining a United Methodist Church."[6]

Schaller is stating one thing clearly—the UMC is not among those groups committed to an "evangelistic approach." Dean Kelley was correct when he said of these declining denominations (including his own UMC), "They will continue to exist on a diminishing scale for decades . . . and will continue to supply some people with a dilute and undemanding form of meaning. . . ."[7] The reason for this lack of meaning is their misunderstanding of the Great Commission. Evangelism and edification, two key principles of the evangelical church growth thinker, are not part and parcel of these denominational leaders. For example, in an interview, one pastor of the UMC stated that their basis for church growth was Matthew 28:19, 20, and then proceeded to state that this *meant* reaching a newer kind of constituency, i.e., the single adult, the single parent, the poor parent, etc.[8] Although it is certain that he does not speak for every UMC pastor, it certainly typifies nonbiblical understanding concerning church growth.

Even at the conference (geographical) level in the UMC this thinking prevails. A speech at Redlands, California, on June 13, 1975, by Bishop Charles F. Golden, reveals this lack of biblical, church growth understanding. Speaking to the 125th Session of the Southern California-Arizona Conference, Bishop Golden talked at length of membership decline and offered the following vague challenge:

Let us seek to achieve a minimum of 10% gain in membership annually for the next six years.

Let each Church become a growing ground in which the call to ministry may find a climate for acceptance and development.

Let us strive to give as much for others as for ourselves in the next six years with a considerable number of our churches moving in this category annually.

Let us make maximum use of the facilities we have established for ministry and service to the total needs of the communities in which we are located.[9]

Bishop Golden did not explain *how* these goals were to be accomplished nor what he meant when he challenged each church to become a "growing ground."

EMPHASIS ON SOCIAL ACTION

Definitions and meanings applied to words become very important as one begins to study what various denominations believe about church growth. At the national level of the UMC (General Conference), in a report made by the General Board of Evangelism to the 1972 General Conference under Rev. Schaller's direction, various solutions were proposed to help stop the loss of members. In the words of the General Board of Evangelism, "No single course of action will be sufficient. Corrective action is recommended at a number of points."[10] But what does it mean to "proclaim and demonstrate . . . the love of Christ to . . . persons living in a variety of life styles"?[11] Or, what does it mean when "the local church should provide opportunity for persons . . . to become involved in some ministry of service, witness, and worship *which will require the best they have to offer at that particular stage of their development"?*[12] From the local church parish on through the national ruling bodies, the United Methodist Church seems to be missing the point of church growth. Just what is the point of church growth or fulfillment of the Great Commission *to the UMC?*

Theoretically the local UMC "exists first of all to reach and help people . . . [and] to help people grow spiritually."[13] Admittedly the wording sounds good, but again in practice what does it mean? The local UMC is said to be fulfilling its true function when five principles are in operation. (This local UMC is called a church in mission.) The first two, already stated, are (1) reaching people and (2) helping them to develop spiritually. The last three are as follows:

> A local church is in mission when it seeks to transform its immediate community. Its first responsibility is to the neighborhood in the midst of which it is set. . . . Whatever it happens to be that promises to improve the total picture in the community about it is a matter of proper concern for that local church that desires truly to be in mission.
>
> A local church is in mission when it maintains the perspective of a world vision, for no local church can afford to forget that it is also a part of the larger world and that however remote some of the problems of the larger world may appear, they are nevertheless its problems also, for it is necessarily a part of all mankind.
>
> A local church is in mission when as a totality it is vitally involved in mission. This means that all the laymen and laywomen must become full and active participants in the Christian enterprise rather than merely spectators or supporters.[14]

The above principles imply that the local UMC has for its main emphasis social action but no real biblical plan or strategy to grow.

SOME EXCEPTIONS

It would be unfair at this point to say that the above statements speak for *all* United Methodist Churches. There are leaders and members in some of these churches who do indeed believe in biblical church growth. Two such evangelical groups within the UMC are the Good News Movement, based in Wilmore, Kentucky, and another group called the Evangelical Missions Council.[15] In fact, members of these two groups and other UMC leaders of evangelism (some 2,300 together) met in Philadelphia the first part of January 1976 for the United Methodist Congress on Evangelism. They heard Presbyterian minister Lloyd Ogilvie and Methodist minister Oral Roberts speak on the Holy Spirit's role in evangelism.[16]

Those United Methodist Churches which are growing today emphasize evangelism and discipleship. Wendell Belew tells of at least three churches that he knows to be growing. Belew writes:

Pastor Charles A. Nowlen, Sr., of the United Methodist Church, Parker, Colorado . . . involved his members in a house-to-house survey of the community and then followed this by leading the laymen in evangelistic training. He utilized neighborhood house meetings, thus "surrounding each person with the love of the church. . . ."[17]

The United Methodist Church of the Good Shepherd, Columbus, Ohio, grew by 121 members in six months, utilizing adult home groups for study, discussion, and witness. But to carry out the personal involvement completely, according to the pastor, *every member* of the church is a task force for specific needs. . . .[18]

Haddonfield United Methodist Church of Haddonfield, New Jersey . . . has added over one hundred people a year for the past ten years and has carried on a remarkable program of ministry in the inner city of Camden, New Jersey.[19]

One of the most exciting and growing churches is Collingswood, New Jersey's First UMC. Listed in *Decision* magazine as one of the "Great Churches of Today," this church exhibits an evangelical zeal which is characteristic of growing churches. For example, four new Methodist churches have grown from this one church. There are midweek Bible studies, a ministry to senior citizens called "Leisure Time," and a coffee house ministry to young people. Their facilities, valued at $1.5 million, are debt-free, allowing some $50,000 to be given annually to missions.[20] The reason for the success of this church is best stated in the words of Philip Worth, their pastor:

Many churches [UMC] consider holding the line on attendance to be a sort of victory today . . . but we are growing and moving ahead. Methodist churches of evangelical persuasion are not experiencing the decline in attendance and finances that has affected so many congregations of the traditional denominations in the last few years.[21]

(It is interesting to note that Pastor Worth previously had been a minister in another UMC in Media, Pennsylvania, which grew from 200 members to 1,200.[22])

UNITED PRESBYTERIAN CHURCH IN THE U.S.A.

What has been said for the UMC corresponds closely to what is seen in the United Presbyterian Church in the U.S.A. (hereafter the UPCUSA). A very exhaustive study on membership decline is still underway by this major denomination in an attempt to determine answers to their obvious loss problems. In November 1974 the General Assembly Mission Council appointed a Special Committee on Church Membership Trends to investigate the loss of its members. Meeting between November 1974 and February 1976, this Special Committee has now published a four-part report dealing with (a) how it went about its task; (b) a summary of the research data developed; (c) the interpretation of the analyzed data; and (d) specific recommendations.

Statistically speaking, this report on Church Membership Trends reveals some very useful information. Greater than the loss of some 500,000 members between 1968 and 1974 referred to earlier, is the decline of the church school (Sunday school) enrollment. The number of new churches being started decreased sharply, and 80 percent of all congregations with over 2,000 members have declined in membership between 1964 and 1974.[23] Of some 1,000 congregations surveyed in this report on Church Membership Trends, some 350 had lost 20 percent of their members; while 350 grew at least 5 percent over the same period.[24]

CONFUSION ON GROWTH

One pastor of a local Presbyterian church cited the fact that "there is really no agreement on what church growth means in the UPCUSA. In fact each leader will tell you something different."[25] Confusion about church growth is apparent in this large, major denomination.

Two very important publications written within the last year deal with the UPCUSA's decline. Looking at them briefly reveals some of the more obvious problems. One of these, written by a nonevangelical Presbyterian, Dr. John R. Fry, is entitled *The Trivialization of the United Presbyterian Church.* In this book, Fry states that the loss of members can be traced to 1967 when the UPCUSA wrote a new Confession of Faith, replacing the orthodox Westminster Confession, and reorganized the total church under the label "Design for Mission." Fry has struck a resounding chord in his book relating to the decline, when he cites the changing of biblical language to something entirely different from the original meaning.

DEPARTURE FROM BIBLICAL TRUTH

The first example that Dr. Fry gives is the meaning of the word *reconciliation.* When the new Confession of Faith was drawn up in 1967, reconciliation was the key word. Fry states, ". . . they [those who wrote the Confession] pictured reconciliation as some mere patching up of differences of opinion . . . they installed reconciliation as the name of life, the name of the church, and the name of God."[26] Fry further adds, "With reconciliation as the operative authority of the Confession, Presbyterians can't really fight over the Confession, or fight over fighting. . . ."[27] Fry, finally, quotes a Presbyterian leader to show how meaningless the word "reconciliation" has become. In the Denver General Assembly in 1972 the moderator (presiding officer), Professor Willard Heckel, proclaimed, "Let us make no mistake; reconciliation is not finding the lowest common denominator . . . but . . . letting every voice be heard."[28]

Thus to the UPCUSA's leaders the word "reconciliation" is not recognized as the work of God in bringing man into a personal relationship with himself through Jesus Christ (2 Cor. 5:18). In fact, reconciliation at work deals primarily with social relationships rather than spiritual realities. An article in *Presbyterian Life*, July 15, 1972, dealing with a grant of $10,000 for the Angela Davis Defense Fund, comfirms this point. The Stated Clerk of the General Assembly, William T. Thompson, was quoted to have said, "Let us seek reconciliation, beginning with open acceptance of the sincerity and commitment of those with whom we disagree. . . ."[29]

MISSING THE POINT

For all the eye-opening statements that John Fry gives about the changing of word meanings, he truly misses the point about the demise of his denomination. He ends his book with an attack upon the evangelicals within his own church, the ones who have a biblical perspective to share. Fry writes:

> They [conservative-evangelicals] want to say that social action is all right *in its place,* but that the more directly mandated activities of preaching, teaching, and evangelism must always be considered the main business of the church. In their bucolic view, the individual sinner, saved by God's grace in Jesus Christ, becomes a different kind of social being. The church's job is to change society by changing its individuals, one by one. You will not catch conservative-evangelicals admitting that society shouldn't be changed, however. All of which is so much sand in our eyes. . . .[30]

> They are a small contingent of Presbyterians whose ability to shout very loudly makes them appear to be an army.

> We see all this fog besetting the church, hear all this sick populist noise, hear so many Jesus Christs it would seem we were in a Methodist revival, only to discover that the fog is not a general climatic condition, sent from On High, but is coming out of a tiny fog machine located in the church basement.

> Yes, despite even the presence of a certain vociferous cell of Presbyterians who fundamentally want to repeal the twentieth century — as a prelude to reinstalling the Bible as the verbally inspired and utterly inerrant Word of God, and *that* as a prelude to preaching the plain Word to lost sinners — I remain optimistic.[31]

The second work which helps us understand some factors in the UP-CUSA's decline is the exhaustive report, referred to earlier, by the Special Committee on Church Membership Trends. This report reveals some key reasons for the denomination's decline. First, people in "rapidly declining" congregations (those with a 30 percent loss of members from 1968-1974) and "typical" congregations (those with a 20 percent loss of members from 1968-1974) were less satisfied with the preaching and their pastors than members in "growing" congregations (those with a 5 percent growth between 1968-1974).[32] Evidently, then, a reason for the decline of these churches is the lack of spiritual leadership and sound biblical teaching.

Second, although the report states that involvement in social issues "is *not* related to growth or decline"[33] (which may be suspect), it does state that "members of rapidly declining congregations are much more apt to feel that involvement in social action has caused disunity or conflict among their members."[34] Thus, it appears a logical deduction that where emphasis upon social action takes priority over evangelism and discipleship a decrease in members will most likely occur. In fact, the study states that in those rapidly declining churches people are least apt to have Bible studies and prayer groups.[35]

A third factor, and closely related to the one previously mentioned, is the meager attempt at "recruitment" by those churches declining in membership. Whereas growing congregations involve elders, deacons, members, young people, and organized groups in everything from training members for personal evangelism to contacting new residents, "rapidly declining" and "typical" congregations only minimally make an effort to recruit new members.[36] The principle of these declining churches is apparent—they are not interested in evangelizing people.

A fourth and final factor related to the decline of the UPCUSA is the whole attitude toward growth itself. In those churches declining in members, the pastors feel far less responsibility for the growth of their congregations than do pastors in growing churches.[37] This is probably a key factor in the total decline of the UPCUSA. For if true biblical church growth comes, it must start with the leadership of godly men dedicated to the Great Commission as their supreme mandate.

SOME EXCEPTIONS

Like the UMC, however, the UPCUSA does have its evangelical churches which are indeed growing. (The report states that 5 percent of those same 1,000 churches are growing. Also, there is a fellowship of evangelical churches in the UPCUSA called Presbyterians United for Biblical Concerns. It would be interesting to discover if those growing churches in the report were part of this fellowship.)

One of these growing churches is the First Presbyterian Church of Pittsburgh where some 2,500 members attend. Although the membership is 2,500, over 8,000 people a week use the facilities at the church. Some 1,000 businessmen from downtown Pittsburgh come every Tuesday at noon to hear Pastor John Huffman expound the Bible. Some 400 women come to the Tuesday Noon Club; and many others use the building also throughout the week. Even Pittsburgh's Chinese community uses the building on Sunday afternoon to hear services in both Mandarin and Cantonese languages. There is an outreach ministry called the Pittsburgh Power and Light Company which ministers to the 28,000 students in downtown Pittsburgh. Moreover, some 30 percent of the church budget is designated for missions.[38]

Equally impressive is the teaching ministry of this Presbyterian Church. There is a "Center of Biblical Studies" for interested Bible students. There is a great ministry in teaching the entire family; there are over 100 shut-in members ministered to by some thirty-five elders.[39] Even the music emphasis is equally important and geared to minister to each person. For as choir director David F. Pressan has rightly said, "If God isn't glorified and if Christ isn't lifted up in our music, then it's just entertainment. The choir communicates the love of Jesus to the congregation. That is its purpose in being here."[40] Indeed this is a picture of a church that can be a pattern to be emulated by the remainder of UPCUSA churches which are failing.

Church Growth Methods

22. Soul-Winning Evangelism

One might ask what other kind of evangelism is there? But only to the fundamentalist is evangelism most clearly understood as soul winning. The United Presbyterian Task Force for new congregations speaks of the priority of the "Ministry of Reconciliation" and yet there is an obvious absence of terms such as: "evangelism," "salvation," or "the new birth," not to speak of "soul winning."[1] As a point of obvious contrast,

> The ministers (especially those belonging to the Baptist Bible Fellowship) of the ten largest Sunday Schools do not speak of evangelism as *witnessing*. Witnessing can be defined as a neutral term whereby we either *become* a witness through our life or give a witness by our testimony. This may simply be telling people what God has done for us, or what He is willing to do for them. The ministers tend to reject the term *witness* in favor of the term *soul winning*. The term soul winning indicates pressing for decisions, giving people the opportunity to accept or reject Jesus Christ. The people in these churches are exhorted to an "action" approach to evangelism, securing results in dealing with the lost.[2]

Although many of the other churches represented may be committed to evangelism, this terminology relates best with the Baptist Bible Fellowship churches. "Capturing Your Town for Christ through the Super-Aggressive, Local, New Testament Church" is the theme of an upcoming "How to Do It" conference for pastors and workers sponsored by the Thomas Road Baptist Church.[3] Soul-winning evangelism by every available means to every available person within each town will be stressed as each local church's responsibility.

> The true fundamentalist church is an aggressive band of born-again Christians who have mutually agreed that the world is going to hell and the drift of this life is governed by the lust of the flesh, the lust of the eyes, and the pride of life. Therefore, strict standards of personal purity are prized. Every man who has not experienced the new birth is lost and going to hell, so the aggressive fundamentalist attempts to win him to Christ, caring nothing of the charge of proselytizing.[4]

Assembly of God author Hodges agrees that "the first and foremost means of spreading the gospel has always been, and will always be, the personal witness of Christians in their contacts with the unconverted . . . and that . . .

each congregation should consider that the unevangelized people in the area are its particular responsibility."[5]

Of those who are committed to biblical church growth, evangelism always plays a dominant role. Paul Benjamin, a colleague of McGavran, warns that "an exploding population makes it imperative that Christians face up to the fact that millions will continue to die in their sins unless congregations change their ways. The harvest is still plentiful and the laborers still few (Matt. 9:35-38)."[6] Benjamin teaches our need to practice two kinds of evangelism, spontaneous and planned. He states that the average American comes into direct contact with at least thirty different people every day, but if we hope to reach every unchurched person in our communities, we must make a planned effort involving house-to-house contacts (Acts 20:20, 21).[7]

McGavran challenges all evangelicals when he cries:

> We need to recover the sense of urgency. Questions about theological definitions there may be. Problems of precise implementation will arise. But neither theoretical nor practical differences must be allowed to dampen the fires of evangelism.[8]

> Continuous passionate evangelization arises from conviction that belief in Jesus Christ—and belief alone, not works—saves a man. Conviction does not arise in hearts which have lost their faith in an authoritative, inspired Bible. The studied neglect of evangelism has, to be sure, several causes; but one of the most potent is loss of Bible-based certainty. When men with a low view of the Bible control a congregation, denomination, council or missionary society, ethical concerns are all their consciences demand. Evangelization inevitably is relegated to a minor position.[9]

One of the most applicable issues to the matter of evangelism and church growth is what Towns refers to as "The Sociological Cycle of Church Growth." Towns believes that each of the ten "fastest growing churches" reported on in his book grew not because of organization, techniques, or methods but because of intangible factors referred to as "inner strength." While each of the ten reported on are now "flaming witnesses for God," he predicts that sometime in the distant future each will deteriorate and erode into liberal edifices. He warns that "the present pastors will be grieved with the prospect and their members will vehemently deny that their church will grow liberal. Yet, death is as inevitable to a church as to every newborn baby."[10] Green warns that other reasons besides doctrine are sufficient to cause the death of a church, although doctrinal deviation will certainly do it.

The church must program for the individual in the context of community. Leadership ought to be watchful for signs of deterioration. Moberg claims the symptoms of disintegration are: "formalism, indifference, obsolescence, absolutism, red tape, patronage and corruption." Since institutions change more slowly than individuals, early awareness of these signs of deterioration is imperative. Purposive control must be exercised before the "gap" occurs between the institution and the constituency.[11]

Hollis L. Green gives reassurance that:

Knowledge of the cycle should not make churchmen pessimistic nor cause them to falter in an effort toward progress. Christians are not building permanent structures or eternal institutions; the objective is to reach men for Christ in a changing world. Program and personnel (and denominations) may change; but the basic motivation and message remain unchanged. The purpose of the church is the same.[12]

23. Research and Scientific Analysis

Again and again in the writings of McGavran and Wagner it is affirmed that church growth is ultimately the work of the Holy Spirit and the sovereignty of God. But their position urges churches to open their eyes and see the facts of growth as God has given them to us. Wagner says that "if we study these churches (growing ones) . . . we can learn more about God and the way He works."[1] He argues that if there is a benefit for a harvester to study harvesting procedures he'll learn more by researching where production is thirty, sixty, and one hundred fold, as the Bible says (Matt. 13:8). Accordingly, someone concerned about growing a church can hardly do better than to study growing churches.[2]

In answering their own question as to why the fields are still ripe and the granaries are still empty, Engel and Norton argue that the cutting blades are missing from the harvesting equipment of the modern church. And what are the cutting blades? "The cutting blades of any Christian organization are a *research-based*, Spirit-led strategy to reach people with the Good News and to build them in the faith."[3] In concluding their thesis, they affirm that "equally important, this strategy must be designed and implemented by a properly functioning Body of Christ. So here you have it—the keys are to be found in the strategy and function of the Church."[4]

Wagner firmly believes in carefully developed strategy for the church today, and defines it.

> Strategy is a mutually-agreed means to achieve the ends which have been determined by a particular group. Good strategy will be concerned with broad principles as well as specific tactics, but it will not lose sight of the determined goal.
>
> Missionary strategy is never intended to be a substitute for the Holy Spirit. Proper strategy is Spirit-inspired and Spirit-governed. Rather than competing with the Holy Spirit, strategy is to be used by the Holy Spirit.[5]

Robert Schuller says, "The secret of success is to find a need and fill it." You find the needs by research and fill them by strategy.

It is understandable in this age, an age in which science has been deified, for some churchmen to react against using the tools of science.

Church growth men are success-oriented, bent upon building churches for Christ regardless of the cost. Thus they are not only accepting of scientifically researched data but also dedicated pragmatists. Wagner makes his case for practical church growth leadership when he states:

It is a common mistake to associate pragmatism with lack of spirituality. Some are rightly afraid that pragmatism can degenerate to the point that ungodly methods are used, and this is not at all what church growth people advocate. The Bible does not allow us to sin that grace may abound or to use means that God has prohibited in order to accomplish ends He has recommended.

But with this proviso, we ought to see clearly that the end *does* justify the means. What else possible could justify the means? If the method I am using accomplished the goal I am aiming at, it is for that reason a good method. If, on the other hand, my method is not accomplishing the goal, how can I be justified in continuing to use it?[6]

Many have been the blessings from the research of this school of thought. Orlando Costas lists several very positive results of the School of World Mission and their work. He explains:

The group approach to evangelism which the Church Growth Movement has propagated has given the church all over the world a new insight into evangelistic strategy. Even in societies where no tribes and clans exist, it is extremely valuable because there are always extended families, kinship groups, and webs of relationships. In fact, the homogeneous group becomes a reality even in a secularized society where people choose their friends on the basis of mutual interests. In such a setting, the idea of multi-individual conversions, of group evangelism, and the homogeneous-unit church is not only relevant but the most viable way to reach people for Christ.[7]

Southern Baptist author Belew agrees that "new churches often find an easy beginning when established upon the common ground that persons have for their place of cultural origin or human likes."[8]

Research has proven workable principles for church growth which transcend cultural barriers. All church growth leaders agree principles are valid for all churches, but methods may have to be radically changed. Schuller affirms:

Any church that really wants to be a part of this vigorous and vital church of the Twenty-First Century can be. But it won't just happen—that church will have to work at it—and will have to *begin* working at it *now*. How? Through the application of certain universal principles.

These principles will work anywhere we work at applying them— they really will.[9]

Baumann urges careful recognition of the difference between methodology and principle when he says, "Mark it well—much is *not* transferable from one setting to another. Principles which are crosscultural must be heeded with particular care. Programs are *not* absolutes; biblical principles are. Take care to distinguish one from the other."[10] In addition he makes two points: (1) No program anywhere is sacred. Structures are either useful or they are not. (2) Principles alone are sacred. They transcend programs and localities."[11]

Donald McGavran summarizes well:

> The churchman should train himself to see the many different varieties of growth and the many factors which play a significant part in each. Then he should resolutely seek for the people whom God has prepared, and use methods of proclaiming and persuading on which God has put His seal of approval.[12]

As a result of the impact and hard work of these committed men, "analytical tools are available for pastors and concerned lay people to determine whether their own churches have desirable growth patterns."[13] Foster Shannon, in his article "Predicting Church Growth," clarifies this:

> Membership growth is, of course, not the only criterion of faithfully fulfilling the purposes of God. Regrettably we currently lack the means to adequately evaluate membership spiritual maturity, the effectiveness of programs of nurture and the relevancy of a congregation's service to persons outside of its own constituency. Let us hope that more precise measures of discipleship in these areas will be developed.[14]

24. Prayer

Although all evangelicals would quickly acknowledge the value and necessity of prayer for effective church growth, it is the Pentecostals who depend most upon this channel of power. Hodges, noted authority for Assembly of God church planting, stresses:

The importance of prayer in establishing a church and maintaining its spiritual life can scarcely be overestimated. Prayer links pastor and people with the living Head of the church. We are colaborers together with God. Prayer makes this partnership a reality and releases the resources of God to enable the church to carry out its ministry.

Prayer has been called the spiritual thermometer of the church.[1]

Prayer may often be encouraged for individuals as a means of growing in their Christian faith, but Pentecostals believe and practice the importance of "corporate" prayer. Hodges adds:

Corporate prayer depends on praying individuals. We cannot be a praying church without having praying people!

Even so, the united prayer of God's people adds a new dimension to individual prayer. Something is accomplished by people coming together in prayer that is not always obtainable when individuals pray alone. United prayer seems to compound the power and benefit of individual praying.[2]

In *Sharpening the Focus of the Church* Gene Getz agrees with the importance of prayer in the life of the church, for he states:

At the time the church was born, one of the most predominant experiences of those who were waiting in the upper room was corporate prayer. In the spirit of unity and "one mindedness," the one hundred and twenty believers "were continually devoting themselves to prayer" (Acts 1:14) as they waited for the Holy Spirit to come as Jesus had promised.[3]

Hodges teaches that this is a valid principle for starting new works today. Earnest prayer by a group of Christians can be greatly used of God to produce a "receptive" climate. In order to plant churches, the spiritual means of prayer must be relied on because the work is a spiritual task. The opposing forces to the gospel are the spiritual powers of darkness, and the value of prayer warriors should not be underestimated.[4]

Citing the beginnings of the Assemblies of God, Hollenweger states that "for the earliest Pentecostals it was more important to pray than to organize."[5] Although this statement would not be totally accurate for all A.O.G. churches today, Palmer from his research acknowledges:

> Pentecostal churches also emphasize and practice prayer more than the other Protestant denominations do. Most of the Pentecostal leaders and pastors interviewed consider the continual practice of prayer and fasting to be a *principal factor in their growth*. While traditional denominations often have difficulty getting a majority of their members to attend a prayer meeting once a week, Pentecostals seem to relish attending several prayer services a week. [In Colombia] besides having regular mid-week prayer meetings, most Pentecostal churches have all night "prayer vigils," and many have daily prayer meetings either in the early morning or evening.[6]

Pastor Mike Johnson of Calvary Temple (A.O.G.), Springfield, Illinois, talked about growth by noting, *"The first key to church growth is prayer.* We have an every-Saturday night prayer group of 400 people who come to seek God. Another key is work. Nothing works by itself. I tell the folks to put legs on their prayers."[7]

Johnson, whose church jumped to an average of more than 2,100 in nine years, built his church on prayer and work. At first he reported that few attended prayer meetings but he continued them, believing that "prayer changes things." And it has! The church experienced an all-time recent high of more than 9,000 at a special service and is listed twelfth in the October 1975 *Christian Life* "Largest Sunday School" listing.[8]

In a recent survey (1974) of growing A.O.G. churches, 121 pastors responded. They were asked to rank forty-four items as to their relationship to growth. Prayer, seen as absolutely indispensable, was listed as the number-one need for church growth.[9]

Twenty-four-hour prayer chains are not innovative to Pentecostals and those with charismatic leanings. Calvary Temple, an interdenominational church in Denver, Colorado, pastored by Dr. Charles Blair, has such a prayer chain, as do others.

Evangel Tabernacle of Louisville, Kentucky, another of the Top 10 churches, was in a recession. While Pastor Waymon Rogers pondered leaving, he felt that God was not through with him.

> He felt impressed to start a prayer meeting around the clock. The people responded and the despair of those days was turned to victory. Evangel Tabernacle had continued to grow, and recently they had over 7,000 on one day. . . . The Louisville church sponsors over a hundred house prayer meetings weekly. They make signs to put on these houses so the community knows where each meeting is. They plan to have over 200 houses of prayer before the year is out. "This is where soul-winning is taking place," the Pastor says.
>
> "This church God built through prayer. We are not against gimmicks

or contests. I suppose we've used every type of program and promotion in the work of the Lord, but it seemed that none of these would work on a permanent basis. When we began the prayer meeting, it was then that things began to change."[10]

Why doesn't every church believe and benefit from the regular habit of the body praying together? For Ed Murphy truthfully states:

There is a mystery in prayer. How do we reconcile prayer as "moving the hand of God" with the Sovereignty of God? Armin Gesswein once gave the only answer that satisfies both my heart and mind. He said, "Do not expect God to do, apart from prayer, what He has said He would do only if we pray." That's good enough for me. I must pray, and pray, and pray again.[11]

25. Bible Teaching and Edification

Bishop Gerald Kennedy of the United Methodist Church was being interviewed along with Dr. Fickett (recent pastor of Van Nuys First Baptist Church) when in answer to a question about whether church attendance was increasing or decreasing, Bishop Kennedy responded, "It is decreasing— definitely on the decline," but then added to the commentator, "Wherever the Bible is preached and Christ is exalted, church growth naturally comes. Attendance in churches like this today [referring to Van Nuys First Baptist] is on the increase."[1] What an indictment to those churches which have left the solid moorings of God's Word to preach a watered-down gospel! How can they grow without the Scriptures being proclaimed?

Hollis Green warns that this is a reason why churches are dying, and lays the blame on the pastor.

> Preaching is the proclamation of the Word of God to men by men anointed of God. Yet proclamation is being downgraded even though the people are still willing to listen. Much of the fault is in the sender and not in the receiver. The problem is not to get the hungry to eat. The problem is to provide sufficient food nutritious enough to meet his needs. A convention of farmers and ranchers would never spend time on "how to get a cow to come to the barn" or "how to get a cow to eat." The program would probably concern itself with improving the feed to take advantage of the appetite that always exists.[2]

While Bible Baptists would certainly agree that Bible preaching is a must, Towns makes an important distinction when he describes the Baptist Bible Fellowship.

> Even though BBF churches are conservative or fundamental in doctrine, theology does not hold the BBF together as in other similar conservative denominations. Most BBF churches believe the orthodox position expressed in the footnotes of the Scofield Bible, and their pastors carry King James Bibles; yet theology is not the primary catalyst. The BBF is a movement of methodology best expressed as evangelism.[3]

John R. Rice well expresses this view when he states that evangelism and not edification is the first duty of every pastor.

> The first aim of every preacher called of God should be to win souls. A minister may say, as an alibi for his powerlessness and fruitlessness: "I am called to be a teaching pastor. My ministry is to the church. I must

feed the flock of God." But that, I insist, is an alibi for outright disobedience to the plain command of God. The Great Commission is still binding on preachers. The Gospel is to be preached to every creature. We are to teach those already converted to go win others.[4]

After referring to the ninety and nine and emphasizing the lostness of the one sheep (Luke 15:4), Dr. Rice submits:

The very term "Pastor" has come to mean looking after Christians, and pastors who win few souls or none, say that they are called to "feed the sheep." And the churches are glad to think that they are God's sheep and that the pastor ought to spend his time in feeding them, teaching them the Word of God and otherwise making himself useful to church members.[5]

The failure in our churches is, first of all, a pastor failure. There is no way to build great soul-winning churches without soul-winning pastors.[6]

Inrig, representing Evangelical Bible Churches, states:

It should also be noted that the main business of assembly life is the equipping and edification of believers. Unfortunately, many churches have focused so strongly upon evangelism that believers have been starved, and church life has become anemic.[7]

By the way of obvious contrast Dr. Lee Roberson says, "The business of the local church is soul winning. The business of the pastor, the song leader, the choir, the Sunday school, the youth organizations is soul winning."[8] Dr. Jack Hyles is committed to evangelism in the church, especially while the trend today is to larger morning crowds. Hyles cites two crucial points.

The first is, I doubt if any preacher will realize his evangelistic potential until he realizes the importance of evangelism *in public worship*. Second, no church can reach its soul-winning potential until it is organized for soul winning and stripped of needless organization.[9]

Gene Getz argues for both evangelism and edification, but in their proper places.

The church therefore exists to carry out two functions—evangelism (to make disciples) and edification (to teach them). These two functions in turn answer two questions: first, Why does the church exist in the world? and second, Why does the church exist as a gathered community?[10]

Hodges, noted Assembly of God expert in church planting, stresses that "every local church should be considered a seedbed that produces Christian workers. In order to attain this, it is necessary that the pastor have a deep desire to develop leadership in his church."[11] He goes on to argue:

The ideal workers' training program includes a strong activity program in the local church, coupled with specialized training in systematic Bible teaching such as is available in a Bible institute. The church in each country should develop a broadbased training program.[12]

Although this may indicate a current trend among Pentecostals to return to a solid teaching ministry, Palmer in his research found that the majority of Pentecostals interviewed based their assurance of salvation on feeling and experience and not the Word of God.[13] Hamilton explains that Pentecostals "having experienced a compelling encounter with the Holy Spirit, come to Scripture and interpret it in the light of that experience, instead of interpreting the experience in the light of Scripture. . . . The controversy with charismatic Christians is not that they are unbiblical, but they are not biblical enough."[14]

Ortiz, a Pentecostal pastor, recognizes the problem of immaturity in his church and calls for discipleship. He believes a great problem in the church today is "the eternal childhood of the believer." He encourages pastors to grow in the Word themselves and then to teach the Scriptures to their people, expecting them to change and become "doers of the Word and not hearers only."[15]

Among the "School of World Mission" men there is no clear emphasis in this area. These Church Growth men emphasize training of workers, but if a pastor spends much time studying, he may not be using his time wisely.[16] Perhaps the reason is simple; this group of church scientists have only recently begun looking into American church growth. On the mission field, programs such as TEE (Theological Education by Extension) are seen as a key principle in church growth, but in the States, given the current seminary profile, putting the need for Bible teaching together with evangelism is difficult for the local church. Evangelism is seen as the priority of the church, but the means are "responsible church members." The Bible churches would agree, believing that Bible teaching and edification is the answer for mobilizing responsible members to evangelism.

McGavran urges faithfulness in proclaiming Christ, and not only proclamation but persuasion. "Church growth follows where Christians show faithfulness in finding the lost. It is not enough to search for lost sheep. The Master Shepherd is not pleased with a token search; he wants His sheep found. The purpose is not to search, but to find."[17] He also recognizes the important element of "feeding" and draws both evangelism and edification together.

> Church growth follows where the lost are not merely found but restored to normal life in the fold—though it may be a life they have never consciously known. Faithfulness in "folding and feeding"—which unfortunately has come to be called by such a dry, superficial term as follow-up—is essential to lasting church expansion.
>
> Faithfulness in proclamation and finding is not enough. There must be faithful aftercare. Among the found, also, there must be fidelity in feeding on the Word.[18]

26. The Holy Spirit

In the study of Pentecostals and charismatics it is clear that the focus on the person, work, and gifts of the Holy Spirit is recognized by their leadership as the main cause for their growing churches. In surveying all kinds of growing churches throughout our country, Wagner asks and answers the question: *"Just what is it that makes churches like these grow?* Of course, it is, in the final analysis, God at work through His Holy Spirit."[1]

The work of a sovereign God in the growth of his church must be seen as the ultimate factor; thus, careful understanding is needed not to usurp the Holy Spirit's proper role. The Holy Spirit is always involved when revival or evangelical awakenings stir even older churches to repentance from sin and resultant renewal and growth. McGavran sees a close relationship between the reviving work of the Spirit and prayer.

> While "an Evangelical Awakening is a movement of the Holy Spirit in the Church of Christ" and thus depends on the initiative of Almighty God, it is usually granted to those who pray earnestly for it. In hundreds of instances, prayer has brought revival. The pattern is the same, first intense prayer, often long continued, then revival.[2]

> In summary we may say that when, driven by their own powerlessness, men turn to God and devote themselves to prayer, He pours out the Holy Spirit on them. Filled with the Holy Spirit, men sometimes experience feelings of great joy and exaltation. Sometimes the chief effect appears to be in mind and conscience. Without emotional accompaniments, the revived dedicate themselves to *be* Christ's people and *do* His will. The gift of the Holy Spirit enables men to confess sin, make restitution, break evil habits, lead victorious lives, persuade others of the available Power, bring multitudes to Christ and *cause the Church to grow mightily.*[3]

Palmer, in his study of Pentecostal churches in Colombia, admits that a major lesson we (non-Pentecostals) can learn about church growth is that our churches must be revived. He concludes his study with these words:

> Our Theme and our goal must be: every church a revived church and every believer a disciple—faithful in Bible study, in prayer, in witnessing, in giving, in serving. The Pentecostals have no special secret of prayer and no exclusive hold on the blessing and power of the Holy Spirit, but they seem to be availing themselves more fully of these divine privileges and provisions. They are an example to us to seek the

Lord more fully and serve Him more faithfully, until we experience greater church growth in our own denominations and churches.[4]

The facts of Palmer's study are clear:

In Pentecostal churches, every believer is not only to seek the baptism of the Holy Spirit, but also the continual filling and power of the Spirit for service. . . . Eugene Kelly, director of the Christian and Missionary Alliance in Colombia, mentions the average Pentecostal's "implicit faith that God will work through him through the power of the Holy Spirit." The Pentecostal's attitude is one of "God and I can do great things together." This is clearly reflected in the words of one Pentecostal pastor, "Any man, any woman, any person can do miracles with the power of the Holy Spirit. Every believer can work miracles because every believer can have the power of the Holy Spirit."[5]

Hamilton sees this emphasis on the Spirit and his gifts as a refreshing change for many of the charismatics in non-Pentecostal churches. He states:

In a time of uncertainty and dissatisfaction with the cold, impersonal, formal worship of the "mainline" denominations, participating in an ecstatic worship is refreshing. For someone weary of academic discussion of theological questions, or impatient with the lukewarm commitment of many members of established churches, speaking in tongues satisfies a hunger for an authoritative, immediate, personal, and powerful religious experience.[6]

While many, it appears, who are in the more staid denominations desire this "new charismatic" work of the Spirit, it seems that some of the Pentecostals appreciate the relief given by a more moderate approach. Hollenweger confirms:

It is well known that there are today many members of the Assemblies of God who have *not* experienced the baptism of the Spirit. These members are under a constant mental pressure. A possible alternative exists for them in those traditional churches which are open to charismatic revival. A change in the dogmatic position of the Assemblies of God can hardly be expected, as they have invested too much energy, zeal and prestige in their Pentecostal theory.[7]

While much may be learned when the Holy Spirit's ministry is stressed, Hamilton uses the word "charismania" to describe the fixation of those who are preoccupied with the gifts and develop a consuming desire for *feeling* and *experience*. He adds that Paul faced "charismania" in Corinth and responded not by rejecting their experience but by holding before the church the objective content of their faith: "I determined not to know any thing among you, save *Jesus Christ*, and him crucified" (1 Cor. 2:2, KJV).[8]

In responding to the criticism of evangelicals concerning the priority they feel should be given to Christ as opposed to the Holy Spirit, Wagner remarks:

Pentecostals agree that Jesus Christ needs to be glorified, but they believe that He is best glorified by a strong emphasis on the person and work of the Holy Spirit. In all fairness it should be mentioned that as far as I have been able to observe Pentecostal teaching and worship, Jesus Christ is honored no less in Pentecostal churches than He is in any other evangelical church in Latin America.[9]

Researcher Elmer Towns asked the pastors of the fastest growing churches in America "if at any time in their life they had an experience with God, apart from salvation, that uniquely equipped them to pastor a fast-growing church?"[10] They all denied any "spiritual experience" with the Holy Spirit apart from salvation which gave them the power to be successful in church growth. Towns therefore reasons:

The charismatic pastors who follow the New Testament pattern of church growth do not claim divine characteristics nor are these qualities attributed to them by their followers. These are regular men who have *appropriated* the spiritual assets available to them for the Christian life and service. These men have incorporated into their lives the spiritual power available to all believers.[11]

There seems, concerning the Spirit's ministry in the church, to be a great need for clarity, truth, and balance. Many churchmen have answered the issue with the cliche, "I pray as if it all depends on the Holy Spirit, and I work as if it all depends on me." But the difficulty is in "practicing what we preach." Robert Girard testifies that hard work with a token acceptance of the Holy Spirit did not satisfy. He writes concerning Our Heritage Church, which he pastors:

Much of what is happening is *no miracle* at all. It can be explained so easily: When I work, it goes. When I don't, nothing happens! Everything can be explained in terms of human effort.

Where is the divine life the New Testament Church had? What *more* do *I* have *to do* to make it happen here?[12]

These frustrations led Pastor Girard to a "rest-and-wait-for-the-Spirit-to-work attitude." In his book *Brethren Hang Loose* he states finally:

The pastors of Our Heritage made one rather drastic rule for our ministry as we began to try to get out of the way and let the Spirit do it.

"Anything in the church program that cannot be maintained without constant pastoral pressure on people to be involved should be allowed to die a sure and natural death."[13]

As a result some programs and traditional aspects of the church life did die. But Girard and associates believe they are experiencing renewal, due to a new awareness and waiting upon the Holy Spirit.

Believing that God desires to work in and through our churches and recognizing the need we have for his power, Harold Cook contends:

We forget, even if we profess to believe it, that the Spirit is the Lord of the harvest. He is the only one who can change a heart. He is the one on whom, in the final analysis, the growth of the church depends. He expects us to work *with Him*, to do *His will*, and He will work *through us*. But all too often we look for Him to work *with us* and to vitalize what are essentially *our plans* and *our efforts*. We need in all sincerity to seek His leadership, realizing at the same time that He uses very human instruments.[14]

27. Lay Involvement and Spiritual Gifts

To some degree and extent an emphasis on lay involvement and spiritual gifts is a common principle of all growing churches, but again the method of implementation varies greatly. Peter Wagner argues that the second vital sign of a growing church is a "well-mobilized laity."[1] Win Arn, leader of Church Growth seminars, writes:

> One thing is certain—if a church is serious about the Great Commission, the involvement of the laity is of utmost importance. The growth of a church is uniquely dependent on the laymen. The pastor who sees his role as an enabler to help the laity discover and utilize their gifts is far ahead of the pastor who tries to run the whole show.[2]

Arn continues by explaining five classes of leadership within the church:

> Class I Leadership: members in the church whose energies primarily turn inward toward maintenance of the organizational structure of the church.
>
> Class II Leadership: members in the church whose energies primarily turn outward toward the non-Christian community in an effort to bring them into the body of Christ.
>
> Class III Leadership: members in the church who are partially paid and whose activities are divided between the church and outside activities.
>
> Class IV Leadership: individuals in the church who are full-time paid personnel viewed as professional staff.
>
> Class V Leadership: denominational, district and/or administrative personnel, usually removed from the immediate scene of the local church.[3]

Murphy, in his volume *Spiritual Gifts and the Great Commission*, agrees with Arn that a growing church should be developing more Class II Leadership than any other but adds that "*all* five varieties of leaders are needed by *all* denominations. The area of most tension has to do with the exact ratio that should be maintained between the five types of leaders."[4] Murphy goes on to state that denominations can be classified by the ratio they maintain in these five classes. A church looking inward is going to develop inward leaders; a church looking outward is going to develop outward leaders.

When giving reasons that churches die, Hollis Green states:

> When the building complex and the church constituency become the field in which to work rather than a force with which to work, the

church is in trouble. Admittedly, a program of Christian growth and development is essential in the training of the young and in the instruction of new converts. The church is to be a base for operations and not the field in which to do all the work.[5]

It appears that one of the constant "drifts" of the local church will be toward institutionalizing or turning inward, and to the degree that that happens, growth will decline.

It isn't difficult to look around a local church and immediately see needs for additional workers, but how to get them is the difficulty. Christian Education leader Kenneth Gangel states:

We face three basic problems in utilizing people in the service of Christ through the church: misuse, disuse, and abuse. The first is a reference to the employing of unqualified teachers and workers; the second, to the many uninvolved Christians that throng our church pews; and the last, to the problem of over-burdened workers in the church.[6]

Evangelical Bible Churches by and large are rapidly moving in the direction of the teaching of spiritual gifts, to properly involve the laity. One of the first books to make an impact in this area was Ray Stedman's *Body Life*. Since this time, spiritual gifts has become a much talked-about topic in many church circles. The layman will find his proper role when the pastor finds his. Stedman, MacArthur, Getz, and others base their case on Ephesians 4:8-12 in which the Apostle Paul says that the gifted men given to the church exist "for the equipping of the saints for the work of service, to the building up of the body of Christ" (NASB). When the minister is directing his efforts at "equipping the saints," then the laity can be expected to discover their spiritual gifts (1 Pet. 4:10, 11) and use them in ministering to one another.

By means of spiritual gifts everyone is a potential minister used by the Holy Spirit to build up his body. Benjamin writes:

If a congregation takes the New Testament idea of ministry seriously, one can no longer speak of a congregation and the minister but rather of a ministering-congregation. . . .

At the present time, over 40 million Americans are worshipping God on Sunday. What would happen in this nation if these 40 million became ministers? What would happen in our world?[7]

The teaching of spiritual gifts emphasizes the worth and contribution of each individual, and in this age of depersonalization, it is imperative that we maintain that emphasis.

Not every member of the body is a nose or an eye and never do we find a member operating alone and healthy. We must know where we fit and how we function and then be willing to use our gifts in conjunction with the direction and power that comes from the head.

One outcome of the charismatic movement is that many Christians now realize a renewed emphasis on the gifts. There is a growing wave of interest among churches and in some cases strong debate over issues concerning spiritual gifts. One of the most exhaustive biblical studies available today is the seminar and manual entitled "Spiritual Gifts" by Dr. David L. Hocking, president of Grace Graduate School, Long Beach, California.

Speaking for the Pentecostal churches of Colombia, Donald C. Palmer emphasizes that gifts and lay involvement are principal factors of their growth. Palmer reports that they "have a very great interest in preparing and motivating every believer to develop his gifts, witness, and serve in the work."[8] He goes on to cite a survey which he took among fourteen denominational leaders and twenty-eight pastors from both Pentecostal and non-Pentecostal churches revealing the major factors in their church growth.

MAJOR FACTORS IN PENTECOSTAL CHURCH GROWTH

Factors	Mentioned by Pentecostals	Mentioned by non-Pentecostals
1. Enthusiasm and activity of the members	15	21
2. Emotionalism that appeals to the masses	2	21
3. Emphasis on healing and miracles	4	12
4. Apprenticeship system of training leaders	3	9
5. Emphasis on the Holy Spirit and prayer	8	8
6. Emphasis on church planting	14	2
7. Self-support system of the churches	5	4
8. Opportunity given to all to participate	0	8
9. Indoctrination system for new believers	4	1
10. Proselytizing activities	0	5

In contrast to congregations where there is little chance for expression, charismatic churches provide many means for their members to be involved. In the chart the first four items cited by non-Pentecostals as growth factors include the individual in the church ministry either through mass-participation, corporate prayer, or direct involvement. Even in their services there is liberty and freedom for each one to express himself.[10]

Ortiz (a charismatic), speaks to pastors about this issue when he deals with the misplacement of the believer.

> Each believer needs to know his place in the body. Most church congregations are not a spiritual building, but a mountain of bricks. There is a difference. However good the materials may be, if they are not situated in their right place and correctly related to one another, there is no building. Each member of the congregation is a brick. The evangelists are continually bringing in new bricks. The pastor encourages this, even teaching classes on soul winning. Bring in more bricks, he urges. But bricks are not a building. Instead of a builder, the pastor now becomes a caretaker of bricks.[11]

Towns indicates a basic difference in Bible Baptist philosophy when he states that the ten largest Sunday schools view their churches as units rather than as groups of individuals. "If you view the church as a unit, discipline, purpose and duty become dominant patterns," he argues and then admits that he is oversimplifying the issue.[12] But he is citing an important point. Although members of Bible Baptist and like churches are involved, they do so because of outward motivation and direction, following the proverb, "Soldiers and slaves ask no questions."[13]

28. Aggressive Leadership

If any principle is common at least in theory to each major group studied thus far it would be the recognition that strong leadership is an important element in building the local church. Of the seven "vital signs" that Wagner lists for a growing church, he says that: "Vital Sign Number One of a healthy, growing church is a pastor who is a possibility thinker and whose dynamic leadership has been used to catalyze the entire church into action for growth."[1] After his survey of four basic types of churches (Soul-Winning, Classroom, Life-Situation, and Social Action) Dan Baumann unequivocally affirms that "any church, regardless of its size, location, or tradition will flourish better with enthusiastic, involved leaders."[2] Harold Cook, speaking from the historical viewpoint, verifies:

> Rarely does outstanding church growth come spontaneously without some strong personality to take the lead. That person may or may not be the originator of the work. He may serve principally as a catalyst. Or he may be just a strong figure around whom the others can rally. But the role he plays is a crucial one.[3]

The question of leadership is in the method of application. How should the strong leader work with his church and staff? Is he to be a backroom strategist and manipulator of men or a commander-in-chief leading the troops and doing every task better than anyone else? Where is the balance to be?

To the Bible Baptists and others, aggressive leadership involves sheer ability to succeed and accomplish outstanding feats. In listing the dangers ahead for Bible Baptists, Towns notes that because of the strong "charismatic" leader, the problem of succession is something the church will have to face, as well as a strong leader's tendency to refuse to allow young leadership to develop. This causes difficulty in extending the spirit and strength of the movement another generation and may often develop a "leadership crisis."[4] Bible Baptist churches are pastor-led and the church's success is measured by the pastor's success. While holding to the view that the congregation is the seat of authority, many BBF pastors boast, "The congregation has never voted me down on one point."[5]

Robert Schuller, having led Garden Grove Community Church to a current membership of over 7,000, agrees:

> Leadership is the key to church growth. If the church is to really succeed in its mission of witnessing effectively to the non-churched

world in the Twenty-First Century, we must develop dynamic, aggressive and inspiring leaders.

And what is leadership? Leadership is thinking ahead, planning for the future, exhausting all possibilities, envisioning problems and dreaming up solutions to them, and then communicating the possibilities and the problem-solving ideas to the decision makers. This is leadership.[6]

He balances this definition with this:

Even a cursory observation would indicate that the average ordained pastor is not a ten-talented man. He may be a good preacher—or a good pastor—but he is generally not strong in both areas. . . . It remains incomprehensible that intelligent church planners could assume that "a single pastor arrangement is the ideal arrangement."[7]

Southern Baptist author Belew comments:

There is little growth of any kind taking place in churches in which the pastor has not played the key role. He should *equip* the saints, but it is not likely they will be *well-equipped* unless he shows them how. In nearly every instance of exciting church growth, the pastor is the major motivator. He informs of why and he shows them where or how.[8]

It is in the "showing them how" that the pastor by example and precept becomes an equipper or enabler. The danger is in doing too much for the flock or not enough of the right thing. "Pastors are not to entertain or maintain the believers, but to mature them. In other words, shepherds are not placed in the flock to give milk to the sheep. God provides milk to every mother to give her child."[9] One of the reasons for the untimely death of a church is the "active pastor-passive sheep" structure that diminishes the role that all should play in the whole work of evangelism.[10] Dr. G. Beauchamp Vick, past president of the Baptist Bible College, pointed out, "You never saw a flock leading a shepherd."

With the additional understanding concerning spiritual gifts available today, many strong aggressive pastors are concentrating on their main gift(s) and encouraging every believer to minister (Eph. 4:11, 12). In *The Problem of Wineskins* Howard Snyder takes this view when he remarks:

Thank God for the superstars! They are of all men most fortunate. But the church of Jesus Christ cannot run on superstars, and God never intended that it should. There just are not that many, actually or potentially, and there never will be. God does not promise the church an affluence of superstars. But he does promise to provide all necessary leadership through the gifts of the Spirit (Eph. 4:1-16).[11]

29. Faith and Goal-Setting

Leadership, faith, and goal-setting are intertwined in the attitudes and actions of a growing church. For whenever someone expresses an active faith, there must be some basis or foundation for his belief. It is in relating a living biblical faith to the problems of growing a church where mainline denominations score the lowest. Belew stresses the real issue when he says: "In order to communicate the gospel and make the church grow, it is assumed that one knows who he is and who Christ is and has a faith which is worthy of propagation."[1] Faith becomes a vision when, by believing God's Word, the leader sees the possibilities for his church to grow and trusts God to overcome the obstacles. A vision is translated into action through goal-setting and planning.

Schuller refers to faith as "possibility thinking" and puts his finger on the crux of growth problems when he states:

> Many of you have heard the statement, "I've got to see it before I believe it." That's a negative-thinking statement if there ever was one, and it's as wrong as can be!
>
> Learn to say it right. Turn it backwards and say, "I've got to believe it before I see it." That's truth! . . . You see, it is God at work in us, giving us the will and the power to achieve His purpose (Phil. 2:13).[2]

For those desiring to start churches, Towns advises that "the most important factor in beginning a church is its conception in the mind of God's man who is motivated by the Holy Spirit."[3] He states that many will follow a pastor with a vision "not for rational reasons, but because the odds are against him and, in fact, appear insurmountable. The charismatic leader appeals to the deep feelings of the populace, and they hope he can somehow 'pull it off.' "[4]

A recent article in *Christian Life* by Towns, entitled, "Nation's Largest 1-Year Anniversary" verifies this truth. The article reports that Pastor Mels Carbonell (Community Bible Church, Seminole, Florida) "set a goal of having the largest first-year anniversary, and at the founding of the church informed *Christian Life* of his intentions."[5] Motivated to action, his people worked with unbelievable dedication and succeeded in reaching an all-time record of 1471. Another outstanding man of faith, vision, and goals is pastor Jerry Falwell who is planning the largest Sunday school and church service in the history of the Christian church. He states, "We are hoping *100,000 persons* will attend."[6] In the same edition of his monthly paper, *Faith Aflame*, he states: "Our ultimate goal is to have a Christian university with 50,000 students."[7]

Our pragmatic scientist of the Fuller school adds this data for the record:

As I study growing churches, it becomes increasingly apparent that a willingness to "risk" is a common denominator. Such churches are willing to believe God for what they cannot see, and to venture beyond their human resources.[8]

So much for faith and specific vision, but where does the establishment of goals fit in? Management expert and director of MARC (Missions Advanced Research & Communication Center), Ed Dayton, concludes:

The Christian's goals are faith's response to God's imperative, and thus reflect an additional dimension, our part in God's plan. . . .

Goals come in all kinds, types and sizes. It's useful to see that some goals have to do with what we want to *be*, and others have to do with what we want to *do*. . . .[9]

Everyone has them, though not everyone is able to state what they are! In one sense to have no goal is a goal in itself. . . .[10]

It appears that the pendulum can swing to two extremes in application of faith and goals. There is truth in both. The contrast is seen in the approach of Bible Baptists with that of the Pentecostal school. On the one hand, Towns notes that in Bible Baptist churches the emphasis is on hard work. Towns says that each leading pastor

testified he had had no special experience to make him holy or that gave him power to build a fast-growing church. Herb Fitzpatrick declared, "I am an average man. Any average man can build a great church if he is willing to work hard, win souls, and be faithful to preach the Word of God." Fitzpatrick went on to indicate, "When I speak of hard work, I refer to man's part. Of course, I realize that God must work and He does so through yielded, dedicated men, but there is no spiritual secret to building a fast-growing church."[11]

On the other hand, according to eyewitness Henry Lord, Pastor Ralph Wilkerson of Melodyland (charismatic-pentecostal) during an evening service stated that "*the Holy Spirit had spoken to him and told him* that he was to raise one hundred thousand dollars for books for the library of the School of Theology."[12] Following the report of the "Holy Spirit-given vision," he then applied highly motivational techniques challenging his church people to exercise "seed faith" allowing God to multiply what they would give.[13]

30. The Sunday School

In liberal circles the Sunday school or church school has fallen on difficult days. Attendance is failing rapidly, and it is hardly the place for "thinking" adults. Yet in the philosophy of fundamentalists and most evangelicals the Sunday school is the most important part of the Christian education program. Sherman Williams, pastor of the Redwood Chapel Community Church of Castro Valley, California, argues:

> Regardless of what else a local congregation did or did not do, it was often judged by its Sunday School, both by unbelievers and by those in the Christian community. The Sunday School was considered a mirror that revealed the effectiveness, or lack of it, of the entire church program.[1]

Dr. Harold L. Fickett, Jr., (former pastor of First Baptist of Van Nuys, California), writing of ten principles of church growth, stated that "it is impossible to build a great church organization of an enduring nature without building a great teaching program through the Sunday School."[2]

According to Towns, the historical perspective of the Sunday school can be extremely valuable in guiding us today.

> Robert Raikes began the Sunday School in 1780, and since the early days, numerical attendance has been used to reflect the strength of the movement. Therefore, Sunday School attendance is the basis of comparison. The next question to face is, "What is a Sunday School?" This question will be more prominent in the next 10 years. Even though some may attempt to make the modern Sunday School a "religious Sesame Street," the definition of Sunday School reflected in the movement begun by Raikes is still valid. 1. The Sunday school involves factual instruction in the Word of God, not employment of the catechism used predominantly in religious education during Raikes' day. 2. The Sunday School employs laymen to teach and administer the program; the clergy teach religious education as was predominant in Raikes' day. 3. The Sunday School centers on the children of the streets, not the children of church members, as in religious education of Raikes' day. As a matter of fact, many clergymen fought the Sunday School, refusing the ruffians access to the church. 4. Finally, the purpose of Sunday School was evangelistic, to bring pupils to Christ. Religious education during Raikes' day centered on edification. The Sunday Schools which will thrive in this decade will be those that

remain true to the original purpose of the Sunday School, which reflects the aim of the New Testament church.[3]

To churchmen, Southern Baptists and Sunday schools have been almost synonymous. Our previous study reflects their heritage of building churches through the Sunday schools. They developed the finest organization anywhere to build Sunday schools. They emphasized quantity and growth, for, according to Flake,

> there is inspiration in numbers, but let it be understood that a school does not necessarily have to have an enrollment of a thousand members to be great. It may be a really great school and have an attendance of a hundred or even less. However, no Sunday school is worthy of being called a great school unless it is reaching a large majority of the people who should attend it. This is true no matter what other claims to efficiency it may have.[4]

Yet Sunday school researcher Towns believes that most Christian educators have been in error concerning the factors which caused their Sunday school growth, for he adds:

> Many Southern Baptists believe "The Laws of Sunday School Growth" published in *The Pull of the People,* by J. N. Barnette [basically the same as Flake's ten steps], caused them to become the largest Protestant denomination in America. I do not agree. Too many schools have organized according to these laws, yet became stagnant. The laws were not causal, but Sunday School growth is the result of the strong evangelistic thrust of Southern Baptist churches. The laws of growth were used to organize and consolidate the gains from evangelistic outreach. The lack of growth in the contemporary Southern Baptist statistics stems from less emphasis on evangelism today than in the past.[5]

Towns continues pointedly:

> Perhaps the greatest reason for decline in Sunday School attendance is its subtle shift in the past few years from evangelism to education. The Southern Baptists built the largest denomination in America on the motto "The Sunday School is the evangelistic arm of the church." In the past 15 years we have seen the Sunday School movement reach a high in attendance and begin its gradual decline. During this time, we have also seen it shift from an evangelistic instrument in the hand of God to a sophisticated "Christian Romper Room."[6]

Among the most aggressive churches in America are the growing Sunday schools of the Bible Baptist Fellowship. Falwell reports that in early stages of Thomas Road Baptist Church it was mainly a preaching center and Sunday school was not emphasized. Falwell was challenged by the great work he saw at Highland Park Baptist Church (Dr. Lee Roberson, pastor) and returned to build a great Sunday school. In defining the purpose of the Sunday school, after this renewed vision, Falwell teaches that "the aim of a Sunday school is therefore the aim of the church. This means that the Sunday school teacher has the aims of the local church. Since the priority of the local church is evangelism, *the main aim of a Sunday school class is evangelism.*[7]

In some of the leading growing Pentecostal churches an emphasis on the Sunday school is lacking. Perhaps it is because Pentecostalism desires a certain amount of freedom for "the Holy Spirit to work creatively."[8] For in the Calvary Chapel Church of Orange County, California (the leading church of the Jesus movement), out of a morning attendance of 10,000 (four services) only about 1,000 are in attendance for the Sunday school. Although there are graded classes there is no curriculum, there are no books and no take-home papers, and each teacher is left to develop his own program and find his own materials.[9]

Christian Center Church of Orange County (Melodyland), another leading charismatic church attended by approximately 10,000 each Sunday, also does not have a growing Sunday school. Pastor Ralph Wilkerson states, "We never have promoted our Sunday School. We have promoted the teaching ministry of the church and we believe in it, and we have the Melodyland School of the Bible to prove it."[10] According to researcher Henry Lord, Wilkerson did not plan to do what was being done by other successful churches.[11]

It is interesting to note that organization, form, training, faithfulness, records, visitation, etc., all necessary to have a growing Sunday school, are each in themselves an aspect of discipline and structure. Likewise, another important part of Sunday school is the development of laymen. Since Robert Raikes's conception and early beginning, Sunday school has been a movement of the committed laity. And if the teachers are going to teach biblical doctrine and truth which agrees with the pastor, someone must see their need for training as a great opportunity for discipleship. The hard work of Sunday school success may appear as a contrast to the "freedom of the Spirit," prevalent in Pentecostal churches.

Contrary to what is seen at Calvary Chapel and Melodyland (leaders in the Pentecostal movement on the West Coast), among many Assembly of God churches Sunday school *is more important* than ever before. Hollenweger, in his monumental work, *The Pentecostals,* says that "the Sunday school is the real backbone of the Assemblies of God and can be regarded as a preliminary stage for all the rest of the school system."[12] He goes on to note that each age group has its own Sunday school magazine, and Sunday school teachers at each level also receive a magazine.[13] In *10 At The Top,* author Lebsack confirms that to every one of the ten Assembly of God churches reviewed, Sunday school is seen as a vital agency for growth.[14]

In his chapter "Celebration+Congregation+Cell=Church," Peter Wagner questions whether a group of people gathering together only for "celebration" (festive worship) is really a church. Wagner defines the "congregation" aspect of church as a group of people, to a maximum of 250, which in sharing together around a common objective lose anonymity. He cites the most common form of "congregation" within a larger church as the Sunday school class.[15] He then concludes with this confirmation concerning the Sunday school: "If a church makes the multiplication of congregations or fellowship groups (or Sunday School classes) a definite part of its planning for growth, the church will almost invariably grow faster."[16]

31. Social Action

Among each group that we have studied there is the recognition that man has eternal and temporal needs. While this truth is common to each church growth school of thought, solutions differ greatly. Controversy runs deep and varied methodology reflects it. A proper perspective in this area is vital for continued church growth. Wagner cites as landmark "the major finding of Dean Kelly's [*Why Conservative Churches Are Growing*] research: Churches that concentrate on developing a philosophy of ministry around social activism tend, in the long run, to *lose* social strength."[1] The invitation to "Come Help Change the World" must be based on biblical principles which result in proper methodology. Kelley's conclusion becomes very strong when his length of research is considered. "He says that he has searched for 20 years for just one case which would disprove the theory, but has not yet found it."[2] Perhaps the extremes could be seen by comparing the contribution of the United Presbyterian Church to the fund for a fair trial for Angela Davis with the simplistic answer of Dr. Lee Roberson to the people at Highland Park Baptist Church, Chattanooga, Tennessee. He said, "If someone has a problem, I have two minutes to spend with him; my time is reserved for reaching the lost." He went on to say, "If a Christian will take advantage of proper Bible study and the fellowship of church attendance, he will not have problems."[3] Dr. Roberson was making a point of priorities, yet revealing a definite position toward what some feel is the proper role of the church today.

Southern Baptist author Belew submits that "the organization needs to be enlarged to admit the possibility of extending itself and the programs of the church out into the streets and into the midst of the needs and hurts of the world."[4] Pastor Dan Baumann, currently growing a Baptist church, argues for relevancy when he proposes:

> Research your community to identify its needs. If you are genuinely willing to seek advice and counsel from your community, you will begin to identify some direction for an enlarged ministry. Meet the needs of your community, and it will beat a path to your door. . . .
>
> Allow the Bible to meet human needs. Every Bible study, Sunday school lesson, and sermon should have as its goal the intersection of God's eternal truth and some clearly defined contemporary situation. Biblical truth without application to where people live is irrelevancy; whereas a study of contemporary need without the clear direction of the Bible lacks authority.[5]

Towns, in describing differences between fundamentalists and evangelicals, states:

> Evangelicals are fast embracing social action as an extension to the gospel ministry. So much so, that they are in danger of losing their emphasis on evangelism. At the same time, fundamentalists see their biblical task as presenting Christ to unsaved people so they can be saved. Social action of the evangelicals takes many forms, such as: the war on poverty, feeding the poor, voter registration, and drives for racial equity. The fundamentalist is not anti-social action, but feels deeply that the transformed individual will ultimately make an impact against social and civil ills. The fundamentalist, however, will not give primary consideration to social action but to soul winning. Dr. Jack Hyles has often said, "We do more social action on our way to win souls than the average liberal church does on purpose."[6]

And as a matter of fact, Hyles and First Baptist activists have come a long way toward fulfilling that statement. With dedication they seek to fulfill the literal application of Luke 14:21 which records the head of the household's command to his slave, "Go out at once into the streets and lanes of the city and bring in here the poor and crippled and blind and lame" (NASB). They have developed phenomenal ministries to the poor through rescue missions, the handicapped, the deaf (over 250 actively involved), the blind and the educably slow (approximately 450 through ten graded Sunday school classes). Plans include a senior citizen's housing complex and an orphanage. All of this "social action" and yet a zealous commitment to soul-winning evangelism. First Baptist has literally proved the words of Melvin Hodges that "there is no greater contribution than to preach the gospel of redemption from sin and to see lives transformed."[7]

Church Growth and the Bible

32. The Biblical Church in the Modern Age

It would be very encouraging if we could report that the institutional church is growing phenomenally. But, of course, the sad truth is that it is not. The institutional church is in deplorable shape and in desperate need of renewal, reorganization, renaissance, and revival.

Snyder, writing as an evangelical who accepts "the entire Bible as fully authoritative," concludes that these suggestions for change are "either heretical or insufficiently radical."[1] He suggests that for a church to change drastically, to return to New Testament principles, to adopt the dynamic of the early Christian church would be unthinkable. "No denomination in its right mind will ever do such a thing, for perfectly good psychological and sociological (if not biblical) reasons."[2]

While advocates of institutional change clamor for attention, all over the world many nontraditional churches and even non-Christian religious bodies *are growing rapidly.* Why? Do history, culture, politics, and economics fan the fires of this religious fervor? How? And if so, is this just a fad, a passing trend, or are there good reasons to believe that such burgeoning growth at the grass-roots level will be with us for some time to come?

McGavran says that "peoples and societies vary in responsiveness. Whole segments of mankind resist the gospel for periods—often very long periods—and then ripen to the Good News."[3] He cites the following factors as common to various peoples' receptivity to the Christian message: (1) New Settlements, (2) Returned Travelers, (3) Conquest, (4) Nationalism, (5) Freedom from Control, (6) Acculturation.[4] Although McGavran speaks here of world missions, his thesis bears on American church growth as well. "One thing is clear, receptivity wanes as often as it waxes. Like the tide, it comes in and goes out. Unlike the tide, no one can guarantee when it goes out that it will soon come back again."[5]

A HISTORICAL PERSPECTIVE

Believing that this current age is very possibly the most "strategic one for the effective proclamation of the biblical gospel," Snyder suggests that history has come full circle and returned "to the spirit of the first-century Roman world."[6] Snyder admits some differences, but his "seven signs of the times" stand as hard evidence for his interesting conclusion:

1. An essentially urban world with cities playing the major cultural role.

2. Unparalleled peace, stability and political unity.

3. The worldwide spread of one predominant culture and language.

4. International travel, communication and cultural interchange.

5. Pervasive social change, with a tendency toward a humanizing, universalist, "one world" outlook; a feeling that mankind is essentially one and shares a common destiny.

6. Widespread religious and philosophical ferment; the mixture and "revitalization" of world views; the rise of new religions; a practical atheism and disbelief in the gods, coupled with an existential mysticism.

7. Moral degeneration.[7]

Dr. Edward Hindson also refers to such conditions during past revival history. He argues that

every major revival came during a time of peace and was followed by war. When God had finished preparing His church for what lay ahead, and when those who rejected his work had confirmed their unbelief, revival would end and war would come. Notice but a few examples:

Great Awakening (1734-1774) ▶ Revolutionary War began in 1776.

Revival of 1805 (1805-1809) ▶ War of 1812

Great Prayer Revival (1857-1859) ▶ Civil War began in 1860.[8]

Are we, the Bride of Christ, being prepared to experience revival before the times of the tribulation grow near and wars and catastrophes increase?

A SCIENTIFIC FAILURE

The god of science has played the role of the Pied Piper. It has led us down the path to the future, promising us utopia through technology, and at the same time taking our billions of dollars as well as a good bit of our faith. But this god science has failed to bring men lasting hope. Indeed, over the years science has induced in man a disbelief in the supernatural and a skepticism toward the transcendent. We plod on behind the Piper, but we are disgruntled and restless. The conditions of the world have worsened: there is inflation, war, hunger, and a shortage of energy. Furthermore, we sense a void of meaning in our lives.

In the muddle of these modern times, if the church is without strength and holds illusions rather than reality, if the church clings only to a form of godliness while denying God's power, then the disenchanted will turn to other gods, other counterfeits.

Francis Schaeffer reminds us that the study of modern science was begun by men who saw and appreciated the beauty of God's creation. He coins the phrase, "modern, modern science," referring to man's idea of placing all of the natural laws into a closed system.[9]

This little phrase changed all of life because it put everything within the machine. If everything is put into the machine, of course, there is no place for God. But also there is no place for man, no place for the significance of man, no place for beauty, for morals or for love. When you come to this place you have a sea without a shore. Everything is dead.[10]

The mocking words of Elijah seem most appropriate to the contemporary followers of the god of science. "Call out with a loud voice, for he is a god; either he is occupied or gone aside, or is on a journey, or perhaps he is asleep and needs to be awakened" (1 Kgs. 18:27, NASB).

ACCELERATION OF CHANGE

Toffler predicted in *Future Shock* that acceleration of change could be one of the greatest enemies of life as we have known it. The world is now beginning to understand the wisdom of that prediction. Now "the rate of change has so skyrocketed upward that more change—and more *significant* change—takes place within one year than occurred in literally hundreds of previous years."[11] Snyder affirms that

history simply cannot continue to accelerate at an ever-increasing rate. Eventually, something drastic must happen. Our civilization is like a jet airplane, accelerating ever faster and faster. But there is a finite limit to how much speed that airplane can withstand. Unless it slows, it will eventually reach the disintegration point. It is not made to transcend the boundaries of space and time and neither is man-made culture.[12]

Still, many church growth leaders advocate change in order to stay abreast of society's needs. They recognize the problem of change in modern life, yet feel that the church must keep up in order to be at all effective.

Michael Tucker has dedicated a chapter in his book to this subject, and has entitled it, "How to Create Change."[13] In a recent survey among Assembly of God pastors, the ability to innovate and create meaningful change was listed number eight in a priority listing of forty-four items concerning church growth.[14]

But it's not enough for the local church to be willing to change. Church growth leaders must produce that change in a nonmanipulative, proper, and biblical way.

THE AGE OF SENSATION

It is the peculiarity of our age that so many dull, drugged-out people continually crave an encounter with genuine feeling, with experience, with what is vaguely termed "reality." How ironic it is that escape from reality is in truth a search for reality, that people dull their senses in order to make them more acute, that men reject the religious but embrace mysticism. Snyder says that "their enchantment [our youth of today] with drugs or oriental mysticsm or the Guru Maharaj Ji is really an acted-out parable. It says, 'Give us a taste of experience.' "[15]

A recent survey of forty-eight university campuses across the nation, involving 9,000 students, revealed that 19 percent seek satisfaction through eastern cults or disciplines. Transcendental Meditation led the field with 11 percent of the students indicating a strong interest or involvement. The survey asked, "What is your belief about truth?" The majority responded that "truth is basically relative" and that there are no absolutes.[16] Concerning the kind of evidence that would most strongly influence these students to believe that Christ was God, the survey reported:

> Although a solid 48 percent of the students surveyed still indicated they would be "strongly influenced to believe that Christ was God" by rational, historical, or testimonial evidence, *a full third of the students rejected the relevancy of that kind of objective evidence at all.* Fifteen percent indicated they would be unconvinced until Christ appeared to them personally and "demonstrated his miraculous power." And another 18 percent flatly stated that "there is no evidence that would strongly influence me to believe that Christ was God."[17]

Both students and adults look to religious counterfeits simply because they offer experiences. And by pursuing experience they have abandoned their belief in absolute truth. Still, people are spiritually hungry. This is the great hope for the church. Can the church provide experience which is both meaningful *and* true?

Author and lecturer, Evelyn Christenson, who believes God's power and meaningful spiritual experience is available through prayer, makes reference to a statement of an occult high priest.

> He said that the churches of America had given up the supernatural. They don't deal in the supernatural; they just deal in plans and programs and social action. He said that every human being is created with a supernatural vacuum, and since Christians aren't doing anything in the realm of the supernatural, he feels that witchcraft is a reasonable substitute for Christianity.[18]

So, the larger issue today is whether or not the church is teaching that the truth of God's Word does *not* teach experience, or teaches *against* experience. But if the church teaches sound biblical doctrine *and supports that with genuine experience in Christ*, then the church will grow.

A DAY OF CRISIS AND UNCERTAINTY

Today, the local church faces a crisis. In many non-church and para-church organizations young people experience a dynamism and vitality which was not apparent ten years ago.[19] Can the same thing happen within the church?

Yes, but there is a price to pay, changes to make, and attitudes to alter.

Engel and Norton in their book, *What's Gone Wrong with the Harvest?*, view the church as God's instrument for this age.

> There is no question that the Church is God's only means for accomplishing His work on earth. Other organizations such as evangelistic movements, broadcasters, publishing agents, and mission societies are best considered "para-church structures," which exist alongside of and parallel to the community of God's people. Although they are helpful in carrying out its purposes, they are *not* the church.[20]
>
> There is no point in talking about fulfillment of God's mission if the Church is entombed in resistance. The answer does not lie in renewal of old forms, because that often is an attempt only to place band-aids on the exterior wounds of the old shell. The key is renaissance. . . . The key, we feel, lies in the discovery of the *principles* of New Testament church organization and function.[21]

Speaking of church renewal, Getz refers to three classes of evangelical Christians: (1) those who desire to change everything always; (2) those who are threatened by change; and (3) those who say change is not the issue, that the issue is how to be "biblical purists."[22] He goes on to say that "in one sense all of these groups are speaking *some* truth—important truth! But in a broad sense, all are wrong—dead wrong! They've all missed the mark. They have fallen short of formulating a philosophy of the ministry that is truly biblical."[23] He continues to emphasize the point that in order to avoid such "tunnel vision" the proper church strategy must be developed by looking through three lenses: eternal Scripture, past history, and present culture.[24]

Getz is correct. The church must be anchored to the fundamental truths of God's Word to give the much-needed "thus saith the Lord." Principles for operation are tested and shaped by holding them up to the mirror of history and by thrusting them into the fire of contemporary culture. Certainly, not to study the history of the church is to assume a position of superiority or ignorance. To run scared of modern culture and to plunge our heads in the sand reduces the church's ability to deal with "felt needs" eye to eye.

We live in an age of wars and rumors of wars, earthquakes, population explosion, hunger and poverty, growing apostasy, and religious and political persecution. In such times, the church ought not be found naked and wanting for strength. The church must raise its voice and proclaim the answer. The church must not cower in the corners of life while false Christs broadcast their heresies with authority. Peter has encouraged us, the church, to give the world the answer, "always being ready to make a defense to every one who asks you to give an account for the hope that is in you, yet with gentleness and reverence" (1 Pet. 3:15, NASB). Our answer is Christ, for "there is salvation in no one else; for there is no other name under heaven that has been given among men, by which we must be saved" (Acts 4:12, NASB).

PROMISED VICTORY

In any contest there is a victor. So it will be in the church's battle in the modern age. The Lord has said, "I will build my church; and the gates of Hades shall not overpower it" (Matt. 16:18, NASB). Notice four important aspects of God's plan.

First, it is his *objective*, not ours, to build the church. Churchmen ought not to question whether it is God's will for this church to be built or for that church to grow. Yes, on occasion it is necessary for some congregations to wave the yellow flag and slow their growth in order to reassess priorities, and sometimes it is important for a church to hoist the white flag and call it quits, if only to reorganize in a different way in a different place. Yet, we need to stand committed to God's objective, that he will build his church, and we must claim that promise regardless of the obstacles. Saucy affirms this prophecy for the church when he explains:

> Although he does not lay down rules for a specific organization, the words "I will build my church" clearly express Christ's intent to establish a new community. The future tense here expresses not only futurity but probably also volition.[25]

Second, the *ownership* of the church is God's, not ours. The living church belongs to Christ. Furthermore, what is true of the body of Christ is true also of the local church. The word *ekklesia* in Matthew 16:18 is most significant:

> The most common use of *ekklesia* . . . is to describe a local church or assembly or congregation or body of believers in the Lord Jesus. It is at the level of the local church that the great realities of God's purposes in Jesus Christ receive visible expression in the world. It should be obvious that Scripture makes no dichotomy between the universal church and the local church. What then is true of the Assembly is to be true of an assembly.[26]

Third, there will be *opposition*. Hocking explains that "the best explanation of 'the gates of Hades' would be that it is referring to death, as the doorway into Hell."[27] Death, Hell, and sin are powerful adversaries of the work of the church. In Revelation 1:18 Christ says that he held the keys of death and Hades. How did he gain this control? Through suffering the cost of defeating the opposition. "From that time Jesus Christ began to show His desciples that He must go to Jerusalem, and suffer many things from the elders and chief priests and scribes, and be killed, and be raised up on the third day" (Matt. 16:21, NASB). It was then that Jesus had to rebuke Peter strongly saying, "Get behind Me, Satan! You are a stumbling block to Me; for you are not setting your mind on God's interests, but man's" (Matt. 16:23, NASB). And what is God's interest? To build his church.

Fourth, the *outcome* is promised. Christ says that the adversaries "shall not overpower it." No opponent will have sufficient power to get the upper hand

and defeat the church. The Apostle Paul said to the Ephesians that they must be "strong in the Lord, and in the strength of His might" (6:10, NASB). He goes on to direct the church to "put on the full armor of God, that you may be able to stand firm against the schemes of the devil. For our struggle is not against flesh and blood, but against the rulers, against the powers, against the world forces of this darkness, against the spiritual forces of wickedness in the heavenly places" (Eph. 6:11, 12, NASB). Satan and his forces will attack the church, but Christ will prevail. Snyder says that "using the world's weapons, the church does not stand a chance. But when the church uses God's weapons (Eph. 6:14-17), it is the world which becomes weak."[28]

The prospects for today's church are bright if it is anchored firmly to biblical principles, aware of the needs and hungers of those who are lost, and going forth wearing the whole armor of God.

33. Pictures of the Church

In the Bible God has described the church by means of images which teach eternal truths. Some believe that the most profound lessons concerning the nature of the church are seen in the Apostle Paul's use of verbal pictures.[1] For anyone serious about the matter of church growth, these pictures represent important issues. Each image speaks to a different kind of growth; each image portrays the church from a different perspective.

THE BODY OF CHRIST

The body of Christ is Paul's most-used description of the church. The Bible teaches that Christ is the head of the body, which is the church. Paul's writings to the church at Ephesus and Colossae often refer to this picture. God has made Christ head over all things (Eph. 1:22). We the members of his body are to grow up in all aspects into him who is the head (Eph. 4:15). Represented by the husband-wife relationship, Christ is also the head of the church, the Savior of the body (Eph. 5:23). Christ is to be first in all things because he is also head of the body, the church (Col. 1:18). Paul rejoiced in his sufferings for the Colossian Christians because he was doing it on behalf of Christ's body which is the church (Col. 1:24). He is also the source and supplier of all growth to the entire body (Col. 2:19). The many members are a part of that one body in Christ and of one another (Rom. 12:5; 1 Cor. 12:12-31).

What do these images tell us about growth?

GROWTH OCCURS WHEN CHRIST HAS FIRST PLACE

The priority for every church and for every Christian is to give Christ first place in everything! In Colossians 1:16-18 the reason for this priority is cited: (1) he produced all things for himself (Col. 1:16); (2) he preceded all things (Col. 1:17); (3) he preserves all things (Col. 1:17b); and (4) he purposes to be first in all things (Col. 1:18). As the head is the center of our lives, so Christ must be given preeminence. The head is always the one who gives directions; the body or members are those who must willingly receive the orders. The growing church today must know how to listen to her head and how to respond when direction is given. It seems reasonable and biblical to assume that if the church would only follow her Lord's instructions, both quantitative and qualitative growth would follow.

226

Early in the history of the church, in Corinth, this biblical principle was voided and the members began following men. They were good men with great ability, but in no way could they avoid the problems of human headship (1 Cor. 1:10-17). They were no longer a body united, but members divided!

Prior to our Lord's ascension he promised to his disciples that the Helper, the Spirit of truth, would be sent from the Father to guide them into the truth and to glorify Christ (John 14:16, 17; 15:26, 27; 16:13, 14). Because the Spirit will never speak apart from the Triune Godhead (John 16:13) there is no fear that he will lead us astray. What he says will be the same as what Jesus would say if he were here in the flesh. Yes, but how will he speak to us? How will the church know what he says? Is it possible that he will give different and conflicting messages to his body? In whatever way he guides us, Scripture affirms that it will be "the truth." Paul affirmed that his word is also truth (2 Cor. 6:7). If each member of his body, beginning with pastors, would acknowledge the lordship of Christ and experience the daily dependence upon the indwelling presence of the Spirit-Helper, there would be no division or conflict within the body.

The primary way for us to communicate to our leader is through prayer. The primary way for him to communicate to us is through his revealed Word. Great emphasis is placed in growing churches upon these "basics." To live without them would be analagous to a football team competing without a huddle and without plays. Perhaps there has been a misunderstanding concerning prayer. Prayer is not just enlisting God's blessings and assistance as we make the decisions. Prayer is our communication system by which we ask him, the Lord of the church, what he wants us to do. It is the means of determining the ministries and methods that the body will engage in. Prayer is the avenue of knowing the thoughts of our head. And make no mistake, our Lord has the winning game plan.

GROWTH OCCURS WHEN THE BODY FUNCTIONS TOGETHER

If the membership of any body is to be successful in accomplishing the goals of its leader, *each part* must be "restfully available" and "instantly obedient." So then, we're going to trust his direction given through his Spirit by his Word, but how will we be able to accomplish such tasks as reaching the world for him? He must equip us, and we must "suit up" for the contest. Unity, diversity, mutuality, as well as special abilities (gifts) are all necessary and available through the ministry of the Spirit and his Word. As Robert Saucy explains concerning spiritual gifts:

> The apostle (Paul) begins his discussion of gifts with the Corinthian church by placing all of the pneumatic gifts under one Lord and Spirit (I Cor. 12:3-5). Therefore, there must be no schism in the body (12:25 ff.) caused by a disorderly display of gifts (1 Cor. 14:33). All of the

227

gifted members are under the same Head and are part of the same body, and such members in a normal body do not oppose each other, thus tearing the body apart.[2]

The Apostle Paul speaks of improper attitudes of pity (1 Cor. 12:15, 16) and pride (1 Cor. 12:21, 22) which need constantly to be dealt with in the minds and hearts of the members, to prevent the functioning of the body from being hindered. There is no room for false concepts of humility nor for exaggerated ideas of self-importance. The words of Paul speak to this issue when he exhorts every Christian "not to think more highly of himself than he ought to think; but to think so as to have sound judgment, as God has allotted to each a measure of faith" (Rom. 12:3, NASB).

If a body is healthy, all of its parts function properly in accord with the others. One practical truth that will maintain this delicate system is the giving of special care, recognition, and honor to the weaker members of the body of Christ (1 Cor. 12:22, 23). Disease and sickness often strike the areas of greatest weakness, and when that happens the entire body is disabled (1 Cor. 12:26).

To fully understand the biblical issues involved in this picture is to realize that many churches are sick and dying because of a great lack of teaching concerning spiritual gifts.

Future pastors are graduating from seminaries today without either knowing their spiritual gift or understanding the doctrine of gifts. How then can they expect to lead a well-ordered, active, and healthy body? It appears that the tendency to discredit the validity of spiritual gifts is disappearing; perhaps it will be replaced with a proper biblical adherence to the teaching of gifts.

> One cannot really understand what the New Testament means when it speaks of the church unless one understands what it teaches about the gifts of the Spirit. Spiritual gifts are primarily a matter not of individual Christian experience but of the corporate life of the church. Gifts are given for, and in the context of, community.
>
> The denial of spiritual gifts really indicates a basic misunderstanding of the nature of such gifts. Those who fear spiritual gifts (and often the problem is, in reality, one of fear) usually conceive of such gifts as highly individualistic, irrational and eccentric manifestations that disturb the unity of the Body of Christ. But such a caricature is not at all what the Bible means by the gifts of the Spirit.[3]

In his references to Col. 2:19 and Eph. 4:15, 16, Saucy remarks: "The body grows through the supply of energy distributed to each part through the Head. As each member, receiving his gift of grace, contributes to the whole, the body grows."[4]

> The truth is that the Body of Christ is designed to teach us that we need one another and that we must care for one another. To the world

we must show ourselves one in Christ, united in love and a shared life. Such a unity is not uniformity or conformity. It is rather a Spirit-given sense of our mutual needs and the recognition that our diversity is both God-given and essential to maturity and health. "Unity, diversity, interdependence." This is not to be just the motto of the local congregation, but its experience under God.[5]

In summarizing this picture of the church as the body of Christ, Radmacher explains that "it is clear that the *source* of all—both unity and nourishment—is Christ himself. The *channels* of the communication, however, are the different members of the body of Christ, in their relation one to another."[6]

THE BUILDING OF GOD

The building of God is in a sense similar to the previous picture. Our bodies are also referred to as buildings and houses (2 Cor. 5:1) in which God dwells (1 Cor. 3:16).

We also know that his building of the church is a growing edifice (Eph. 2:21), similar to the body illustration, which is "built up" with spiritual gifts (1 Cor. 14:12; Eph. 4:12, 16). For the sake of illustration, spiritual gifts can be viewed as mortar which joins the "living stones" (1 Pet. 2:5) together. These bricks or living stones must be carefully "fitted together" for maximum growth (Eph. 2:21). In looking at the "growth principles" found in this picture, additional biblical issues are clarified.

GROWTH OCCURS WHEN CHRIST DWELLS IN THE BUILDING

The purpose of the building is not only to grow but to exalt Christ as his indwelling presence is manifested. Paul warned the Corinthians to take care of their individual bodies because they were the temple of God (1 Cor. 3:17; 6:19, 20). Kent writes:

Each convert, whether he be Jew or Gentile, adds to the growth of the structure. And this structure is no less a holy temple, for God dwells within it. If the Jewish temple at Jerusalem suggested Paul's figure, it is important to note that he chose the word that denoted the sanctuary proper, rather than one that described the outer courts and buildings. It was this inner sanctuary which was regarded as God's dwelling place.[7]

A building is constructed not to be empty but to house a tenant, and this marvelous building is to house the Lord! "Let it be said again," writes Chafer, "Israel *had* a building in which God was pleased to dwell; the Church *is* a building in which God is pleased to dwell."[8]

It cannot be taught too often that Christ, the living God is to "dwell in your hearts through faith" (Eph 3:17, NASB). He desires to settle down and be at home, speaking, guiding, moving about freely, exercising his Lordship in every area of our lives. To the extent that Christ is seen in each stone he will be seen in the building of his church.

GROWTH OCCURS WHEN BUILDERS BUILD PROPERLY

One of the important biblical issues concerning church growth is who are the builders and how are they to build? In Ephesians 2:20, Paul cites the apostles and prophets as builders of the church. Whether this text in its first sense refers to the apostles and prophets as *the* foundation or as *laying* the foundation is in question. But the fact remains that the apostles did lay the beginnings of many churches.

To the church at Corinth Paul admits that "as a wise master builder [architect] I laid a foundation" (1 Cor. 3:10, NASB). Saucy explains that "the apostle has laid the foundation by teaching the doctrines of Christ and bringing men into a relationship with him who is the only foundation that is laid. The church is not built upon a man or a creed but upon the person of the living Christ."[9]

In addition to those who found churches by the teaching of the sound doctrine of Christ there is need for many more builders. This building will not be finished until the rapture, but will it not be exciting if contemporary builders "put the roof on"? In the 1 Corinthians passage Paul is quite clear that many builders are involved: "But let *each man* be careful how he *builds* . . ."; "Now if *any man builds* upon the foundation . . ."; and (a phrase repeated four times) "*each man's work* . . ." (1 Cor. 3:10-15, NASB). Everyone who is a "living stone" can also be a builder and should be, for the biblical building crews are saints who are equipped for the work of service, to the building up of the body of Christ (Eph. 4:12).

As any builder knows, good help is hard to find, and in fact must be carefully trained and equipped to do the job. A well-trained building crew can get the job finished in half the time it might take unskilled novices. Paul urged the Corinthians to learn how to build a lasting church and to take the care to do it right. Today we need places of instruction within the local church which will adequately train our new apprentices how to become journeymen for God in the greatest construction task on earth.

GROWTH OCCURS WHEN QUALITY MATERIAL IS USED

Every building begins with the ground first. In fact in many instances thousands of dollars and hours of time are invested in preparing the soil even before the foundation can be laid. The soil is of utmost importance for it must receive the foundation (cf. parable of the sower in Matt. 13).

The foundation is then laid, and it must be Jesus Christ alone (1 Cor. 3:11). Paul had previously determined before coming to Corinth that he would be an expert in one field, and that was "Jesus Christ, and Him crucified" (1 Cor. 2:2,

NASB). Is it any wonder that his message and preaching were demonstrations of the Spirit's power? (1 Cor. 2:4). Church planters must know and preach about the historical person and work of Jesus Christ. There is no other effective way to build a church.

After the foundation is firmly settled, the first row of blocks or stones are then placed. The first one sets the standard for the remaining ones. In this case our Lord Christ is also the cornerstone. Lenski affirms the importance of this stone which is

> . . . set at the corner of a wall so that its outer angle becomes important. This importance is ideal; we may say symbolic: the angle of the cornerstone governs all the lines and all the other angles of the building. This one stone is thus laid with special, sometimes with elaborate ceremonies. It supports the building no more than does any other stone. Its entire significance is to be found in its one outer angle. Its size is immaterial and certainly need not be immense. It is thus also placed at the most important corner, in or on the top tier of the foundation, so as to be seen by all.[10]

As the bricklayer takes his setting and draws his line for the entire building from the cornerstone, so every believer by design is to be formed to the pattern set by Christ. It is this One "rejected by you, the builders, but which became the very corner stone" (Acts 4:11, NASB). that all believers are to look to for direction and example (Heb. 12:2).

Now at this point the floors of the building are ready to be constructed. The building material for the local church referred to by Paul in 1 Corinthians 3:12 includes a choice of quality materials (gold, silver, precious stones) or nonquality materials (wood, hay, stubble). Because of the ultimate test yet future ("for the day will show it"), the builders are admonished to make sure that, as the building is fitted and joined together, quality material is relied upon. And what is this material? It is none other than believers, who are properly allowing the cornerstone to set the course for their life-styles. In 1 Corinthians 3:9 Paul refers to them as a building of God. Boyer explains:

> Certainly the context makes the primary application to *people*. They [the materials] represent persons being built into the church. This is not to be understood, however, as a mere adding of another brick to the wall by getting another convert to Christ. Remember, these people are "living stones." They themselves grow, so that the temple grows and is edified as its people grow. Thus, the minister's work is twofold: He builds (1) by getting new people into the building, and (2) by getting those in the building to increase in stature and maturity. And since both of these tasks are accomplished by a ministry of teaching, there is some truth to the interpretation often encountered in the commentaries that the works here refer to the *doctrines* of the church leaders. Doctrine, however, is involved only secondarily, as it affects persons.[11]

The problem in understanding this illustration of building material comes when we attempt to press it further than the main truth. Questions, such as "What is a 'wood' or a 'silver' person?" or "Do the 'perishing' materials represent unsaved people?" lead us into areas of speculation that lose sight of the central lesson of good building practices.

The people are the work (1 Cor. 9:1), and the work has no value unless it centers in people. Since believers are the real building, then only a foolish builder would use his people to build anything else except other believers. The end and substance of a man's work for Christ must be people. The staying power of the church, the permanence of the building in the face of testing is the "mark of excellence" that Christ desires. While the main concern of the builders is quality, a building cannot be constructed without a *quantity* of material.

Getz summarizes:

> "Be careful how you build!" warned Paul. A church can be weak and immature—constructed of wood, hay and stubble. Or it can be strong and mature—composed of gold, silver and precious stones (1 Cor. 3:10-15). If it is immature, it reflects impatience, jealousy, strife, divisions, pride, arrogance, and unbecoming behavior. If it is mature, it reflects a growing love, a unity of faith, and a steadfast hope. [12]

THE BRIDE OF CHRIST

The bride of Christ is used to describe the church in only a few New Testament passages but not without great meaning: "Come here, I shall show you the bride, the wife of the Lamb" (Rev. 21:9, NASB); "For I am jealous for you with a godly jealousy; for I betrothed you to one husband, that to Christ I might present you as a pure virgin" (2 Cor. 11:2, NASB); and in the extended passage of Ephesians 5:23-32.

Radmacher describes a correct view of the bride of Christ when he states that "the church, the bride of Christ, includes all those who have put their faith in Christ in this age of grace which had its beginning at Pentecost and will continue until the Bridegroom comes to receive His bride unto himself to consummate the marriage." [13]

GROWTH OCCURS WHEN WE REALIZE CHRIST'S LOVE

Someone has well said that "we are unable to love someone else until we first realize that someone loves us." In Ephesians 5, Paul pens a love letter from which the church should never stop swooning. The Apostle John wrote that "God is love" (1 John 4:8) and that he proved his love to us, his bride, on the cross (1 John 4:9). Even though Paul illustrates the love of Christ for his church by painting a picture of a husband's love for a wife, the illustration falls short. The love of Christ for his church far exceeds anything known in human relationships. "Never has a husband loved as Christ loved the church." [14]

The first biblical issue seen here in its effect on the growing church is the proclamation and demonstration of Christ's limitless love. When we, his church, fail to live by his standards and thereby "please" him, we often conclude that it is because we don't love him enough, but in reality it is because we fail to realize how much he loves us. The Scripture is clear: Christ loves us in spite of ourselves and not because of performance or on the basis of what we are. He loves because he is God (Rom. 5:8). It was on the basis of this principle that Peter could exhort fellow Christians to "keep fervent in your love for one another, because love covers a multitude of sins" (1 Pet. 4:8, NASB).

For the church to believe and accept this principle requires the kind of faith that comes only from hearing the word of Christ (Rom. 10:17). According to the passage in Ephesians 5, Christ intends to love us to himself and in the process to cleanse and perfect his bride. Like Paul did to the Ephesian church, so church leaders today should pray for their flock that they "may be able to comprehend with all the saints what is the breadth and length and height and depth, and to know the love of Christ which surpasses knowledge" (Eph. 3:18, 19, NASB).

GROWTH OCCURS WHEN WE RESPOND TO CHRIST'S LOVE

The Apostle John explained that "we love, because He first loved us" (1 John 4:19, NASB). Response to someone who refuses to stop loving you is natural. Recognizing that he is controlling all of the experiences of this life to prepare us for an eternity with him, one could reason that it would be an easy thing to respond. However, the issue is the kind of response. Christ our Lord desires subjection to him in every area. The church is totally dependent upon him for life and health, for sustenance and protection, and yet, blinded by our sinful nature, we still desire to run our own lives.

Saucy confirms that "the life of the church in each member is to be arranged under the headship of Christ. Their authority and leadership are found in Him. His thoughts and attitudes must be theirs."[15]

The daily creed of the bride must be "whatever He desires I will do, wherever He leads I'll go, however He wants to change me I'll respond." To the church, the bride of Christ, love is Lordship! Thus we must teach it, preach it, and live it that others also may be "rooted and grounded in love."

THE FLOCK OF GOD

The flock of God is one of the most picturesque illustrations of the church. It highlights several issues which are critical for growth. Paul used this picture in reference to the Ephesian church and its responsible elders when he said, "Be on guard for yourselves and for all the flock, among which the Holy Spirit has made you overseers, to shepherd the church of God which He purchased with His own blood (Acts 20:28, NASB). Peter also used the illustration when he wrote the elders to "shepherd the flock of God among you, not under compulsion, but voluntarily, according to the will of God; and not for sordid gain, but with eagerness; nor yet as lording it over those allotted to your charge, but proving to be examples to the flock (1 Pet. 5:2, 3, NASB). Jesus made clear application to the flock and the shepherd in that very descriptive passage in John 10.

GROWTH OCCURS WHEN CHRIST IS RECOGNIZED AS THE CHIEF SHEPHERD

Total responsibility and authority belong to Christ for the oversight of his sheep. Peter referred to Christ as the Chief Shepherd who when he appears will reward his faithful undershepherds (1 Pet. 5:4). The understanding of this issue is as crucial for the undershepherd as it is for the flock. For, as Christ told Peter so plainly, the task is to "Shepherd *My* sheep" (John 21:16, NASB, author's italics). The ownership of the flock is clear. The church belongs to Christ. Pastors are working for him and will someday give an answer concerning the sheep allotted to their temporary care (Heb. 13:17).

Perhaps more care should be taken that local flocks are not referred to as "my church" or "Brother So and So's church" but always "the church he pastors." If the sheep know (by hearing and seeing) that the undershepherd is mindful of this important fact and that he receives his direction from the Chief Shepherd, they will be more willing to follow.

GROWTH OCCURS WHEN THE UNDERSHEPHERDS ADEQUATELY PROVIDE FOR THE SHEEP

The illustration of sheep as people throughout the Scripture may not be the most flattering but it is nevertheless accurate. The Word of God consistently indicates that the church is like a flock of sheep constantly needing food, protection, and direction. Radmacher remarks that "long lists of specific items could doubtless be listed at this point, but it seems that they could all be summarized under provision, particularly the provision of spiritual food."[16]

However, prior to the feeding or providing ministry of the undershepherd is the task of "finding." McGavran strongly asserts:

God wants countable lost persons found. The shepherd with ninety-nine lost sheep who finds one and stays at home feeding or caring for it should not expect commendation. God will not be pleased by the excuse that His servant is doing something "more spiritual" than searching for strayed sheep. Nothing is more spiritual than the actual reconciliation of the lost to God.[17]

The great commission then can be seen in *shepherd terminology* (a McGavranism): *finding* (making disciples), *folding* (baptizing), and *feeding* (teaching).[18]

"Finding" results in maturity for the lost one and for the whole flock. No one can deny that when lost sheep are added to the flock there is growth (Luke 15:1-7).

If the church follows the scriptural example of the church in Acts for adding to the body, membership growth will also result from "folding." "So then, those who had received his word were baptized; and there were added that day about three thousand souls" (Acts 2:41, NASB).

The third aspect, "feeding," results in qualitative or perfecting growth. When charging the Ephesian elders, Paul reminded them, "For I did not shrink from declaring to you the whole purpose of God" (Acts 20:27, NASB). He urged them to protect the flock as he had done to them: "For a period of three years I did not cease to admonish each one with tears" (Acts 20:31, NASB). And finally, he commended them to God and "to the word of His grace, which is able to build you up" (Acts 20:32, NASB). Paul was satisfied that he had faithfully fed the flock at Ephesus. And how had he accomplished that? By giving them the Word of God. The shepherd must know where to find the food, and he must regularly supply it for his flock, leading them to satisfy their hunger and thereby causing them to grow.

In further defining the responsibilities of the shepherd's role of protection and discipline, it is interesting to note the importance of the rod and the staff (Psa. 23:4).

> The staff was a long, crooked stick used for pulling back straying sheep, while the rod was a stout piece of wood about three feet long with a lump on one end; it was used as a weapon against wild beasts and robbers. It was also the practice of some shepherds to lay down across the opening of the fold during the night so that their bodies became literally the protecting door.[19]

While Scripture is clear that each Christian has a responsibility to rectify offenses against another brother (Matt. 18:15 ff. and Gal. 6:1), it is equally clear that the undershepherd must be able to exhort, refute, and reprove (Tit. 1:9, 13). No longer are we armed with the staff or the rod but with the faithful Word which is totally adequate "and profitable for teaching, for reproof, for correction, for training in righteousness" (2 Tim. 3:16, NASB).

Here the obvious biblical issue is that we must have undershepherds who tend the sheep. The many functional and administrative tasks of the church plant and programs are very successful in diverting the pastors from their chief area of responsibility. Reorganization may be the answer, but there appears to be a constant "pastorless drift," and the warning of Paul and Peter should be nailed on the wall of every pastor's study: "*Shepherd the flock of God!*"

One practical issue which speaks volumes to today's busy pastor is the example that Jesus gave us when he said, "He calls his own sheep by name" (John 10:3, NASB). Also "the sheep follow him because they know his voice" (John 10:4, NASB), and "My sheep hear My voice, and I know them, and they follow Me" (John 10:27, NASB). It is a challenge to be able to call each Christian in the church by name! It is a challenge to be with them enough that they know their shepherd's voice! It is a challenge to have lived Christ before them so that they now trust enough to follow! These are the burning issues of the pastorate. But if they are faced and pastors do the work of shepherding, the church will grow.

An additional issue that is being brought to light today by church growth thinkers is the maximum size of the flock. Just how many sheep can one shepherd know, feed, love, protect, and direct? New Testament evidence abounds that a plurality of elders existed in cities where churches were established. In Ephesus there were elders (Acts 20:17) of the church. In Lystra, Iconium, and Antioch Paul and Barnabas "appointed elders for them in every church" (Acts 14:23, NASB, author's italics). In Titus 1:5, Paul directed Titus to "appoint elders in every city" (NASB, author's italics). Should sheep have more than one shepherd or should shepherd and sheep be carefully allotted to each other (1 Pet. 5:3)?

Wagner urges large churches to consider decentralizing into "flock-congregations" in which the major characteristic would be that everyone is supposed to know everyone else.[20] He states that "if properly decentralized, they [the congregations] can contribute to church growth in a much more powerful way. This decentralization takes two forms: (1) multiplication of congregations and (2) a higher degree of self-government."[21] He further suggests that "the *maximum optimum growth* of a congregation is limited by its primary objective of fellowship,"[22] and he agrees with Larry Richards's figure of 250 as absolutely maximum.[23]

Richards was one of the first to suggest this in his book *A New Face for the Church*, and several large and rapidly growing churches are successfully working an adaptation of his smaller "growth group" concept.[24] Gene Getz at Fellowship Bible in Dallas, Texas, calls their concept "mini-programs," while Dan Baumann, pastor of Whittier Area Baptist Fellowship dubs their growth groups "circles of concern."

> They are voluntary mini-Christian communities of 5 to 7 families that meet regularly. Each Circle has a Bible study, discussion leader and a co-leader who coordinates social function. The circles are intended to become an intimate, concerned community with an emphasis on "sharing with" and "caring for" each other.[25]

Dr. Robert H. Schuller, pastor of the 8,000-member Garden Grove Community Church, has been most successful in establishing a shepherding plan for his entire church. The Pastoral Care Program instituted over seven years ago depends on some 500 lay ministers of Pastoral Care. The Garden Grove Community Church is divided into four geographical units, called areas, which in turn are divided into divisions. Each division is comprised of zones including from eight- to ten-member families living in close geographical proximity.

The lay ministers are considered the "nervous system" of the church.

They show concern to the families of the church and serve as a communication line concerning illness, bereavement, and joyful occasions among the members. They also seek to encourage each member to participate fully in the church's programs.[26]

Among many churches this practical implementation of the "shepherd-sheep" concept is taking on a greater importance.

GROWTH OCCURS WHEN
THE SHEEP FOLLOW THE SHEPHERDS

Assuming that the organizational structure has been clarified (that's assuming a lot), and that the sheep know who their shepherd is (a godly spiritual leader), and that the sheep will follow, then the church will grow. Peter writes, "For you were continually straying like sheep, but now you have returned to the Shepherd and Guardian of your souls" (1 Pet. 2:25, NASB). Isaiah also reminds us of our sheep nature when he says, "All of us like sheep have gone astray, Each of us has turned to his own way" (Isa. 53:6, NASB).

For the sheep to know of the shepherd's provision and protection and still not follow is to fail to obey clear scriptural direction. Saucy's remarks well conclude this point.

> Essentially, the sheep can provide nothing for itself and can only prosper as it follows the direction of the shepherd. Its only obligation is to submit to his leading and authority. Thus the church is directed as the flock of God to submit to His authority and that of the chief Shepherd. Because this direction is communicated through the Word and the ministry of the undershepherds which God has placed in the church, the members are exhorted to "obey them that have the rule over [literally, lead] you, and submit, yourselves" (Heb. 13:17). As even the leaders of the church are sheep, they also are obligated to submit ultimately to the chief Shepherd.[27]

THE GARDEN OF GOD

The Garden of God is a collective phrase which describes several organic illustrations found in the New Testament of church growth. Tippett remarks that "the teaching of Jesus was charged with expectation of growth."[28] He classifies them into various types of imagery and refers to fields "white for harvest" (John 4:35, NASB) and the mustard seed parable (Matt. 13:31, 32) as well as other examples.[29]

A garden is a cultivated field where seed is sown and plants are grown which are expected to produce crops for the farmers. In 1 Corinthians 3:6-9, the description of the church as a cultivated field is used. In John 15, the illustration of Christians as branches is used, and Christ is portrayed as the life-giving vine.

GROWTH OCCURS WHEN
THE LABORERS WORK TOGETHER WITH GOD

In the church at Corinth, a church that was schismatic and idolized its leadership, Paul taught the beauty of seeing the church leaders for what they are: ministers or servants, colaborers, and fellow-workers with God. According to Paul, each laborer had his own special ministry, but in reality God was the one causing the church to grow (1 Cor. 3:6). Therefore it is wrong to give any human the credit for building a church, for the Sovereignty of God is the ultimate cause (1 Cor. 3:7). As a matter of fact, if two or more "farmers" are working a garden, one planting and the other watering, the church is instructed to view them as a team, although each will be rewarded individually by the Lord. "Now he who plants and he who waters are one; but each will receive his own reward according to his own labor" (1 Cor. 3:8, NASB). It is important to note that both laborers are working together for one purpose — the crop! Therefore they are to complement one another rather than compete.

The biblical issue is clear. As every growing flock needs more than one shepherd and must somehow divide the responsibility of the sheep, so growing gardens will flourish if several farmers can work together.

Some may argue that Paul preceded Apollos just as one who plants comes before one who waters. While that is true, do not fail to miss the obvious lesson of the passage, that both Paul and Apollos were fellow-workers of God (1 Cor. 3:9).

Costas underscores the concept of partnership with God when he explains:

Perhaps one of the strongest images of church growth is suggested by the New Testament concept of stewardship, particularly the idea of fellow worker. In 1 Cor. 3:9 and again in 2 Cor. 6:1 Paul refers to the Christian as God's fellow worker (Greek *sunerquoi*). . . .

The role of fellow worker implies tremendous privilege but also great responsibility. It suggests the idea of a responsible person whom God has brought in as a junior partner and has given oversight of his work and from whom he expects a responsible rendering of accounts (cf. 1 Cor. 4:2). . . .

Behind the idea of fellow worker lies not only the concept of responsibility but also of resources. God does not entrust us with a task without giving us adequate resources to fulfill it. In both the parables of the pounds and the talents the master gives the servants financial resources to invest for the kingdom. Paul speaks of the giving of gifts to the church "for the work of ministry, for building up the body of Christ" (Eph. 4:11, 12). We can assume that if God sees his coworkers as cultivators, builders, soldiers, fishermen, stewards, harvesters, and shepherds, surely he provides the resources for us to use in the expansion of the kingdom under the direction of his Spirit.[30]

238

Working together for growth includes our responsibility vertically to God as well as horizontally with others. Building a partnership with God is essential for biblical church growth. In addition, building a growing church is too large a task for any one individual.

Concerning a plurality of elders working together as a team, Murphy refers to this practice when he states:

> The Scriptures refer to such men (1 Tim. 5:17, 18). They fulfilled a function somewhat similar to that of the modern pastor. The New Testament practice of a plurality of elders was not violated by this arrangement. These men were leaders of pastoral teams.

But can shepherds effectively work together if their flock grows larger than one can oversee? Is it practical that one field should be tilled by more than one farmer? Is this principle valid for the contemporary, growing church ministry? Murphy argues that it is.

> It is often claimed such a plurality of leadership is almost impossible to effect. It may work in a tribal situation where the concept of leadership by a group of elders is part of the cultural motif, we are told. In an urban situation it is unworkable. Urbanites are too individualistic. A group of elders sharing equal authority would be in constant conflict. Such men could never agree on the handling of a church. Someone has to have the authority and make the final decisions, it is claimed.
>
> While there is some truth to this objection, it ignores two facts. One, there are just too many actual situations in which it has worked to dismiss it as unworkable. Two, among any group of leaders, one or two men will always rise above the rest and carry more authority. Their authority will be accepted, indeed, even delegated by the others.
>
> This is the type of leadership the New Testament calls for. Without violating the plurality of elders in the local church, a few outstanding men will come to the surface above the others.[32]

GROWTH OCCURS WHEN
THE BRANCHES ABIDE IN THE VINE

At every turn and with every illustration concerning the church, the Scriptures teach of our dependence upon Christ who is our only source of life and growth. The picture of the vine and the branches given in John 15 is pregnant with meaningful application. There are two central issues to be considered. One is the process or factors causing the growth, and the other is the produce or fruit that results.

Jesus commanded Christians to abide in him, for it is impossible for branches to produce fruit apart from the vine. "Abide in Me, and I in you. As the branch cannot bear fruit of itself, unless it abides in the vine, so neither can you, unless you abide in Me" (John 15:4, NASB). Dr. C. I. Scofield's note on abiding is helpful.

To abide in Christ is, on the one hand, to have no known sin unjudged and unconfessed, no interest into which He is not brought, no life which He cannot share. On the other hand, the abiding one takes all burdens to Him, and draws all wisdom, life and strength from Him. It is not unceasing consciousness of these things, and of Him, but that nothing is allowed in the life which separates from Him.[33]

"Practicing the presence of Christ," knowing that he is real, experiencing a vital faith-walk with Jesus moment by moment and day by day is mandatory for productive life-filled branches. While many authors may say it differently, the biblical issue of abiding in Christ must be communicated in a practical way to each member of the growing church. When certain branches "lose touch," the resulting productivity of the vine's potential is reduced from what it could be.

According to the text, the clearest way to know whether one is abiding in Christ or not is seen in Christ's teaching concerning his words. In John 15:7, Christ joins the concept of abiding in him with abiding in his words. He further explains in verse 10 that you will be abiding in his love if you are keeping his commandments. He exemplifies this by his own obedience to his Father's commandments.

As if we, the branches, must have everything spelled out (and we do), Christ assured us of the positive benefits of joy that would accrue to our lives (John 15:11). He also gave a very practical barometer by which we constantly can measure our "abiding level." "This is My commandment, that you love one another, just as I have loved you" (John 15:12, NASB). In order to grow and produce the fruit of the vine, a healthy church must demonstrate observable love one to another which is another result of abiding in him.

Every church can experience an increase in fruit if more of its members actively abide in him. We must understand that while both the vine and branches are necessary, the fruit-producing power flows only one way, from the vine to the branches.

The second issue relating to the growing church is the matter of producing the fruit. Dr. Chafer summarizes the results of abiding as "pruning (v. 2), prayer effectual (v. 7), joy celestial (v. 11), and fruit perpetual (v. 16)."[34]

It is important for us, the garden of God, to constantly remember our purpose of fruit bearing. Christ reminded his disciples, "You did not choose Me, but I chose you, and appointed you, that you should go and bear fruit, and that your fruit should remain" (John 15:16, NASB). Christ is affirming the central purpose of every Christian's life. The sole purpose of a branch is to produce fruit, and a fruitless branch is considered worthless. Is it any wonder when depression comes and joy is gone that it is often found to be a result of not fulfilling our reason for being? Desert experiences come to the life of every branch. They appear to be inevitable, yet they *are* alterable. Dynamic life can flow again; but first, pruning is necessary.

What is the fruit that we are to produce? Some say it is winning souls. Certainly Christians should be active in evangelism. But there is general agreement among writers on the church that this fruit (singular) is best described by the fruit (singular) which the Holy Spirit produces (Gal. 5:22). Basically it is the life of Christ, the vine, flowing through the branches, and demonstrated by the nine qualities cited by Paul in Galatians 5:22. It is "Christ in you, the hope of glory" (Col. 1:27, NASB). The quality of an individual's changed life, in the final analysis, is the undeniable apologetic. It is this fruitbearing of the vine in and through the branches that causes others to be drawn to the Savior. In reality then, if it is good fruit (love, joy, peace, patience, kindness, goodness, faithfulness, gentleness and self-control), others will know and also come to be grafted into the life-giving vine. Then the fruit of the Spirit will produce fruit in soul winning.

GROWTH OCCURS WHEN
PRODUCING BRANCHES RESPOND TO PRUNING

After referring to his Father as the vinedresser, Christ explained that the Father prunes every branch that is bearing fruit in order that it may bear more fruit (John 15:2).

The Greek word for "prune" means "cleanse." It signifies a purging process of all that may reduce or prevent additional fruit.[35] Fruit-bearing Christians ought never to believe that God cannot yet expand their field of effectiveness and continue to develop their potential all through life. Saucy remarks:

> Again the pertinency of this particular metaphor is seen in the fact that no tree requires such extensive pruning as that of the vine, and yet it is the characteristic of the vine, that even though it is severely cut back, it does not die but grows again.[36]

Donald Grey Barnhouse cites an amazing example of this lasting potential fruitfulness.

> In Hampton Court near London, there is a grapevine under glass; it is about 1,000 years old and has but one root which is at least two feet thick. Some of the branches are 200 feet long. Because of skillful cutting and pruning, the vine produces several tons of grapes each year. Even though some of the smaller branches are 200 feet from the main stem, they bear much fruit because they are joined to the vine and allow the life of the vine to flow through them.[37]

Pruning as experienced in a believer's life can best be understood as the loving discipline from the Father. Purging, cleansing, or discipline is the result of the Father's love (Prov. 3:11, 12) and is ultimately for our good and additional fruit bearing. In Hebrews 12:10, 11, the Scripture shows how discipline produces fruit.

> For they [earthly fathers] disciplined us for a short time as seemed best

to them, but He disciplines us for our good, that we may share His holiness. All discipline for the moment seems not to be joyful, but sorrowful; yet to those who have been trained by it, *afterwards it yields the peaceful fruit of righteousness* [NASB, author's italics].

In John 15 it is clear that it is the Father, the vinedresser, who does the pruning (also seen in Hebrews 12). Hollis Green, adapting this concept, urges churchmen to think of the church as a living organism similar to a tree or a vine. He sees the church as a garden in which pruning is delegated by the Chief Vinedresser to subordinates who take a role similar to that of the undershepherd.

Green sees the need for regular pruning of policies, programs, and organizational structures that may be diseased or not as productive as they should be. This is accomplished by cutting back certain parts for better growth. He warns that this kind of change always results in the "setback of pruning" which may be the phobia that keeps churchmen from administering this necessary cure.[38] Green encourages regular pruning of the living church so that more fruit will be produced. He explains:

> Fruit bearing always takes place on new growth. It is this aspect of administration that should be the primary concern of churchmen. The fruit bearing apparatus must be kept in operation. New growth in the fruit bearing area also produces foliage. Foliage has a direct relationship to the food supply and the healing of wounds caused by pruning. In horticulture it is suggested that the pruning should take place as close to the main branch as possible so the growth tissue surrounding the wound may form new tissues to heal the wound. Since food moves down through the stems and comes from leaves above the wound, the wound must be in position near this food supply if healing is to occur. The implication here is one of distance. Pruning must be done close to the foliage and food-moving mechanism if the plant is to survive.
>
> Arbitrary and indiscriminate pruning at a distance from the main branch leaves a stump because the healing of the wound cannot occur. When church leaders prune or tamper with the fruit bearing mechanism of the church, it must be done with due caution and careful planning. The ultimate objective of repairing the wound and nurturing the whole body into a productive unit must be considered.
>
> Where churchmen do not have the courage to prune, disease gnaws at the fruit bearing areas, and the process of strangulation cuts off the flow of life to the superstructure. Without the courage to prune, it is only a matter of time until fruit bearing stops and the slow but sure process of death destroys the foliage, the superstructure and even the roots. The tree may stand but it is dead. There is no shade for the weary traveler and no fruit for the hungry. The structure is there, the organization is there, but the life is gone. This is the sad plight of many churches.[39]

THE FAMILY OF GOD

Peter stated that believers "are being built up as a spiritual house" (1 Pet. 2:5, NASB), and Paul explained the church to Timothy as "the household of God" (1 Tim. 3:15, NASB). To the Ephesian Christians, Paul emphasized that both Jews and Gentiles through Christ became a part of God's family (household — Eph. 2:19). In fact, an entirely new family, different from anything previous, was initiated by the cross. "For He Himself is our peace, who made both groups into one, and broke down the barrier of the dividing wall . . . that in Himself He might make the two into one new man, thus establishing peace, and might reconcile them both in one body to God through the cross" (Eph. 2:14-16, NASB).

According to John's gospel, "But as many as received Him, to them He gave the right to become *children* of God" (John 1:12, NASB, author's italics). And so it is because we are sons that Paul said, "God has sent forth the Spirit of His Son into our hearts, crying, 'Abba! Father!' " (Gal. 4:6, NASB). Vine states that according to the Gemara (a Rabbinical commentary)

> slaves were forbidden to address the head of the family by this title. "Abba" is the word framed by the lips of infants, and betokens unreasoning trust; "father" expresses an intelligent apprehension of the relationship. The two together express the love and intelligent confidence of the child.[40]

As a result of Jews and Gentiles entering the family of God, wherever the gospel was taken, a new institution was formed. As the great commission was fulfilled, a local expression of God's family came into being. People who before had no relationship to each other now were members of a household, the church. They were brothers and sisters, loving, helping, encouraging, teaching, and sharing with one another. The relationships and purposes God has for his family demand order and direction, unity and oneness in order that it will grow properly.

GROWTH OCCURS WHEN
ORDER AND EFFECTIVE LEADERSHIP ARE PRESENT

Regardless of our various backgrounds of nationality, parentage, economic standards, etc., the message of Scripture to the born again is "Welcome to the family of God!" (Eph. 2:19). Every believer, once he becomes a part of the household of God, has full family privileges.

In Paul's instructions to Timothy concerning church order, structure, and effectiveness, the importance of the household concept is stressed. In 1 Timothy 3 Paul compared the managing of a man's family with the qualifications necessary for New Testament church leadership and service (1 Tim. 3:4, 5, 12). One of the tests for the overseer of the church is whether he can properly lead and care for the needs of his own family. Paul's main intent is not programs nor concern for the house building itself. His message is whether or not the person under consideration as overseer can meet the basic needs of people. Engel and Norton warn of a wrong emphasis at this point.

The role of the pastor is not one of getting things done through people; rather, it is one of *developing* people into men and women of God. A focus on *using people* in the program of the church is a vicious and nonbiblical dead end.[41]

Every family needs a father, every building program needs a general contractor, and every flock needs a shepherd. As Paul stresses to Timothy, the ingredient to look for in a potential leader's or minister's home is submission of the family and an effective operating chain of command (1 Tim. 3:4). In verse 15 Paul clarifies the importance of his previous instruction when he explains, "I write so that you may know how one ought to conduct himself in the household of God, which is the church of the living God, the pillar and support of the truth" (NASB).

The church's welfare is based, then, on the welfare of its constituent families. Church leaders must set the example by properly loving their wives and disciplining their children.

GROWTH OCCURS WHEN UNITY AND ONENESS ARE EXPERIENCED IN OUR HOMES AND CHURCHES

Paul taught the Christians at Galatia that differences are removed and all are *one* in Christ (Gal. 3:28). Sometimes, however, becoming one in Christ will divide a family rather than unite it. "Therefore if any man is in Christ, he is a new creature; the old things passed away; behold, new things have come" (2 Cor. 5:17, NASB). When one person in a family comes to Christ, the church should pray and plan to evangelize the entire family for Christ. This builds unity in the home and as a result builds the church.

Scripture is encouraging at this point, for the first incidents of non-Jewish salvation involved whole families. In Acts 10 Cornelius and his whole household trusted Christ. In verse 2 the Scripture shows that entire families can be prepared to receive Christ, for they were all "God-fearers." In Acts 10:24, when waiting for Peter, Cornelius was busy inviting his relatives and close friends, who, upon hearing the message, believed (Acts 10:44-48). The Philippian jailer and his family also were saved, accepting Christ individually and yet professing him together (Acts 16:31-34).

McGavran explains these blessings as "people movements."

What I am affirming is that conversion does not have to be the decision of a solitary individual taken in the face of family disapproval. On the contrary, it is better conversion when it is the decision of many individuals taken in mutual affection. *Multi-individual* means that many people *participate* in the act. Each individual makes up his mind. . . .

Mutually interdependent means that all those taking the decision are intimately known to each other and *take the step in view of what the other is going to do.* This is not only natural; it is moral. Indeed, it is immoral, as a rule, to decide what one is going to do regardless of what others do. Churchmen in Afericasia frequently say to inquirers, "Since Jesus Christ is the Savior, the pearl of great price which you have found, and since you are a loyal member of your family, you do not want to enjoy salvation secretly all by yourself. The first thing you want to do is to share your new-found treasure with your loved ones. The person who loves the Lord most will try most to bring his intimates to Him. Andrew went and found his brother Simon. You do the same."

In a people movement, members of the close-knit group seek to persuade their loved ones of the great desirability of believing on Jesus Christ and becoming Christians. Often they will defer their own decision in order to be baptized together. . . .

Conversion means participation in a genuine decision for Christ, a sincere turning from the old gods and evil spirits, and a determined purpose to live as Christ would have men live. The individual decisions within a people movement exhibit all these marks. It is *a series of multi-individual, mutually interdependent conversions.*[42]

As the family's unity and oneness are seen in evangelism, so they are evident in edification. Peter wrote that the prayers of a Christian husband could be hindered and not answered if his relationship with his wife is not biblically correct (1 Pet. 3:7). In fact, Paul wrote that a Christian marriage is to follow the pattern of Christ's love for the church (Eph. 5:25). It was evident and widely reported than an unbiblical family relationship existed in the church of Corinth (1 Cor. 5:1). Obviously there have been many such examples where the growth of a local church has been hindered by families not living as a testimony of Jesus Christ.

When it was necessary to correct problems within the local body of Christ, Paul told Timothy to handle church problems in the way he would deal with problems in a family relationship. In 1 Timothy 5 Paul gives principles to follow in resolving family problems of both the home and the church. In fact, he seems to move from the church to the home and back again, explaining the application of the same truths. When dealing with an older man, respect is always important, and he is to be exhorted as one's own father (1 Tim. 5:1). An older woman is to be treated as a mother, younger men as brothers, and younger women as sisters (1 Tim. 5:1, 2). What practical advice for oneness and growth today! After all, the local church of believers *is* a family, and it does consist of fathers, mothers, brothers, and sisters in the Lord (Matt. 12:49, 50).

A proper emphasis upon the family is not easy for the church to maintain, yet it is possible. Our supreme example, the Lord Jesus himself, was also tested in this area. While on the cross, accomplishing the mission for which he came, Jesus remembered to care for the needs of his own mother! (John 19:26, 27).

Larry Richards has attempted to bridge the gap between the theory of "the church ought to" and "the church is able to."

> This concept of the family-as-a-unit is a key one. Too often families are, in fact, loose associations of individuals whose basic needs are met outside the home. The biblical picture, and one stressed more and more by contemporary social scientists, is that the most basic needs—those dealing with personality development of both the adult and child—must be met within the family structure. Secular writers today note that a family unit will develop and mature much as an individual grows and matures.
>
> Thus our study team is on firm ground when they see, as part of the church's ministry, strengthening the family in its unit functions. . . .
>
> The church, the team felt, should provide these minimum ministries: counseling, training for parenthood, reorganization of church meetings into a weekly "family night" program, and variety in the Sunday evening service with the meeting designed to minister to specific family needs (a demonstration of family worship, for instance). . . .
>
> The reason for much of the failure [of the family] can be attributed directly to our churches. Today most church ministries are focused almost exclusively on individuals. Family units are broken down into individuals in nearly all our agencies. Any sharing (and very little takes place in our pulpit-centered and teacher-centered services) is outside the family structure.[43]

The use of household and family pictures in the Scripture shows us the desirability of adequately meeting not only individual needs but the needs of this basic social unit in both evangelism and edification. As there must be oneness on the physical family level, so there must be unity on the spiritual family level. When this biblical issue is satisfied within the church today, growth will result.

SUMMARY

The victory is secure and the promise is guaranteed for the church of Jesus Christ in spite of the contemporary problems of our world. For the local assembly of "called-out ones" to experience the reality of this hope today requires men and women committed to biblical principles of church life.

The implications found in the pictures and metaphors of the church revealed in Scripture are far reaching. In every case the church is illustrated as a living organism. Even in the example of the building the church is composed of "living stones."

We must properly instruct believers that the church is not a building occasionally inhabited by people. Rather, we are the building of God, and we are constantly inhabited by his Spirit.

As we view the pictures that God has revealed to us in his Word, care must be taken not to "pragmatize" the truth to a place of secondary importance. The problems that we face today are going to be solved by men dedicated to building churches God's way. Inrig pointedly remarks:

> But reform is not enough, even in the twentieth century. There are many well-meaning Christians who see the diverse needs of contemporary churches, and advocate change. But change, especially change on the basis of pragmatism, is simply not sufficient. Unless change is guided by definite biblical principles, today's reforms will be tomorrow's problems. It is not enough that method or practice "works" by the standards we use to measure such things. If a work is to last and have permanent value, it must be done in God's way.[44]

34. The Purpose of the Church

Since the initial prediction of God the Father to Abraham that "in you all the families of the earth shall be blessed" (Gen. 12:3, NASB), until the explosive events of the day of Pentecost (Acts 2), the church had been a hidden mystery. Paul, in writing to the church of Ephesus, explains that "He [God] made known to us the mystery of His will" (Eph. 1:9, NASB). In chapter 3:3-6 Paul confirms that this sacred secret, hidden during Old Testament times is "that the Gentiles are fellow-heirs and fellow-members of the body, and fellow-partakers of the promise in Christ Jesus through the gospel" (Eph. 3:6, NASB). What then are the purposes that God intended for his church?

THE EVANGELISM AND SATURATION OF THE WORLD

The first purpose of the church is to spread the gospel and evangelize all who will accept Christ as Lord and Savior. It seems impossible to miss this clear directive of the Scriptures. Christ's command of Matthew 28:19, 20 is in essence emphasized again in Luke 24:47, 48, Mark 16:15, and Acts 1:8. Also, in John 20:21 Christ sends his disciples into the world as the Father had sent him. The Apostle Paul, referring to all believers, states that Christ "gave us the ministry of reconciliation" (2 Cor. 5:18, NASB). He confirms on the basis of Christ's finished work that "He has committed to us the word of reconciliation. Therefore, we are ambassadors for Christ, as though God were entreating through us; we beg you on behalf of Christ, be reconciled to God" (2 Cor. 5:19, 20, NASB).

Dr. George Peters verifies the mandatory purpose of evangelism for the church.

> In the light of the totality of revelation, evangelism is the central thrust of the Bible. God is minded to make Himself known and to have the good news of the salvation in His Son communicated to all mankind. For this purpose He encoded His message in the Bible by revelation and inspiration of the Holy Spirit in an infallible manner. For this purpose He also called out in the Old Testament the people of Israel and in the New Testament the church of God. These are not institutions in themselves nor for themselves. They are institutions by the sovereign calling of God and for the purpose of His glory. This glory, however, manifests itself chiefly in the good news of the salvation in Christ Jesus, His Son, the only Savior and Lord. Toward this end the

chief energies of the Holy Spirit operate. Herein lies the supreme mission of the church.[1]

A survey of the book of Acts shows the natural commitment New Testament Christians had to evangelism. The Jerusalem church evangelized in the market place, in homes, in the synagogues, in jail, before rulers and kings, everywhere throughout the city. The high priest proved the extent of their witness when he said, "You have filled Jerusalem with your teaching" (Acts 5:28, NASB).

As a result of their aggressive, bold saturation evangelism, "all the more believers in the Lord, multitudes of men and women, were constantly added to their number" (Acts 5:14, NASB). The church grew!

THE EDIFICATION AND STRENGTHENING OF BELIEVERS

After explaining God's eternal purpose which was fulfilled in Christ, Paul stresses the unlimited power available to the believer through his Spirit (Eph. 3:16-20). He confirms that this power is to have a life-changing effect upon believers and is to transform their everyday walk. Paul exhorts the Ephesians on the basis of God's indwelling power, to practice their position in Christ (Eph. 4:1). Explaining how their walk should change, Paul emphasizes first the unity and functioning of this new body (Eph. 4:3-16). He then advocates a complete change of life-style, turning from incorrect thinking patterns (4:17, 18), sinful habits (4:19-23), falsehood (4:25), anger (4:26), stealing (4:28), improper communication (4:29-32), and moreover, grieving the indwelling Holy Spirit (4:30).

Understanding what changes God desires in us is one thing, but seeing it accomplished is another. What part does the church as a functioning organism play? How are believers to be strengthened and enabled to glorify and exalt their God? God desires an end product that will adequately reflect his image to others, and therefore he also reveals the process.

In the life of the first local body of believers Luke describes one of the basic purposes of the church when he records that "they were continually devoting themselves to the apostles' teaching and to fellowship, to the breaking of bread and to prayer" (Acts 2:42, NASB). The verses immediately following confirm the growth that resulted. The believers were strengthened and unbelievers were saved. As they dedicated themselves to the objective of growing in their faith, their simple yet powerful program worked.

While Luke reported what happened in the Jerusalem Church, Paul carefully unfolded the basic principles to the Ephesian Church.

In Ephesians 4:8-16, Paul unfolds several principles which form the means by which the church can glorify God. Since God desires the church to reflect himself to the world, men and women must first be changed. Therefore, Paul explains that God gave gifted men (vv. 8-11) for the purpose of equipping the

249

believers (church) to minister, which will result in the church being edified or built up (vv. 11, 12). The results are specifically cited in verse 13 when Paul refers to unity, knowledge of Jesus, maturity, and growth, which express the fullness of Christ.

Understanding this basic purpose of the church will result in the practical demonstration of stability in the face of false teaching and the proclamation of the truth in love (vv. 14, 15).

The illustration of the body is so appropriate to the understanding of this concept. Every part is necessary and has its own individual role to perform. Crucial to the accomplishment of this goal is that pastors and people properly fulfill their scriptural roles. When this occurs, God's Word promises "the growth of the body for the building up of itself in love" (Eph. 4:16, NASB).

Kent remarks:

> If even one Christian fails to develop spiritually, the church as a whole is not as strong as it ought to be. By growing spiritually as we ought, the unity of the body of Christ is preserved, the witness of the church in the world is maintained, and the growth of the church as a whole is accomplished.[2]

THE EXALTATION AND SATISFACTION OF GOD

The church that successfully evangelizes and effectively edifies will bring glory to God. Paul taught that God the Father "chose us in Him before the foundation of the world," and that "He predestined us to adoption as sons through Jesus Christ to Himself" (Eph. 1:4, 5, NASB). Why did he do this? The Scripture confirms that it was an act of his own goodness, "according to the kind intention of His will" (v. 5, NASB). Three times in chapter 1 of Ephesians Paul repeats the supreme motive of God for his church, "to the praise of His glory" (Eph. 1:6, 12, 14, NASB). Our redemption through Christ made possible the fulfillment of God's plan for his own glory. While there are other aspects of God's purpose, such as providing a dwelling place for himself (Eph. 2:22), revealing his wisdom to rulers and authorities in the heavenly places (Eph. 3:10), and securing a bride for the future (Eph. 5:27), the thrust of purpose is that which exalts, glorifies, and brings satisfaction to himself.

Paul emphasizes this main objective in his prayer of doxology when he says, "To Him be the glory in the church and in Christ Jesus to all generations forever and ever. Amen" (Eph. 3:21, NASB). No one else deserves the glory for the church.

The Corinthian church was glorifying everyone else except the One who deserved the honor and praise for this new institution. They were exalting the experiences of having the Holy Spirit and following human leaders who were only used by God to establish their local church. As a result Paul stated the supreme purpose of the corporate church in terms that every individual could understand. "Whether, then, you eat or drink or whatever you do, do all to the glory of God" (1 Cor. 10:31, NASB).

MacNair remarks that "the broadest expression of the universal purpose of the church is that the church exists for the glory of God."[3] He reasons that "this task of giving honor and glory to God is basic to everything in life and therefore basic to the church."[4]

Stedman agrees that "the first task of the church is not the welfare of men, important as that may be and much as it enters the picture. . . . The first aim is to live to the praise and glory of God."[5]

The supreme purpose of the church and the most challenging one to practice is the matter of exalting and worshiping God. Teaching and building the church to individually and corporately glorify, honor, praise, worship, thank, adore, and reveal our God is the greatest task of all. "Now to the King eternal, immortal, invisible, the only God, be honor and glory forever and ever. Amen" (1 Tim. 1:17, NASB).

CONCLUSION

Today it appears that a church seldom finds a balance among the activities of exaltation, edification, and evangelism. Somehow they must be connected in a logical sequence. The basic purposes of the church include three directions: toward God, toward itself, and toward the world.

If we envision two main objectives (edification and evangelism) for the church, we normally conclude that when they are being fulfilled God will be glorified. If there exists a wrong emphasis on evangelism, the growth of believers in maturity will be hindered, for there will be total concentration on "giving it out" without a proper concern for "taking it in." On the other hand, if edification becomes the only "reason for being" then the excitement of sharing Christ will dwindle and the church will lose the vibrant life that it should have. Believers must be constantly challenged by the teaching ministry and example of godly leaders to maintain the proper motivation (to glorify God), developed through a ministry to both believers and nonbelievers. A true understanding of the basic purposes of the church is the foundation for growth in quality and quantity.

35. The Priority of the Church

To have well-defined purposes suggests that a church has a good grasp as to why it exists. Purpose asks, "Why are we here?" and characterizes basic objectives. If a church is not fulfilling its purposes, obviously its priorities will also be incorrect. Priorities go beyond purposes and reflect the most important issues or activities. To operate on the basis of a priority listing affects how you will spend the most productive hours of your time as well as where you will use the greatest amount of energy. If a personal priority for a Christian is to "love God with all his heart" then there must be some practical way in which that is realized in his life. Time alone with God in the morning hours, obeying his word, putting him first in every consideration, etc., would be specific examples. So it must be with his church.

In the last hours of our Lord's ministry he spoke to the eleven disciples, saying, "All authority has been given to Me in heaven and on earth. Go therefore and make disciples of all the nations, baptizing them in the name of the Father and the Son and the Holy Spirit, teaching them to observe all that I have commanded you; and lo, I am with you always, even to the end of the age" (Matt. 28:18-20, NASB).

THE GREAT COMMISSION IS THE PRIORITY OF THE CHURCH

McGavran touches on the problem of the "many tasks" when he states:

> In mission today many tasks must be carried on together; yet the multiplicity of good activities must contribute to, and not crowd out, maximum reconciliation of men to God in the Church of Jesus Christ. God desires that men be saved in this sense: that through faith they live in Christ and through obedience they are baptized in His name and live as responsible members of His Body. God therefore commands those of His household to go and "make disciples of all nations." Fulfilling this command is the supreme purpose which should guide the entire mission, establish its priorities, and coordinate all its activities.[1]

On this issue of understanding the Great Commission, needless to say the church is not in agreement. Some equate the Great Commission with helping the hungry and meeting the social needs of people. Others struggle to balance the tension between evangelism and edification. It seems illogical that Christ in one of his last major directives would have given a confusing message. But different interpretations and "hobby horses" do exist.

Coleman, in his classic book, *The Master Plan of Evangelism*, stresses the priority of making disciples on the basis of the pattern Jesus set in his ministry. He says:

> Perhaps His total number of devoted followers at the end of His earthly ministry numbered little more than the 500 brethren to whom Jesus appeared after the resurrection (1 Cor. 15:6). . . . Jesus doubtless would not be considered among the most productive mass evangelists of the church. . . . He had to devote Himself primarily to a few men, rather than masses, in order that the masses could at last be saved. This was the genius of His strategy.[2]

In relating the principle of discipleship to today's church, Coleman says that the current obsession with numbers and the lack of concern for the preservation of new converts is a failure of the church, and he explains:

> Surely if the pattern of Jesus at this point means anything at all it teaches that the first duty of a pastor as well as the first concern of an evangelist is to see to it that a foundation is laid in the beginning upon which can be built an effective and continuing evangelistic ministry to the multitudes. This will require more concentration of time and talents upon fewer men in the church while not neglecting the passion for the world. It will mean raising up trained leadership "for the work of ministering" with the pastor (Eph. 4:12). A few people so dedicated in time will shake the world for God. Victory is never won by the multitudes.[3]

There is, however, another imperative in the last commands of Jesus. Its emphasis is upon *world* evangelism, the preaching of the gospel to every creature (Mark 16:15, 16; Luke 24:47; Acts 1:8). Reflecting this necessary emphasis, one writer explains:

> Edification is absolutely necessary, but in the list of God's priority, evangelism comes first. . . . The 10 churches in this book place evangelism primary in purpose, hence they are growing. Their methods may differ, but their mandate is unmistakable: They are to "Go into all the world and preach the gospel to every creature" (Mark 16:15).[4]

Peters wrestles with this problem when he writes:

> There is no question that world evangelism is the will of God and the design of the New Testament. Thus a tension is set up between the time-absorbing, individual, personal care needed for the deepening of the spiritual life of the believer—the making of disciples on the one hand—and the imperative, inner Spirit-motivation of world evangelism willed by the Father, commanded by the Son, and directed by the Spirit on the other (John 16:8, 11; 12:32).
>
> Such tension is not contradiction, but the divine pressure that re-

leases within believers their best. This tension finds its focus, intensity and solution in the church as an organism and as an institution. The church is God's creation for both of the above purposes — the making of disciples and the evangelization of the world. This is portrayed in the book of Acts and propositionally stated by Paul in Ephesians 4:11-16.[5]

There are many verses in the book of Acts in which both concepts are apparently brought together very naturally (Acts 2:46, 47; Acts 6:7; Acts 9:31; Acts 18:8-11). Thus Peter affirms:

> The church is God's instrument to mobilize, discipline and equip God's saints that they might perform nobly in the world the task of evangelizing. Only thus will the church fulfill her purpose. Only thus will the tension between the two imperatives in the Great Commission be resolved. Only thus will the world be evangelized. Such is the biblical basis of total mobilization and total evangelism.[6]

Virgil Gerber says:

> The central imperative of The Great Commission is to MAKE DISCIPLES. This means bringing men and women to Jesus Christ so that they give Him the all-inclusive "yes" of submission and faith.
>
> All the other action words in these verses are helping verbs. They are "going," "baptizing," and "teaching."[7]

Looking closely at the Great Commission and combining the thrust of the other texts as well (Mark 16:15; Luke 24:47, 48; Acts 1:8), three central issues for the church appear. They are (1) the Church "proclaiming and evangelizing," (2) the Church "perfecting and edifying," and (3) the Church "planting and expanding."

THE CHURCH PROCLAIMING AND EVANGELIZING

ACTION AND MOBILIZATION

The first issue that the church must face in order to proclaim and evangelize is that of *action and mobilization*. In the Matthew passage the helping verb or participle "going" is first. It could be translated "as you are going" or "while you are going." In the Mark passage the concept of going is also presented in participle form. It would be translated the same "while you are going." "Going" is not specifically mentioned either in the Luke or Acts passage; rather it is assumed. Christ never questioned or doubted that his true disciples would *go* into all the world; thus the "go" of the Great Commission is not set forth as an imperative, but assumed to be an inward motivation to evangelize the world. Hollis Green explains:

> It is not an order to "go," it is a plan of action for individuals who are in the process of "going." The "good news" of the gospel impels those who receive it to share their experience with others. . . . The Commis-

sion was for followers already in motion. The "go ye" was placed automatically in the heart of New Testament converts. Conversion became their motivation.[8]

The word for going, *poreuomai* (only in participle form), according to Vine means

> to go on one's way, to proceed from one place to another (from *poros*, a passage, a ford, Eng., *pore*), is always used in the Middle Voice in the N.T. and the Sept., and is the most frequent verb signifying to go; it is more distinctly used to indicate procedure or course than the verb *eimi*, to go (not found in the N.T.)[9]

A question with serious implications for the church today is "Who is to be going?" Obviously from the context, the eleven disciples were specifically meant, but when Christ said, "And lo, I am with you always, *even to the end of the age*," it is clear that all other true followers throughout time were included. Hodges remarks:

> Emphasis must be continually placed on the participation of the total body of believers in evangelism. Great spiritual awakenings are always characterized by the zealous witnessing and fervent prayer participation by the body of Christian believers. As a revival loses its original impetus, the tendency is to place more responsibility in the hands of a few leaders. The activities tend to move out of the homes, the streets, and the open air, and into the church building. The pastor assumes more and more of the responsibility for evangelism until the congregation's activity is mostly that of spectators. Thus the evangelistic activity of the church tends to stagnate.[10]

Wagner, as a result of his many experiences and research, reports that often efforts at "total mobilization" have failed, resulting in negative influences on church growth.

Wagner also explains that new Christians, "while they are going," have a greater potential to witness than older, more mature believers. The simple reason that they have a multitude of family relatives and friends who are immediate prospects. The person who has been a Christian longer has developed more friendships with believers than nonbelievers. In many cases, he has either "left them" or they have "left him."[11]

The imperative "go" implies that the main thrust will be outside the church building, Peters asserts:

> The major effort of evangelism is done *by* the church but not *in* the church; by *all* members and not only by a professional man or team. This, no doubt, is the biblical order and pattern.
>
> It is evident that if this world is to be evangelized, it will have to happen outside of the church buildings. The world is the field and not the church building. We must win the people in the world in which they find themselves, if they are ever to enjoy the salvation of God and

become members of the church of Jesus Christ.[12]

Peters quotes from the writings of Charles W. Kingsley to prove his position concerning "revolutionary New Testament Christianity" in evangelism.

During an encouraging all-day men's retreat, when men with their pastors and church leaders dared face their barrenness and accepted the challenge of the theme of growth, "Double in a Decade," a burdened Canadian layman stood to his feet and cried, "But under our present methods it took us over a half century to double. What are we going to do differently that will cause this growth?"

This is a good question. It calls for a drastic reorganization, a revolution of our thinking, our motives, our program.

Our evangelistic strategy of "building-centered evangelism" and "enlistment evangelism" falls far short of the New Testament. Both of these concepts have one glaring flaw that hinders our church from ever becoming the instrument of the Great Commission.

Gene Edwards said, "The flaw is this: The only people who can be won to Christ by these two methods are those who will deliberately get up, get dressed, go down to the auditorium, and willing expose themselves to the preaching of the Word. Most people will not do this! Today our *church building* concept of evangelism is the greatest single hindrance to world evangelization—not because we have the church buildings, but because we have failed to get out of them."

In many new communities across our nation, we have built new physical structures without building New Testament outreach. Imagine a farmer building a barn in a new field and expecting the barn to harvest the crop.

"We must get the right perspective," Edwards exhorts. "Realize the evangelism is not to be centered inside but outside the church building. Church is not a place to bring the converts into. It is a battle station to send Christians out from!"[13]

We need to change from being an inviting church to being an invading church. The church is to prepare its members to "go out" into the community and win people to Christ where they live and work. Church centripetalism must be changed to church centrifugalism.[14]

Benjamin's remarks indicate the faulty growth concepts held by many.

Comparatively speaking, few congregations today are following the New Testament principle of gathering and scattering. A study of congregational life in most religious groups usually reveals a "come-type" attitude. The faithful are exhorted weekly through the sermon, in the worship folder, and by the church paper to be "faithful to services." Much emphasis is placed upon "keeping up the attendance." A high attendance in proportion to the average is cause for elation, whereas a low attendance is cause for sagging spirits.[15]

256

The issue of mobilization and action depends upon every believer "going" into the world and proclaiming Christ. But to conclude on the basis of previous arguments that evangelism should *not* occur in the church is to make a great error. The problem again is one of holding two concepts in tension and getting the task of world evangelization accomplished. To say that Christians should not bring converts or even non-Christians into the assembly is to add to Scripture and in fact contradict it. In order for the normal Christian to be active in sharing his faith, he must not only hear the Word in the teaching ministry at the assembly, but he must feel an atmosphere and see examples of evangelism.

In the parables of Jesus there is an emphasis on both going and bringing. In Matthew 22:1-14 Christ likens the kingdom of heaven to a wedding feast, teaching of the coming marriage of the church to Christ (Eph. 5:27; Rev. 19:7-9). The issue of the parable is getting the guests to come. Verse 9 includes a command to go (imperative), find, and invite people to the wedding feast. In Luke 14:16-24, Christ speaks of a certain man giving a dinner who had invited many to come. But they would not come and gave many excuses. In verse 21 the head of the household commands his servant to "go out and bring in" the poor and crippled and blind and lame. And again in verse 23, "Go out into the highways and along the hedges, and compel them to come in, that my house may be filled" (NASB). Some may object to the argument, for in both cases the dinner will be in heaven and not in the church assembly as such. But the point is clear that they must come to Christ wherever he is and receive the proper wedding garments (Matt. 22:11-14; Rev. 19:8).

In the early church it is clear that "church buildings" as such did not exist until the second or third century.[16] The Christians gathered in at least three different places for instruction and fellowship. They (believers) met *in the temple*, as is clear from Acts 2:46; 5:20, 25, 42; and they also gathered together in the outer court known as the portico (Acts 5:12). The word used here for temple (*hieron*) according to Radmacher "is the whole compass of the sacred enclosure, the temple precincts, including the outer courts, the porches, porticoes, and other buildings in which the people gathered for worship.[17] The Scripture is clear that evangelistic preaching and conversions took place in that same location (Acts 3:1-4; 4; 5:20-25,42).

The believers also met in *homes* for instruction and fellowship (Acts 2:46; 12:5,12; Rom. 16:5; 1 Cor. 16:19). But the record includes the fact that the proclamation message took place in homes (Acts 5:42; Acts 20:20,21). In Acts 20 Paul is clear that he was teaching the elders of the Ephesian church *as well as* bearing witness to both Jews and Greeks concerning "repentance toward God and faith in our Lord Jesus Christ. . . . from house to house." Green in his excellent study, "Evangelism in the Early Church," affirms;

there was no such clear-cut distinction between the work of the evangelist and the teacher. This is, in fact, apparent throughout the period from St. Paul to Origen. Both of them evangelized through teaching the Christian faith. Origen's school at Alexandria was originally intended to inculcate basic Christian teaching. At the age of eighteen he was already leading this school "for elementary instruction in the faith." But it was an evangelistic agency as well as a didactic one.[18]

Green also verifies that many unbelievers through the early centuries came to know Christ during instruction-type meetings in homes.[19]

Christians also met in the *local synagogue*, for in James 2:2 we read, "For if a man comes into your assembly [synagogue] with a gold ring . . ." (NASB). In a town or city where many Jews would become saved often they would use the synagogue as the meeting place for the newly planted church.[20] As we investigate the record of the churches in the book of Acts we see a pattern established of evangelizing in the synagogues (Acts 13:15-44, Antioch in Pisidia; Acts 17:1-4, Thessalonica). Michael Green's remarks are pertinent:

> The synagogue provided the seedbed for evangelism among the Jews. Wherever there were Jews, there were synagogues, and all loyal Israelites were expected to attend weekly; furthermore, they attracted a number of "godfearers" among thoughtful Gentiles. Here was a ready-made congregation for Christian missionaries to address.[21]

The example of the church at Corinth provides another proof that evangelism and edification can both occur *within* the church. In 1 Cor. 14:23-25 it is obvious that unbelievers might at any time enter the local assembly and the result of a proper experience would bring conviction and "he will fall on his face and worship God."

Wagner, referring to Latin American Pentecostals, gives us a contemporary example of urging believers to evangelize outside the church but also inside the church.

> Those who analyze what they are doing theologically [Latin American Pentecostals] will tell you that they are only obeying Jesus' commands to go and preach the gospel to every creature. But they stress the word *go* in contrast to many others who expect unbelievers to *come*. They are aggressive in their evangelism while slower growing churches are invariably more passive. They untiringly proclaim the message of salvation to the lost, but they are not satisfied with proclamation only. They believe in persuading their unbelieving friends to commit their lives to Christ and become responsible members of His church.
>
> This last phrase, "responsible members of His church," is a key concept in unlocking the secrets of Pentecostal growth. To a very high degree, Pentecostals are church-centered, and this increases their effectiveness.
>
> By "church-centered," I do not mean that they are ingrown and introverted — just the opposite! They know that Christ has commanded

them to "make disciples," and they also know that disciples are made from those out there in the world. If Pentecostals were centripetal (inward-moving), they wouldn't grow. They are, instead, centrifugal (outward-moving), intent on meeting unbelievers on their own ground, and there persuading them to become disciples of Jesus. They do not expect the people to come to the gospel; they diligently take the gospel to the people.[22]

But contrary to some modern churchmen who hold the "go" concept to the exclusion of any "come" concept, Wagner affirms that many Pentecostals are led to Christ not only outside the church buildings but inside as well. In referring to the high percentage of "decisions" who become "disciples," Wagner states:

They make their decision right there in the church. The church, in a sense, is the spiritual delivery room for their new birth. Church members, not a visiting preacher from outside, are the obstetricians.[23]

Thus it has been demonstrated that the action of soul-winning can be done anywhere and anyplace where someone will go sharing the message of Christ with unbelievers who will listen and respond. The problem is not that people are not going, for our contemporary life-style certainly disproves that, rather it is that Christians are not proclaiming and evangelizing.

ANNOUNCEMENT AND MESSAGE

In order for the church to successfully fulfill the Great Commission it must understand its message and unceasingly proclaim it. The Apostle Paul shared his burden for the non-Christian Jew or Gentile when he said, "how then shall they call upon Him in whom they have not believed? And how shall they believe in Him whom they have not heard? And how shall they hear without a preacher?" (Rom. 10:14, NASB).

In order to adequately meet the need of proclamation, the church must understand three great words and their meanings. Those words include: (1) to tell the good news *(euaggelizesthai)*, (2) to proclaim or preach *(kerussein)*, and (3) to bear witness to the facts *(marturein)*.[24] The gospel must be proclaimed or announced; it consists of the best news man has ever heard; and it can be affirmed by facts which are thoroughly trustworthy.

Although there is a certain amount of overlap in the usage and meaning of these terms, there remain important practical distinctions.

Evangelism, of the gospel, deal mainly with the message itself. Peters explains the three forms of the word evangelism.

1. The word for "gospel," literally *evangel*, means "good news." It is found seventy-six times in the New Testament. The Anglo-Saxon form of it was Godspell, that is God-story, indicating that the Gospel concerns the great acts of God.
2. The verb *evangelize* means "to bring," or "to announce," or "to pro-

claim good news." It appears fifty-one times in the New Testament.

3. The word *evangelist* describes the person involved in telling the good news. It occurs only three times.[25]

An evangelist is a gifted person (Eph. 4:11) as seen in his superior ability to evangelize (proclaim with results) the evangel or gospel. Paul refers to the basic gospel message in 1 Cor. 15:1-4.

Now I make known to you, brethren, the gospel which I preached to you, which also you received, in which also you stand, by which also you are saved, if you hold fast the word which I preached to you, unless you believed in vain. For I delivered to you as of first importance what I also received, that Christ died for our sins according to the Scriptures, and that He was buried, and that he was raised on the third day according to the Scriptures [NASB].

Paul also notes the manner in which he presented it to them. He says it includes words "which I preached to you." To "preach" or "proclaim" is taking the role of a herald announcing a message with the full authority of his Lord.

Kittel affirms that "it is demanded, then, that they [the heralds] deliver their message as it is given to them. The essential point about the report which they give is that it does not originate with them. Behind it stands a higher power. The herald does not express his own views. He is the spokesman for his master."[26]

A herald in the Greek world was expected to have a strong voice and to be trustworthy for the deliverance of his message. The New Testament usage of the word "to preach," however, "does not mean the delivery of a learned and edifying or hortatory discourse in well-chosen words and a pleasant voice. It is the declaration of an event."[27] This is an important distinction, for all can herald the message. Paul stresses this when he writes to the Corinthian church. "And my message and my preaching [heralding] were not in persuasive words of wisdom, but in demonstration of the Spirit and of power" (1 Cor. 2:4, NASB). The issue here is that the believers must be *telling*. Without the heralds fulfilling their charge, the lost will never hear.

Dr. Bill Bright, president of Campus Crusade for Christ, recently affirmed that there is a great spiritual hunger today, contrary to what some Christians may believe. He explained that according to their (Campus Crusade) surveys across our nation "one out of two will receive Christ if the gospel is properly communicated by a person that is trained and filled with the Holy Spirit."[28]

Peters, after referring to the many methods of gospel presentation in the New Testament, submits:

It is well to note that the method of presentation is not the determining factor. The important fact is that no evangelism has happened until the good news has been *told*. The presence of the Christian and the humblest and most helpful service of a Christian in itself is not

260

evangelism. This may prepare the way for effective evangelism. But presence in itself is not sufficient.[29]

Telling or heralding assumes that one knows the message and also know how to properly communicate it so as to produce the intended result. In the process of "making disciples," every church and every believer should train and be trained in the art of heralding the good news. Their lesson can only be considered well-learned when they are successful in teaching others how and what to proclaim (2 Tim. 2:1, 2).

The need of training and teaching others to evangelize is more apparent when we consider the third concept, "to witness." Michael Green explains:

> It is primarily a legal term and was frequently used in Greek to denote witness to facts and events on the one hand, and to truths vouched for on the other. In both cases the personal involvement and assurance of the man making the witness was an important element.[30]

When Christ challenged his disciples to a proclamation ministry, he stated, "You are witnesses of these things" (Luke 24:48, NASB). In the immediate context, Christ had made reference to the Old Testament Scriptures and how they proved that he was indeed the Messiah. Getz affirms:

> As you trace this word ["to witness"] through the book of Acts it is obvious that in context it takes on a strong "apologetic" syndrome. Both Peter and Paul, the two apostles whose communication is described by this word, were attempting to convince their hearers that Jesus Christ was truly the Messiah promised in the Old Testament. They were not simply presenting the gospel but were attesting and giving evidence from the Old Testament as well as from their own personal experience that Jesus was the Christ.[31]

Since we are talking about the combination of facts and personal experiences which attest these truths, it is imperative that someone teach a believer the necessary facts. Christ, in the Luke 24 passage, was obviously performing that role, and he promised after his teaching that the indwelling presence of the Holy Spirit would empower them to "make disciples."

Becoming a disciple then includes learning scriptural facts which verify the claims of Christ along with instruction concerning the positive communication of the "good news." All of this teaching and proclaiming must be done in the power of the Holy Spirit (Acts 1:8).

Hollis Green sees the importance of the issue of telling when he concludes:

> Proclamation must have priority. Not necessarily pulpit preaching but proclamation: teaching, witnessing, declaring the "good news." The pulpit has its place, but somehow every believer must feel a responsibility to carry the "good news" everywhere. This must have priority in a program of growth in a local church. Unless proclamation of the "good news" has priority in the life of every believer, the true purpose of the church will be thwarted.[32]

One of the major hindrances to reaching "all the nations" is clearly all the believers who are not participating in the church's mandate. Is a believer a real disciple who is not sharing his faith and not continuing the reproductive cycle? Certainly not an obedient disciple, for Christ did not only give his Commission to the eleven or to certain full-time gifted "preachers" but to all who would follow him. Somehow the clarity of this message has been lost within the walls of the institutionalized church, for it appears that leaders are not processing disciples either. If the world is going to be permeated with the gospel of Christ, the church (institutional) must give the full responsibility for the Great Commission back to the believers in the church.

ACCOMPLISHMENT AND MAKING DISCIPLES

Just how successful should believers intend to be, in this matter of evangelizing the world? On the one hand we do know that every person will not come to Christ, while on the other hand we do not know who will. Many Christians today, whether they admit it or not, are neutral. A neutralist is one who believes that he is responsible to proclaim but not to persuade. To search is his responsibility but the finding is up to God. McGavran, one of the most dogmatic opponents of this position, is committed to persuasion. He states:

> We do not believe the neutralist position is *theologically* sound. It is out of harmony with the mainstream of Christian revelation. Christ's words and deeds contradict it. The apostles and the early Church would have repudiated it.[33]

Following the example of the Apostle Paul whose regular theme was the sovereignty of God, we must be impressed with his zeal, especially when he writes, "Therefore, we are ambassadors for Christ, as though God were entreating through us; we *beg* you on behalf of Christ, be reconciled to God" (2 Cor. 5:20, NASB). Paul's enthusiasm and sincerity was evident in his challenge to King Agrippa, who, upon hearing his piercing message, replied, "Almost thou persuadest me to be a Christian" (Acts 26:28, KJV).

Weld and McGavran, in their programmed learning text, *Principles of Church Growth*, summarize this position in simple terms.

> It is possible to preach to deaf ears. A common experience is to proclaim the gospel in almost empty churches. A mere homiletic exercise doesn't accomplish God's purposes. If I drop my keys while opening a door, just looking for them is not sufficient. I must continue until I find them. There is a biblical illustration to the same effect. It is not sufficient to look for the lost sheep. God wants it to be found. His purpose is finding, not seeking. Some "sheep" don't want to be found. If they continue in their rebellion against God without repenting, God's servant is not responsible for their condemnation. But he is obligated to seek the lost with intelligence and zeal, doing all that he can to find them.[34]

As we examine the Great Commission, we see that Christ did not command that we "attempt" to make disciples. He gave direction to each follower that he or she is to plan to succeed at the process of reproduction. If we are not "making disciples," something is wrong. Either we are ignorant of the message or how to properly communicate it, or our zeal is not great enough, or we're just plain disobedient. Peters affirms:

> Christ commissioned us to invite and to compel people to come in. There is an urgency in the motivation and tone of the announcer of the good news that arrests and attracts, draws and compels the listener. It is an encounter of men for decision, not only to listen but to consider. Evangelism never leaves man neutral; it compels him to take a position for or against Christ.[35]

Em Griffin, communications professor at Wheaton College, deals with the ethics of persuasion and explains the following ethical standard. "Any persuasive effort which restricts another's freedom to choose for or against Jesus Christ is wrong."[36] He adds that there are some persuasive techniques which are in reality manipulation and not in harmony with the Christian message. He further explains:

> But avoiding persuasion altogether is a luxury unavailable to the Christian. He takes seriously the right of each individual to choose, and he desires that God's way be a live option for every man. Without his persuasive effort, another might not be free to choose for Christ. He knows that no man is an island, and that to decide not to influence is to decide to let others' influence hold sway. The passive, silent Christian is, perhaps, more unethical than the other person.[37]

Virgil Gerber, a student of the Great Commission, has developed a concept known as "body evangelism." Contrary to other methods or types of evangelism, "body evangelism" emphasizes church growth to the point that participating churches are urged to discard any method which does not measurably contribute to its increase.[38]

If a local body of believers understands and fulfills their responsibility to proclaim and evangelize, thus making disciples, the church will grow.

THE CHURCH PERFECTING AND EDIFYING

As we study the Great Commission in the light of New Testament practices, it is clear that one who believed was expected to be baptized as well as become attached to the local assembly of believers. Thus, after the lost are sought and found, they must be folded. Tippett explains that it was McGavran who initially

> differentiated between quantitative growth by conversion from paganism or from the world, which he called "discipling," and qualitative growth within the Church, which he called "perfecting." It must

be insisted that both of these are essential to church growth theory, and each has its biblical base.[39]

After referring to many passages that teach the growth of individual Christians and the necessary perfecting growth of a local church, Tippett remarks:

Discipling and perfecting, then, are different but related kinds of growth—one the quantitative intake due to evangelistic outreach, the other the qualitative development to maturity within the congregation. Without the former the congregation would die. Without the latter it would produce neither leaders nor mature members. Without maturity and leadership there would be no organic growth of "the Body."[40]

THE PURPOSE OF BAPTISM

Although infant baptism has become an issue among some today, it cannot be disputed that the New Testament teaches that baptism is for believers. Personal faith in Jesus Christ was an indispensable prerequisite to baptism. In the following passages, water baptism is seen as the natural first step of obedience for the new disciple who has placed his faith in Christ: Acts 2:41; 8:12; 8:35-39—although verse 37 is not found in the most reliable Greek manuscripts, there can be no doubt that the eunuch had believed prior to his baptism; 9:18; 10:47; 16:14, 15; 16:33, 34; 18:8; 19:4, 5. F. F. Bruce states that "the idea of an unbaptized Christian is simply not entertained in the New Testament."[41]

It is important to the understanding of the Great Commission to distinguish between Spirit baptism and water baptism. According to 1 Corinthians 12:13, Spirit baptism is the act of the Holy Spirit by which he places every believer into the body of Christ. Romans 6:1-10 refers to this work of God as do other similar passages.

Water baptism is the obvious meaning of the Great Commission, for the simple reason that no man can "Spirit-baptize" another. Water baptism is the outward symbol of Spirit baptism. Scriptural evidence indicates that a person's profession of faith was immediately followed by water baptism, thus the time factor between Spirit baptism and water baptism would have been minimal. To take one example (Acts 2:41, 42), it is clear that as soon as the 3,000 believed the proclaimed message, they took the initial step of faith which made them candidates for water baptism. If we follow the order of the Great Commission and the order of the New Testament church in Acts, the perfecting-teaching ministry does not really begin until after baptism.

The consistent and uniform witness of Scripture is that any person is saved or justified by faith alone. Although water baptism is always closely related to the time of forgiveness in the New Testament, it is not a requirement or a work necessary for salvation. Inrig clarifies:

Those verses which might seem to imply saving efficacy for baptism are misunderstood if they are construed to make baptism a work which brings salvation. Baptism is the outward, visible confession of faith, expressed in action, not words. Without faith, baptism is valueless. With genuine faith, baptism is the dramatic expression of inner reality. To profess faith and to refuse baptism in the apostolic period is to throw doubt on the reality of that profession.[42]

Baptizing in the early church resulted in believers being added to that particular fellowshipping group of believers, as is evident in Acts 2:41, 42, 47. Beyond the issues of personal faith and baptism, the New Testament adds no other requirements for church membership. While there is no definite reference to church membership as such in the Scriptures (only a listing or numbering of widows—1 Timothy 5:9), there is the specific usage of the word "added" in the book of Acts. Hocking explains:

The word is used in four places in the book of Acts, 2:41 and 47, 5:14, and 11:24. The word in Greek for "added," *prostithemi*, is a compound word connecting the preposition, *pros*, meaning "toward," with the verb, *tithemi*, meaning "to place" or "to set." The Greek writers make use of this verb to signify that act by which cities, towns or provinces changed their masters, and put themselves under another government. Thus, the word is not merely a mathematical numbering. If based on Greek usage, it carries the sense of placing oneself under a new command or authority, leaving the old authority. This would certainly be a beautiful picture of the transition from being under Judaism and the law, to being under Christ. Literally, the word means "to place forward," that is, the placing of certain things next to things already in existence, for the increase of that which is already in existence.[43]

The New Testament church, in its simple straightforward obedience to Christ's last directive, recognized that believers who were brand new disciples were to be perfected after becoming one in Christ, not before. In reality, no congregation reaches the fullness of maturity, having achieved perfection to the limits of possibility. Weld and McGavran boldly clarify the issue.

The least perfected Church is better than the pagan people from which its members came. If their faith is sincere and if they receive adequate instruction, congregations will always improve. We can trust that the Holy Spirit will work through the Bible to demonstrate the implications of the Christian faith in every aspect of life. Sometimes less perfected congregations grow more. This is partly due to the fact that the Christianity which they profess is something simple that the common man can achieve. It is also due to the contact that these Christians have with parents and friends who have not yet been converted. Although they lack extensive knowledge of the Bible and don't always show the fruit of the Holy Spirit, they often produce more evangelistic fruit than better prepared Christians. And their evangelistic fruit is genuine even though imperfect.[44]

THE PROGRAM FOR PERFECTING

Once a fellowshipping member of the body of Christ and of the local assembly, the new disciple-learner must become a responsible Christian. In the words of Jesus this step is *"teaching them* [the new disciples who have been baptized] to observe all that I commanded you." This clarifies who the learners are, the subject material, and the identity of the teachers.

Whereas C. H. Dodd, in his book *The Apostolic Preaching and Its Development*, carefully drew a line between the preaching message and the teaching message, many current scholars are taking exception to his view. Those who were being taught could well be among others who were being preached to at the same time. Skinner states:

> There is no truth in the assertion that the apostles either preached the gospel *or* taught the church. In Jesus' own *teaching* as well as that of the early church, the *preaching* element is very prominent, often linked together within the same passages. [After referring to other authors and Scriptural references he concludes that] from such a perspective we may affirm that there is always a didactic element implicit within the apostolic evangelistic preaching.[45]

While it is true that the proclamation message is necessary for someone to become a believer, it may well be included in the teaching message directed primarily to believers. In fact, the Great Commission ought to clarify this issue, for it commands us to be making disciples as we are going, baptizing, and teaching.

It is interesting to note that believers were called disciples before they were called Christians, which occurred at Antioch (Acts 11:26). Thus it is obvious that one of the problems today is understanding what it means to be a disciple. If taken in its simplest meaning, the emphasis of the Great Commission is on evangelism. If taken to mean a strong mature believer, then the Great Commission results in an emphasis on edification.

Murphy, in stressing a theology of discipleship, explains:

> The Great Commission speaks of making disciples, not just converts. A disciple is one who believes in the doctrine of his teacher and follows him. The idea of following Christ is implicit in the word *disciple*. Professions of faith, therefore, that do not produce followers of Christ do not represent the New Testament concept of evangelization.[46]

Ortiz, in his study of the New Testament church, learned the meaning of a word that revolutionized his life and the life of the church he pastors. The word was "disciples." He explains, "We learned that a disciple is one who learns to live the life his teacher lives. Then, with his life, he teaches others to live the life he lives."[47]

In Acts 6:1, 7 the immediate result of the teaching and preaching of Jesus was a numerical increase of disciples. In Acts 9:18 and following, the Scripture records that Saul/Paul immediately associated with the disciples and immediately began fulfilling the Great Commission. According to Acts 9:25, 26, he had already gathered some new disciples around him, yet he was so new to the faith himself that the disciples in Jerusalem did not believe that he was a disciple. In the account of Paul and Barnabas at Derbe it appears that a new believer as well as a seasoned follower can be called a disciple. "And after they had preached the gospel to that city and had made many disciples, they returned to Lystra and to Iconium and to Antioch" (Acts 14:21, NASB). While it is not stated how long Paul and Barnabas remained in Derbe, the inference is a short time.

Perfecting is definitely a part of the Great Commission, but only after the "making of disciples" is a reality. In the example of Acts 2:41, 42, 3,000 disciples experienced perfecting by "continually devoting themselves to the apostles' teaching and to fellowship, to the breaking of bread and to prayer" (NASB). Here there are four simple elements which in a sense all make up the program of perfecting. It was a specific fulfillment of Christ's instructions.

The apostles' teaching. This is first in priority. The simple truth is that the New Testament church was continually devoting itself to the teachings of the apostles. This same doctrine is available to us by the inspiration of the Word of God resulting in the complete written revelation. This teaching is absolutely necessary for the growth of new disciples. For Peter said it well, "Like newborn babes, long for the pure milk of the word, that by it you may grow. . . ." (1 Pet. 2:2, NASB).

This doctrine of the apostles included "all that I commanded you" (Matt. 28:20), for it was the teachings of Christ, as well as additional revelation imparted by the Holy Spirit.

The fellowship. This is the word *koinonia*, and means a "joint-participation" or something that we share in common. Ultimately that which we share in common is Christ himself—the real essence of a disciple. MacArthur explains the three kinds of unity which result from understanding and experiencing true fellowship. They are:

> Positional unity, secured by the baptism of the Spirit; ultimate unity, secured by the Resurrection; and practical unity, which is presently unsecured but can be secured by the ministering of spiritual gifts and the sharing of love in fellowship.[48]

This practical fellowship that these new believers experienced resulted in literally a sharing of everything (Acts 2:42-45).

It is in the realm of fellowship that the community of Christians takes on the dimension whereby each believer is involved in perfecting others. According to the Ephesian 4:11-16 passage, growing up into Christ or maturity is dependent upon every joint and every part working properly, supplying its contribution to the whole, resulting in growth. Reflecting upon the pastor's role in perfecting, Skinner explains:

The word in Ephesians 4:12 for "perfecting," *katartismon* . . . suggests equipment for usefulness. Jesus encountered James and John "perfecting" their nets; that is, mending, repairing, and equipping their nets for service. The pastor's task is to make his congregation useful, to fit each member for his appropriate place in the program of Christian service.

Each church will therefore need a well-planned program to train people to exercise their gifts and to discharge their functions.[49]

The breaking of the bread. This was an additional element of the edifying ministry of the church. This phrase most certainly refers to the communion. Paul's example of breaking the bread with believers at Troas (Acts 20:7, 11) also indicates communion. The meaning of the breaking of bread is best understood by the words of Jesus, "This do in remembrance of me" (Luke 22:19; 1 Cor. 11:24, 25). Saucy remarks:

> Based upon common participation in Christ and His salvation, there is also in the Lord's Supper a communion of believers in the unity of His body (1 Cor. 10:16). These two thoughts of the remembrance of Christ and the fellowship with the members of His body are the focuses of the celebration of the Lord's Supper.[50]

As the breaking of the bread causes believers to remember Christ's past sacrifice of redemption, it also has reference to his present fellowship and future coming.

The prayers. According to the book of Acts, the early church was a praying church. The believers were meeting for prayer in Acts 1:14; 2:42; 3:1; 6:4; 12:5; 16:13, 16. Prayer became one of the key reasons for the growth of the early church. Commenting on the type of "prayer meetings," Gene Getz states:

> Evidently, New Testament "prayer meetings" did not usually involve "periods of prayer" or a "time" or an "evening" or a "day" set aside for prayer, though on occasions this was done. Rather, the normal process involved prayer, interwoven into a variety of experiences, as believers met together to be edified. And most significantly, prayer at the vertical level was frequently prompted by needs at the horizontal level. Prayer was oriented around human relationships and needs, which gave it meaning and vitality at the divine level.[51]

As we understand the program for perfecting that the early church continually participated in, it is plain that the central figure was the one who gave the Great Commission. The apostles' doctrine included the teaching of Christ. The times and occasions of fellowship involved the sharing of Christ. The breaking of the bread centered specifically on remembering Christ and his finished work, while the seasons of praying resulted in continued communication with Christ. Each segment of this simple program met real physical and spiritual needs, and as a result the church grew.

Both ministries (proclaiming and perfecting) are indispensable to a balanced growing church, for in reality we must advance in both directions at once. Tippett, giving warning, states:

> there is an undesirable kind of "perfectionism" which must be avoided—a self-satisfied perfectionism which shuts off the congregation from the world, encloses it, and robs it of outreach. The congregation guilty of this is static. It is worse than static—it is dying. The marks of true perfection or maturity in Christ are the various forms of Christian outreach.[52]

The issue that some churches lose sight of is that the Great Commission is framed in such a way that it must be self-perpetuating. Those who are followers, while being perfected, are also going, baptizing, and teaching the new disciples to do the same. "It is a continuous process by which men who are converted to Jesus Christ relate themselves to each other and become responsible, reproducing church members. These disciples go out to make other disciples, baptizing, teaching, and relating them to the church also."[53] Gerber, in stressing the point of the ultimate evangelistic goal, remarks:

> Thus evangelism in the New Testament does not stop with reaching people with the Gospel nor with the proclamation of the Gospel nor with public professions of faith in the Gospel nor even with relating them to the church through baptism and teaching.
>
> The evangelistic goal is not fulfilled until these new converts become reproducing Christians who complete the cycle and guarantee the continuous process of evangelism/church growth.[54]

Perhaps the tension is drawn even tighter when Weld and McGavran ask a hypothetical question. "But if you were a leader in a congregation that had to choose between opening a new evangelistic effort in another town or building a school for the children of evangelicals, which would you choose? Why?"[55]

To many today, if the church is "perfected" or "renews" itself, growth will occur and multitudes will be saved. McGavran, speaking for the church growth theory, boldly declares:

> That is not the New Testament way. Had God the Holy Spirit waited till the Jewish Christian community at Jerusalem all by itself broke the barrier to the Gentiles, He would have waited a long time. Instead, the fresh advance of the Christian faith, the new relevancy to the Gentile world was achieved by baptizing hordes of those who in the year 50 A.D. were outside the Church.
>
> Renewal to the New Testament Church did *not* come by creating cells of Jewish Christians so vitalized, so Christian that they were able to overcome their ethnocentrism and Jewish pride and see that Gentiles (all men) were able to be saved simply by faith in Jesus Christ, rather than by obedience to the law. *Renewal came by church growth*, by bringing new races into the Church, by multiplying churches around the Mediterranean.

We should not conclude, therefore, in narrow partisan fashion that "renewal is not the first need of the Church, that is expansion." We should conclude that today the great need of the world and the supreme commission of our Lord is simultaneous advance both in discipling and in perfecting, in both church growth and church renewal. Nations must be won. We must demonstrate what being a Christian in this new world in process of creation means. Both must be done simultaneously.[56]

THE CHURCH PLANTING AND EXPANDING

In our study of the Great Commission as the priority for the church today we have seen the importance of evangelism and edification being carried on in a continuous pattern. Further study of Christ's marching orders to his church reveals a similar command to expand. In Matthew 28:19 the command includes discipling "all the nations" or peoples. Mark 16:15 includes the entire world as the sphere and every creature (person) as the goal to which the gospel is be proclaimed. Luke 24:47, 48 directs us that the message of Christ's offer of forgiveness for sins is to be taken into all the nations beginning from Jerusalem. Acts 1:8 teaches that when filled with the Holy Spirit, believers are to witness of the facts of salvation to the most remote, farthest point of the earth. It is with this in mind that Virgil Gerber concludes that "the ultimate evangelistic goal in the New Testament, therefore, is twofold: (1) To make responsible, reproducing Christians, [and] (2) responsible, reproducing congregations.[57]

A COMMITMENT TO MULTIPLY LOCAL CHURCHES

Beginning with the great dispersion of the Jerusalem believers recorded in Acts 8, the disciples successfully multiplied congregations and planted additional churches. In fact "new congregations were planted in every pagan center of the then-known world in less than four decades."[58] As the believers were scattered, so was the seed of the gospel that would take root in various national soils. In Acts 9:31 a geographical broadening takes place so that believers are placed (as directed in Acts 1:8) "throughout all Judea and Galilee and Samaria" (NASB). Based on the understanding of the eleven disciples and the success that resulted from their obedience, it is evident that planting local churches in every city throughout the world is God's plan.

The dynamic church-planting efforts of the Apostle Paul, Barnabas and Silas, Timothy, and others who were all early disciples verifies the concept of local church expansion to which the eleven were committed.

High on the list of practical issues that face the growing church today is the commitment and planning that are necessary to begin other works. Costas agrees that:

Another principle of church growth strategy is the concentration on congregational multiplication in established church situations rather than in increasing the membership role of one local congregation. Wagner says that "the best way for a church to grow . . . is to be active in reproducing itself." He warns that such an enterprise is bound to be costly. It will cost people, time, money, and identification, but the fruit it will produce will make the sacrifice worth while.[59]

Palmer, reporting on church growth in Columbia, confirms that the reason certain groups are exploding with growth is because of their commitment to plant new churches.

The Assemblies of God concentrates on the *campo blanco* system, the Foursquare church on branch Sunday schools, the Panamerican Mission on home Bible-study groups and out-stations, and the United Pentecostal Church on preaching points. But by whatever name these outreach points are called, the goal is the same: to multiply local churches. Glen Kramer of the Assemblies of God summarizes this emphasis:

"Our *principal goal always* is to evangelize and establish churches. We are local-church centered. Some denominations have their emphasis on education and other ministries; our emphasis is on local churches."[60]

Concerning church multiplication in Thailand, Paul Davis, one of 800 missionaries of the Christian Missionary Alliance Church, writes:

From the day God said to Adam and Eve, "Be fruitful, multiply, replenish the earth," multiplication has been the secret of the growth of the human race, until this geometric progression has reached the staggering proportions of a population explosion.

Christians will lose the race to tell the world of Christ unless we are converted from our dedication to mere addition which slowly increases an organization, and begin diligently to apply to the living Church the principle of multiplication, so characteristic of the growth of a living organism.

Our experience in Thailand seems to indicate two dangers: (1) we aim too low—individual; (2) we aim too high—the district organization, the national organization.

Even when we grasp the simple fact that multiplication is the secret of the growth of the church, we need to ask—a multiplication of what? Not committees, not high offices, not even individual believers as such. We must apply our secret at the level of the local church. To start rapid growth by multiplication, we must encourage our own local church (be we pastor, layman, or missionary) to reproduce itself in another part of the city or in a neighboring town or village.[61]

Engel and Norton believe that one believer winning another is not enough. They state that "it is a demonstrated principle of church growth that Chris-

271

tianity gains in a society only to the extent that the number of existing churches is multiplied. Multiplication of new congregations of believers, then, is the normal and expected output of a healthy body."[62]

Southern Baptist author Belew, however, indicates potential problems when he remarks:

> Church growth may not always be determined by the number of church units organized. Two churches of very small membership and weak leadership will probably be little more effective than a larger one. On the other hand, dynamic church growth is not produced by very large churches who have committed most of their Christian witness to the staff members whom they employ.[63]

In a recent address, Dr. Charles L. Chaney, a Southern Baptist executive, unfolded an aggressive plan to multiply new churches within the states. The plan which he presented to Southern Baptists calls for the establishment of 2,431 churches in the North Central States.

In his challenge he wrestles with the arguments against starting new churches and identifies the movement as "the new Anti-Missionism." He maintains that the antimission spirit takes one of three forms. (1) *The Common Sense Syndrome* — which is the argument that there are already too many small struggling churches. (2) *Jackhylitus* — which is not meant to disparage the great job Jack Hyles is doing but describes the feeling among some that small churches are inferior and can't compare in many areas to the large growing churches. (3) *The One-for-One Strategy* — which can be summarized in the goal of having one large strong church in each city and that's sufficient.[64]

Concerning the problem of the large church versus the small church (an issue of concern today), Dr. Chaney states:

> Don't think that I'm against large churches. Before this century is out we will have several churches in these NCS [north central states] with more than 2,000 members. But the whole SBC has only 141 churches this size. With four or five exceptions, most are about 100 years old. Give us in the NCS 25 more years and we will have several large churches.
>
> Let me remind you that big churches come from little churches — nowhere else. That is true in two ways. All big churches were at one time small. But, every large church is composed of hundreds of Christians that were won to Christ in small churches. Every church in the SBC with more than 3,000 members is surrounded by hundreds of smaller churches that share Christ in every socio-economic stratum of the society. Hundreds of little Baptist churches preaching the Gospel to all different people that make up our society make large churches more likely to occur.[65]

Dr. Chaney concludes his inspiring challenge by encouraging each church to plan to begin another church or chapel by the end of 1978.[66]

A STRATEGY TO MULTIPLY LOCAL CHURCHES

The history of missions indicates that specific planning and goal-setting for the multiplication of new churches has not been the norm, at least since the days of Paul. But rather it has been common to assume that church growth will automatically happen without planning for it. Therefore, somewhat like spontaneous combustion, churches will be planted and grow according to God's timetable. As long as the church carries on the whole program of God in the world, church growth really doesn't matter.[67] McGavran challenges this as a common assumption that is a serious mistake, and adds that "church growth seldom comes without bold plans for it."[68]

> If we believe that expansion is the principal mission of the Church and that all secondary activities should contribute toward this goal, we must make definite plans to reach the desired objectives and measure our progress toward them. Without plans it is possible to float aimlessly, swept along by the currents of popular ideas or by many other pressures or influences.[69]

McGavran adds, "Only those who disregard the evidence can believe that church growth is a by-product of multifaceted mission. The assumption is contrary to the New Testament practice."[70] Several authors, including Weld, McGavran, Michael Green, Roland Allen, and others, refer to the strategy that the Apostle Paul used in his church planting endeavors. The Apostle Paul concentrated his efforts on cities, which were centers of communication, transportation, and commerce. Paul planned to begin churches. He would often go to the synagogue seeking to win his Jewish countrymen first (Acts 13:5 — Salamis; Acts 13:14 — Pisidian Antioch; Acts 14:1 — Iconium; Acts 17:1, 2 — Thessalonica; Acts 18:4 — Corinth). Paul gained a hearing with the Jews who attended the synagogues and later continued with the Gentiles (God-fearers) who also had heard of him and his message. As the Scripture indicates, before Paul reached Thessalonica he had been practicing his plan for starting churches, to the point where Acts 17:2 records, "And according to Paul's *custom*, he went to them, and for three Sabbaths reasoned with them from the Scriptures" (NASB, italics added).

Michael Green explains:

> The strategy of a man like St. Paul was basically simple: he had one life, and he was determined to use it to the greatest extent and at the best advantage possible in the service of Jesus Christ. His vision was at once personal, urban, provincial and global.[71]

From Paul's own words we know that he was a committed planter of churches, for he writes, "And thus I aspired to preach the gospel, not where Christ was already named, that I might not build upon another man's foundation" (Rom. 15:20, NASB).

Referring to the rapid and wide expansion of the early church, Roland

Allen emphasizes "spontaneous expansion," although he does explain the issue of organization as well.

> The Church expanded simply by organizing these little groups [early disciples] as they were converted, handing on to them the organization which she had received from her first founders. It was itself a unity composed for a multitude of little churches, any one of which could propagate itself, and consequently the reception of any new group of Christians was a very simple matter. By a simple act the new group was brought into the unity of the Church, and equipped, as its predecessors had been equipped, not only with all the spiritual power and authority necessary for its own life as an organized unit, but also with all the authority needed to repeat the same process whenever one of its members might convert men in any new village or town.[72]

What is keeping the contemporary North American churches from returning to the same pattern? Are there too many barriers in the twentieth century for local churches to assume the major responsibility in planting other congregations? Are we to say that while the example of the New Testament churches proves that church planting is the chief method of fulfilling the Great Commission, we can and should no longer follow that course? Murphy believes that young churches can parent new congregations and that we must return to this biblical practice. He states:

> Many churches complain that they do not have the necessary financial resources nor the highly trained leaders necessary for further church expansion. This is unscriptural. A new church, experiencing the power of the Holy Spirit and motivated along New Testament lines, can multiply cells of believers without dependence on missionaries or ordained ministers. The early churches did not depend on foreign missions for financial aid before planting more churches. Neither did the apostles import ordained men from Jerusalem or Antioch to pastor the hundreds of new churches being planted all over the Roman Empire. Pastors were found within the churches themselves. Local men, gifted by the Holy Spirit, were given on-the-job training by the apostles and other leaders, and thrust out to work.[73]

Palmer, speaking from a denominational perspective, reasons:

> Usually people and organizations achieve what they aim for, and this is true in missions as well. If the emphasis is on institutions and secondary ministries, then these will generally develop and prosper more than the churches. If a denomination's emphasis is on education, the greater results will be seen in its schools and students. But if the emphasis of a denomination is on planting and building up local churches, the result will more likely be growing churches that reproduce themselves.[74]

McGavran, whose concern and interest is clearly the multiplication of new churches, believes the sequence of the Great Commission makes it so. Since the command to "make disciples of all the nations" precedes "teaching them to observe all," he argues:

> Only churches which exist can be perfected. Only babies who have been born can be educated. Only where practicing Christians form sizable minorities of their societies can they expect their presence seriously to influence the social, economic, and political structures. The Church must, indeed, "teach them all things," but first she must have at least some Christians and some congregations.[75]

The local church today in its obedience to Christ's commands must return to a New Testament commitment and strategy to plant new churches. Church expansion as a goal must become part and parcel of the leadership and laity. Programs of home Bible studies on the local level, cooperation with mission agencies, and support of seminary graduates should all be seen as contemporary avenues to church multiplication.

Snyder believes that while small groups (the house-to-house method of Acts 5:42) are not a panacea, they are an essential component to Christian experience and growth. He states that the small group is the only structure dynamic enough to keep pace with the needs of our society and result in a significant evangelistic ministry.[76] He cites the following eight advantages of the small group structure in our urban world.

1. It is flexible.
2. It is mobile.
3. It is inclusive.
4. It is personal.
5. It can grow by division.
6. It can be an effective means of evangelism.
7. It requires a minimum of professional leadership.
8. It is adaptable to the institutional church.[77]

And it can be added that the small group structure can be used effectively in starting a new church.

SUMMARY

Why are we here? Where are we going? How are we going to get there? These are questions that the church should be constantly asking, while studying carefully the principles of Scripture for the answers. A clear statement of purpose should be widely communicated within each local church. Priorities of the ministry and specific objectives which fulfill the Great Commission should also be disseminated. Research-based strategy, plans, and goals resulting in proclamation, perfection, and planting efforts should be revised on a regular basis. Every possible effort should be made to evangelize not only the immediate community but to extend the outreach impact of the church to the ends of the earth. Evangelism and edification must be seen as two equal and necessary "reasons-for-being" which cause growth and bring glory, honor, and praise to God.

Christians make two false assumptions regarding church growth. First, some believe that if the church is growing in spiritual character, an automatic expansion in numbers will result; that quality will lead to quantity. This is not necessarily so. The second false assumption, a reversal of the first, is that churches which are growing in numbers automatically are growing in Biblical maturity. It is possible for a stagnant congregation to have individuals growing in grace and truth. Both congregations are growing, but neither has the full blessing of God.[78]

Since Jesus came "to seek and to save that which was lost" (Luke 19:10, NASB) and to build his church, we must also view the two as interrelated. As the local church is successful in accomplishing these tasks, the blessing of God will be evident and the church will grow!

Authorities Talk about Church Growth

36. Three Growth Principles for a Soul-Winning Church

C. Peter Wagner

Dr. C. Peter Wagner is associate professor of Church Growth at the School of World Mission and Institute of Church Growth, Fuller Theological Seminary in Pasadena, California. He is also senior consultant and board member of Pasadena's Fuller Evangelistic Association.

Peter Wagner serves as a charter member of the Lausanne Continuation Committee and is a former missionary to Bolivia (1956-71). His two latest book releases are **Your Spiritual Gifts Can Help Your Church Grow** (Regal) and **Our Kind of People** (John Knox). Other published books include: **Your Church Can Grow, Look Out! The Pentecostals Are Coming, Church/Mission Tensions Today,** and others.

A Phi Beta Kappa honors graduate of Rutgers University, Dr. Wagner also attended Fuller Theological Seminary (M. Div., M.A.), Princeton Theological Seminary (Th.M.), and University of Southern California (Ph.D.).

As Jesus explained it, there was one reason above all others for deciding to leave the glories of heaven and come to earth to live and to die. He put it this way: "For the Son of Man is come to seek and to save that which was lost (Luke 19:10, KJV). After he had instructed his disciples for three years, made the atonement on the cross, and risen from the dead, his very last words to those who would carry on his work were: "Ye shall be witnesses unto me . . ." (Acts 1:8, KJV). The Great Commission constitutes the marching orders of the followers of Jesus Christ.

That is why I consider it of utmost importance that every church professing loyalty to Jesus Christ be a soul-winning church. Winning souls in itself, however, is not quite enough. True commitment to Christ carries with it a simultaneous commitment to the body of Christ. Jesus' Great Commission tells us to go and make *disciples* of all nations (Matt. 28:19, 20). Disciples are those who accept Christ, who are baptized, and who continue as responsible members of a local church. When this biblical principle is clearly seen and acted upon, a soul-winning church will also be a *growing* church. All too many churches give lip service to soul winning, and some even invest substantial quantities of time, energy, and money in soul winning, but year after year show little or no membership growth.

Why does such a thing happen? Church growth is complex, but through the years that I have been studying the growth dynamics of American churches, I have come to the conclusion that there are three principles above all that must be followed if a church is to grow.

PRINCIPLE 1: A DEDICATED PASTOR
WHO WILL LEAD HIS CHURCH INTO GROWTH

Jesus himself is the great shepherd of the sheep. His undershepherd in each local church is the pastor. Whereas each individual Christian person is directly accountable to Jesus Christ, when it comes to the *church*, no one is as accountable as the pastor. This is one of the reasons why, as I have studied growing churches, I have found that a pastor who is willing and able to lead his church in growth is the first vital sign of a healthy church.

To be perfectly frank, many churches are not growing because their pastor does not want them to grow. He is often not willing to pay the price for growth. What are the chief aspects of this price for growth that scare some pastors off?

The first price to pay for growth is hard work. Identify a growing church and you will identify a hard-working pastor. The routine of the status quo is all too comfortable for many pastors, so they decide they are working hard enough. Pastoring a growing church may be enjoyable, but it is not easy. This is why church growth is not high on the agenda of many of today's pastors.

A second price that pastors must pay for growth is that they must be willing to share leadership. By this I do not mean the top leadership. There should be only one senior minister. Many churches have attempted a plurality of elders concept of leadership, and only a few of them have succeeded in sustaining vigorous church growth. Furthermore, most of those who have can clearly identify a "first among equals" who functions as the undisputed top leader even though he might not have the title.

The leadership that must be shared is on two levels: the staff level and the lay level. Growth-minded pastors must be willing to delegate responsibilities to other professionals whom they hire as staff colleagues. This does not apply to churches up to around 200 active members, but it is essential if the church is to grow through the 300 or 500 mark and beyond. Besides the staff, gifted lay leadership needs to be discovered and trained and put to work. Unfortunately, many pastors (a) do not have the ability to lead a staff effectively and (b) are threatened silly by strong lay leadership. Such a person is not destined to lead a church into much significant growth.

A third part of the price that pastors must pay for growth is a willingness to have church members whom they cannot personally pastor. This for many is not only a difficult, but an insurmountable barrier. They have been brought up in the rural or small church tradition that the pastor must take direct responsibility for the personal needs of every church member. Every home is called on at least once or twice a year. Members who go to the hospital expect one or a series of pastoral visits. The pastor provides premarital counseling for all young couples. He visits every Bible study group, addresses prayer circles, and says grace for the women's tea. He marries people and buries them. He consoles parents of wayward children. He is a shepherd to all.

Again, for a church of up to 200 this may be feasible. But if the church continues to grow, the pastor must be willing to move from what has been called a "shepherd" attitude to a "rancher" attitude. A rancher sees to it that all the people are properly cared for and counseled and consoled, but he himself does not attempt to do it personally. He recruits and trains others who are gifted for that task so that his energies can be used for more crucial and specialized leadership roles.

PRINCIPLE 2: A CONGREGATION MOTIVATED FOR GROWTH AND WILLING TO PAY THE PRICE

While I have yet to see a vigorously growing church where the pastor does not want the church to grow, I also have yet to see one in which the congregation does not want their church to grow. The active participation of the people of God is crucial for church growth. But while both pastor and people are essential, the order must not be reversed. A congregation that wants growth with a pastor who does not is an unlikely prospect for growth.

Just as there are certain prices that a pastor must pay for growth, there are also prices that the people of the congregation must pay if their church is to grow. What are some of them? What are some of the characteristics of a growth-oriented congregation?

The first characteristic of a growth-oriented congregation is a willingness to follow growth leadership. The people of the congregation honor, love, and follow the leader God has given them. I once heard a pastor say to a group, "There are only two requirements for membership in my church: pay your tithe and love your pastor." The remark was meant to be humorous and it did draw a laugh. But there was a good deal of truth behind it, since his church then had about 3,000 members and was growing rapidly.

Many churches don't grow because a strong-minded group of lay leaders has gained control of them and they have long since decided not to surrender their leadership to any pastor. Their usual tactic for preserving that control is to change pastors every two to five years. This is highly effective in prohibiting any pastor from usurping their leadership power. It is equally effective in keeping a lid on the growth of the church.

The second characteristic of a growing congregation is its willingness to pay the bills. Stingy, miserly, penny-pinching Christians are not conducive to growth. Admittedly, some church growth is quite economical, and I believe such models as the house church movement are likely to increase over the next ten years. Nevertheless, most church growth in America has, does, and will cost money—plenty of it. Growth usually means a sanctuary, surplus parking areas, Christian education units, staff salaries, choir robes, audio visual material, office supplies, buses and vans, and more. Christians in growth-oriented congregations know this and are willing to tithe their income and add generous offerings to that to make it happen. They also end up happier, more attractive Christians because in the process they discover that they cannot outgive God.

The third characteristic of a growing congregation is that the people are willing to readjust their fellowship patterns. One of the major reasons why people stay in a church once they have joined is that they find there a quality of love and fellowship that can be found nowhere else. Christian fellowship is highly important in church growth. But it should never be considered the ultimate value. If it is, it can get in the way of winning the lost to Jesus Christ.

Many churches fail to make newcomers feel welcome. Warm and loving fellowship groups have been formed in which people enjoy each other very much. That is the good news. But although they would never verbalize it, they really do not want strangers in the group. That is the bad news. Many churches which have aggressive soul-winning programs and which report high yearly baptisms but still fail to grow are weak in this area. New church members seek in vain to enter a fellowship group and in three to six months they are gone. Most of them don't even bother to say goodbye.

PRINCIPLE 3: A CHURCH WHICH UNDERSTANDS WHERE IT IS AND WHERE IT WANTS TO GO

This last principle needs to be examined more by churches having growth problems than by those which are showing vigorous growth. Growing churches already know where they are and where they are going. They are doing things right and God is blessing them. They are in good health, and healthy churches do not need a physician.

But churches which have been growing only slightly or not at all should be deeply concerned with their health. They need to realize that there is something wrong, and they need to get to the bottom of it. Up until recently there has been very little skilled outside help available for ailing churches. Church leaders have known whom to call if they or their children have awakened with a rash or a fever or chest pains or dizziness. But they have had no one to call if their church has begun to show symptoms of ill health. Many, in fact, can't even recognize the symptoms when they do show up.

This situation is now being cared for. We have available an increasing body of knowledge concerning both the vital signs of a healthy, growing church and the diseases frequently seen in an unhealthy, nongrowing church. Skilled and experienced Christian workers are now being employed by denominations, districts, and interdenominational agencies which can fairly rapidly diagnose the health of a given church and make suggestions as to what to do about the situation. One organization has even developed and marketed a sort of do-it-yourself "Diagnostic Clinic" that can be used by pastors to get a better understanding of what might ail their churches.[1]

Once a church has an accurate picture of its own health and growth opportunities, it should set specific measurable goals for growth. A faith projection answering the question, "How many people can we trust God to bring to himself and to bring into membership in our church in the next five years?" is a powerful instrument for future growth. The Bible says that "without faith it is impossible to please [God]" (Heb. 11:6, KJV). Making a projection and holding each other accountable for attaining it is one obvious way that the faith dynamic has been used of God in many, many churches. To grow well, a church needs to understand where it is and where it wants to go.

I believe that Jesus wants to see every one of his churches healthy and growing. He wants souls being saved and new Christians enjoying the thrill of worship and fellowship and the power of the Holy Spirit in their lives. There is no better example of this happening than in that church formed in Jerusalem on the day of Pentecost. Part of its life-style was that "the Lord added to the church daily such as should be saved" (Acts 2:47, KJV). With God's help this also can be a description of your church.

37. Why Some American Churches Are Growing and Some Are Not

Donald A. McGavran

Dr. Donald A. McGavran is senior professor of Missions and was founding dean of Fuller Seminary's School of World Mission and Institute of Church Growth from 1965-1971.

Recognized as the father of the modern Church Growth movement, Dr. McGavran served as a missionary executive in India (1923-1955). After founding the Institute of Church Growth at Northwest Christian College in 1961, he founded the School of World Missions at Fuller Theological Seminary (Pasadena, California).

Among the many books written by Donald McGavran are **Church Growth and Group Conversion, The Bridges of God, How Churches Grow, Church Growth and Christian Mission, Understanding Church Growth, How to Grow a Church** and **Back to Basics in Church Growth.** He is editor of **Global Church Growth Bulletin.**

Dr. McGavran is a graduate of Butler University (B.A.), Yale Divinity School (B.D.), Indianapolis College of Missions (M.A.), and Columbia University (Ph.D.).

God is granting a revival to his people in the United States. As we plan and pray for our congregations and denominations to rebound in the area of growth, it will help us to see why some of them are growing and some are not.

Direct your attention to eighteen denominations here in America. Between 1964 and 1974, nine grew and nine declined. The Disciples of Christ declined most—a whopping 34 percent. The Episcopal Church declined 19 percent. The Reformed Church and the three United Churches shrank 10 to 12 percent apiece. Three Lutheran denominations decreased by 4 to 6 percent.

The nine denominations which grew are worth careful study. Their *median* growth was 33 percent. In an America where the old, powerful denominations were registering 33 percent *loss*, these churches were registering 33 percent *gain*. Pentecostal churches did about as well as the others, though no better than the others. Churches cannot offer lack of Pentecostal emphasis as a reason for nongrowth. The Salvation Army, the Nazarenes, the General Conference Baptists, and the Alliance all grew well. These are earnest Christians, but not Pentecostal. Their congregations grew for reasons possible to any church made up of earnest Christians.

Note that the Southern Baptists grew at only 18 percent. When a denomination gets to be 11 million (as they were in 1964) it suffers from built-in antigrowth factors. Many of its congregation pass away. Many congregations get set in their ways and remain content with tolerable decline. All the antigrowth factors which assailed the 11-million-member United Methodist Church also assailed Southern Baptists. Nevertheless, Southern Baptists grew 18 percent, which was 28 percent more than the United Methodists.

The Alliance grew very well. Its growth cannot be credited to its being small, because scores of small denominations in America plateaued and were quite happy not to grow. Neither smallness nor largeness has anything to do with whether churches grow or decline. The Alliance was simply doing those things which make churches grow. It strictly eschewed those things which make churches decline.

In America the very best denominations are often the least growing. Many respectable denominations manned by educated ministers are not growing. They support their seminaries well, maintain high standards, carefully teach the Bible to their members, build beautiful churches, stress brotherhood, and play an important part in civic affairs. But they pay little attention to propagating the gospel. It is regrettably true that the best denominations are often the least-growing.

The subject of this chapter gains a certain piquancy from this fact, that the best often grow the least. It ought not to be so. I am convinced that it is not necessarily so. Indeed, the truly best churches—including your own—*can* generate those convictions and multiply those activities which make churches grow. The truly best churches can eliminate those attitudes and activities which inhibit and prevent church growth.

I lay before you, then, five great reasons why some American churches are growing.

REASON 1: THEY BELIEVE THAT GOD WANTS HIS CHURCH TO GROW

They demonstrate this belief by praying for church growth. If we would know what a person considers really important, let us observe what he prays for. What is considered unimportant seldom enters into prayer. What is considered supremely important automatically is laid before God. Even skeptics pray on the battlefield.

When a congregation or a denomination is possessed by an inner vision of the tremendous difference it makes for human beings to be in Jesus Christ and observe the tremendous loss suffered by those who live without conscious faith in him, *then* it pours out ardent prayer that lost sons and daughters return from the far country to their Father's house. *Growing churches pray for growth.* They align themselves with God's unswerving purpose to save men and women through faith in Jesus Christ. They beseech God to grant his grace to multitudes now living on the pitiful resources available to worldly people, and to turn them toward the light.

Growing churches also regularly pray that Christians may become skillful finders of lost sheep and responsible stewards of the grace of God. They bathe in prayer every activity of the church intended to incorporate men and women into living churches. They petition that the power of the Holy Spirit will operate *beyond* our poor efforts, working a deliverance greater than we had dared imagine.

Prayer can be taught by every congregation, every minister, and every denomination. As your churches turn their attention to the redemption of mankind, make sure that all prayer from the pulpit, all devotional manuals, and all catalogs of prayer are purposefully filled with prayer for specific *church growth* — the winning of certain individuals, the churching of certain populations, the empowering of the hundreds of evangelistic task forces which your denomination will soon be forming and setting to work. Pour out great prayer for all leaders, that they may kindle a flame of concern for the starving multitudes perishing in a famine of the Word of God. This famine is made more terrible because we who have abundant supplies of the bread of heaven often live just across the street from those who are starving. And many of us find it difficult to believe they are really hungry, let alone starving.

By way of contrast with all this, declining churches seldom pray for church growth. They pray (often at great length) for members of the church who are sick. They pray for building funds. They pray for missionaries out around the world. They pray for the governors of our country and the spread of peace. *But they pray little for church growth.*

Observe carefully the prayers of your churches, your colleagues, and yourselves. If your observations confirm mine, take whatever steps are needed to make your congregation noted for its powerful prevailing prayer that unbelievers may come to salvation.

Rapid growth of the church must be seen again, as in apostolic times, to be pleasing to God. He wants ripe fields reaped to the last sheaf. The Savior — not secular hunger for numbers — constrains obedient Christians to harvest.

Growing churches also demonstrate their conviction that God wants his church to grow *by preaching for church growth.* They pray for church growth and they preach for church growth.

The Scriptures are full of magnificent passages which require burning, life-changing evangelism. "I came to seek and save the lost," our Lord declared, and there are tens of thousands of these poor people within driving distance of most of our congregations.

In the amazing high priestly prayer of our Lord recorded in John 17, we read that he said, "As thou hast sent me into the world, I have sent them into the world" (v. 18, NEB). The purpose of the sending is clear. Five times in that prayer, our Lord declares that the *basic purpose* of his appointing and teaching and sending his disciples was that "the world may believe that Thou didst send Me." When the world learns *that* and believes it, the world will experience both an individual and a corporate salvation. Telling men *that* is still the basic purpose of Christ's sending out his servants. There are *hundreds* of such passages, which are there to be expounded. They are not isolated proof texts, but are part of the main thrust of all Scripture. It is God's intent that the Church—the body of Christ, the household of God—should *multiply and ramify throughout the earth*, to bless mankind and to move societies toward righteousness. Growing churches preach this effectively, persuasively, and repeatedly.

Growing churches develop, teach, and give an honored position to a *theology of church growth*. Our generation has been exposed to a plethora of specialized theologies—of liberation, of brotherhood, of justice, and of many other good ends. If these specialized theologies have a place—and they do—how much more should a basic theology of evangelism, on which all these others depend, be honored and taught in American churches and seminaries.

I emphasize the point because the decline of some mainline churches coincides with the spread of anti-evangelism, antichurch growth theologies. Recently, a theologian of the Reformed Church in America (RCA), one of the numerous plateaued denominations, published a blast against church growth, alleging all the tired theological rationalizations why Christians should not be concerned about it. But he had not reckoned with the new wind blowing. The editor of the RCA's *Church Herald* spread across a whole page a letter from Dr. Win Arn, ably defending the position that evangelism and church growth are the essence of any true theological understanding of the Christian faith. Specialized theologies are, alas, being proposed as *substitutes* for a basic theology of evangelism and church growth. This serious error is a major contributing factor in the decline of some American churches.

REASON 2: GROWING CHURCHES INTEND CHURCH GROWTH

Because growing churches believe God wants church growth, they determine to grow. Of course, the conversion of persons and the growth of the church is the work of the Holy Spirit. Those who intend church growth are simply responding to the leading of the Holy Spirit. He moves the church; and the church, filled with the Holy Spirit, sets about the work of God with renewed zeal. Looked at from the divine point of view, we can say that as church growth sweeps America, God is pouring out his Spirit. Looked at from the human point of view, we can say that the empirical church is girding itself for growth.

Such intent manifests itself in a mighty multiplication of work specifically aimed at church growth. Men live at 10 percent of their efficiency. Churches do too. Few congregations work at top speed. No congregation is working twenty-four hours a day. Few are working eight. Every congregation has a large reservoir of power which it has yet to tap. Whatever it is doing, it can do more. Most of the time it can do much, much more. If it is putting twenty hours a week into realistic evangelism, its 500 members could easily put in 200 hours. Indeed, if only fifty of the 500 were to put in four hours a week (one evening) they would put in 200 hours of evangelism.

I was talking to a district superintendent of a denomination in the Philippines which has been showing marked growth. He said, "We figure that for every convert who sticks, our people put in a thousand hours of personal work." Let me assure you that no amount of orthodox belief and no amount of prayer unaccompanied by work will be honored by God. If our programs must be bathed in prayer, it is equally true that our prayers must be bathed in work. American churches are called to magnify their evangelistic labors. That is what an unstoppable passion to share the love of God means.

Dr. Peter Wagner, so greatly used by God in America today, has recently written that church growth men must be prepared to pay the cost of church growth.

A fruitful new concept in church growth being advocated by David Wasdell of England deals with the intent to grow. He says that growing churches create an adequate "church growth task system." Every congregation has three task systems—that which deals with the public worship of God, that which raises perhaps a $100,000 a year, and that which reaches out to the whole world.

A congregation which has these and does *not* have a *task system focused on the growth of the church* does not grow. The church growth task system must be adequate. This means that it must be adequate for that particular congregation, at its particular point in history, with its particular leaders, and its particular resources of Spirit and flesh. As American churches gear for growth, each must ask itself, "Has our congregation a task force designed specifically for finding the unchurched and winning them to ardent life in Christ?"

A simple way to estimate the intent to grow is to count the number of men and women putting in regular time every week *out there* calling on the multitudes of masterless, shepherdless men and women, boys and girls, and doing everything possible to bring them to a knowledge of the Savior. I call these "Class Two" leaders. How many Class Two leaders do you have in your congregation, in your conference, in your district? How many hours are they putting in every week? Have you designed a system of training these essential workers which makes them effective in their work? Do you make sure that such training and such sending forth gets done whether anything else gets done or not? If the intent is to grow, let me assure you that nothing you do will be of greater value than to train and deploy a task force for church growth, and to keep it blessed, month after month, year in and year out.

I said that the second reason churches grow is that they *determine* to grow. Any real determination speedily discovers that *measuring* church growth is a very helpful activity. How much has taken place? In what sectors of the church has it taken place? How much is now taking place? How much will you project for the coming year? The coming five years?

This facet of the intent to grow is so obvious that I shall not stress it. Let me observe, however, what a flood of light Dr. Hunter cast on the real problem when he wrote to the United Methodists:

> The basic reason for our net loss is *not* that we are losing more people out the back door than we used to. Our rate of losses has been relatively the same since 1949. Our problem is that fewer people are coming in the front door. For instance, in the late '50s we brought in some 400,000 per year. Today we bring in about 230,000.

Exact measurement tells us where the difficulty lies. The brain scan tells the surgeon exactly where the tumor is. Class Two leaders can measure the many different aspects of church growth and portray these to the whole congregation and its leaders in graphs, charts, tables, and pictures. Everyone should see where evangelistic efforts may be spent to best advantage.

Intent to grow must never be mere words. It must be incarnated in deeds, recorded in hours spent, and sufficiently exercised so the whole body glows with radiant energy. Growing churches work at church growth.

When one turns to American churches which are not growing, he finds them *not doing* what makes churches grow. They do not feature church growth in their national magazines. They do not throw the spotlight on their churches and ministers whom God is blessing with church growth. Sometimes they minimize growth or actually denigrate it. Their national assemblies, synods, and conventions pass multitudinous resolutions about everything else but church growth—and the secular press picks up such actions and broadcasts them. The impression members get is that the really important issues are other than that of discipling unbelievers.

When I examine church budgets, I find that rarely is even a tenth of the income devoted to evangelism and church growth. Sometimes out of a budget of a couple of hundred thousand, $500 is allocated to an annual week of evangelism. A recent nationwide computer-selected survey of 5,000 pastors indicated that in planning for the coming year more than half the pastors gave a low priority to evangelism and church growth. The pastors are secure. Their people are content. Their budgets are adequate and they are looking after the flock. Some pastors fear church growth, knowing it will bring more work and more problems. It seems simplistic and yet I believe it is true, that *most nongrowing churches neither want to grow nor intend to grow. They are contentedly doing those things which do not lead to growth.* It is as simple as that.

REASON 3: GROWING CHURCHES
RECOGNIZE SOCIAL REALITIES

I am asking, "Why are some American churches growing?" My third answer is that in devising a growth strategy for their churches they *recognize the social realities* and teach these to their members, leaders, and task forces.

Church growth does not take place in a vacuum. It occurs in an enormously complex society, which is really a kaleidoscope of changing parts. Society is constantly changing. Society is in revolution. Each generation establishes a new place for itself. The Irish a hundred years ago and the Italian immigrants eighty years ago were a depressed part of the American population. Not today! The 1980 agnostic segment of the American elite quite frequently had mothers and fathers who were devout Baptists, Episcopalians, or Presbyterians. Society is not an unchanging mosaic. It is a kaleidoscope. Every piece is on an express train. Many pieces are going in different directions. This is the social reality.

Growing churches recognize this social reality — both the separate strands and pieces *and* the fact that each one is changing at a different rate and in a somewhat different direction. American churches are growing in this highly mobile milieu.

In addition to believing that growth is commanded by God and to determining to grow, growing churches recognize the current social realities and adjust their prayers and growth activities to the real scene.

Paul, the apostle to the Gentiles, recognized the social realities. He knew the best way to win the Gentiles was to start with those "devout persons" who were greatly attracted to the God of Israel but were not ready to go all the way and become circumcized Jews, keeping the full law. Devout persons welcomed the good news that men were saved by faith not by law. They could become followers of the Savior without culturally becoming Jews. These Gentile believers had multitudes of close relatives who were not allied to the synagogues, who were not devout persons. And across the bridge of family relationships, the gospel flowed to them also. The Apostle to the Gentiles had to start with the *Jews*. That was the social reality.

Today we must identify the social realities of our industrial urban society. Let us observe the complex social systems and behavior patterns of our congregations. Let us take advantage of the insights of the sociologists and management experts so abundantly available. Let us take seriously the social structure of small groups and the dynamics which create change in small groups and harness these to the spread of the gospel and the multiplication of churches.

Here in America, ethnic enclaves are enormously important for the growth of all churches. In Los Angeles the Korean, Amerindian, and Greek communities are cases in point. A couple of years ago I was speaking to the General Conference Mennonites in Calgary, Canada. The Mennonites formed an ethnic enclave in that part of Canada. In certain rural areas they were almost the whole population. Everyone was already a Mennonite and there could be no church growth. In the burgeoning cities, however, as second- and third-generation Mennonites moved to town and as some of them married out of the Mennonite community, many were being lost. The city churches of the Mennonite persuasion were growing, but were not conserving nearly all their people. A nearby denomination was growing considerably. Most of its converts were lost Mennonites. It was not stealing sheep. It was gathering lost sheep.

Ethnic enclaves are enormously important. In the half-million-member Japanese community only 50,000 are Christians of any sort. At least 450,000 Japanese Americans are growing up as non-Christians, most of them as secularists. The massive program of evangelization, which is required to present the gospel adequately to this gifted and able people, is not being mounted. They are not being won, either into Anglo churches which welcome Japanese members, or into Japanese congregations which maintain an ethnic identity. Why not put enough prayer and muscle into evangelization of Japanese Americans—a highly specialized kind of evangelism—to increase 50,000 Japanese American Christians to 200,000?

The Spanish-speaking community of at least 25 million in the United States is another significant enclave. Out of 25 million Spanish-name Americans, maybe 250,000 are biblical Christians. If the wealthy American churches were to *intend* church growth among this fine people and ardently *pray to God* for his blessing in finding and shepherding his lost sons and daughters, it should be quite possible that *many million* Spanish-name Americans would find new life in Christ—righteousness, brotherhood, peace, purity, and blessedness—in a multitude of old and new congregations.

But social structure means much more than ethnic enclaves. Much of the native white population is unchurched and growing up materialistic, hedonistic, and substantially pagan.

A single congregation, the Church of Christ at White Station in Memphis, recently published a four-page bulletin on Church Planting Priority Areas in Georgia. Listen to a few of the remarkable facts it dug up. (Any congregation could easily amass similar information. Denominational headquarters could put such information on computers. Indeed, this is exactly what the Southern Baptists have done). Here are the facts the Church of Christ discovered:

> Madison County is the most populous in the largest unevangelized block of counties in Georgia. It has 13,517 residents, 86 percent of whom are white. The white population is growing and the blacks are becoming less numerous. More than 43 percent of all the residents—about 6,000—are unaffiliated with any form of Christianity.

That is the social reality. Let me assure you that in the cities of almost all states, the proportions are even more startling. Might we believe that tremendous church growth in these receptive segments of the population ought to be a subject of our prayers and an object of our confident expectation? Does our Lord's caution, "You have not because you ask not," apply to us?

Nongrowing congregations and denominations refuse to see social realities. The fact of the matter is that the majority of their members are better educated, better off, live in the suburbs, and are employed in professional and administrative positions. We have somewhat class-bound churches which have less and less contact with the native born white dweller, the private tenant, and the white proletariat in general. The existing Church has little ability to reproduce in the "low" sector of society. Its desire to evangelize these people is even less. Nongrowing churches do not recognize social realities. They take shelter behind doing good to poor people and demanding social justice in Korea and South Africa!

REASON 4: GROWING CHURCHES CREATE MULTITUDES OF SUBSTRUCTURES OF BELONGING

It is impossible for anyone to know a thousand people intimately. Oh, we are friendly with a thousand. Good politicians cultivate a manner of greeting which makes them appear "the best of friends" to tens of thousands; but men and women really know and are really intimate with only a few. That is one reason why the family is such a basic unit. It is where we know and are known and yet love each other.

Consider the normal experience of a visitor to a church. He comes into a congregation of 500. At a suitable place in the service, those who sit near him greet him and shake his hand. That is a friendly church. Yet he *really knows* no one there. He is not likely to stay. He has not gotten into "a substructure of belonging." He has not gotten into a family. If he is already a good Christian and is resolved to make this church his home, he may stay around long enough to get into some small group where he knows the others and is known by them; but if he is not already a good Christian, he is quite likely to drift out about as fast as he drifted in.

If, on the contrary, the visitor is helped into a suitable substructure of belonging, then he is likely to stay. He meets not 500 people, but a dozen. He shares in their conversation. He participates in their activity. He becomes known as a person. Perhaps the substructure is a choir, a Bible study class, a weekly coffee klatch, a group repairing the church, or a group taking a census of Appalachians, French Canadians, or Filipinos living in their city. Perhaps it is a small Sunday school class or an action group. What the group *is* makes little difference, provided it suits his or her talents and interests, and provided a sense of belonging is soon developed.

Congregational growth occurs best where there are many substructures of belonging. If the visitor does not join this one, he does join that. He becomes a member of this church by becoming a known and welcomed member of some small group. The multiplication of such substructures of belonging is one good way to encourage the growth of the church. A main reason why small churches grow better than large churches is that, in the beginning church, everyone knows everyone else and everyone has a sense of belonging. The whole congregation becomes a substructure of belonging.

REASON 5: GROWING DENOMINATIONS
PLANT MULTITUDES OF NEW CHURCHES

For more than thirty years an influential notion has formed the policy of many denominations, namely that several weak congregations ought to unite to form one strong one. The ecumenical movement greatly encouraged this notion. Instead of several congregations competing for the same thousand persons, it has been said, the Baptists, Methodists, Presbyterians, and Disciples should unite into one strong community church. There are, no doubt, communities where this notion is valid; but it was applied in many more than these few communities—and it is *not* universally valid. On the contrary, the case for *new* churches is strong.

Each denomination ought to engage in deliberate, skillfully planned multiplication of congregations. Let me name four substantial considerations bearing on planned parenthood for churches.

First, sheer numbers of the unchurched prove that America needs many more churches. Making a generous estimate, there are some 60 million practicing Christians in America today. That leaves 160 million who are either nonpracticing Christians or openly non-Christians. Those who estimate what kind of television programs will secure maximum hearing and thus sell maximum advertising obviously believe that most Americans are *not* practicing Christians. A hundred and fifty million buy violence, sex, and soap.

Inconceivable numbers of men and women, boys and girls are *not* being won into existing congregations. New congregations, free to experiment with new approaches, relatively unburdened with past images of what the church is, are certainly one way to approach the unchurched two-thirds of the American population.

Second, hundreds of exclusive homogeneous units now in America prove that thousands of new churches are needed. American society is not composed of one kind of people. It is composed of hundreds of different units. The members of these units will not join churches made up of members of some other unit. University professors will not join congregations dominated by factory laborers. Greek Americans (two million of them) very seldom join WASP congregations. Those who live in $200,000 homes like to belong to churches where other members live in similar opulence. American churches ought to place glowing congregations in every homogeneous unit. That will require at least 100,000 new churches.

Third, most great cities in America have substantial sections which are

293

seriously underchurched. I walk home from the seminary several times a week through three miles of Pasadena streets on which hundreds of Chicano youth are playing. In all that area there is no congregation which caters primarily to these fine people. Each one of us knows of unchurched sections of our cities where there really ought to be a church of that *kind* of *people*.

Fourth, streams of immigrants flow into America year after year — Portuguese, Korean, Argentinian, Haitian, French Canadian, Italian, Chinese, and many others. These immigrants will join neither Anglo congregations nor older congregations of their own racial and linguistic background which have become acculturated to the American scene. Furthermore, most existing American congregations will not actively seek new immigrants and provide that care and linguistic accommodation which they crave. Add to the immigrants coming in legally hundreds of thousands coming in illegally and it is clear that if these are to be churched in the first few years when they are approachable, a major church-planting enterprise must be mounted by American denominations. Let us do our share in the great discipling which ought to take place. These incoming multitudes desire to become Americans, and we must give them every opportunity to become *Christian* Americans.

CONCLUSION

As we study why some American churches are growing, we come to a pleasant conclusion. They are growing for reasons which all real Christians can heartily second. This is one of the great discoveries of the Church Growth movement. Churches grow not for odd, unusual, exotic, or questionable reasons, but because God wants his church to grow. They pray for church growth, they intend and work for church growth, they recognize the social realities in the midst of which God has set them to work, they create multitudes of substructures of belonging in each of their congregations, and they plant multitudes of new churches. To be sure, there are other reasons for growth, but these five are very important. I hope they will commend church growth to you. Church growth is a delightful and fruitful enterprise. All hope for a transformed world and a great movement toward righteousness rests on and arises out of multitudes of sound Christian churches, branching throughout the families of mankind, both in America and in the uttermost parts of the earth.

38. The Sunday School's Fight for Life

Dr. Win Arn and Dr. Charles Arn

Dr. Win Arn is executive director and president of the Institute for American Church Growth in Pasadena, California. He conducts seminars, training sessions for individual churches, continuing education for pastors, and has assisted churches in over fifty Protestant denominations.

A pioneer in new concepts for religious films, he has produced over thirty films and numerous other visual resources for the advancement of teaching church growth. Dr. Arn has served as director of Religious Education for seven years in Baptist and Congregational churches. Other administrative service was as director of Christian Education for the California Conference of Covenant Churches.

Teaching experience includes: professor of Religious Education at Western Evangelical Seminary, Portland, Oregon; professor of Religious Education at Western Conservative Baptist Seminary, Portland, Oregon; and as guest lecturer at Fuller Theological Seminary and Biola Seminary.

Dr. Arn has studied with the School of World Mission and Church Growth at Fuller Seminary, Pasadena, California (1972-74); received the Master of Religious Education from Eastern Baptist Seminary in 1950 (Philadelphia); and the Doctor of Religious Education from Eastern Baptist Seminary in 1954.

Books authored with Dr. Donald McGavran include: **How to Grow a Church, Ten Steps for Church Growth,** and **Back to Basics in Church Growth.** He is also co-author with his son, Dr. Charles Arn, of **Growth: A New Vision for the Sunday School.** Dr. Win is publisher of the periodical **Church Growth: America.**

Dr. W. Charles Arn is vice-president in charge of Research and Development with the institute for American Church Growth (Pasadena, California).

Over the past five years Dr. Arn has had a substantial part in developing resources and seminars now successfully being used throughout many congregations in the area of church growth. He is co-author of the book **Growth: A New Vision for the Sunday School.**

Today, after 200 years as a growing institution, the Sunday school is in a desperate struggle for its very existence.

Total Sunday school, church school, and Sabbath school enrollment in American churches has declined from 40,508,568 in 1970 to 32,607,421—a 24 percent decadal decline. This decline, moreover, is in spite of an apparent trend of renewed growth in church membership. Total church membership, during this same period, grew over 16 percent.[1] *But in nearly every major Protestant denomination, Sunday school and church school enrollment is declining!* Such a significant decline has never before occurred in the history of the Sunday school.

What has happened since Robert Raikes held the first Sunday school in "Sooty Alley" of Gloucester, England, in 1780, and John Wesley adopted the Sunday school in his own mission as "one of the noblest instruments to be seen in Europe for some centuries"?

In America the Sunday school found fertile soil. Between 1827 and 1860 most denominations officially took this new organization under their wing. Through the rest of the ninetenth century the embryo continued to grow as more and more churches discovered the unique value of the Sunday school.

Then the first third, and particularly the second third, of the twentieth century saw American Sunday schools skyrocket in unprecedented growth. As both rural and urban churches began to flourish, new Sunday schools were established at a record pace. Large Sunday school conventions were held and Christian educators were in great demand. Sunday school growth seemed to happen with little or no effort. The first sixty years of the twentieth century became the "Golden Age of American Sunday Schools." Churches, too, enjoyed unprecedented growth.

But as the century moved into the 1960s, with few noticing, growth patterns began to change. In many Sunday schools enrollment began to plateau. Worship attendance stabilized or started a slight decline. Membership followed. The decline didn't happen in every Sunday school or denomination at once. Nor was there a "Black Sunday" that educators recall as the turning point. But the tide had turned. The "Great Depression" of the growth of many American Sunday schools and churches had begun.

The decline of the Sunday school accelerated into the 70s. Mainline and evangelical Sunday schools alike found the cancer of decline difficult to arrest. In 1974 national Sunday school enrollment dipped, for the first time in history, to less than the expected growth rate based on national population increase.

Today, at the outset of the 1980s, after 200 years as a growing institution, the Sunday school is in desperate times:

Of forty-two major Protestant denominations in America last year, twenty-four reported at least some degree of growth in confirmed church membership. Of that same forty-two, only twelve registered any growth last year in their Sunday schools; and only one has shown a steady pattern of growth in recent years.[2] Research has also shown that in *every* Protestant denomination, Sunday school enrollment — as a proportion of total church membership — is steadily declining.

MAINLINE SUNDAY SCHOOL DECLINE

Mainline congregations and denominations, in the last decade, have taken a beating in Sunday school/church school enrollment. In ten years the Christian Church (Disciples of Christ) has lost 302,780—over 45 percent of its enrollment.

The Lutheran Church, Missouri Synod has declined from 885,567 enrollment in 1969 to 638,074—a 28 percent loss; compared to approximately 1 percent gain in church membership during the same period.

The United Presbyterian Church in the U.S.A. since 1970 has lost over 30 percent of its enrollment.

Church school enrollment in the United Methodist Church exceeded U.S. population growth until 1964. But since its peak, the denomination has lost 2,524,365 from the church school.

In overview, while mainline church membership has been dropping in recent years, church school enrollment in these denominations has been declining at a much greater rate.

EVANGELICAL SUNDAY SCHOOL DECLINE

The cancer of decline in Sunday school enrollment does not stop with mainline churches, but includes many denominations classified as "evangelical." For example, the Christian and Missionary Alliance has grown nearly 40 percent since 1970. Sunday school enrollment has dropped 8 percent.

The Church of the Nazarene has grown 33 percent since 1965 and shown steady membership growth every year since. In the last year reported, the denomination lost 24,441 from Sunday school. The year before enrollment declined by 28,429.

The Assemblies of God have grown 64 percent in church membership since 1965. But in recent years enrollment growth in the Sunday school has stopped.

The Free Methodist Church, growing at a decadal rate of 16 percent, is declining by 6 percent in Sunday school enrollment.

The Mennonite Church, in ten years, has grown from 85,343 to 97,142—13 percent. Yet in the same period it has declined over 14 percent in Sunday school.

Even the huge Southern Baptist Convention, in the three most recent years reported, lost over 120,000.

A similar pattern of membership growth together with Sunday school decline is occurring in the Baptist General Conference, The Wesleyan Church, Salvation Army, Evangelical Covenant, Mennonite Brethren, Church of God (Anderson), and most other "growing" denominations. (See graph.)

This unmistakable decline of the Sunday school in both mainline and evangelical bodies is also reflected in the shrinking number of Americans being exposed to Christian education. In 1952, 6 percent of those surveyed had received no religious training as a child. In 1965 that percentage had grown to 9 percent. In 1978, 17 percent indicated they had received no religious training.[3]

Indeed, the diagnosis for the Sunday school, that once great and thriving institution of the American church, may be rapidly approaching terminal. The question must be asked, "Is there really a future for the Sunday school?" As the nation moves toward secularism, as the Christian education of children, youth, and adults continues to decline, is there any hope?

SUNDAY AND CHURCH SCHOOL ENROLLMENT IN U.S.

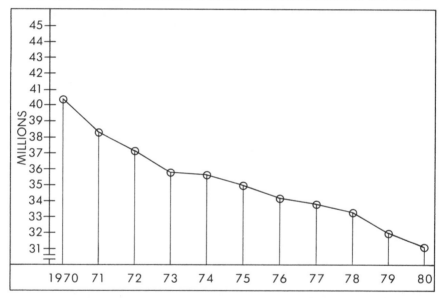

HOPE FOR THE SUNDAY SCHOOL!

Yes! There is hope for the Sunday school.

Despite these sobering statistics on national Sunday school trends, there is the first light of a new dawn. There are children, youth, and adult education programs today that are enlisting new members and growing with explosive vitality in every denomination and in every area of the country. These Sunday schools are reaching, winning, and discipling people into active fellowship within the life of local churches. Today, while some Sunday schools are fading into oblivion, others are thriving with contagious vitality.

Why?

Can it be that the quality of teaching makes all the difference in a growing Sunday school?[4] Or do growing Sunday schools require several dozen buses and pandemonious quarterly attendance contests? Can education classes that provide meaningful Christian growth and development become contagious and turn enrollment decline into active new growth?

New knowledge on why *churches* grow or decline has emerged from the study of American church growth. During the 1970s considerable research and attention was focused on the growth and decline of churches, as well as developing strategy to stimulate new growth. And as denominational executives and local pastors have been learning and applying church growth theory, substantial progress is being made. The new growth principles pioneered in the church growth movement and disseminated by such organizations as the Institute for American Church Growth (Pasadena, California), have been greatly used by God for the growth of his Church.

But what of the Sunday school? Research conducted by the Institute for American Church Growth now indicates that a growing *church* does not, by any means, ensure a growing Sunday school. Even as membership patterns in many churches seem to be turning from decline to growth, the Sunday school continues to plummet. Can the church growth movement provide any insights to the current problems of the Sunday school?

A major new book is soon to be released on the numerous unique applications of church growth to the Sunday school (*Growth: A New Vision for the Sunday School*, by Win Arn). Here is one of the significant findings: A major difference between Sunday schools that are not growing can be stated simply —*purpose*.

Church growth research indicates that *the "purpose for being" is nearly always different in declining Sunday schools than in growing ones.*

INWARD FOCUSED SUNDAY SCHOOLS

The reason for being, in most declining Sunday schools, is exclusively for ministry to existing Christians and nurture to members of existing churches.

While a concern for the spiritual health, the personal growth, and the social fellowship of Christians within existing Sunday schools is necessary, in declining Sunday schools these concerns have become the entire preoccupation of the classes and curriculum.

What happens when the priority of Christian education focuses exclusively on nurture of existing Christians? People are urged to participate in the Sunday school because it will help *them*. The church is thought of as a refuge for intimate fellowship with other believers; a personal and spiritual center where *believers* are nurtured to spiritual maturity. Programs, activities, and curricula are focused almost exclusively on the personal concerns of the people. In inward-focused Sunday schools, growth, by reaching out to un-churched people in the community, is assumed to be an automatic by-product of Christian nurture. Larry Richards verbalizes such a view:

> As the first concern of the church we must retain the nurture of the Body. For this is God's order . . . as we grow to His likeness, His love will motivate us, His concern will energize us, and the evidence of His Presence enable us to witness in power.[5]

This assumption is wrong! The belief that Sunday school growth will natu-rally result from personal growth and spiritual development of existing mem-bers is one of the primary reasons that many Sunday schools today are declining. Such self-centered education *does not* motivate people toward in-volvement in the church's mission of growth and outreach. On the contrary, education that concerns itself with only the spiritual nourishment of its own members contributes significantly to a "self-service mentality" that effec-tively seals off the Sunday school from the outside world.[6]

Dr. Kenneth Van Wyk, director of a growing Christian Education pro-gram at Garden Grove Community Church (Garden Grove, California), underscores this point:

> In my judgment, nurture-oriented education commits the serious error of making an end out of something that is meant to be a means. By definition it is self-centered and therefore suffers from a basic introver-sion. It violates the example given us in Christ's teaching and life where ministry on behalf of others is central and primary.[7]

In most declining Sunday schools the programs, curricula, activities, and training do not reflect the priority of outreach required by Christ.

OUTWARD-FOCUSED SUNDAY SCHOOLS

The purpose of most *growing* Sunday schools, on the other hand, is quite different. Outward-focused Sunday schools exist *primarily* to participate in Christ's Great Commission and to train and equip laity for ministry to the world. While concern for spiritual growth and nurture of existing Christians is an important part of the curricula and activities, it is seen as a means to an end, not an end in itself:

> Christian Education is missionary education by definition. It is partici-pation in Christ's invitation to join in God's mission to the world. . . . God's mission, His purpose and plan for the world is that He desires all men to be saved and come to the knowledge of the truth (1 Tim. 2:4).[8]

Outward-focused Sunday schools, in contrast to inward-focused Sunday schools, see evangelism and education as two sides of the same coin, two tasks to achieve one goal. Carrying out Christ's commission—to reach and disciple lost people—is the motivation for education in most growing Sunday schools.

Evangelism is the chief work of the Sunday school. In fact, Christian Education cannot be Christian unless it is evangelistic. To fail here is to fail in our primary reason for existence.[9]

Two research studies shed additional light: In a comparison between growing church schools and sharply declining ones in the United Methodist Church, Dr. Warren Hartman of the Board of Discipleship found that nearly twice as many lay people in growing church schools saw the church school as a place for winning persons to Christ.[10]

The Institute for American Church Growth surveyed 250 pastors and executives from various denominations, inquiring, "What are the reasons for the present decline of the Sunday school?" One of the two most often listed reasons was: Classes not concerned with reaching/recruiting new people.

In outward-focused Sunday schools each class and each department has high priority for seeking, reaching, teaching and discipling people. Creative strategies that "fit" the Sunday school are devised to identify and reach receptive new people. The focus of the entire organization, events, classes, and activities of growth-centered Sunday schools are for one purpose—making disciples. And the result is growth. God gives the increase!

HOW TO GROW A SUNDAY SCHOOL

It would be a mistake to conclude that in order to turn a Sunday school around from decline to growth, a concern for spiritual nurture and personal growth must be abandoned in pursuit of a "mission emphasis."

Christ did not abandon his disciples after they agreed to follow him. He spent much time and effort teaching them and encouraging them in their new life. The spiritual growth and maturity of Christ's disciples were essential for him to carry out his goal.

Yet, Christ's goal was not to develop a "class" of spiritual giants. The training and teaching of his disciples was a means to an end—preparing them to be effective in reaching and winning others. The Book of Acts is replete with accounts of the growth of the early church and the central role of Christ's "students" in building the church.

The difference between an inward-focused and an outward-focused Sunday school, and in most cases a declining Sunday school and a growing one, is simple. One sees Christian growth and spiritual maturity as an end in itself. The other also sees growth and maturity as an essential part of Christian education. But it is not the goal, it is the supporting foundation. The goal is making disciples.

Campbell Wyckoff nearly twenty years ago stated the simple implication of priorities facing the Sunday school:

All education clearly implies a process toward an end. The end, the goal, gives it direction. Purpose, to a large degree, determines what shall be included in the educational process, what shall be stressed, and what shall be played down or omitted.[11]

Church and Sunday school leaders, for the most part, continue to have a strong commitment to the Sunday school. And well they should have. The Sunday school provides many unique contributions to the life of a local church that are essential for growth.

1. The Sunday school is a great source of evangelistic outreach to friends and relatives of existing members.

2. The Sunday school provides the opportunity for establishing and developing personal relationships, which, in turn, greatly support the incorporation of new members into the life of the church.

3. The Sunday school provides a unique opportunity to teach Bible knowledge and to study the implications of the Christian life in today's world.

4. The Sunday school is a natural structure to create new classes which appeal to a wide spectrum of new people.

5. The Sunday school provides a system for the church to minister to the entire family and to include every age group in this ministry.

6. The Sunday school is the most natural organization within the church for training and equipping large numbers of laity for the work to which Christ called his Church.

The time has come to take a fresh look at the Sunday school, to see our Sunday schools through growth eyes. This means, above all, to see with clear understanding the purpose to which we are called. Our past history has a rich heritage. The future could be equally as bright. Let us, in obedience to Christ, go into all the world and make disciples.

WHERE ARE THE SUNDAY SCHOOLS GOING?

	PERCENT DECLINE	PERCENT GROWTH
S.S. ⟶ (solid arrow)	50 40 30 20 10	10 20 30 40 50
CHURCH MEMBERSHIP ⟶ (open arrow)		
ADV. CHRISTIAN		
AM. LUTH.		
ASSY OF GOD		
BAPT. GENERAL		
BRETHREN		
C. & M.A.		
CHRISTIAN CH. (D.O.C.)		
CHR. REF		
CHR. OF GOD (ANDER.)		
CH. OF THE BRETH.		
EPISCOPAL		
EVAN. COV.		
EVANG. FREE		
FREE METH.		
LUTH. CH. IN AM.		
LUTH CH. (M.S.)		
NAZARENE		
PRESBY. CH.		
REFORMED		
SALV. ARMY		
7th DAY ADV.		
SO BAPT.		
UN. CH. OF CHRIST		
UN. METH.		
UN. PRESBY.		

SUNDAY/CHURCH SCHOOL AS
PROPORTION OF CHURCH MEMBERSHIP

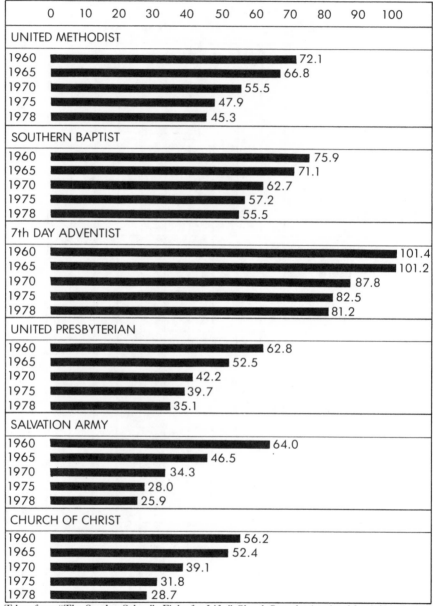

	0	10	20	30	40	50	60	70	80	90	100

UNITED METHODIST

1960	72.1
1965	66.8
1970	55.5
1975	47.9
1978	45.3

SOUTHERN BAPTIST

1960	75.9
1965	71.1
1970	62.7
1975	57.2
1978	55.5

7th DAY ADVENTIST

1960	101.4
1965	101.2
1970	87.8
1975	82.5
1978	81.2

UNITED PRESBYTERIAN

1960	62.8
1965	52.5
1970	42.2
1975	39.7
1978	35.1

SALVATION ARMY

1960	64.0
1965	46.5
1970	34.3
1975	28.0
1978	25.9

CHURCH OF CHRIST

1960	56.2
1965	52.4
1970	39.1
1975	31.8
1978	28.7

Taken from "The Sunday School's Fight for Life," *Church Growth: America*, March/April 1980. Used by permission.

39. Building a Growing Church

Leon Kilbreth

Leon Kilbreth is the leading Sunday school evangelist among Southern Baptists. He is a layman and a supermotivator. A disciple of J. N. Barnette, quoted by Billy Graham as the most effective evangelist in the twentieth century in starting Southern Baptist Sunday schools, Kilbreth has influenced more than 400 churches, more than 20,000 conversions, and enlisted more than 800 Sunday school teachers in his Sunday school revivals.

He has been a successful business man, the president of a professional baseball league, mayor of a city, a board of education president, and is author of **How to Win Souls.** After attending Southern Baptist Theological Seminary in Louisville, Kentucky, he served the strategic Ninth and O Baptist Church and the Beth Haven Baptist Church in Louisville, Kentucky. Others include the Miami Springs Baptist Church of Miami, Florida, and Florida Street Baptist Church of Greensboro, North Carolina.

There have been thousands of pages written on church growth. The books and authors are too numerous to mention. There have been scores of suggestions and multitude of ideas, perhaps most of them true and helpful.

It is my observation that most pastors and church leaders are reading so much, about so many different methods, programs, and principles that most of them are confused and bewildered by the mass of materials and the notions of thousands of authors. The more simple the approach, the less complicated the plan, and the easier the implementation, the far more likely you are to communicate a strategy of consistent growth with quality results.

Let me suggest three major categories for priority consideration as a base for developing a strategy and a philosophy. These categories will enable you to develop a plan, a program of methods and actions that will produce a constant year-by-year growth spiral resulting in both quantity and quality.

The most important ingredient in any church is evangelism. Evangelism is far more than outreach, more than growing attendances. It is more than conversions and baptisms. It is also spiritual growth which is accomplished by teaching, training, and developing. It is making disciples.

AN APPEALING PULPIT

The most important ingredient in growing an aggressive evangelistic church is *an appealing pulpit*. This doesn't mean an *appeasing* pulpit. Appeasement is never appealing. Appeasers in the end are the most unappealing leaders in the world. An appeasing pulpit will never result in growing an aggressive evangelistic church. I've never seen an evangelistic church that moved from plateau to plateau year by year with consistent quality growth unless that church was blessed with the leadership of a special man of God. Take a look at them today!

The pulpit is the "nerve center" of every ministry of the church. It turns on or off the power that lights the flame of evangelism. It must feed, it must inspire, it must motivate, it must instruct, it must correct, it must challenge, it must minister, it must love, and it must develop.

Where do new leaders come from? Where does motivation and inspiration come from—inspiration to visit, to win souls, to serve, to plan, and to discover God's will?

There is a growing hunger in the membership of thousands of churches for an appealing pulpit—not a refined, well-educated, well-mannered, well-organized, sophisticated, eloquent, brilliant pulpit, but a pulpit where a man of God stands—a humble man who walks with God and preaches from a burdened heart, not a man who keeps the congregation informed on current events. An appealing pulpit has a man who is motivated by a concerned compassion for a white harvest. It has a man with a burning desire to reach people not by word of mouth, but by action and personal example. An appealing pulpit has a man who is a prophet of God, not the president of some civic organization. It has a man with courage and boldness, that speaks with conviction in such a manner that you know it comes from God. An appealing pulpit has a man who has a plan to evangelize his community, a man who is fearless in his leadership, judgments, and decisions, one who leads and doesn't conform to the whims and wishes of a few influential members. An appealing pulpit has a man who is a living example of what he preaches, a man who is honest, truthful, humble, and touchable, and a man who cries and repents when there are not decisions for Christ when he preaches.

This is an appealing pulpit! This is a pulpit that builds a growing evangelistic church. This is a pulpit that produces fellowship. This is a pulpit that inspires, motivates, and brings lasting commitment. This is a pulpit that fans the flame of evangelism. This is a pulpit that creates a vision, that produces dedicated leadership. This is a pulpit that inspires witnessing, personal soul winning and outreach. This is a pulpit that produces conviction, conversions, baptisms, and godly living. This is a pulpit that causes homes to stay together. This is a pulpit that inspires good planning and the execution of these plans. This is a pulpit that attracts a frustrated world which seeks to find a sincere man of God who has some answers. This is a pulpit that commands confidence and assurance within the body—a confidence which allows the pastor to implement strategies and make decisions that are necessary for building a growing evangelistic church.

Unless there is a drastic change in the pulpits of our land, you can forget revival and evangelism and the local church will grow weaker. The local church will recapture the attention of the world only when the church becomes different from the world.

If we are to build growing, exciting evangelistic churches which will attract people and move the church into a position of great influence, which will allow us to take advantage of our last opportunity to win a lost world, then there is one thing for sure: We must see every church led, guided, inspired, fed, and challenged by an appealing pulpit.

Building a growing evangelistic church doesn't come by mastering the right methods and principles. Neither does it come by implementing certain programs or activities. It is not the result of bigger buildings, larger staffs, and increasing budgets. We have all of these. And these may be a necessary part. But with all of these, building a growing evangelistic church will never happen in any local church until there is an appealing pulpit!

Let the men of the pulpit accept this challenge! Let the pulpit admit that we must be willing to submit to self-examination—to ask ourselves, "Has my pulpit lost its appeal? Is it producing fruit? Is it building a growing evangelistic church?" I challenge you to review your results!

AN AGGRESSIVE OUTREACH

The major thrust of an evangelistic church will be an aggressive outreach. Aggressive means: Always on the attack, constantly charging forward, never easing the pressure, without let-up, always on the offensive. This means every hour, every day, every week, every month, every year, without ceasing!

Aggressive outreach is:
1. Locating every prospect
2. Assigning every prospect
3. Visiting every prospect
4. Cultivating every prospect
5. Bringing every prospect
6. Teaching every prospect
7. Winning every prospect
8. Developing every prospect

This must be the strategy that saturates the subconscious mind of every leader.

Every individual, every home, every block, every neighborhood, every street, every lane, and every highway becomes a mission field. This kind of strategy calls for us to do all our planning in light of the cross. We cannot be stopped by criticism, persecution, suffering, sacrifice, leadership, or a bad location. An aggressive outreach never notices a bad location.

Our battle cry must be, "Never retreat in the face of difficulties. We will advance as conditions permit. If conditions don't permit, we will create those conditions."

An aggressive outreach will overcome barriers, obstacles, handicaps, and tradition. An aggressive outreach calls for the employment of proven methods and a constant recruiting and training of new leaders. You must have 20 percent new leadership each year, trained and motivated, ready for service.

You must emphasize your Sunday school! An aggressive outreach has its beginning in a healthy, growing Sunday school. The Sunday school is the base of evangelism. A growing Sunday school is the greatest opportunity for evangelism that a local church can have. It will feed a steady flow of new prospects into the bloodstream of your Sunday school and worship services every week. This will generate a momentum which produces excitement, a new spirit and fellowship that results in crowds, growing attendance, conversions, baptisms, and decisions.

Sad, but true, it is a fact that the tremendous potential power of the Sunday school is being sapped today because church leaders are allowing inferior programs and activities to weaken the Sunday school. The results and evidence of this are on every hand.

An aggressive outreach is an aggressive bus ministry. It includes a major emphasis on reaching adults. It requires a definite plan for starting new departments and classes. An aggressive outreach must have an aggressive Sunday school enrollment plan.

Aggressive outreach means the wise use of the media—television, radio, newspapers, and all types of advertising. Also, it means *wise* employment of special days and attendance campaigns.

Aggressive outreach is enthusiasm and excitement about your church wherever you go. It is an example before your neighbors; it is joy and a positive attitude. It is victory in your heart and a cheerful disposition at church and on the street. It is a song in your heart and on your lips.

The power that fuels aggressive outreach comes always from a group of dedicated, faithful people who have and believe in a ministry of prayer. This doesn't mean the entire church will be involved (as great as that would be). But in every evangelistic church you will find a group of prayer warriors who know what the power of prayer can do, and with faith they engage in an aggressive prayer ministry.

Aggressive outreach means being able to say, "My church is in the battle of reaching people, using every tool, vehicle, instrument, method, and resource at its command, with one aim—to reach every unenlisted and lost person and confront them with Jesus as Savior and Lord.

AN ATTRACTIVE TEACHING MINISTRY

You cannot grow a superaggressive evangelistic church without an attractive teaching ministry!

Thousands of people are engaged in Bible study outside the local church today because they have found an attractive Bible study elsewhere! The greatest attraction you can have around a New Testament church is an attractive teaching ministry. It will not only *draw* people, it will *hold* people. The fact that most Sunday schools average only 40 percent or less of their enrollment is proof positive that we have not developed an attractive teaching ministry in our churches.

Most Sunday schools remain stagnant and fail to keep a high level of attendance because of poor, unattractive teaching, and not meeting the needs of the pupils.

Reaching people today isn't the number-one problem of the church. Winning and baptizing people isn't the number-one problem. We can reach people in great numbers! We can enroll people in great numbers in our Sunday schools! But our greatest problem is that we cannot hold them! We cannot keep them coming; we cannot activate them and develop them. They attend a few times, they may even enroll in our Bible study, but they soon become chronic absentees, for they find little to hold them. Their hunger for Bible study is not met.

For example, the largest Baptist church in the world today has 20,000 members. Yet, over 11,000 of their members are not enrolled in their Bible study program. Over 50 percent of their members haven't been attracted to their Sunday school. Thousands of their members do not tithe. Thousands never attend on Sunday evenings, thousands never witness or win a soul. There is far more to building an evangelistic church than adding large numbers to the membership.

Then let's further expand the truth. Southern Baptists, who may be one of the last remaining major denominations that still has some interest in growing aggressive evangelistic churches, find themselves afflicted with a great blight. With a membership of over 13 million members, they have over 7 million not enrolled in their Sunday schools. This is around 58 percent. These 7 million have not been attracted to their Sunday schools. These 7 million are dead wood to the local church. They make little or no contribution, yet these churches continue on in a desperate attempt to add thousands more to their church membership. If we can't minister, develop, and cultivate those we have, why do we think God would give us any more?

You see, one of our major mental blocks today is this: we have let creep into our leadership thinking that "there are only a few really good teachers around." We attach quality to small numbers or only a few. So we add greater and greater numbers to the enrollment of a few teachers, who soon are over their head. These lay people with hundreds of pressures and responsibilities of home, job, and church are lucky just to prepare and appear before their class to teach on Sunday morning. So the class has no ministry, few visits, no cultivating, no meeting of needs. Because the teachers have such a large enrollment, the task frustrates them, so our church leaders continue on crying and moaning, "We don't have enough teachers. God only calls a few." Would God give us the task of teaching every nation and then only call a few to teach? Every born-again, Spirit-filled Christian is a potentially great Bible teacher! The fact is that our pastors and church leaders are so busy with secondary things that they've never taken the time to pray out these people, enlist them, train them, develop them, motivate them, and give them the greatest task they could have.

If I were a pastor, one of my two great priorities would be to select, elect, train, and motivate a corps of Holy Spirit-filled Bible teachers. You can grow a tremendous aggressive evangelistic church anywhere if you will concentrate on developing an attractive Bible teaching ministry in your Sunday school.

We need to develop thousands of lay people, develop their teaching skills, train them how to minister, show them how to cultivate and how to make disciples. This takes patience and hard work. It takes time and a definite purpose.

Our teachers need to see that teaching is a seven-day-a-week responsibility. It is more than a thirty-minute class session on Sunday morning. The single greatest aim behind every discussion of the Word of God by the teacher should be to make disciples! "My word will accomplish whereunto it is sent."

Week by week, verse by verse, chapter by chapter, book by book, sentence by sentence, phrase by phrase, the Sunday School teacher should be able, through the convicting power of the Holy Spirit and by example, to:

— Inspire and motivate his class to witness and visit;
— Inspire and motivate his pupils to serve, to minister, to love, to pray;
— Inspire and motivate his class to enroll, to cultivate and bring new members;
— Inspire and motivate his pupils to experience the revelation that true Christianity is more than a decision to accept Christ, but also a commitment to follow Christ;
— Inspire and motivate his pupils to reach out and experience the joy of the abundant life through obedience and total stewardship.

From the classrooms should come all new Bible teachers. Good teachers beget good teachers. From our Sunday school classrooms should come our deacons, our preachers, our soul winners, our faithful visitors and witnesses, our Sunday school directors, our servants, and our missionaries.

An attractive teaching ministry produces new disciples and field hands who are necessary in the reaping of the harvest and the growing of an aggressive evangelistic church.

40. What Is a Mature Church?

Gene A. Getz

Dr. Gene A. Getz is associate professor of Christian Education and Practice Theology at Dallas Theological Seminary. Along with several businessmen he began the Fellowship Bible Church of Dallas in 1972. The church is composed of four congregations that meet in one building—a Friday night church, a Sunday morning church, a Sunday afternoon church and a Sunday night church.

A graduate of Moody Bible Institute, Rocky Mountain College (A.D.), Wheaton College (M.A.), and New York University (Ph.D), Dr. Getz is also author of several books, including **The Measure of a Church, The Measure of a Man, Building Up One Another,** and **Sharpening the Focus of the Church.**

"But if he does not listen to you, take one or two more with you, so that by the mouth of two or three witnesses every fact may be confirmed. And if he refuses to listen to them, tell it to the church" (Matt. 18:16, 17, NASB).

Obviously, Jesus was using the word "church" to refer, first, to the larger and total body of Christians he was going to call out to be his own people. He was not speaking of building a single church in a particular geographical area, but rather a single church that was made up of all believers everywhere.

When Jesus said to tell it to the church, he was referring to a specific group of Christians located in a particular area—a group that could listen to a report and take action on that report. It is clear, from his directive and his expectation from those who were listening to that directive, that Jesus was referring to a local assembly of believers.

Again, when Paul wrote that Christ is head of the church and that Christ loved the church and gave himself for her (Eph. 5:23, 25, KJV), he was referring to the universal church. But when he wrote "to the church of God which is at Corinth" or when he referred to the doctrine which he taught "everywhere in every church," he was clearly referring to local groups of believers (1 Cor. 1:2; 4:17, KJV).

At times it is difficult to differentiate between the two uses of the word *ekklesia* in the New Testament. But for the most part it is quite clear that the word is primarily to refer to a local assembly. This use of the word is far more prevalent in the New Testament. Alfred Kuen believes that out of the 115 times the word *ekklesia* is used in the New Testament, about ninety of them refer to the local churches.[1]

In the New Testament, then, "the universal church was the universal fellowship of believers who met visibly in local assemblies,"[2] but these "local assemblies" were also called churches, even though they were visible manifestations of the one true church.

Also, it's important to note that the Bible never classified a church as a "building." Thus today, the word "church" is not used correctly by most Christians. We often speak of the church that is "located at Fourth and Main Street," whereas in the New Testament sense, *the body of believers* who assemble at Fourth and Main are the church. But note! These believers are the church whether they are assembled or not. It is their position in Christ and their relationship to one another that make them a New Testament church.

But culture changes and so does language. In New Testament days they had no special buildings they called "churches." Rather, they met in houses, or earlier, in the Jewish temple and synagogues. But, eventually, with the use of special buildings as a meeting place for the church, it followed naturally that the building would also be called a "church." Though the word "church" was never applied to a building in the New Testament, it certainly is not wrong to call a building a church, as long as people realize that the church, in the New Testament sense, is really not the building but the people who use the building as a place to be edified and built up in Jesus Christ.

WHEN IS A LOCAL CHURCH A "CHURCH"?

It is easy to get bogged down with peripheral issues and questions. And there does not seem to be a clear-cut way to define a local church.

For example, is it when you have a constitution and regular meetings? Is it when you have baptized believers who partake regularly of the Lord's Supper? Is it when you have church officers such as elders and deacons? Should numerous norms be present in order to have a local church? It certainly does not include a certain level of maturity, for the Corinthians were carnal, but Paul called them a church. Further, it does not seem necessary to have spiritual leaders before you call a body of believers a church, for it is clearly implied that groups of believers throughout Lystra, Iconium, and Antioch were called "churches" even before elders were appointed (Acts 14:21-23, KJV).

When, then, can a body of believers be called a church? I personally tend toward a simple definition: a body of believers can be called a church whenever that group meets together regularly for mutual edification. Jesus said in the context of talking about church discipline, "For where two or three are gathered together in my name, there am I in the midst of them" (Matt. 18:20, KJV). And it is clear what Tertullian felt Jesus meant, for he said: "Where there are two or three people, even laymen, there is a church."[3]

WHEN IS A LOCAL CHURCH A "MATURE CHURCH"?

When talking about a "mature church," we can only really talk about local churches. True, the universal church is in the process of maturing and some-day it will be totally mature—when we all are with Christ in heaven. But the only way we can measure a church is by what we can see, and, as will be shown, this is the only way New Testament believers could measure the maturity level of a body of believers in a particular location.

If a "church" is a body of believers that meets together regularly for a mutual edification, how then can we determine when that body becomes mature? Or, more personally, what criteria can we use to measure ourselves to see if we have arrived at some degree of maturity?

VARIOUS VIEWS OF MATURITY

Some say a mature church is an active church! They evaluate progress by the number of meetings held each week and by the number of different kinds of programs going on.

Some say a mature church is a growing church! As long as new people are coming and staying, they believe they are a maturing church. As long as the pastoral staff is enlarging, they believe "all is well."

Some say a mature church is a giving church! As long as people are contributing financially to the ongoing program of the church and supporting its many ventures, they believe it is a maturing church.

Some say a mature church is a soul-winning church! They say this is proof positive. When people are bringing others to Christ regularly, when we can account for regular professions of faith and regular baptisms, then for sure we have a New Testament church.

Some say a mature church is a missionary-minded church—a church that supports missions around the world, designating a large percentage of its overall budget to world evangelism.

Some say a mature church is a smooth-running church—a church whose organizational machinery is oiled with every degree of regularity. It is a finely tuned machine with job descriptions, eight-hour days, coffee breaks, and punch cards. Everyone does what he was hired to do—on time and efficiently.

Some say a mature church is a Spirit-filled church. This is the church that is enthusiastic and dynamic. It has lots of emotion and excitement. Everyone in it knows what his gifts are and uses them regularly.

And finally, some say the ultimate mark of maturity is the big church, with thousands coming to Sunday school and church every Sunday. Matur-ity, to them, is represented by a large paid staff, scores of buses that pick up children every week, multiple programs, a radio and television ministry, a

Christian day school, a Christian college and seminary, and oh, yes, a printing press to prepare its own literature.

Unfortunately, some people really believe that what I have stated are actually biblical marks of maturity. And let me hurry to say that many of these things *will* be present in a mature church. There *will* be activity! Normally, the church *will* be growing numerically! People *will* be sharing their material possessions! People *will* be leading others to Jesus Christ and supporting missions! The church *will* be well organized! There *will* be a sense of enthusiasm and excitement! And certainly there *will* be a number of ministries that develops out of a dynamic New Testament church!

But unfortunately, all of these things can be present without having a mature church. When measured by biblical criteria, a church may be found seriously wanting, in spite of all activity, busyness, and organizational structure.

A BIBLICAL STANDARD FOR MATURITY

The Bible is very clear regarding the criteria for measuring the maturity level of the local church. Paul summarized it in his letter to the Corinthians and illustrated it in several of his other letters.

Paul's letter to the Corinthians. "And now these three remain: faith, hope and love. But the greatest of these is love" (1 Cor. 13:13, NIV).

Paul made it particularly clear in his New Testament correspondence what thrilled and encouraged him about certain churches. It was the manifestation of these three qualities and virtues—faith, hope, and love—in each local body of believers.

Paul's letter to the Ephesians. "For this reason I, since I heard about your faith in the Lord Jesus and your love for all the saints, have never stopped giving thanks for you, remembering you in my prayers. . . . I pray also that the eyes of your heart may be enlightened in order that you may know the hope to which he has called you, the riches of his glorious inheritance in the saints . . ." (Eph. 1:15, 16, 18, NIV).

Paul's letter to the Colossians. "We always thank God, the Father of our Lord Jesus Christ, when we pray for you, because we have heard of your faith in Christ Jesus and of the love you have for all the saints—the faith and love that spring from the hope stored up for you in heaven, and which you have already heard about in the word of truth, the gospel that has come to you. All over the world this gospel is producing fruit and growing . . ." (Col. 1:3-6, NIV).

Paul's letter to the Thessalonians. "We always thank God for all of you, mentioning you in our prayers. We continually remember before our God and Father your work produced by faith, your labor prompted by love, and your endurance inspired by hope in our Lord Jesus Christ" (1 Thess. 1:2, 3, NIV).

"We ought always to thank God for you, brothers, and rightly so, because your faith is growing more and more, and the love every one of you has for each other is increasing. Therefore, among God's churches we boast about your perseverance and faith in all the persecutions and trials you are enduring" (2 Thess. 1:3, 4, NIV).

It is clear from Paul's letters to various New Testament churches that the thing that pleased him, the thing that he thanked God for again and again, was what he heard about the development of faith, hope, and love—but especially love. In fact, as we've seen from Paul's second letter to the Thessalonians, he would actually hold up certain churches that had developed these marks of maturity as examples to other churches.

A DEFINITION OF FAITH, HOPE AND LOVE

Faith describes the confidence and trust that a local body of Christ has in its head, Jesus Christ.

Hope describes doctrinal insight and stability, particularly in respect to our present and future relationship to God through Jesus Christ.

And love—a very profound concept in the New Testament—describes the relationships that should exist in a local church as well as the way that local groups should relate to all men. In essence, love is the manifestation of Christ-like behavior by a functioning body of believers.

THE TWENTIETH-CENTURY CHURCH

If Paul sat down today to write a letter to the average church—to your church—how would he begin that letter? What would he thank God for? Would it be for the activities in the church? Would he refer to numerical growth? Would he begin the letter by thanking God for a large budget? For soul-winning efforts? For a finely-tuned organization? A charismatic emphasis? Huge edifices? Or would he thank God for the corporate faith, the corporate hope, and above all, the love for one another and all mankind that exist in the church? Would he actually be able to find many churches that measure up to this biblical criteria?

ACTION STEP

If you are a church leader, give your people an opportunity to respond to the message in this chapter by completing the following statements:

1. I thank God for my church because . . .
2. I believe my church could become more mature if . . .

41. Factors in Church Growth in the United States

Tetsunao Yamamori

Dr. Tetsunao Yamamori is director and professor of Intercultural Studies at Biola College, LaMirada, California. He also serves as adjunct professor at the School of World Mission, Fuller Theological Seminary, in American Church Growth and Japanese studies.

Dr. Yamamori is former director of the Institute for World Studies and Church Growth at Milligan College and dean of Northwest Christian College. In addition to numerous journal articles, he has published, among others, **Church Growth in Japan, Introducing Church Growth,** and **Church Growth: Everybody's Business.**

He received his B.A. from Northwest Christian College, B.D. from Texas Christian University, and Ph.D. in Sociology of Religion from Duke University.

Over the last two decades I have constantly concerned myself with the question of how God brings people of varied cultural backgrounds to faith and obedience. No two cases of church growth are alike. The growth pattern of a church in the Punjab, India, differs substantially from that of a church in Tokyo or in Garden Grove, California. Yet, repeated case studies show that several factors, corporately functional to growth, are found in many of the rapidly growing churches. The following factors are influential in the United States.

A GROWTH-ORIENTED PHILOSOPHY OF MINISTRY

A church likely to grow possesses a clearly delineated philosophy of ministry bent on growth. The pastor regularly articulates the philosophy from the pulpit. The lay leaders are convinced that this growth philosophy is firmly lodged in the very heart of God who does not desire that any believing soul should perish. They know that God intends the gospel of Jesus Christ to be believed and obeyed. This philosophy drives every member of the church to witness to the unsaved in order that they be saved. A growing church considers evangelism and church growth a way of life. It is not unusual for a rapidly growing church to begin new congregations as part of its evangelistic outreach. The growth philosophy affirms the expansion of God's kingdom through multiplying churches.

DYNAMIC WITNESSING MEMBERS

A church likely to grow is made up of numerous dynamic witnessing members in actual and frequent contact with non-Christians in the community. A

316

church of this kind has generally developed an effective method of constantly enlisting and training workers whose primary efforts are directed outward to non-Christians in the community. The pastor exerts his influence to make sure that a proportionately large number of "outreach laymen" are recruited, trained, and sent out into the community. A nongrowing church, in contrast, mobilizes its lay leaders primarily for the maintenance of the church as an institution — serving on various committees, teaching Sunday school classes, and making sure that all other needs are met for the smooth operation of the church. Churches grow when the efforts of dynamic witnessing Christians are constantly directed toward non-Christians in the community.

THE CHURCH'S UNDERSTANDING
OF ITSELF AND ITS COMMUNITY

A church likely to grow has an accurate knowledge of its own membership constituency and its community. The leaders of a growing congregation know the growth pattern of their church. They know, for example, what kind of people constitute their membership. It is important for the church to know the sociologically discernible facts about its members. Research shows that people most likely to join a particular church are those within the community who most approximate its membership. A growing church knows who and what kind of people have joined the congregation for the last several years; that is, the church knows among whom it is most effective. The church, therefore, seeks to find and reach those within the community who are the most likely to respond to the claims of Christ through its outreach efforts.

RESPECTING THE LINES OF COMMUNICATION

A church likely to grow respects the lines of communication. The line of communication is generally good between two intimates, such as between relatives or friends. The gospel flows best from one member of a family to another or between two friends. Research shows that an overwhelming majority of any congregation have become Christian or have joined a particular church because of their Christian relatives or friends. Now, the strategic importance of this phenomenon is obvious. Churches grow by respecting the lines of communication — by reaching the friends and relatives of new converts and of new members by transfer, if they are not active, practicing Christians.

THE CONSTANT SEARCH FOR GOD'S BRIDGES

A church likely to grow is in constant search for God's bridges and upon their discovery develops strategies to reach them. The patriarch of church growth thinking, Dr. Donald McGavran, uses the phrase "bridges of God" as referring to the segments of society that are responsive to the gospel. God's bridges in a given community may be people who are experiencing or have recently experienced stress or crises. People who have recently lost loved ones or who have recently gone through a divorce are often among the most receptive. God's bridges may be people who have experienced dissatisfaction. For example, during the sixties there was a massive turning to Christ of drug users who had become dissatisfied with themselves. They then became known as "Jesus people." God's bridges may be recent immigrants such as the Koreans in Southern California among whom churches are multiplying rapidly today. Growing churches are constantly looking for receptive people whom God has prepared for harvesting.

Though America's ethnic "islands" are currently largely untouched by the gospel, I am convinced that the decade of the eighties will see the turning to Christ of a large segment of ethnic America. Protestant churches in America (which number almost 300,000) have generally been using the "come to us" (assimilationist) approach to evangelize their ethnic neighbors (including the "white ethnics" of Eastern and Southern Europe). Very few ethnics have joined the predominantly white Anglo-Saxon Protestant churches by crossing their cultural, linguistic, racial, and class barriers. America's ethnic population will not be won if Protestant churches follow their present approach. However, evidences abound that perceptive churches are earnestly trying to surmount their white, middle-class limitations and to reach out to their ethnic neighbors. These churches will succeed in their efforts if they observe the following guidelines: (a) abandon the notion that the "come to us" approach is the only right way; (b) focus on the goal of evangelizing, rather than Americanizing or "civilizing," the undiscipled persons in each ethnic group; (c) acknowledge the heterogeneous nature of persons even *within each ethnic group* and remember that they are differentiated socioeconomically, and often linguistically, generationally, and geographically; (d) recruit and train *indigenous* full-time and unpaid lay ministers who will mobilize their laity for ethnic evangelism; (e) utilize the strong ethnic communal ties (friendship and kinship) to the advantage of spreading the gospel; (f) develop parachurch organizations for ethnic evangelism (i.e., missionary organizations working within America having the specific purpose of winning these unchurched persons of various ethnic groups); (g) start numerous ethnic churches, Sunday school classes, and evangelistic home Bible study fellowships; (h) use the indigenous (heart) language of the ethnic unit being evangelized; (i) evangelize each ethnic group to its fringes; (j) conduct research to identify the responsive as well as the resistant areas within ethnic groups and subgroups; (k) set immediate and long-range goals for ethnic church growth at local, judicatory, and denominational levels: (l) pray that the Holy Spirit will empower your church to realize the lostness of every person without Christ and to act decisively for ethnic church growth.

SYSTEMS OF INCORPORATION AND TRAINING

A church likely to grow develops effective systems of incorporating and training new members. The church which loses more members than it takes in per annum is obviously not growing. The growing church welcomes new members and quickly incorporates them into various fellowship groups where they are made to feel at home and are invited to become productive members in pursuit of the church's redemptive ministry. Sunday school classes, small interest groups, and Bible study fellowships all function for a growing church as beachheads for evangelistic activities and as buffers against membership leakage. It is largely in these small groups that new members are given instruction and care in order that they may grow in grace, increase in the knowledge of the Lord Jesus Christ, engage in his mission, and become responsible members of his church. Churches grow when they take in new members, incorporate them into well-functioning fellowship groups, nurture them to become productive and responsible members, and retain them.

A HIGH PREMIUM ON PRAYER

A church likely to grow places a high premium on prayer and consequently upon the work of the Holy Spirit. I am yet to see a rapidly growing church which has not emphasized intense prayer on the part of its members both individually and corporately. A growing church is prayer-led and Spirit-filled. Prayer is the lifeblood of effective evangelism. It prepares the hearts of both the proclaimers and the proclaimed. Through prayer, ordinary Christians become bold in witnessing. Their hearts are tuned in to the heart of God who desires eternal life for every human being. They pray for specific individuals by name. They do all they can to make the gospel of salvation known to their friends, relatives, and those whose lives intersect with theirs. Yet, after all that is humanly possible has been done, they pray and remain expectant in the confidence that God through his Spirit will culitivate and harvest the souls of men and women in his own time.

42. Evangelism

D. James Kennedy

Dr. D. James Kennedy serves as a pastor of the Coral Ridge Presbyterian Church in Ft. Lauderdale, Florida. For nine years the congregation is reported as being the fastest-growing Presbyterian church in the United States. The church has grown in eighteen years to 4,800 members and reports a peak attendance of over 9,000 in three morning services.

He is author of the books **Evangelism Explosion** (now translated into almost a dozen languages), **Truths That Transform, This is The Life, Spiritual Renewal** and **The God of Great Surprises.** His academic training includes: B.A., University of Tampa; M. Div. cum laude, Columbia Theological Seminary; M. Th. summa cum laude, Chicago Graduate School of Theology; and Ph.D., New York University.

SURVEYING THE PROGRAM

The program of training laymen for the task of evangelism is one which grew out of the specific problems and specific situation of the Coral Ridge Church in Fort Lauderdale, Florida, and yet the program contains within it some "readily transferable techniques" which have been and can be used by other congregations. We believe that the principles contained in this program represent some of the basic principles of the New Testament concerning the matter of evangelism, though by no means does it exhaust all of the biblical teaching and possibilities of evangelism. It should be stated here, at the outset, that this is a program of personal lay evangelism and does not begin to encompass many of the other sound and biblical methods of evangelism, such as mass evangelism, pulpit evangelism, etc.

Realizing that laymen are perhaps the most strategic and also the most unused key to the evangelization of the world, we have endeavored to build a program which will motivate, recruit, and train men and women to do the job of evangelism, and then to keep them doing it. This, of course, is not an easy task, as most every pastor can testify. And yet it would seem that the basic principles of New Testament evangelism would require that this mobilization of the laity take place. Let us look for a minute at some of these principles.

EXAMINING THE PRINCIPLES

Christ's first instructions to his new followers in the first chapter of Mark were, "Come ye after me, and I will make you to become fishers of men." His last words on this earth to his disciples were, "But ye shall receive power, after that the Holy Ghost is come upon you: and ye shall be witnesses unto me both in Jerusalem, and in all Judea, and in Samaria, and unto the uttermost part of the earth." Christ thus began and ended his ministry with the command to be witnesses and fishers of men. This thrust of his teaching is summed up in the Great Commission where Jesus commands his followers to go into all of the world and preach the gospel to every creature. The first and obvious principle then is that the church is a body under orders by Christ to share the gospel with the whole world.

But the question then arises, How is this to be done and by whom? We believe that one of the greatest victories that Satan has ever scored against the church is the idea which he had foisted off on probably 90 percent of the Christian church, that it is the task of ministers and evangelists only to share the gospel of Christ and that this is not the job of laymen. So successful has Satan been with this stratagem that it has been estimated that probably 95 percent of our church members never lead anyone to Christ. Thus the army of Christ has been more than decimated, and the response from the pew has been "let clerical George do it." I am thankful that today there is an obvious trend in the opposite direction, as more and more laymen and churches are realizing and accepting their responsibility to witness. The second important principle then is that the laymen as well as the ministers must be trained to evangelize. Over 99 percent of the church is made up of laymen. Therefore, if they are AWOL there is little doubt but that the battle will be lost.

It was the witness of the entire early Christian church that produced such a tremendous impact upon the world. In Acts 8:4 we read, "Therefore they that were scattered abroad went every where preaching the word" (KJV). But some have said, "Does not this refer to the apostles? After all, what do laymen know about such things?" A standard exegetical axiom is that "a text without a context is a pretext." Thus, this text has been ripped from its context and used as a pretext for idleness on the part of multitudes of laymen. But let us examine its context. In Acts 8:1 we read, ". . . they were all scattered abroad . . . except the apostles" (KJV). Therefore we see that according to the emphasis of this passage those that went everywhere preaching the word were everyone except the apostles. And the term translated "preaching the word" is from the Greek verb *evangelizomai* which means, of course, to evangelize. Thus we see that in the early church all of the laymen went everywhere "evangelizing." This is the lost ideal that we are striving to regain.

We have seen what needs to be done and by whom; now let us ask, How are we going to get them to do it?

There have been hundreds of thousands of messages preached on the responsibility of Christians to witness, and yet there is a striking absence of any formidable army of lay witnesses. Something, therefore, must be missing. This brings us to our next important principle, namely, "Evangelism is more caught that taught." This oft repeated cliche rather accurately describes what is missing in most attempts at teaching laymen to evangelize and also fairly well describes the method that Christ used to teach his followers. I have asked thousands of ministers how many of them have preached sermons on the need to witness and have taught classes on this subject. Most of them have raised their hand, but when I have asked how many of them make a habit of taking their people with them when they go out to evangelize, only 3 or 4 percent will usually respond. I once questioned a group of ministers, missionaries, and teachers, and found that only about one and one-half percent of their members were regularly engaged in leading people to Christ. Then I discovered that only three of these people took their laymen with them when they went to evangelize. The average person can no more learn to evangelize in a classroom than he can learn to fly an airplane in the living room. The missing link of modern evangelistic training, which was so thoroughly provided by Christ, is "on-the-job training."

These are the most basic principles that we feel need to be understood and accepted if a church is to have an effective program of evangelism.

REVIEWING THE HISTORY

This program grew out of the experiences I had in starting this church, which was a Home Mission project and which is now eighteen years old. I came directly to this work from seminary and though I preached evangelistically and though I had taken all of the courses offered at seminary on the subject of evangelism and read many books besides, I found that the sophisticated people of Fort Lauderdale did not respond to my message from the pulpit. I was totally lacking in both confidence and know-how as far as confronting individuals face to face with the gospel was concerned. After eight or ten months of preaching, the congregation had gone from forty-five to seventeen people, and I was a most discouraged young minister. About this time I was invited to Decatur, Georgia, to preach ten days of evangelistic services. Happy to get away from my Fort Lauderdale fiasco, I accepted the invitation. When I arrived, the pastor told me that I would be preaching each night, but more importantly, he said, we would be visiting in the homes each day — morning, noon, and night — to present the gospel to people individually. I was petrified, for I knew that I had no ability whatsoever to do this. However, the next morning we went out. After about a half-hour of my stumbling attempts at evangelism, the pastor took over the conversation and in about fifteen or twenty minutes led the man to Christ. I was astonished but did not realize even then the impact that this was to have on my life. For ten days I watched this pastor lead one person after another to Christ — a total of fifty-four individuals during those ten days. I went back to Fort Lauderdale a new man, and I began to do just what I had seen done. People responded. Soon dozens, scores, and then hundreds accepted Christ. The principle of "on-the-job" training had been applied to my life and had produced its results.

I then realized that there was a definite limit to the number of people that I myself could see, and that what I ought to do was to train others to do the same thing. What I then foolishly did is the same thing that thousands of others no doubt have done: I organized a class on witnessing. I gave them six lessons and sent them out. They all went home terrified! I waited a few months and tried again. This time I gave them twelve lessons—again no success. A few more months, and another series, more elaborate, more complex; fifteen weeks—again no results. I do not know of one single adult that was brought to Christ by one of these laymen as a result of these witnessing classes.

Finally it struck me like a bolt of lightning—I myself had had classes for three years and had not learned how to witness. It was not until someone who knew how had taken me out into people's homes that I finally got the confidence to do it myself. Thus I began the program which has continued for the past fifteen years. It began by my taking out one individual until he had confidence to witness to others. And I then did the same with another, and another. And so it has grown. After the people are trained, they in turn can train others.

MOTIVATING THE CHRISTIANS

Often when an evangelism program is envisioned a pastor will begin by preaching on the subject and then inviting everybody who is willing to take part to come on some specified night to begin the program. This is the way that we tried at first to motivate people and recruit them, but we found that it was not very successful. The basic motivation will no doubt begin from the pulpit with sermons on the responsibility, privilege, and necessity for witnessing for Christ. The great texts already mentioned, and others, should certainly be preached with clarity and forcefulness. However, our experience would teach us that the actual recruiting should not be done from the pulpit, but rather should be done on an individual, person-to-person basis.

RECRUITING THE WORKERS

When Christ called his apostles, he first prayed all night and then called them specifically by name. Now an apostle was one sent forth with a commission. The term has both a narrow and a wider meaning. In its narrow sense it refers only to the twelve apostles whom Christ first called. In its broader sense it refers to every Christian who has been sent forth by Christ with a Great Commission. We would therefore recommend that after much prayer the minister select several people whom he would like to take with him to learn how to evangelize. (I might add at this point that we have changed from going out two by two, to going out by threes. The reason for this was that it solved the problem of what to do about women in a program of this sort. To send out two women at night in a large modern city can be quite dangerous; to send out one woman with somebody else's husband can be dangerous in a different way; to send out only husbands and wives defeats the purpose of multiplication.)

We have selected Wednesday morning from 9:00 to 12:00 and Wednesday and Thursday evenings from 7:15 to 10:30 as our time of visitation. In each case we have a report-back meeting which I feel is quite important to prevent discouragement. At these times we hear the reports of the work of the day. These report sessions help reduce drop-outs due to discouragement; workers have an opportunity to have their spirits lifted by returning to hear others whom God has blessed that night or morning.

We have two training programs a year, the first beginning early in September and the second in February, each running about four-and-a-half months. We also hold three six-day clinics annually for ministers. Again all of these details will vary according to local customs and circumstances.

I did not want to begin a program in this small way with only one or two individuals, but wanted rather to train a whole class of evangelists at one time. The result was that I ended up with none. However, if you begin with a few, you can grow in not too much time into a large body of witnesses. At the end of the four-and-a-half-month training program each of these four trained individuals would recruit two more workers and the minister also would recruit four more. Now there would be the original four plus their eight, making twelve, plus the minister's new four, making sixteen, plus the minister, or a total of seventeen. After the next class, the sixteen laymen would get thirty-two more, making forty-eight, plus the minister's four, which makes fifty-two, plus the minister, making fifty-three. And soon it could grow to a hundred, two hundred, etc. The people are recruited by personal visits at which time the program is explained by the trained individual in detail, and then they are invited to a dinner which will consist of a greater explanation of the goals and principles and reasons for the program, plus testimonies of what has been accomplished. Then they are asked to commit themselves to the entire four-and-a-half-month training program or else not to start. Paul said, "I am afraid of you, lest I have bestowed on you labor in vain."

TRAINING THE EVANGELISTS

Our program consists of three types of training.

Class instruction. These classes, lasting about half hour each, are held once a week on the day the people come to the church for visitation. They meet together for class instruction for a half hour and then go out into the field.

During this class instruction there is a brief lecture on the topic of the week, assignments are given for study during the following week, and the class is divided into two's where they practice what has been learned during the previous week.

Homework assignments. A detailed notebook has been prepared containing instructions in how to present the gospel logically and interestingly. Assignments are given each week, consisting of portions of the gospel to be learned. These are checked and recited each week at the class.

On-the-job training. The third most important part of the training is the "on-the-job training." Here each trainee goes out with a trained individual and listens as this trained person endeavors to lead someone to Christ. This is the vital, indispensable element of training.

PRESENTING THE GOSPEL

Our basic approach is neither apologetic, defensive, or negative. It is a simple, positive statement of the good news of the gospel. We have found that most Christians do not know how to make an intelligible, forceful, and interesting presentation of the gospel itself. Such a presentation is included in the training materials, and the people are encouraged to learn it and use it as a guide as they begin to present the gospel of Christ. Later it is no doubt adapted to the individual personality to which many additions or subtractions are made, as the case may require. But most people need something to start with.

The essential things which we are trying to teach our people are: how to get into the gospel, how to find out where the person is spiritually, how to present the gospel itself, and how to bring the person to a commitment to Jesus Christ.

In teaching the trainees the presentation of the gospel itself, we proceed in the following manner. First we have them learn the outline of the gospel, which might be considered as the skeleton. Second, we have them learn Scripture verses which give muscle, so to speak, to the outline. Third, we have them learn illustrations which flesh out and make clear and understandable the outline of the gospel.

In having the trainees learn the Gospel, we do not have them memorize the entire presentation but rather have them first learn the outline and then gradually build on to it. First we have them add just enough so that the bones of the outline don't rattle. Then we have them give a three-minute presentation of the gospel. And then we enlarge it to five minutes and then to eight. We continue to enlarge the presentation until they are able to present the gospel anywhere in a minute or an hour, depending on what the particular situation warrants. We provide them with a long presentation of the gospel as well as a shorter one; these are used as resource materials from which they can build their own presentations. In this way it becomes their own. We encourage them to work on it, practice it, and give it until indeed they own it and can give it with authority.

PRESERVING THE FRUIT

A program of evangelism such as this generates a tremendous need for follow-up. It has produced a need for additional secretaries and ministers on our staff, but the main responsibility for follow-up rests with the individual who has led the person to Christ. In our training notebook we have a rather elaborate section on follow-up principles and procedures. In essence the follow-up procedure involves several individual return visits wherein the new convert is established in Scriptures and assured of his salvation. We use a variety of materials and recommend highly the Navigator follow-up material. After several personal visits we then endeavor to get them into a small Bible study group which will consist of several more mature Christians plus four or five newer Christians. These classes of six or eight people then provide the spiritual incubator in which the newborn babe will live out the first few months of his Christian life.

Follow-up procedures are not completed until the convert has been taught to study God's Word, to pray, to live the Christian life, and to walk with Christ. Then he is encouraged to come into the evangelism program to learn how to win others to Christ. Yet at this point the follow-up still is not complete, for he must be taught not only how to reproduce but also how to disciple his new convert until he has matured to the place where he (that new convert) also is able to bring somene else to Christ. This emphasis of spiritual multiplication, looking past the first generation to the second, third, and fourth is the secret of an expanding and multiplying evangelistic ministry. In just a few years this has produced instances of great, great, great, great, great, great, great grandchildren in the faith. The acid test of any follow-up procedure will ultimately be: Is it producing spiritual grandchildren and great grandchildren? If not, then something is amiss and somewhere the process is breaking down.

MULTIPLYING THE RESULTS

Christ said, "The field is the world." I believe that our field should be the world, that every church, every individual, has a worldwide responsibility. I do not believe that any church can settle for anything less than worldwide evangelism as its own responsibility. Is it utterly unrealistic? I think not. Eleven men, indeed a very small church, have succeeded in carrying the gospel to most every nation on the earth. And the march of those eleven men goes on today. I do not believe, however, that it necessarily must take hundreds or thousands of years for the impact of the gospel to spread around the world. The process of spiritual multiplication can grow with the rapidity of the physical population explosion that we are seeing today. Our goal then is to reach the world for Christ.

How can this be done?

First, we must realize that our responsibility extends beyond Coral Ridge, or Fort Lauderdale, or even Florida, or the United States. But how are we to meet this responsibility? We have proceeded in this manner. In addition to training an increasing number of people in our own church, we have also trained a good many other churches in the city and the immediate area. In addition to this, we have three clinics annually where we have been bringing down hundreds of ministers for six days of intensive training, both in classroom instruction and on-the-job training, going out with our trained laymen. This has proved very successful and these ministers have gone back to their churches with a new vision for evangelism and a new zeal for training their people to do the work of ministry.

This program has already jumped the boundaries of the United States, and such programs are being conducted in a number of other nations. We hope that in the not too distant future that there will be churches in every nation which will see the vision of training their laymen, until a vast army of tens of millions of Christian lay evangelists has been raised up. This is our goal. This is our challenge. And by the continual supply of the Spirit of Christ we trust that it shall be done.

Soli deo Gloria.

Taken from *Vine Life* magazine. Used by permission.

43. Discovering Growth Possibilities

E. S. Anderson

Dr. Andy Anderson is a church growth consultant serving the Growth Section, Sunday School Department, Sunday School Board of the Southern Baptist Convention in Nashville, Tennessee.

As developer of the Action Sunday school enrollment plan, he leads national growth conferences frequently for the Southern Baptists as well as other denominations. More recently, he has developed the growth tool now known as the "growth spiral."

He is a graduate of Atlanta Bible Institute (B.A.) and Luther Rice Seminary (B.Div., Th.M., and D.Min.) Jacksonville, Florida. Anderson is author of **The Action Manual, Fasting Changed My Life,** and is editor of an introductory New Testament Greek course used for home study.

A native of South Carolina, Anderson served as pastor of Riverside Baptist Church, Ft. Myers, Florida, for nineteen years before moving to the Baptist Sunday School Board.

Your Sunday school can have a fantastic future! Your church can reach and develop more disciples than ever before!

Do you believe those two statements? Do you want them to become true? Then read on; this short chapter has big ideas for you.

It will excite your hope, lift your expectations, inspire dreams, and place in your hands the tools with which to bring your dreams to reality. Welcome to Sunday school growth through use of the Sunday School Growth Spiral.

WHAT IS SUNDAY SCHOOL GROWTH?

Numerical increase. While this is not the only area of growth, numerical increase is an area where growth is measurable. Some churches grow only 5 to 10 percent in one year, while others may grow 300 percent in the same time; both are reaching more people for Bible study.

A balance of quantity and quality. Quantity and quality should be as Siamese twins to a church; neither should outweigh the other.

No church should be interested in quantity alone; it should have a concern for quality as well. If it strives for quantity without good teaching, it fails; if it emphasizes quality at the expense of reaching the unreached, it loses its quality.

"There is a great debate today about the nature of church growth. The battle lines are usually drawn between what is called Qualitative Growth versus Quantitative Growth," says Charles Chaney and Ron Lewis in their book, *Design for Church Growth.*[1]

" 'The key question is not how churches can grow numerically,' " they quote one spokesman, " 'but how they can grow in grace.' " Indeed, the Bible underscores the need for growth to Christian maturity (Eph. 4:15; Col. 1:10; 1 Pet. 2:2; 2 Pet. 3:18). But this debate may be only a smoke screen to rationalize little or no numerical growth.

A church grows when its members grow in grace. The growth is largely unmeasurable. A church grows when people repent, believe in Jesus Christ, and are baptized and added to the church. This kind of growth is measurable. But the two are not mutually exclusive.

Not either/or but both/and is what is demanded. Qualitative growth and quantitative growth are inseparably related.

Qualitative growth produces quantitative growth, else something is wrong with its quality. Quality that does not produce quantity is counterfeit.

Quantitative growth makes qualitative growth possible. There has to be some quantity before there can be quality. Qualitative growth can only exist after the fact of quantitative growth.

Quantitative growth that does not end in qualitative growth will disappear.

Without the dimension of quality, quantitative growth cannot take place.

WHY IS SUNDAY SCHOOL GROWTH NEEDED?

The population explosion demands it. Population increases unbelievably. From the beginning of man's creation until 1959, world population had reached two-and-a-half-billion people. Within thirty years from that date another two-and-one-half-billion people will have been added. Our world is crowded! Some of the increase is in the United States, for population here is not yet stable.

Since Jesus wept over the multitudes of people two thousand years ago, how his heart must break over the billions today who need his love and forgiveness. How he must delight in seeing even one of his churches committed to reaching some of these unreached multitudes.

As world population increases dramatically, churches should enlarge their visions of growth! "Enlarge the place of thy tent, and let them stretch forth the curtains of thine habitations: spare not, lengthen thy cords, and strengthen thy stakes; for thou shalt break forth on the right hand and on the left" (Isa. 54:2, 3, KJV).

Healthy churches produce it. Enrolling new people in Bible study contributes to the spiritual growth of an entire church. Bible study grows churches! Without Bible study there is little hope of winning the increasing multitudes and developing believers. Growing strong churches means promoting Bible study and then bringing in the people. "Compel them to come in!" (Luke 14:23, KJV).

In order to live, churches must grow. When they cease to grow, they begin to die. As P. E. Burroughs once said, "Like bicycles, churches can stand up only as they continue to run. There can be no standing still!"

Lost people wait for it. With few exceptions, lost people never come to church of their own accord. Nor does the Bible command them to come. It does command the saved to go to the lost.

"It is as natural for an unregenerated person to stay away from your church as it is for water to run downhill," observed J. N. Barnette. "Therefore, it stands to reason that the church must go to these people, love them into its fellowship, teach them and win them by the Word of God."

A new awareness expects it. The Action Sunday School Enrollment plan, used by thousands of churches, has created a new awareness of the possibility of numerical growth. Church after church, using the open enrollment idea, Action's basic concept, have increased Sunday school enrollment dramatically. While some, through neglect of sound Sunday school organization and procedures, have failed to hold some gains, the interest and concern for growth still becomes even greater. The growth spiral does not supercede Action; it moves forward from its technique of reaching and helps plan for and produce further solid growth.

Compassion motivates it. The forward movement of the church begins with the fuel of concern, compassion, and commitment.

One spark of spiritual fire can do more to prove the power of God than a whole library written on the subject. The most common cause of failure is a lack of commitment. We must use the talents we have. The meadows and forests would be silent if no birds sang except those who sang the best.

WHY DON'T SOME CHURCHES GROW?

Barriers to growth do exist. But they can be overcome! Recognize them. Move over or around them.

Small number of unreached people. More obvious a hindrance to church growth is the limited population of a church field. In rural communities there may be few people; in some locations there may be few of the "type" people a church wishes to reach. A church may be so "uptight" about "undesirables" and reaching its own kind that hundreds of families go unreached, untouched, and forever lost to the gospel of Christ.

Cultural differences. Many churches will not cross cultural and language barriers. Yet, should not every person hear the gospel in his own language, culture, and tradition? Will he not respond more quickly and easily? Then why shouldn't a church cross these barriers, refuse to be limited by type staff, building, strategy, location, or program? Limited capacities and resources indicate that not all persons can be reached by one manner. To insist that all do so is to limit growth.

Unworthy Christian conduct. Disunity in a church surely will kill or chill its evangelistic outreach. A house divided against itself cannot promote conversion and growth. It breeds hatred and jealousy instead of loving concern and compassion. Church members who are disgruntled, unhappy, and dissatisfied hinder progress and growth, both numerical and spiritual. Un-Christian conduct dishonors Christ, "turns off" lost people, and causes the church's witness to become powerless. A New Testament church cannot grow in this kind of soil.

"Not every person has by nature a personality that adjusts well to others. However, every Christian can, through the power of the Holy Spirit, reflect the love of Christ in all his relationships with others."

Limited faith. "Without faith, it is impossible to please him" (Heb. 11:6, KJV).

Faith in Christ is indispensable. Christian leaders must have complete faith in Jesus Christ. They cannot possibly lead others to a saving faith in Christ unless their own faith in him is indisputable and uppermost. Christian workers must have an unshakable conviction that Christ is the answer to every human need and that we are not only saved by his power, but are kept by his grace. It is hard for a church to grow when its members have a shaky uncertainty concerning their faith.

Faith in others is a necessity. To be a good worker or leader in a New Testament church, one must not only have faith in Christ, one must also have faith in others. There is good in everyone if it is sought for, discovered, and brought out. One of the major values of the Sunday school is an enlistment agency for uncovering and developing the potential talent for service within each redeemed individual.

God has a purpose for every life. And that purpose can and should be found. Believing in others means helping persons find and follow that purpose to the glory of Christ.

Faith in oneself is a prerequisite. "I can do all things through Christ which strengtheneth me" (Phil. 4:13, KJV). Strong Christians can and should develop self-confidence. A person must have faith in himself, because he will seldom accomplish that which he does not believe he can do.

A. V. Washburn says in his book, *Outreach for the Unreached*,[2] "If a person accepts a place of service because he feels confident that God led him to it, then he can claim with assurance every resource of God to strengthen him for the task."

Inadequate organization. Without the addition of new teaching units, churches cannot experience growth. If organizations, like cornerstones, are set in concrete, the church will not grow. Needs of people precede, but also should dictate the establishment of organizational patterns. The more people to be reached, the larger the organization should become.

Fred Smith, one of America's great management consultants, says: "The difference in a good organization and a bad organization is structure. There *must* be a good structure. But the difference in a good organization and a great organization is motivation." When we become enthusiastic and excited about reaching people, our churches and their organizations will rise to the necessity of meeting the needs of the people—both physically and spiritually.

A church must provide adequate space, a sufficient number of classes, excellent Bible teaching, and attractive programs; when it reaches the people and brings them in, their needs can be met adequately. The above are vitally essential to sustain growth.

Failure to plan. Sometimes a preacher or teacher justifies lack of studying and planning by saying, "Oh, I just let things roll and God takes care. I just open my mouth and the Lord puts the proper words in it." This seems to relieve them of responsibility for proper preparation and planning, also for failure.

Some Sunday schools seem to operate in a similar manner, never setting goals, never planning calendars of activity, never developing visitation programs, enrollment emphases, or enlargement campaigns. They hope to grow by some magic.

Churches showing significant growth and producing great fruit in souls redeemed and lives transformed are those churches that plan and prepare to attempt great things.

Over twenty centuries ago Jesus left his command to disciple the entire world. When a church, taking seriously his command, plans how to reach more people, the Holy Spirit surely will inspire the planning and bless the actions planned.

Planning for effective church growth through effective Bible teaching in the Sunday school organization cannot be overemphasized.

Vision. "Where there is no vision, the people perish" (Prov. 29:18, KJV).

Let us paraphrase the words of Nehemiah, Ye see the distress of these communities—how they lie in waste and the people are scattered abroad, as sheep not having a shepherd. Come, let us organize Sunday schools in these communities that we be no longer guilty of neglect and that these communities be no longer a reproach to us. The God of heaven, he will prosper us—therefore, let us arise and save these neglected communities.

There is a malfunctioning of the eyes when one eye is nearsighted and the other is farsighted. Without a proper diagnosis and lens prescription, seeing becomes difficult for the one afflicted. However, we should all be so afflicted in our spiritual vision, nearsighted so as to look inwardly and grow strong base churches—with straight Bible teaching and preaching and a fervor for winning those in our midst who have been brought in through visitation and Sunday school enrollment. Then on the other hand, we should have a farsighted vision—looking out beyond our own church field to neglected communities of lost and backslidden people who need churches and Sunday schools within walking distance of where they live.

Misplaced priorities. A financier in a federal savings and loan institution was also chairman of the finance committee in the church to which he belonged. He compared the financial priorities of a church with those of a family. "First of all," he said, "the home needs must be met. In the home, the rent has to be paid, groceries bought, medical needs supplied, utilities paid, and of course, the tithe. Secondly, the other creditors must be paid, and lastly any luxury items that might be under consideration can be purchased.

"The same priorities should hold true for a church," he continued. "First of all, the home base is provided for, mortgage, utilities, salaries, mission gifts. These must be met. Then all other bills and obligations must be taken care of. Then luxury items can be considered. That is, things which we can use but do not necessarily have to have in order to exist as a church."

J. N. Barnette said, "The success of any church is to a great degree bound up with the finances. If a church is behind with running expenses, the spirit of the members is dampened; if spasmodic appeals are made from time to time to meet current bills, a church will soon have a low rating in the thinking of the people. The lack of a sound, practical, result-filled financial system cripples all the work in a church" and hinders further growth.

No desire to grow. Not all churches want to grow. With growth comes change, and to many people change is painful. "I like things the way they are," someone may say. "If too many new people come in I won't know anybody. Our classroom is all fixed up with new rugs and drapes. If we grow, we may have to change rooms."

"We don't need all those bus kids messing up our nice, clean walls," another may say. "It doesn't look right for our classes to be meeting in the auditorium. Things used to be so quiet, now it's too noisy around our church."

When the Action program was in its infancy and I was still a pastor, hundreds of calls and letters came in daily with orders for the Action Manual and materials. One small church had received the Manual, but had returned it to me with an attached note that read: "Dear Brother Andy: Enclosed please find Action Manual, unused. We are not going to do the program in our church, as we have decided we do not want to grow."

This man's candid honesty is to be appreciated. He openly expressed what so many pastors and church leaders feel and would never verbalize. Growth does bring a greater responsibility, hard work, and sometimes even pain. It is much more comfortable to remain "as is."

WHY SHOULD A CHURCH DESIRE A GROWING SUNDAY SCHOOL?

It is God's will. "What then is Apollos? What is Paul? Servants through whom you believed, as the Lord assigned to each. I planted, Apollos watered, but God gave the *growth*" (1 Cor. 3:5-7, RSV).[3]

"Praising God and having favor with all the people. And the Lord *added to* their number day by day those who were being saved" (Acts 2:47, RSV).

"Built upon the foundation of the apostles and prophets, Christ Jesus himself being the cornerstone in whom the whole structure is joined together and *grows* into a holy temple in the Lord" (Eph. 2:20, 21, RSV).

People wait to be reached. How can a church be satisfied to exist in a community of unsaved people and continue to conduct "business as usual"? People without Jesus Christ as Savior are lost. The church's primary task is pointing men to Jesus.

Charles E. Jefferson suggests that a good definition of a Christian would be, "A builder of the church of Jesus Christ."[4] Practically every believer must in the final analysis trace his own personal salvation back to some one of Christ's churches. Out of love and gratitude to Christ and his church, we are motivated to a growth commitment.

Not only do the lost need Christ, but Christ certainly needs the lost. Without these people for whom Christ died, the church would lack certain elements for its building and growth—certain living stones so vitally needed for the construction of Christ's church.

The task is so large. The United States itself is a needy mission field. There are about 185,000,000 Americans who have no systematic Bible study. The responsibility of the churches is to reach, teach, evangelize, and disciple every one. Specific plans must be provided to reach *this* generation. To reach these people would require more than 750,000 new Sunday schools the size of those existing today.

Parachurch movements have their values, but the church—the organization established in the New Testament—is the unit on which God is depending. The Great Commission was given to the church!

The love of Christ impels growth. "For God so loved the world, that he gave his only begotten Son, that whosoever believeth in him should not perish, but have everlasting life" (John 3;16, KJV).

No one could be saved without his matchless love. Christians must be involved in sharing this love with the peoples of the world.

Paul tells us that "Christ also loved the church, and gave himself for it" (Eph. 5:25, KJV).

"This statement goes deeper than may at first be thought. It means more than that he *died* for it, more than that he 'purchased it with his own blood.' In very fact he *gave himself* for it. He *spent* his strength in the making of it. He gave himself to the building of it. The purchase price was far greater than his death; it included also his life! He gave himself to the gathering and preparing of living stones and to the building of these stones into his church."

THE LONGING TO HELP PEOPLE

A Christian is one who has been forgiven of his sins, given a new life and an assurance of an eternal home in heaven. The non-Christian continues beneath the weight of his sins, has no life in Christ, and has no assurance of heaven as his future home. Those who have experienced salvation have a longing to reach the unsaved.

John Sisemore in his book, *The Ministry of Visitation*, says: "Christianity is an out-going religion. To follow Christ in spirit and practice is to feel a deep concern for those who are lost."[5]

There is also a desire to assist "babes in Christ" to grow. Arthur Flake reminds us that "in every church there is one or more persons suited to every task. The gifts of the members are as varied and different as the tasks. "Unto every one of us is given grace according to the measure of the gift of Christ" (Eph. 4:7, KJV). "And he gave some, apostles; and some, prophets; and some, evangelists; and some, pastors and teachers" (Eph. 4:11, KJV).

"As it was in the New Testament times, so it is today. In all our churches we have capable people of varied gifts and talents who, if *enlisted* and *trained*, are amply able to do valiant service for Christ. It is up to us to assist these new Christians to grow in grace and in knowledge — to help them discover their spiritual gifts that they may be of service to Christ and his church."

Knowing how to grow is a motivation to grow. Growth comes to those who are willing to outbelieve, outlive, outpray, and outdie, if necessary, the status quo. We should not be afraid to take a big step if one is needed, but we cannot cross a chasm in two small jumps.

A. V. Washburn said, "Jesus recognized that workers are the essential element of success. 'The harvest truly is plenteous, but the labourers are few; pray ye therefore the Lord of the harvest, that he will send forth labourers into his harvest' (Matt. 9:37, 38, KJV). All that stands in the way of victory is the enlistment of an abundance of workers.

"There are no limitations to the power of God, but he has restricted himself in his relationships with people. He has elected to bring about his will and way in the world through human instrumentality. People — leaders God can use — are indispensable. The changing of individuals, or society, of world conditions is ultimately dependent on usable channels of personality.

"The longer one studies Sunday School work, the more he realizes that the basis for growth and improvement lies in what the workers really see in Sunday School. If Sunday School work appears to them as a small task and having little stature, then workers are not willing to give more than a margin of their time and strength to do it." As a Christian grows in his conception of the work of the church and its organizations, he grows in his ability to perform the tasks. "Walk worthy of the vocation wherewith ye are called," said the Apostle Paul (Eph. 4:1, KJV).

It is marvelous just to know that as Christians we have the opportunity of sharing our lives, our insight into God's Word, our hope and dreams, and our ideals with the unbelievers and the babes in Christ. There is no better investment, no better way to spend one's life.

Pastor. The secret of large worship service attendance is a large Sunday school attendance. P. E. Burroughs said, "It is not really a question whether the people will come to hear the preaching; it is rather a question whether being already in the building, the people will remain for public worship and to hear the pastor's message."

In the 1920s, a pastor who preached to great crowds on Sunday morning said, "Some people give me credit for being an attractive preacher; it is true that large crowds wait on my ministry. The explanation is simple and very easy; our Sunday school draws upwards of 1,000 people to our building every Sunday morning. When the Sunday school closes its service some 200 officers and workers in the Sunday school are alert, seeking to induce the people to remain to hear me preach." The pastor smiled and continued, "Any man who could not get a congregation with that backing, ought not to try to preach. Even a wooden man ought to command a fair audience under such conditions."

A pastor must live *in* his Sunday school and live *for* it. He must build up his Sunday school and build himself into it. As a result the Sunday school will build him and his church. A growing Sunday school will put lost people and church members into the worship services. It won't work any other way. Ninety percent of an average Sunday morning congregation come through the Sunday school.

Dr. George Truett was much a part of his great Sunday school in the First Baptist Church, Dallas. He said so many times, "Next to the dear wife of my heart and next to the sweet children God has given me, I hold most dear the company of men and women who teach in my Sunday School."

A pastor *must* be the head of his Sunday school. He *must* be committed to its growth—spirtually and numerically. Charles Jefferson in his book, *Building a Church*, says, "Preachers are ordained, not to attract an audience, but to build a church."[4] As people study the Word in Sunday school, they are eager for a greater understanding of its meaning. Thus the pastor with his expertise in Bible interpretation and exposition can build upon and supplement the Sunday school teaching. The spirit, conception, and plans of a pastor will quickly be reflected in the Sunday school organization. Then as the Sunday school grows, the church grows. This cannot be overly emphasized.

The pastor's commitment should be as follows:

Begin or continue a daily devotional experience.

Concentrate on expository preaching.

Take personal direction of the Sunday school.

Take personal direction of the visitation program.

Take personal direction of the soul-winning program.

Use the Sunday School Growth Spiral.

Minister of education. The minister of education certainly must have a vision of the worth of the Sunday school in growing a church if a church is to make the most possible progress.

The man or woman who holds this important position will work under the direction of the church and in cooperation with the pastor. He shares in the work of every officer and teacher, and provides all the resources at his command to help them to more effectively work. He will work with the church staff and will provide guidance, assistance, and encouragement to the Sunday school director.

If there is indifference among the workers, the minister of education should help overcome it with his enthusiasm. If there is a lack of spiritual fervor, he should set a good example by his dedication of life and talents in growing a church.

His commitment should be as follows:

Develop or continue a daily devotional experience.

Plan and promote a weekly officers/teachers meeting.

Personally direct the visitation program with pastor.

Personally direct the soul-winning program with pastor.

Personally work with pastor in building the Sunday school.

Use the Sunday School Growth Spiral.

Leaders and workers. Before a church can grow not only must the pastor and the minister of education be committed to growth, but the church and Sunday school leaders and workers also must be sold on it. Only workers with such a commitment can be used for growth.

Sunday school officers, leaders, and teachers determine the rate of growth in a Sunday school. No other group can do this. They are at the head of the procession, and the Sunday school moves along at the same rate of speed as these leaders move.

Dedicated leaders and workers will train and prepare willingly, will visit absentees and prospects regularly, enrolling those not presently enrolled in Bible study, calling on the sick and the needy, pointing those who are lost to the Savior. Such commitment will grow a great church.

The Sunday School leadership should:

Support the pastor and staff in Sunday school growth.

Support the visitation program.

Support the soul-winning program.

Accept and use the Church Growth Spiral.

Pray, specifically, for God to bless.

The Church Growth Lists

44. The 100 Largest Churches and Sunday Schools

As was mentioned in Part I, which elucidated certain conclusions drawn from the statistical material presented here in Part VII, the researchers originally wanted to list 400, not just 100, large churches and Sunday schools. "Large" churches were arbitrarily designated as those with membership or attendance of 1200 or more. Curiously, there were not 400 "large" churches to be found, and the researchers have since settled upon 100 large churches and Sunday schools for these lists.

This may be a blessing in some sort of disguise. While the researchers desired these lists to be comprehensive, there is also something to be said for usefulness, and there is no question that the conciseness of a "100" list is more practical than the bulk of a "400" list. And, still, a "100" list remains comprehensive enough to provide an accurate profile of the large congregations of America.

It should be said also that the researchers wanted to look at more than just Sunday school growth. Elmer Towns, one of the researchers, had given much attention to Sunday school growth in his book, *The Ten Largest Sunday Schools* (Baker). In addition, his book, *America's Fastest Growing Churches* (Impact), examined growth among independent Baptist churches only. The researchers hoped to put together lists that would be more extensive and comprehensive than these already published.

Consequently, the researchers measured growth in five areas: church membership, church giving, attendance at Sunday morning preaching services, Sunday school enrollment, and Sunday school attendance.

Another reason for these criteria is that the annual listing of the 100 largest Sunday schools was not deemed by the researchers to be a true picture of a church's growth. It is possible for a church to bus in vast numbers of children for Sunday school and appear to grow; in fact, such a church may have a very small adult membership and the offerings may not be comparable to other large congregations. With these lists it is possible for someone to find a church listed high in Sunday school attendance but listed low or not listed at all in church giving or church membership. By comparing the placement of churches on these lists, one can sketch a rather accurate portrait of a church, one which can be of great value and use.

To conduct the research, fourteen major denominations were contacted for computer printouts, records, or yearbooks; from these sources tabulations were carried out. Also evangelical denominations, usually associated with

NAE (National Association of Evangelicals), were evaluated from statistics provided by individual Sunday school leaders or from the annual yearbook. Furthermore, an extensive mailing was made to independent churches — those not associated with any denomination. The source of these mailings was supplied by Elmer Towns. Finally, advertisements were listed in the magazines that had large circulation among churches; this was an attempt to locate large, independent churches unknown to the researchers. Periodicals used included the *Journal-Champion* (circulation, 40,000) and the official magazine of the International Christian Education Association (circulation, 100,000).

As a result of the comprehensive and thorough investigation by the researchers, it is felt that this listing of 100 churches in five categories is a complete and accurate assessment of the large churches in America today.

100 LARGEST CHURCHES: CHURCH MEMBERSHIP (1979-1980)

1. Highland Park Baptist Church	Chattanooga, Tennessee	54,989
2. First Baptist Church	Hammond, Indiana	52,255
3. First Baptist Church	Dallas, Texas	21,137
4. Thomas Road Baptist Church	Lynchburg, Virginia	17,000*
5. First Southern Baptist Church	Del City, Oklahoma	14,210
6. Concord Baptist Church	Brooklyn, New York	12,000
7. First Baptist Church	Van Nuys, California	11,614
8. Bellevue Baptist Church	Memphis, Tennessee	11,508
9. First United Methodist Church	Houston, Texas	11,384
10. First Baptist Church	Houston, Texas	11,133
11. Mount Olivet Lutheran Church	Minneapolis, Minnesota	10,640
12. First Baptist Church	Lubbock, Texas	10,595
13. First Baptist Church	Jacksonville, Florida	10,214
14. Temple Baptist Church	Detroit, Michigan	10,088
15. Garden Grove Community Church	Garden Grove, California	9,553
16. First Baptist Church	San Antonio, Texas	9,404
17. First Baptist Church	Amarillo, Texas	9,347

18.	Christ Temple of Faith	Inkster, Michigan	9,163
19.	Highland Park United Methodist Church	Dallas, Texas	9,148
20.	First Baptist Church	Hollywood, Florida	8,343
21.	North Phoenix Baptist Church	Phoenix, Arizona	8,248
22.	Lovers Lane United Methodist Church	Dallas, Texas	7,979
23.	Dauphin Way Baptist Church	Mobile, Alabama	7,806
24.	First Baptist Church	Atlanta, Georgia	7,705
25.	Travis Avenue Baptist Church	Fort Worth, Texas	7,441
26.	Kansas City Baptist Temple	Kansas City, Missouri	7,000
27.	Collegiate Corporation	New York, New York	6,974
28.	Highland Park Presbyterian Church	Dallas, Texas	6,960
29.	First Baptist Church	Wichita Falls, Texas	6,826
30.	South Main Baptist Church	Houston, Texas	6,812
31.	Cottage Hill Baptist Church	Mobile, Alabama	6,742
32.	First Baptist Church	Tulsa, Oklahoma	6,674
33.	First Baptist Church	Midland, Texas	6,545
34.	First Baptist Church	Jackson, Mississippi	6,489*
35.	Village Presbyterian Church	Prairie Village, Kansas	6,454
36.	Hyde Park Baptist Church	Austin, Texas	6,375
37.	St. Luke's United Methodist Church	Oklahoma City, Oklahoma	6,367
38.	Boston Avenue United Methodist Church	Tulsa, Oklahoma	6,247
39.	Walnut Street Baptist Church	Louisville, Kentucky	6,224
40.	First Baptist Church	Fort Smith, Arkansas	6,166
41.	St. John Lutheran Church	Des Moines, Iowa	6,154
42.	Castle Hills Baptist Church	San Antonio, Texas	6,151
43.	Cliff Temple Baptist Church	Dallas, Texas	6,089
44.	First United Methodist Church	Richardson, Texas	6,067
45.	First Baptist Church	Oklahoma City, Oklahoma	5,992
46.	Dawson Memorial Baptist Church	Birmingham, Alabama	5,985

47. St. Luke's United Methodist Church	Houston, Texas	5,947
48. Trinity Baptist Church	San Antonio, Texas	5,915
49. First United Methodist Church	Fort Worth, Texas	5,887
50. First Baptist Church	Baton Rouge, Louisiana	5,865
51. The Chapel in University Park	Akron, Ohio	5,800
52. First Baptist Church	Pasadena, Texas	5,798
53. Columbus Avenue Baptist Church	Waco, Texas	5,796
54. First Baptist Church	Lawton, Oklahoma	5,726
55. Beverly Hills Baptist Church	Dallas, Texas	5,694
56. First United Methodist Church	Lubbock, Texas	5,659
57. Roswell Street Baptist Church	Marietta, Georgia	5,655
58. Memorial Drive United Methodist Church	Houston, Texas	5,584
59. Park Cities Baptist Church	Dallas, Texas	5,536
60. First United Methodist Church	Dallas, Texas	5,502
61. Los Gatos Christian Church	Los Gatos, California	5,500
62. Zion Lutheran Church	Anoka, Minnesota	5,500
63. Curtis Baptist Church	Augusta, Georgia	5,484
64. Madison Church of Christ	Madison, Tennessee	5,355
65. Sagamore Hill Baptist Church	Fort Worth, Texas	5,354
66. New Testament Baptist Church	Hialeah, Florida	5,335
67. First Colorado Springs United Methodist Church	Denver, Colorado	5,314
68. First Baptist Church	Arlington, Texas	5,261
69. Tower Grove Baptist Church	St. Louis, Missouri	5,190
70. First United Methodist Church	Shreveport, Louisiana	5,123
71. First Baptist Church	Orlando, Florida	5,100
72. Memorial Drive Presbyterian Church	Houston, Texas	5,100
73. Coral Ridge Presbyterian Church	Ft. Lauderdale, Florida	5,085
74. Paradise Baptist Church	Los Angeles, California	5,076

75. Plymouth Park Baptist Church	Irving, Texas	4,923
76. First Baptist Church	West Palm Beach, Florida	4,920
77. St. Peter Lutheran Church	Arlington Heights, Illinois	4,902
78. First Baptist Church	Abilene, Texas	4,865
79. First Baptist Church	Columbia, South Carolina	4,830
80. Broadway Baptist Church	Fort Worth, Texas	4,822
81. Rehoboth Baptist Church	Tucker, Georgia	4,781
82. Wieuca Road Baptist Church	Atlanta, Georgia	4,742
83. Park Avenue Baptist Church	Nashville, Tennessee	4,729
84. First Baptist Church	Waco, Texas	4,717
85. St. Mark Lutheran Church	Davenport, Iowa	4,640
86. First Baptist Church	Tallahassee, Florida	4,629
87. First Baptist Church	Beaumont, Texas	4,605
88. Leawood Baptist Church	Memphis, Tennessee	4,597
89. First United Presbyterian Church	Tulsa, Oklahoma	4,552
90. Mount Carmel Christian Church	Decatur, Georgia	4,548
91. Tallowood Baptist Church	Houston, Texas	4,530
92. First United Methodist Church	Orlando, Florida	4,504
93. Shiloh Baptist Church	Washington, D.C.	4,500
94. First English Lutheran Church	Mansfield, Ohio	4,464
95. Trinity United Methodist Church	South Central, Nebraska	4,463
96. Peachtree Road United Methodist Church	Atlanta, Georgia	4,461
97. Bible Baptist Church	Savannah, Georgia	4,458
98. Lavon Drive Baptist Church	Garland, Texas	4,449
99. East Grand Baptist Church	Dallas, Texas	4,438
100. Second Baptist Church	Houston, Texas	4,431

Note: The Cathedral of Tomorrow, Akron, Ohio, pastored by Rex Humbard, **does** belong within the above listing. However, due to difficulties of record-keeping and the unavailability of hard statistics, The Cathedral of Tomorrow could not be listed. Readers should be aware that interviews with the church's staff have verified that The Cathedral of Tomorrow should be considered one of the 100 largest churches in the category of church membership.

*These figures are not verified, but are estimates based on research and interviews.

100 LARGEST CHURCHES:
FINANCIAL INCOME (1979-1980)

1. First Baptist Church	Dallas, Texas	$7,200,000
2. Bellevue Baptist Church	Memphis, Tennessee	$4,998,351
3. First Baptist Church	Hammond, Indiana	$4,153,752
4. North Phoenix Baptist Church	Phoenix, Arizona	$3,600,000
5. Grace Community Church	Sun Valley, California	$3,500,691
6. First Baptist Church	Houston, Texas	$3,417,676
7. Los Gatos Christian Church	Los Gatos, California	$3,000,000
8. First Southern Baptist Church	Del City, Oklahoma	$2,953,000
9. First Baptist Church	Van Nuys, California	$2,800,000
10. Calvary Temple	Denver, Colorado	$2,637,044
11. First Baptist Church	Atlanta, Georgia	$2,568,209
12. First Baptist Church	Amarillo, Texas	$2,324,602
13. First Baptist Church	Jacksonville, Florida	$2,276,983*
14. Calvary Temple Baptist Church	Savannah, Georgia	$2,195,092
15. Calvary United Presbyterian Church	San Francisco, California	$2,151,172
16. Garden Grove Community Church	Garden Grove, Calfornia	$2,100,000
17. South Main Baptist Church	Houston, Texas	$2,044,081
18. First Evangelical Free Church	Fullerton, California	$2,016,500
19. First Assembly of God	Rockford, Illinois	$2,000,000
20. Wieuca Road Baptist Church	Atlanta, Georgia	$1,983,886
21. Lovers Lane United Methodist Church	Dallas, Texas	$1,970,566
22. Hyde Park Baptist Church	Austin, Texas	$1,966,746
23. The Peoples Church	Willowdale, Ontario	$1,950,000
24. Tallowood Baptist Church	Houston, Texas	$1,902,129
25. Christ Temple of Faith	Inkster, Michigan	$1,900,000
26. First Baptist Church	Lubbock, Texas	$1,890,354
27. Calvary Assembly	Winter Park, Florida	$1,888,500

28. Grace Community Church	Tempe, Arizona	$1,870,902
29. Beverly Hills Baptist Church	Dallas, Texas	$1,803,932
30. First Baptist Church	Jackson, Mississippi	$1,777,506
31. Highland Park Baptist Church	Chattanooga, Tennessee	$1,745,253*
32. Park Cities Baptist Church	Dallas, Texas	$1,729,766
33. First Baptist Church	Midland, Texas	$1,726,192
34. Blackhawk Baptist Church	Fort Wayne, Indiana	$1,700,000
35. First Assembly of God	Lakeland, Florida	$1,700,000
36. First Baptist Church	Orlando, Florida	$1,700,000
37. First Wesleyan Church	High Point, North Carolina	$1,700,000
38. Collegiate Corporation	New York, New York	$1,680,343
39. Highland Park United Methodist Church	Dallas, Texas	$1,673,702
40. Dawson Memorial Baptist Church	Birmingham, Alabama	$1,666,373
41. Highland Park Presbyterian Church	Dallas, Texas	$1,642,722
42. First Baptist Church	Tulsa, Oklahoma	$1,639,101
43. The Chapel in University Park	Akron, Ohio	$1,627,352
44. People's Church	Fresno, California	$1,618,000
45. Central Church	Memphis, Tennessee	$1,615,000
46. Walnut Street Baptist Church	Louisville, Kentucky	$1,598,238
47. Green Acres Baptist Church	Tyler, Texas	$1,590,140
48. First Baptist Church	Shreveport, Louisiana	$1,589,431
49. First Baptist Church	Wichita Falls, Texas	$1,576,500
50. Dauphin Way Baptist Church	Mobile, Alabama	$1,507,000
51. Scott Memorial Baptist Church	San Diego, California	$1,507,000
52. First Baptist Church	Lubbock, Texas	$1,501,886
53. Calvary Temple Church	Springfield, Illinois	$1,500,000
54. Paradise Baptist Church	Los Angeles, California	$1,500,000
55. New Testament Baptist Church	Hialeah, Florida	$1,500,000*
56. Concord Baptist Church	Brooklyn, New York	$1,500,000

57. Village Presbyterian Church	Prairie Village, Kansas	$1,459,205
58. Ponce de Leon Second Baptist Church	Atlanta, Georgia	$1,441,518
59. First Assembly of God	New Orleans, Louisiana	$1,424,055
60. Peachtree Presbyterian Church	Atlanta, Georgia	$1,413,301
61. Broadmoor Baptist Church	Shreveport, Louisiana	$1,387,758
62. Curtis Baptist Church	Augusta, Georgia	$1,384,758
63. Mount Olivet Lutheran Church	Minneapolis, Minnesota	$1,356,169
64. Riverside Baptist Church	Denver, Colorado	$1,354,581
65. Memorial Drive Presbyterian Church	Houston, Texas	$1,331,048
66. Broadway Baptist Church	Memphis, Tennessee	$1,325,017
67. Mount Paran Church of God	Atlanta, Georgia	$1,300,000
68. First Baptist Church	Longview, Texas	$1,298,706
69. Trinity Baptist Church	San Antonio, Texas	$1,297,772
70. First Baptist Church	Columbia, South Carolina	$1,289,709
71. Braeswood Assembly of God	Houston, Texas	$1,288,416
72. First United Presbyterian Church	Pittsburgh, Pennsylvania	$1,286,225
73. First Presbyterian Church	Greensboro, North Carolina	$1,286,135
74. Allandale Baptist Church	Austin, Texas	$1,282,010
75. Briarlake Baptist Church	Decatur, Georgia	$1,278,703
76. First Baptist Church	San Antonio, Texas	$1,278,058
77. Cottage Hill Baptist Church	Mobile, Alabama	$1,271,000
78. First Presbyterian Church	Houston, Texas	$1,258,532
79. Broadmoor Baptist Church	Jackson, Mississippi	$1,256,565
80. First Baptist Church	Tyler, Texas	$1,252,798
81. First Baptist Church	Abilene, Texas	$1,237,392
82. Second Presbyterian Church	Memphis, Tennessee	$1,235,533
83. Grace United Presbyterian Church	Peoria, Illinois	$1,235,336

84. Shepherd of the Valley Lutheran Church	Phoenix, Arizona	$1,235,278
85. St. Mark Lutheran Church	Davenport, Iowa	$1,234,205
86. Menlo Park United Presbyterian Church	Menlo Park, California	$1,233,580
87. First Baptist Church	Pasadena, Texas	$1,222,916
88. Castle Hills Baptist Church	San Antonio, Texas	$1,211,847
89. Broadway Baptist Church	Memphis, Tennessee	$1,207,805
90. Northway Baptist Church	Dallas, Texas	$1,203,413
91. First United Presbyterian Church	Aurora, Illinois	$1,202,095
92. College Avenue Baptist Church	San Diego, California	$1,200,000
93. Huffman Assembly of God	Birmingham, Alabama	$1,200,000
94. First United Methodist Church	Houston, Texas	$1,199,608
95. Peachtree Road United Methodist Church	Atlanta, Georgia	$1,197,293
96. Calvary Baptist Church	Shreveport, Louisiana	$1,197,028
97. First United Presbyterian Church	Colorado Springs, Colorado	$1,191,797
98. First Baptist Church	Arlington, Texas	$1,191,628
99. First Baptist Church	Bartlesville, Oklahoma	$1,188,054
100. St. Luke's United Methodist Church	Houston, Texas	$1,177,795

100 LARGEST CHURCHES: CHURCH ATTENDANCE (1979-1980)

1. First Baptist Church	Hammond, Indiana	13,000
2. Thomas Road Baptist Church	Lynchburg, Virginia	8,000*
3. Highland Park Baptist Church	Chattanooga, Tennessee	7,000*
4. First Baptist Church	Dallas, Texas	6,000
5. The Chapel in University Park	Akron, Ohio	6,000*

6. Garden Grove Community Church	Garden Grove, California	5,800
7. Mt. Olivet Lutheran Church	Minneapolis, Minnesota	5,610
8. First Baptist Church	Jacksonville, Florida	5,200
9. Coral Ridge Presbyterian Church	Fort Lauderdale, Florida	5,000*
10. Bellevue Baptist Church	Memphis, Tennessee	4,700
11. Madison Church of Christ	Madison, Tennessee	4,469
12. Calvary Temple Church	Springfield, Illinois	4,400
13. The Chapel in University Park	Akron, Ohio	4,300
14. North Phoenix Baptist Church	Phoenix, Arizona	4,300
15. Los Gatos Christian Church	Los Gatos, California	4,200
16. Calvary Assembly of God	Winter Park, Florida	4,122
17. First Baptist Church	Atlanta, Georgia	4,000
18. Akron Baptist Temple	Akron, Ohio	4,000*
19. Temple Baptist Church	Detroit, Michigan	4,000*
20. Christ Temple of Faith	Inkster, Michigan	3,700
21. First Assembly of God	New Orleans, Louisiana	3,700
22. Westside Assembly of God	Davenport, Iowa	3,700
23. People's Church	Fresno, California	3,700
24. First Assembly of God	Lakeland, Florida	3,700
25. Calvary Community Church	San Jose, California	3,533
26. Grace Community Church	Tempe, Arizona	3,500
27. College Church of Christ	Searcy, Arkansas	3,400
28. Roswell Street Baptist Church	Marietta, Georgia	3,350
29. First Baptist Church	Van Nuys, California	3,300
30. Paradise Baptist Church	Los Angeles, California	3,000
31. Cottage Hill Baptist Church	Mobile, Alabama	3,000
32. Canton Baptist Temple	Canton, Ohio	3,000*
33. Peninsula Bible Church	Palo Alto, California	3,000
34. Concord Baptist Church	Brooklyn, New York	3,000
35. First Southern Baptist Church	Del City, Oklahoma	3,000
36. Evangel Tabernacle	Louisville, Kentucky	3,000
37. High Street Baptist Church	Springfield, Missouri	3,000*

38. Indianapolis Baptist Temple	Indianapolis, Indiana	3,000
39. Park Cities Baptist Church	Dallas, Texas	3,000*
40. Landmark Baptist Temple	Cincinnati, Ohio	3,000*
41. First Baptist Church	Lubbock, Texas	2,954
42. Cottage Hill Baptist Church	Mobile, Alabama	2,900
43. Broadway Church of Christ	Lubbock, Texas	2,874
44. First United Methodist Church	Dallas, Texas	2,832
45. First Baptist Church	Orlando, Florida	2,800
46. First Evangelical Free Church	Fullerton, California	2,800
47. Trinity Church	Lubbock, Texas	2,800
48. First United Methodist Church	Houston, Texas	2,761
49. Christ United Methodist Church	St. Petersburg, Florida	2,709
50. Mount Paran Church of God	Atlanta, Georgia	2,672
51. Grace Brethren Church	Long Beach, California	2,644
52. Walnut Street Baptist Church	Louisville, Kentucky	2,600*
53. First Baptist Church	Amarillo, Texas	2,580
54. First Baptist Church	Hollywood, Florida	2,500
55. First Baptist Church of Van Nuys	Van Nuys, California	2,500*
56. The Peoples Church	Willowdale, Ontario	2,500*
57. First Assembly of God	Oklahoma City, Oklahoma	2,436
58. Highland Church of Christ	Abilene, Texas	2,400
59. Concordia Lutheran Church	San Antonio, Texas	2,350
60. Gospel Light Baptist Church	Walkertown, North Carolina	2,350
61. Central Church	Memphis, Tennessee	2,300
62. First Assembly of God	North Hollywood, California	2,300
63. Central Assembly of God	Joplin, Missouri	2,272
64. North Cleveland Church of God	Cleveland, Tennessee	2,250
65. Emmanuel Faith Community Church	Escondido, California	2,200*
66. First Baptist Church	San Antonio, Texas	2,200*

67. Sunset Church of Christ	Lubbock, Texas	2,198
68. Scott Memorial Baptist Church	San Diego, California	2,162
69. Fairhaven Church	Chesterton, Indiana	2,112
70. First Assembly of God	Rockford, Illinois	2,100
71. Calvary Baptist Church	Hazel Park, Michigan	2,100*
72. Kansas City Baptist Temple	Kansas City, Missouri	2,100
73. Bethany First Church of the Nazarene	Bethany, Oklahoma	2,089
74. Highland Park United Methodist Church	Dallas, Texas	2,005
75. Abundant Life Memorial Church	Indianapolis, Indiana	2,000*
76. Allandale Baptist Church	Austin, Texas	2,000
77. Allapattah Baptist Church	Miami, Florida	2,000*
78. Bethany Bible Church	Phoenix, Arizona	2,000*
79. Briarlake Baptist Church	Decatur, Georgia	2,000*
80. Broadmoor Baptist Church	Shreveport, Louisiana	2,000*
81. Calvary Temple	Denver, Colorado	2,000*
82. Christ Church of Northgate	Seattle, Washington	2,000
83. Christian Life Center	Santa Rosa, California	2,000
84. College Avenue Baptist Church	San Diego, California	2,000
85. Dauphin Way Baptist Church	Mobile, Alabama	2,000
86. Dawson Memorial Baptist Church	Birmingham, Alabama	2,000*
87. Faith Chapel	La Mesa, California	2,000
88. First Assembly of God	Tacoma, Washington	2,000
89. First Baptist Church	Pomona, California	2,000*
90. First Baptist Church	Merritt Island, Florida	2,000*
91. Evergreen Christian Center	Olympia, Washington	2,000
92. First Baptist Church	Riverdale, Maryland	2,000*
93. First Baptist Church	Midland, Texas	2,000*
94. First Christian Church	Canton, Ohio	2,000*
95. First Presbyterian Church	Colorado Springs, Colorado	2,000*
96. First United Methodist Church	Tulsa, Oklahoma	2,000
97. Forrest Hills Baptist Church	Decatur, Georgia	2,000*
98. Hyde Park Baptist Church	Austin, Texas	2,000

99. Limerick Chapel	Limerick, Pennsylvania	2,000*
100. Massillon Baptist Church	Massillon, Ohio	2,000*

Note: The Cathedral of Tomorrow, Akron, Ohio, pastored by Rex Humbard, **does** belong within the above listing. However, due to difficulties of record-keeping and the unavailability of hard statistics, The Cathedral of Tomorrow could not be listed. Readers should be aware that interviews with the church's staff have verified that The Cathedral of Tomorrow should be considered one of the 100 largest churches in the category of church attendance.

*These figures are not verified, but are estimates based on research and interviews.

100 LARGEST CHURCHES:
SUNDAY SCHOOL ENROLLMENT (1979-1980)

1. First Baptist Church	Hammond, Indiana	23,446
2. First Baptist Church	Dallas, Texas	10,867
3. First Baptist Church	Jacksonville, Florida	9,592
4. Calvary Temple Church	Springfield, Illinois	6,488
5. North Phoenix Baptist Church	Phoenix, Arizona	6,317
6. First Baptist Church	Del City, Oklahoma	5,952
7. Bellevue Baptist Church	Memphis, Tennessee	5,872
8. First Baptist Church	Houston, Texas	5,799
9. First United Methodist Church	Richardson, Texas	5,618
10. Central Assembly of God	Joplin, Missouri	5,563
11. Cottage Hill Baptist Church	Mobile, Alabama	5,458
12. First Baptist Church	Amarillo, Texas	5,453
13. Fairhaven Church	Chesterton, Texas	5,248
14. Orlando Calvary Assembly of God	Winter Park, Florida	5,217
15. Eastwood Baptist Church	Tulsa, Oklahoma	5,068
16. First United Methodist Church	Fort Worth, Texas	5,007
17. Trinity Baptist Church	San Antonio, Texas	4,905
18. Dawson Memorial Baptist Church	Birmingham, Alabama	4,854
19. New Testament Baptist Church	Hialeah, Florida	4,844
20. Dauphin Way Baptist Church	Mobile, Alabama	4,640
21. Broadway Baptist Church	Memphis, Tennessee	4,611
22. Allandale Baptist Church	Austin, Texas	4,564

353

23. Tallowood Baptist Church	Houston, Texas	4,555
24. Garden Grove Community Church	Garden Grove, California	4,520
25. First United Presbyterian Church	Colorado Springs, Colorado	4,469
26. First Baptist Church	Atlanta, Georgia	4,411
27. First Baptist Church	Lubbock, Texas	4,410
28. Hyde Park Baptist Church	Austin, Texas	4,271
29. Lovers Lane United Methodist Church	Dallas, Texas	4,144
30. First Baptist Church	Orlando, Florida	4,077
31. Park Cities Baptist Church	Dallas, Texas	4,064
32. Madison Church of Christ	Madison, Tennessee	4,023
33. First Baptist Church	Pasadena, Texas	3,781
34. First Baptist Church	Van Nuys, California	3,752
35. Highland Park Presbyterian Church	Dallas, Texas	3,747
36. Casa View Baptist Church	Dallas, Texas	3,695
37. Ninth & O Baptist Church	Louisville, Kentucky	3,666
38. Green Acres Baptist Church	Tyler, Texas	3,664
39. First Baptist Church	Ferguson, Missouri	3,649
40. Westside Assembly of God	Davenport, Iowa	3,604
41. First Baptist Church	Fort Smith, Arkansas	3,567
42. Leawood Baptist Church	Memphis, Tennessee	3,567
43. South Main Baptist Church	Houston, Texas	3,526
44. Plymouth Park Baptist Church	Irving, Texas	3,490
45. First Baptist Church	Jackson, Mississippi	3,482
46. Memorial Drive United Methodist Church	Houston, Texas	3,469
47. First Baptist Church	Midland, Texas	3,412
48. Bible Baptist Church	Savannah, Georgia	3,409
49. Tower Grove Baptist Church	St. Louis, Missouri	3,409
50. First Baptist Church	Wichita Falls, Texas	3,402
51. Travis Avenue Baptist Church	Fort Worth, Texas	3,399
52. Roswell Street Baptist Church	Marietta, Georgia	3,375
53. The Chapel in University Park	Akron, Ohio	3,300

54. Shiloh Terrace Baptist Church	Dallas, Texas	3,288
55. Lakeview Temple	Indianapolis, Indiana	3,188
56. Broadmoor Baptist Church	Shreveport, Louisiana	3,157
57. First Baptist Church	Ferguson, Missouri	3,152
58. First Baptist Church	Richardson, Texas	3,139
59. First United Methodist Church	Houston, Texas	3,129
60. Wieuca Road Baptist Church	Atlanta, Georgia	3,105
61. Highland Park United Methodist Church	Dallas, Texas	3,089
62. First Baptist Church	Arlington, Texas	3,026
63. Scott Memorial Baptist Church	San Diego, California	3,015
64. Sagamore Hill Baptist Church	Fort Worth, Texas	3,007
65. First Baptist Church	Carrollton, Texas	3,006
66. Christ Temple of Faith	Inkster, Michigan	3,000
67. Curtis Baptist Church	Augusta, Georgia	3,000
68. First United Methodist Church	Shreveport, Louisiana	2,981
69. Walnut Street Baptist Church	Louisville, Kentucky	2,978
70. First Baptist Church	San Antonio, Texas	2,944
71. Calvary Temple Baptist Church	Savannah, Georgia	2,940
72. First Baptist Church	Kenner, Louisiana	2,937
73. First Baptist Church	Tulsa, Oklahoma	2,922
74. First Baptist Church	Paris, Texas	2,917
75. Rehoboth Baptist Church	Tucker, Georgia	2,875
76. First Baptist Church	Euless, Texas	2,870
77. First Baptist Church	Irving, Texas	2,863
78. First Baptist Church	Columbia, South Carolina	2,858
79. First Assembly of God	Lakeland, Florida	2,852
80. Paramount Baptist Church	Amarillo, Texas	2,837
81. Calvary Community Church	San Jose, California	2,829
82. First Baptist Church	Bossier City, Louisiana	2,827
83. Bethany First Church of the Nazarene	Bethany, Oklahoma	2,800
84. Lavon Drive Baptist Church	Garland, Texas	2,780
85. First Baptist Church	Pensacola, Florida	2,771

86. First Assembly of God	Rockford, Illinois	2,756
87. First Baptist Church	Lafayette, Kentucky	2,717
88. Two Rivers Baptist Church	Nashville, Tennessee	2,710
89. Ward United Presbyterian Church	Livonia, Michigan	2,697
90. Parkway Baptist Church	Jackson, Mississippi	2,660
91. First Baptist Church	Raytown, Missouri	2,657
92. First Baptist Church	Garland, Texas	2,644
93. First Baptist Church	Baton Rouge, Louisiana	2,641
94. First Baptist Church	Winter Park, Florida	2,637
95. Castle Hills Baptist Church	San Antonio, Texas	2,634
96. St. Luke's United Methodist Church	Houston, Texas	2,630
97. First Baptist Church	Greensboro, North Carolina	2,628
98. Briarlake Baptist Church	Decatur, Georgia	2,617
99. First Baptist Church	Lawton, Oklahoma	2,579
100. Canterbury United Methodist Church	Birmingham, Alabama	2,577

100 LARGEST CHURCHES:
SUNDAY SCHOOL ATTENDANCE (1979-1980)

1. First Baptist Church	Hammond, Indiana	15,101
2. Highland Park Baptist Church	Chattanooga, Tennessee	11,000
3. Thomas Road Baptist Church	Lynchburg, Virginia	8,000*
4. Akron Baptist Temple	Akron, Ohio	6,700*
5. First Baptist Church	Dallas, Texas	6,600
6. Westside Assembly of God	Davenport, Iowa	4,925
7. Calvary Temple Church	Springfield, Illinois	4,908
8. Concord Baptist Church	Brooklyn, New York	4,800
9. Canton Baptist Temple	Canton, Ohio	4,574
10. Calvary Assembly	Winter Park, Florida	4,348
11. Landmark Baptist Temple	Cincinnati, Ohio	4,315*
12. First Southern Baptist Church	Del City, Oklahoma	4,100
13. First Baptist Church	Jacksonville, Florida	3,828
14. First Assembly of God	New Orleans, Louisiana	3,487

15. Westside Assembly of God	Davenport, Iowa	3,400*
16. Madison Church of Christ	Madison, Tennessee	3,357
17. Los Gatos Christian Church	Los Gatos, California	3,352
18. Grace Community Church	Sun Valley, California	3,258
19. The Chapel in University Park	Akron, Ohio	3,200*
20. North Phoenix Baptist Church	Phoenix, Arizona	3,113
21. Indianapolis Baptist Temple	Indianapolis, Indiana	3,100*
22. Temple Baptist Church	Detroit, Michigan	3,100*
23. First Assembly of God	Lakeland, Florida	3,050
24. Bellevue Baptist Church	Memphis, Tennessee	3,000*
25. First Baptist Church of Van Nuys	Van Nuys, California	2,850*
26. North Cleveland Church of God	Cleveland, Tennessee	2,739
27. Grace Community Church	Tempe, Arizona	2,593
28. Central Assembly of God	Joplin, Missouri	2,572
29. Dauphin Way Baptist Church	Mobile, Alabama	2,561
30. Garden Grove Community Church	Garden Grove, California	2,475
31. Huffman Assembly of God	Birmingham, Alabama	2,460
32. First Baptist Church	Amarillo, Texas	2,416
33. First Assembly of God	Oklahoma City, Oklahoma	2,400
34. Calvary Temple	Denver, Colorado	2,400*
35. Forrest Hills Baptist Church	Decatur, Georgia	2,400*
36. Trinity Baptist Church	Jacksonville, Florida	2,400*
37. Calvary Community Church	San Jose, California	2,381
38. High Street Baptist Church	Springfield, Missouri	2,381*
39. Gospel Light Baptist Church	Walkertown, North Carolina	2,325
40. First Baptist Church	Riverdale, Maryland	2,308*
41. Scott Memorial Baptist Church	San Diego, California	2,257
42. First Baptist Church	West Hollywood, Florida	2,252
43. Lakeview Temple	Indianapolis, Indiana	2,242

44. First Presbyterian Church	Colorado Springs, Colorado	2,235
45. The Chapel in University Park	Akron, Ohio	2,200
46. Cottage Hill Baptist Church	Mobile, Alabama	2,152
47. Broadway Baptist Church	Memphis, Tennessee	2,148
48. Allandale Baptist Church	Austin, Texas	2,123
49. Averyville Baptist Church	Peoria, Illinois	2,100*
50. The People's Church	Willowdale, Ontario	2,100*
51. Fairhaven Church	Chesterton, Indiana	2,073
52. Travis Avenue Baptist Church	Fort Worth, Texas	2,047*
53. College Church of Christ	Searcy, Arkansas	2,030
54. First Baptist Church	Lubbock, Texas	1,997
55. Tallowood Baptist Church	Houston, Texas	1,989*
56. Evangel Tabernacle	Louisville, Kentucky	1,980
57. Kansas City Baptist Temple	Kansas City, Missouri	1,968
58. The Open Door Church	Chambersburg, Pennsylvania	1,916
59. First Baptist Church	Van Nuys, California	1,910
60. Hyde Park Baptist Church	Austin, Texas	1,901
61. First Baptist Church	Orlando, Florida	1,898
62. Allapattah Baptist Church	Miami, Florida	1,893*
63. First Baptist Church	Pomona, California	1,882*
64. Grace Brethren Church	Long Beach, California	1,877
65. Willamette Christian Center	Eugene, Oregon	1,860
66. Park Cities Baptist Church	Dallas, Texas	1,850*
67. Bethany First Church of the Nazarene	Bethany, Oklahoma	1,849
68. Central Gospel Temple	St. Catherine, Ontario	1,849
69. Massillon Baptist Church	Massillon, Ohio	1,842*
70. First Baptist Church	Atlanta, Georgia	1,822
71. Broadway Church of Christ	Lubbock, Texas	1,800
72. Paradise Baptist Church	Los Angeles, California	1,800
73. College Avenue Baptist Church	San Diego, California	1,800*
74. Dawson Memorial Baptist Church	Birmingham, Alabama	1,800*
75. Lima Baptist Temple	Lima, Ohio	1,800*
76. Tucson Baptist Temple	Tucson, Arizona	1,785
77. People's Church	Fresno, California	1,777

358

78.	Good Shepherd Baptist Church	Tampa, Florida	1,756*
79.	Trinity Church	Lubbock, Texas	1,750
80.	Tri-County Assembly	Fairfield, Ohio	1,750
81.	Moline Gospel Temple	Moline, Illinois	1,722*
82.	Capital Christian Center	Sacramento, California	1,701
83.	Roswell Street Baptist Church	Marietta, Georgia	1,700
84.	South Sheridan Baptist Church	Denver, Colorado	1,700*
85.	Sunset Church of Christ	Lubbock, Texas	1,694
86.	Mount Paran Church of God	Atlanta, Georgia	1,673
87.	First Baptist Church	San Antonio, Texas	1,650*
88.	First Assembly of God	Concord, North Carolina	1,645
89.	Florence Baptist Temple	Florence, South Carolina	1,645
90.	Bible Baptist Church	Savannah, Georgia	1,604
91.	First Baptist Church	Elkhart, Indiana	1,600*
92.	Christ Temple of Faith	Inkster, Michigan	1,600
93.	New Testament Baptist Church	Hialeah, Florida	1,581
94.	First Baptist Church	Long Beach, California	1,578*
95.	First Baptist Church	Columbia, South Carolina	1,578*
96.	Bethesda Baptist Church	Brownsburg, Indiana	1,561*
97.	Highland Church of Christ	Abilene, Texas	1,526
98.	Anchorage Baptist Temple	Anchorage, Alaska	1,520
99.	Garnett Road Church of Christ	Tulsa, Oklahoma	1,512
100.	Bethany Bible Church	Phoenix, Arizona	1,508*

*These figures are not verified, but are estimates based on research and interviews.

45. The Sunday School Growth Awards for the Fifty States

THE FASTEST GROWING SUNDAY SCHOOLS

Englishmen went wild 200 years ago when Robert Raikes, editor of the *Gloucester Journal*, published the results of his experimental school in Sooty Alley. Politicians, ministers, and laymen immediately jumped aboard the Sunday school bandwagon. Within five years, there was a Sunday school in every major English town; within thirty years, 1,300,000 (one-third of the population) were enrolled in Sunday school.

Each year in the U.S., the listing of fastest growing Sunday schools brings an almost equally excited response from both pastors and laymen. When the awards are announced during the Mid-America Sunday School Association Convention, delegates cheer the winning Sunday school from each state. The large auditorium is darkened, and spotlights converge on the platform where the representative from each state, including Hawaii and Alaska, receives a five-foot silk banner. Spontaneous applause breaks out for each of the fifty schools as the crowd recognizes the work of God growing in many denominations and in every state of the Union.

Later, delegates line up, and most of them have the same response: "We're going to try to be the fastest-growing Sunday school in our state next year!" And after the convention, letters and phone calls pour in, helping the staff find the fastest growing Sunday school in each state for the next year.

The list of the fastest growing Sunday school in each of the fifty states reveals that Sunday school continues to grow and be an effective tool to teach the Word of God.

In a day when most Americans think the Sunday school is out-of-date, the statistics reveal that the movement is vibrant.

The fastest growing Sunday school is located in the massive Calvary Temple, Winter Park, Florida, having grown last year from an attendance of 3188 to 4234, for a total growth of 1046 on an average Sunday over the previous year. This is the fifth year Calvary Temple has led all of Florida. Only a few years ago, they were an average church school with a few hundred members. But the big Sunday schools were not the only winners. At the other end of the growth cycle was the Community Bible Church of S. Burlington, Vermont, with a growth of just thirty new people per week.

Also, baby churches won the award. In Michigan the Heritage Baptist Church was less than a year old when the awards were passed out. Dr. David Wood began the church in a suburb of Grand Rapids, and six months later, the Sunday school is averaging over 400. However, the total average attendance was 181, making Heritage the fastest growing in the state of Michigan.

The Sunday school awards demonstrate that churches in all types of situations can grow: inter-city, rural, suburban, and small towns. Also, all types of denominations placed winners on the list, including twenty-one Baptist, thirteen Assembly of God, three Church of God, one Nazarene, one Presbyterian, plus a number of independent churches.

Since no denomination has a corner on growth, the question is asked, What does it take to motivate a Sunday school to become the fastest growing in its state? According to Dr. Elmer Towns, who guided the research, "Each winning Sunday school had one ingredient—determination—they planned to be the fastest growing in their state. Growth does not come naturally. These winning Sunday schools programmed for it by planning contests, campaigns, and special days."

Kids love the excitement. "We've got seventy-four!" a mop-headed third grader called to his pastor as the Sunday school bus approached the front door of the church. Yet the excitement of the masses does not crowd out the personal touch. A little first-grade girl was among the seventy-four packed on the bus. She began to cry when she became lost in the crowd on the steps. "I'll help you find your class," a high school bus worker consoled while hugging her.

There were other characteristics for the fastest growing Sunday school. In every growing Sunday school there was at least one person who had given aggressive leadership for outreach. Usually that person announced attendance goals and motivated the congregation to diligent work.

"Of course," Towns said, "no one person alone can produce growth. These fast-growing Sunday schools are characterized by teachers who pray, visit, and follow-up absentees. Other workers drive Sunday school buses, check rolls, lead singing, and unselfishly give themselves to do thousands of small jobs that require attention to reach the masses."

These growing Sunday schools have returned to the basics of religious education. They preach the old-fashioned gospel. They use traditional techniques such as memory work, puppets, pictures, lectures, flannelgraph, chorus-singing, Bible games, flashcards, and chalk illustrations. They insist that it is still important that children learn the Word of God.

Perhaps the spirit of these Sunday schools is personified by Pastor M. C. Johnson who founded Calvary Temple, an Assembly of God Church in Springfield, Illinois, ten years ago. When he first read the listing of the nation's fastest growing Sunday schools, he wrote Dr. Towns that his Sunday school would be one of the largest in America, as well as the fastest growing, by 1980. Last year the weekly average in his church grew by 641 over the previous year, raising their average Sunday school attendance to 4379. The Sunday school that was begun ten years ago has become one of the ten largest in the nation.

FASTEST GROWING SUNDAY SCHOOLS—1979

		1978	1979	Gain
ALABAMA	Calvary Baptist Temple Montgomery, AL	850	1652	802
ALASKA	Anchorage Baptist Temple Anchorage, AK	1559	1835	276
ARIZONA	Tucson Baptist Temple Tucson, AZ	1650	1785	135
ARKANSAS	Trinity Church of Little Rock (Nazarene) Little Rock, AR	141	254	113
CALIFORNIA	Scott Memorial Baptist Church San Diego, CA	2000	2161	161
COLORADO	First Presbyterian Church Colorado Springs, CO	1918	2235	317
CONNECTICUT	Gospel Tabernacle North Haven, CT	189	216	27
DELAWARE	First Baptist of New Castle New Castle, DE	1120	1167	47
FLORIDA	Calvary Temple Winter Park, FL	3188	4234	1046
GEORGIA	Evangel Temple Columbus, GA	653	781	128
HAWAII	Faith Baptist Church Kailua, HI	250	475	225
ILLINOIS	Calvary Temple Springfield, IL	3738	4379	641
INDIANA	Gospel Center Missionary Church South Bend, IN	486	533	47
IOWA	Fellowship Baptist Church Marshalltown, IA	399	502	103
KANSAS	Midway Baptist Church Wichita, KS	211	252	41
KENTUCKY	Eastland Parkway Church of God Lexington, KY	375	453	78
LOUISIANA	First Assembly of God New Orleans, LA	1884	2557	673
MAINE	Bible Believing Church Gray, ME	0	60	60
MARYLAND	Evangel Temple Baltimore, MD	384	485	101
MASSACHUSETTS	Grace Chapel Lexington, MA	834	1002	168
MICHIGAN	Heritage Baptist Church Kentwood, MI	New	181	181
MINNESOTA	First Baptist of Rosemont Rosemont, MN	725	800	75
MISSISSIPPI	Mountainview Baptist Church Raymond, MS	90	165	75
MISSOURI	Central Assembly Christian Life Center Joplin, MO	1974	2127	153

MONTANA	Fairview Baptist Church Great Falls, MT	232	330	98
NEBRASKA	Bible Baptist Church Lincoln, NB	171	309	138
NEVADA	Parkdale Baptist Church Las Vegas, NV	108	216	108
NEW HAMPSHIRE	Bethel Assembly of God Portsmouth, NH	236	266	30
NEW JERSEY	Open Bible Baptist Church Williamstown, NJ	854	1088	234
NEW MEXICO	First Assembly of God Carlsbad, NM	289	304	15
NEW YORK	Perth Bible Church Amsterdam, NY	760	973	213
N. CAROLINA	Cedar Creek Church of God Fayetteville, NC	133	179	46
N. DAKOTA	Grand Forks Assembly of God Grand Forks, ND	241	311	70
OHIO	Town Blvd. Church of God Middletown, OH	762	1157	395
OKLAHOMA	Woodlake Assembly of God Tulsa, OK	839	921	82
OREGON	Church of Open Bible Medford, OR	568	716	148
PENNSYLVANIA	South Hills Assembly of God Bethel Park, PA	677	866	199
S. CAROLINA	Florence Baptist Temple Florence, SC	1190	1445	255
S. DAKOTA	First Assembly of God Sioux Falls, SD	294	354	60
TENNESSEE	Lighthouse Baptist Church Antioch, TN	160	320	160
TEXAS	Braeswood Assembly of God Houston, TX	860	993	133
UTAH	Berean Baptist Church Ogden, UT	50	88	38
VERMONT	Community Bible Church S. Burlington, VT	290	328	30
VIRGINIA	Liberty Baptist Church Suffolk, VA	61	166	105
WASHINGTON	Neighborhood Church Bellevue, WA	516	626	110
W. VIRGINIA	Briscoe Run Baptist Church Parkersburg, WV	721	812	91
WISCONSIN	Elmbrook Church Waukesha, WI	297	354	160
WYOMING	Sunnyside Baptist Church Cheyenne, WY	675	711	36

FASTEST GROWING SUNDAY SCHOOLS—1980

		1979	1980	Gain
ALABAMA	First Assembly of God Montgomery, AL	547	1055	508
ALASKA	Anchorage Baptist Temple Anchorage, AK	1424	1741	317
ARIZONA	Grace Community Church Tempe, AZ	2725	2995	270
ARKANSAS	Hot Springs Baptist Temple Hot Springs, AR	222	305	83
CALIFORNIA	Los Gatos Christian Church Los Gatos, CA	3094	3669	575
COLORADO	First Presbyterian Church Colorado Springs, CO	2235	2334	99
CONNECTICUT	Grace Baptist Church Milford, CT	135	160	25
DELAWARE	First Baptist of New Castle New Castle, DE	1050	1104	54
FLORIDA	Calvary Assembly Winter Park, FL	4234	4711	477
GEORGIA	Sherwood Baptist Church Albany, GA	485	805	320
HAWAII	Lanakila Baptist Church (means Victory) Waipaku, HI	350	620	270
IDAHO	First Church of the Nazarene Nampa, ID	863	948	85
ILLINOIS	Calvary Temple Church Springfield, IL	4379	4702	323
INDIANA	Christ Gospel Church Evansville, IN	3011	3784	773
IOWA	Sunnyside Temple Waterloo, IA	804	973	169
KANSAS	College Church of the Nazarene Olathe, KS	918	1097	179
KENTUCKY	Eastland Parkway Church of God Lexington, KY	335	442	107
LOUISIANA	First Assembly of God New Orleans, LA	2309	2691	382
MAINE	Easton Wesleyan Church Easton, ME	103	124	21
MARYLAND	Church of the Open Door Westminister, MD	205	340	135
MASSACHUSETTS	First Assembly of God Worchester, MA	247	326	79
MICHIGAN	Riverview Church of God Riverview, MI	794	1143	349
MINNESOTA	Bloomington Assembly of God Bloomington, MN	521	581	60

MISSISSIPPI	Northside Assembly of God Biloxi, MS	165	227	62
MISSOURI	Central Assembly Christian Life Joplin, MO	2121	2495	374
MONTANA	Old Fashioned Baptist Church Butte, MT	75	110	35
NEBRASKA	Omaha Gospel Tabernacle Omaha, NB	508	610	102
NEVADA	Carson City Church of God Carson City, NV	34	55	22
NEW HAMPSHIRE	Sunshine Baptist Church Newport, NH	38 (Feb.'79)	102	64
NEW JERSEY	Lighthouse Tabernacle Mt. Holly, NJ	209	315	106
NEW MEXICO	First Family Church Albuquerque, NM	266	388	72
NEW YORK	Perth Bible Church Amsterdam, NY	948	1139	192
N. CAROLINA	Trinity Assembly Charlotte, NC	482	695	213
N. DAKOTA	First Assembly of God Fargo, ND	415	498	83
OHIO	Town Blvd. Church of God Middletown, OH	1147	1604	457
OKLAHOMA	Williams Memorial Church/Nazarene Bethany, OK	385	503	118
OREGON	Harvest Baptist Temple Medford, OR	275	400	225
PENNSYLVANIA	Bethany Wesleyan Church Cherryville, PA	704	832	128
RHODE ISLAND	Greater Rhode Island Baptist Temple Johnston, RI	205	278	73
S. CAROLINA	Northwood Assembly Charleston Hts., SC	355	531	176
S. DAKOTA	First Assembly of God Brookings, SD	96	139	43
TENNESSEE	Lighthouse Baptist Church Nashville,TN	295	476	181
TEXAS	Allandale Baptist Church Austin, TX	2085	2611	526
UTAH	Mountainview Christian Church Sandy, UT	77	105	28
UTAH	Valley Assembly of God Salt Lake City, UT	238	266	28
VERMONT	The Salvation Army Burlington, VT	25	44	19
VIRGINIA	Calvary Road Baptist Church Alexandria, VA	250	500	200
WASHINGTON	Valley Fourth Memorial Church Spokane, WA	307	525	218

WEST VIRGINIA	First Assembly of God Beckley, WV	707	786	79
WISCONSIN	Brookfield Assembly Brookfield, WI	414	473	59
WYOMING	The Salvation Army Sheridan, WY	29	71	42

46. America's Ten Largest Sunday Schools

Another interesting statistical analysis explores the change in Sunday schools over a decade's time. This following list takes the top ten Sunday schools as of 1969 and looks at their growth or decline as of the year 1979.

Interestingly, the first six churches on this list did register increases in their Sunday school enrollments. Some might expect the largest Sunday schools to have reached a peak or a saturation level. These figures indicate that this is not necessarily true: of these ten only two Sunday schools declined — and the decline totalled only 353.

AMERICA'S TEN LARGEST SUNDAY SCHOOLS

TEN LARGEST IN 1969	1969	1979	Difference
1. Akron Baptist Temple, Akron, Ohio	5,762	*6,700	+1,062
2. Highland Park Baptist Church Chattanooga, Tennessee	4,821	11,000	+6,179
3. First Baptist Church Dallas, Texas	4,731	6,703	+1,972
4. First Baptist Church Hammond, Indiana	3,978	15,101	+11,123
5. Canton Baptist Temple Canton, Ohio	3,581	*4,574	+993
6. Landmark Baptist Temple Cincinnati, Ohio	3,540	*4,315	+775
7. Temple Baptist Church Detroit, Michigan	3,400	*3,100	—300
8. First Baptist Church Van Nuys, California	2,847	*2,850	+3
9. Thomas Road Baptist Church Lynchburg, Virginia	2,640	*8,000	+5360
10. Calvary Temple Denver, Colorado	2,453	*2,400	—53

*These figures were not supplied by the church but are based on estimates that came from research and interviews.

NOTES

1. This chapter was prepared as a paper to be read to some of the United Methodist Sunday school administrators and editors, Nashville, Tennessee, August 1979. Parts of this chapter first appeared in *The Successful Sunday School and Teachers Guidebook*, Elmer L. Towns (Carol Stream, Illinois: Creation House, 1975), chapter 1.
2. Sunday school growth is measured by five criteria: (1) growth in attendance, (2) growth in enrollment, (3) growth in financial income, (4) growth in physical facilities, and (5) growth in programs and services to individuals. Spiritual growth is not immediately implied in these criteria, yet in must not be neglected. Even though some consider spiritual growth as unmeasurable, its resulting change in attitudes, values, and actions can be measured through observation and tests. The purpose of this chapter is not to convey the factors and causes associated with spiritual growth, but their impact should not be ignored.
3. These factors are not all evident in evident in every growing Sunday school, nor could all these factors pass rigorous New Testament scrutiny as the causal influences that produce a New Testament Church
4. Some have called the large churches the "super-aggressive churches," their locations are called "church campuses," and their sociological dynamic movement has been attributed to "synergism." The authority of their pastors is attributed to charismatic leadership defined as "personal magnetism used by leaders to accomplish a predetermined goal in their organization or movement." See the following: Elmer Towns, *America's Fastest Growing Churches* (Nashville: Impact Books, 1973), p. 193. Elmer Towns, *Church Aflame* (Nashville: Impact Books, 1971). *Christian Life*. September or October editions, 1968-1977. The annual listing of the 100 largest Sunday schools appeared in this magazine each fall for ten years.
5. Elmer Towns, *The Ten Largest Sunday Schools* (Grand Rapids: Baker Book House, 1969), p. 11.
6. *Christian Life*, September 1968.
7. When a church loses its unique Christian message, it loses its reasons for existence. The author believes liberal theology tends to eliminate the supernatural and, as a result, humanizes the Christian community. When this happens, outsiders perceive the liberalized church as having little difference from their political club or bowling league.
8. With the passing of time, older denominations tend to centralize their authority in committees and paid professionals. The people perceive the church is no longer theirs and turn their endeavors elsewhere. See Elmer Towns, *Is the Day of the Denomination Dead?* (Nashville: Thomas Nelson, 1973), chapter 7, "Growth of Bureaucracy."
9. Growth tends to come from the establishment of new units in existing churches and the planting of new churches. These new forces produce excitement and personal commitment by the congregation to make the church succeed. Older congregations have little or no vision to build new buildings, reach new neighborhoods, and pay off their mortgages. They tend to settle down and die on the vine.
10. The mainline churches have been quick to experiment with innovations in doctrine, teaching techniques, management, and building design. But when it comes to advertisement and/or publicity that leads to evangelistic outreach, very little has been done in innovation and expenditures.
11. Quoted by Rev. Larry Richards at the Greater Chicago Sunday School Association, Spring 1968.
12. The growth of most large fundamental churches seemed to level out. However, the small and mid-sized church continues to grow as we approach the 80s, just as the larger church grew ten years ago. One wonders if these churches will also stop growing when they reach

their saturation point, brought on by some of the self-limiting factors of fundamentalism.

13. Larger Sunday school attendance in 1969 was attributed to the personal relationship of teacher and pupil. The weekly pressure of taking roll in class and follow-up of absentees by the teacher produced a higher attendance, especially in a time when the mood of the country was contrary to attending the services of the institutional church. However, during the past ten years, both church and Sunday school attendance have grown. But, attendance at the Sunday morning church service has grown more rapidly than attendance at the Sunday school hour.

14. Churches that are nonconservative in theology have not been active in busing outreach. First, because they do not accept the fact that man is a sinner who is lost and needs redemption. This theological basis mandates that a church/Sunday school use every possible means to reach every person possible. Hence, Sunday school busing is an answer to that need. Second, churches that accept the philosophy of nurture rather than evangelism, will not tend to employ Sunday school busing.

15. During World War II, rationing boards made allocations for churches with Sunday school buses. However, at the beginning of the war there was a moratorium on public transportation for church attendance. The public outcry caused a review, and Sunday school buses were given adequate allocations. The writer feels the same factors will prevail should America again enter a period of gas rationing.

CHAPTER 2, SUNDAY SCHOOL AND CHURCH GROWTH IN THE EIGHTIES

1. When one changes the message of Sunday school, it is only natural that he has changed the nature of Sunday school. There is a discernible difference between the aims, expression, and methods of Sunday schools that teach a liberal theology and those that teach a conservative theology.

2. The author perceives declining attendance as a cause and effect relationship that is attributable to liberal education in the pulpit and/or Sunday school curriculum.

3. The author believes there is a unique tie between the learning psychology of revelation and its original communication to man. Just as the Spirit of God became involved in the process of inspiration, so the Spirit of God becomes involved in the process of illumination. True biblical interpretation cannot be effective without the process of spiritual illumination.

4. "And it came to pass, when Jesus had ended these sayings, the people were astonished at this doctrine: For he taught as one having authority, and not as the scribes *(Matt 7:29, KJV)*.

5. The authority of the Sunday school teacher is not internally inherent. He receives his authority from being Spirit-filled and knowledgeable of the Word of God. Because of his maturity in Jesus Christ and his godly living, the Sunday school teacher becomes an authoritative person.

6. Just as we learn from nature that a neglected farm will not naturally produce fruit but will devolve into a state of uselessness, so a Sunday school will not naturally grow, but, if left to itself, will devolve to a state of uselessness.

7. "Beforetime in Israel, when a man went to inquire of God, thus he spake, Come, let us go to the seer: for he that is now called a Prophet was beforetime called a Seer" *(1 Sam. 9:9, KJV)*.

8. Elmer Towns, "Riding One Bicycle at a Time," *Journal Champion,* 15 June 1979, vol. 2, no. 3, p. 2. The article indicates that a Christian school does not always cause church growth to plateau. If church leaders will recognize the causes and counteract them, the church can continue growing.

9. These laws of Sunday School growth are: (1) Sunday schools grow in proportion to their workers at a ratio of 10:1, (2) Sunday schools grow when they have adequate facilities, (3) new units will produce more workers and growth than old units; therefore, there must be a continual dividing of units for multiplied growth, (4) Sunday schools must grade by ages for growth, (5) Sunday school growth is directly tied to visitation.

10. Elmer Towns, *The Ten Largest Sunday Schools* (Grand Rapids: Baker Book House, 1969), pp. 5-9.

CHAPTER 15, FUNDAMENTALISM
1. Carey McWilliams, "The New Fundamentalists," *The Nation*, 5 June 1976, pp. 686, 687.
2. Pat Horn, "The New Middle-Class Fundamentalism," *Psychology Today*, September 1976, pp. 24, 25.
3. Jerry Falwell and Elmer Towns, *Church Aflame* (Nashville: Impact Books, 1971), pp. 37, 40.
4. Elmer L. Towns, *America's Fastest Growing Churches* (Nashville: Impact Books, 1972), pp. 10, 11.
5. Garry Wills, "What Religious Revival?" *Psychology Today*, April 1978, p. 80.
6. Elmer Towns, "The Small, Personal Sunday School," *Christian Life*, April 1971, p. 48.
7. Jackson W. Carroll (ed.), *Small Churches Are Beautiful* (New York: Harper and Row, 1977), p. 16.
8. Elmer Towns, "America's Largest Sunday Schools Are Growing," *Christian Life*, August 1970, p. 16.
9. Elmer Towns, "Sunday Schools in the U.S.—The 100 Largest, '76," *Christian Life*, October 1976, pp. 38-45.
10. Hollis L. Green, *Why Churches Die* (Minneapolis: Bethany Fellowship, 1972), p. 95.
11. Gerald H. Anderson *et al.*, *Mission Trends No. 2: Evangelization* (New York: Paulist Press and Grand Rapids: Wm. B. Eerdmans, 1975), p. 61.
12. Elmer Towns, "Trends in Sunday School Growth," *Christian Life*, October 1976, p. 37.
13. Anderson, *Mission Trends*, p. 66.
14. Elmer Towns, *Christian Life*, October 1976, pp. 38-45.
15. "Churches Leaving the SBC," *The Sword of the Lord*, 28 June 1974, p. 4.
16. George Marsden, "Defining Fundamentalism," *Christian Scholar's Review*, vol. 1, no. 2 (Winter 1971), p. 141.
17. Harold Lindsell, *The Battle for the Bible* (Grand Rapids: Zondervan, 1976), p. 37.
18. Daniel B. Stevick, *Beyond Fundamentalism* (Richmond: John Knox Press, 1964), p. 24.
19. *Ibid.*, p. 20.
20. *Ibid.*, pp. 29, 30.
21. *Ibid.*, p. 31.
22. Elmer Towns, "Trends Among Fundamentalists," *Christianity Today*, 6 July 1973, p. 12.
23. John R. Rice, *Come Out or Stay In* (Nashville: Thomas Nelson, 1974), p. 95.
24. Elmer Towns, "What Do We Communicate?", *Christian Life*, May 1969, p. 33.
25. C. Allyn Russell, *Voices of American Fundamentalism* (Philadelphia: The Westminister Press, 1976), p. 31.
26. Louis Entzminger, *How to Organize and Administer a Great Sunday School* (Ft. Worth: The Manning Company, 1949), p. v.
27. *Ibid.*, p. iii.
28. "Sunday School Newsmakers of the Decade," *Christian Life*, October 1977, p. 33.
29. C. Peter Wagner, *Your Church Can Grow* (Glendale: Regal Books, 1976), p. 18.
30. J. Robertson McQuilken, "Making the Numbers Count," *Moody Monthly*, June 1977, p. 30:
31. Elmer Towns, "Sunday Schools in the U.S.—the 100 Largest, '76," *Christian Life*, October 1976, pp. 38, 39.
32. "Sunday School Newsmakers of the Decade," *Christian Life*, October 1977, p. 33.
33. Elmer Towns, "America's Fastest-Growing Sunday Schools," *Christian Life*, November 1974, p. 35.
34. Elmer Towns, "Sunday Schools of the Decade," *Christian Life*, October 1977, pp. 30, 31.
35. John R. Rice, *The Sword of the Lord*, 9 September 1977, p. 13.
36. John R. Rice, *The Sword of the Lord*, 21 April 1978, p. 2.
37. "Sunday School Newsmakers of the Decade," *Christian Life*, October 1977, p. 33.
38. Elmer Towns, *America's Fastest Growing Churches* (Nashville: Impact Books, 1972), p. 7.
39. Elmer Towns, "50 Largest Sunday Schools in the U.S. Today," *Christian Life*, October 1969, pp. 44-49.

CHAPTER 16, THE FULLER FACTOR
1. Robert T. Coote, "Church Growth: Shot in the Arm for Evangelism," *Evangelical Newsletter*, vol. 2, no. 14 (9 May 1975), p. 4.

2. C. Peter Wagner, "American Church Growth Update, 1974," *United Evangelical Action*, vol. 33, no. 1 (Spring 1974), pp. 15, 16, 36.

3. C. Peter Wagner, "Mission and Hope: Some Implications of the Theology of Jurgen Moltmann," *Missiology*, vol. 2, no. 4 (19 October 1974), p. 468.

4. James H. Montgomery, "Resistant, Neglected or Turned Off?" *Church Growth Bulletin*, vol. XV, no. 1 (September 1978), p. 217.

5. C. Peter Wagner, "Mission and Hope," *Missiology*, p. 462.

6. Ralph D. Winter, *The Grounds for a New Thrust in World Missions* (South Pasadena: William Carey Library, 1977), p. 28.

7. David B. Barnett, "AD 2000: 350 Million Christians in Africa," *International Review of Missions*, vol. LIX, no. 233 (January 1970), pp. 49, 50.

8. C. Peter Wagner (ed.), *Church/Mission Tensions Today* (Chicago: Moody Press, 1972), p. 137.

9. C. Peter Wagner, *Your Church Can Grow* (Glendale: Regal Books, 1976), p. 170.

10. Alan R. Tippett, "Anthropology and Post Colonial Mission Through a China Filter," *Missiology*, vol. 1, no. 4 (October 1973), p. 470.

11. Donald McGavran, *The Bridges of God* (New York: Friendship Press, 1955), p. 3.

12. Arthur F. Glasser, "Timeless Lessons From the Western Missionary Penetration of China," *Missiology*, vol. 1, no. 4 (October 1973), pp. 448, 449.

13. Ted W. Engstrom, *What in the World Is God Doing?* (Waco: Word Books, 1978), pp. 22, 23.

14. *Ibid.*, p. 20.

15. Roger S. Greenway, "Mission to An Urban World," *Church Growth Bulletin*, vol. XII, no. 1 (September 1975), p. 475.

16. "Local Church Reaches 100,000 Membership," *Global Church Growth Bulletin*, vol. XVII, no. 1 (January/February 1980), p. 9.

17. Engstrom, *What in the World*, p. 162.

18. C. Peter Wagner, *Look Out! The Pentecostals Are Coming* (Carol Stream: Creation House, 1973), pp. 131, 132.

19. C. Peter Wagner, *Stop the World I Want to Get On* (Glendale: Regal Books, 1974), p. 9.

20. Wagner, *Look Out! The Pentecostals Are Coming*, p. 82.

22. Wagner, *Look Out! The Pentecostals Are Coming*, p. 89.

23. *Ibid.*, p. 61.

24. Winfield Arn, C. Peter Wagner, and James H. Montgomery, "Church Growth Flourishes In America," *Church Growth Bulletin*, vol. XIII, no. 2 (November 1976), p. 88.

25. Donald A. McGavran and Winfield C. Arn, *Ten Steps for Church Growth* (San Francisco: Harper and Row, 1977), p. 47.

26. Donald A. McGavran and Winfield C. Arn, *How to Grow a Church* (Glendale: Regal Books, 1974), pp. 135, 136.

27. Arn, Wagner, and Montgomery, "Church Growth Flourishes," p. 87.

28. Mimeograph copy mailed to this writer by Dr. McGavran.

29. McGavran and Arn, *Ten Steps for Church Growth*, pp. 7, 8.

30. Donald H. Gill, "Apostle of Church Growth," *World Vision*, vol. 12, no. 7 (September 1968), p. 11.

31. John K. Branner, "McGavran Speaks on Roland Allen," *Evangelical Missions Quarterly*, vol. 8, no. 3 (Spring 1972), p. 173.

32. McGavran and Arn, *Ten Steps for Church Growth*, p. 5.

33. Wagner, *Your Church Can Grow*, p. 14.

34. *Ibid.*, p. 11.

35. Medford Jones, "American Church Growth Explored," *Church Growth Bulletin*, vol. VI, no. 2 (November 1969), pp. 30, 31.

36. Wagner, *Your Church Can Grow*, p. 17.

37. "Equipping the Saints for the Work of Ministry," *Church Growth: America*, vol. 4, no. 1 (September/October 1978), p. 6.

38. Arn, Wagner, and Montgomery, "Church Growth Flourishes," pp. 88, 89.

39. *Ibid.*, p. 89.

40. J. Robertson McQuilkin, *Measuring the Church Growth Movement* (Chicago: Moody Press, 1973), pp. 73-76.

41. C. Peter Wagner, " 'Church Growth': More Than a Man, a Magazine, a School, a Book," *Christianity Today*, vol. 18, no. 5 (7 December 1973), pp. 11, 12, 14.
42. Donald A. McGavran, *Understanding Church Growth* (Grand Rapids: William B. Eerdmans, 1970), p. 170.
43. Wagner, *Your Church Can Grow*, p. 12.
44. Donald A. McGavran, "Why Neglect Gospel-Ready Masses?" *Christianity Today*, vol. 10, no. 5 (29 April 1966), pp. 17-19.
45. Donald A. McGavran, "Focus and Reflection," *In Focus* (Waco: Word, Inc., 1976), vol. 1, no. 10, p. 2.
46. C. Peter Wagner, "World Baptists: 3,176,954 New Members and Standing Still!" *Church Growth Bulletin*, vol. X, no. 4 (March 1974), pp. 401-3.
47. McGavran, *The Bridges of God*, pp. 113.
48. Wagner, *Your Church Can Grow*, p. 63.
49. *Ibid.*, p. 63.
50. Alan R. Tippett, *Church Growth and the Word of God* (Grand Rapids: William B. Eerdmans, 1970), p. 58.
51. McGavran and Arn, *Ten Steps for Church Growth*, p. 31.
52. Donald McGavran (ed.), *Eye of the Storm: The Great Debate in Mission* (Waco: Word Books, 1972), p. 57.
53. McGavran and Arn, *Ten Steps for Church Growth*, p. 12.
54. McGavran and Arn, *How to Grow a Church*, pp. 45, 47.
55. C. Peter Wagner, "American Church Growth Update 1974," p. 40.
56. McGavran and Arn, *Ten Steps for Church Growth*, p. 78.
57. McGavran, *Understanding Church Growth*, pp. 214, 215.
58. Charles H. Kraft, "North America's Cultural Challenge," *Christianity Today*, vol. XVII, no. 8 (19 January 1973), p. 6.
59. McGavran, *Eye of the Storm*, p. 61.
60. McGavran and Arn, *Ten Steps for Church Growth*, pp. 10, 11.
61. *Ibid.*, p. 114.
62. Wagner, *Your Church Can Grow*, p. 47.
63. McGavran and Arn, *How to Grow a Church*, p. 35.
64. Eric S. Fife and Arthur F. Glasser, *Missions In Crisis: Rethinking Missionary Strategy* (Downers Grove: Inter-Varsity Press, 1961), pp. 187, 188.
65. Wagner, *Your Church Can Grow*, p. 49.
66. Donald McGavran, *How Churches Grow* (London: World Dominion Press, 1959), pp. 166-168.
67. C. Peter Wagner, "American Church Growth Update, 1974," p. 37.
68. Win Arn, "Let My People Grow!" *Eternity*, vol. 26, no. 5 (May 1975), p. 14.
69. C. Peter Wagner, "What Makes Churches Grow?" *Eternity*, vol. 25, no. 6 (June 1974), p. 17.
70. Neil Braun, *Laity Mobilized* (Grand Rapids: William B. Eerdmans Publishing Company, 1971), pp. 81, 82.
71. Wagner, *Your Church Can Grow*, p. 69.
72. McGavran and Arn, *Ten Steps for Church Growth*, pp. 112, 113.
73. Arn, "Let My People Grow!" p. 58.
74. Braun, *Laity Mobilized*, p. 95.
75. McGavran, *The Bridges of God*, pp. 139, 140.
76. Engstrom, *What in the World Is God Doing?*, p. 198.
77. John Stetz, "Biggest Little Church in the World," pp. 78-83.
78. "Local Church Reaches 100,000 Membership," *Global Church Growth Bulletin*, p. 9.
79. McGavran, *Understanding Church Growth*, pp. 192, 193.
80. E. LeRoy Lawson and Tetsunao Yamamori, *Church Growth: Everybody's Business* (Cincinnati: New Life Books, n.d.), pp. 122, 123.
81. Melvin L. Hodges, *Growing Young Churches* (Chicago: Moody Press, 1920), p. 74.
82. Donald McGavran, "New Methods for a New Age in Missions," *International Review of Missions*, October 1955, p. 402.

83. Branner, "McGavran Speaks on Roland Allen," p. 170.
84. Braun, *Laity Mobilized*, pp. 98, 100.
85. McGavran, *Understanding Church Growth*, pp. 190, 191.
86. McGavran, *How Churches Grow*, p. 29.
87. Wagner, *Your Church Can Grow*, p. 158.
88. McGavran and Arn, *How to Grow a Church*, p. 107.
89. Wagner, *Stop the World I Want to Get On*, p. 93.
90. McGavran and Arn, *Ten Steps for Church Growth*, pp. 5, 6.
91. Glasser, "Timeless Lessons From the Western Missionary Penetration of China," pp. 460, 461.
92. McGavran and Arn, *How to Grow a Church*, p. 88.
93. Wagner, *Your Church Can Grow*, p. 50.
94. McGavran and Arn, *How to Grow a Church*, p. 80.
95. McGavran, *Understanding Church Growth*, pp. 150-152.
96. Glasser, "Timeless Lessons From the Western Missionary Penetration of China," pp. 461, 462.
97. McGavran and Arn, *Ten Steps for Church Growth*, pp. 121, 122.
98. McGavran, *Understanding Church Growth*, pp. 266, 267.
99. Wagner, *Your Church Can Grow*, pp. 97-109.
100. C. Peter Wagner, "How to Diagnose the Health of Your Church," *Christianity Today*, vol. XVII, no. 8 (19 January 1973), pp. 24, 25.
101. Foster H. Shannon, "Predicting Church Growth," *Church Growth: America*, vol. 2, no. 2 (March/April 1976).
102. Charles L. Chaney and Ron S. Lewis, *Design For Growth* (Nashville: Broadman Press, 1977).
103. DuBose, *How Churches Grow in an Urban World* (Nashville: Broadman Press, 1978), p. 17.
104. Donald A. McGavran, "Loose the Churches. Let Them Go!" *Missiology*, vol. 1, no. 2 (April 1973), p. 91.
105. Wagner, *Your Church Can Grow*, p. 143.
106. McGavran, *How Churches Grow*, pp. 38, 39.
107. Wagner, *Stop the World I Want to Get On*, p. 46.
108. Wagner, "Mission and Hope: Some Missiological Implications of the Theology of Jurgen Moltmann," p. 473.
109. McGavran and Arn, *Ten Steps for Church Growth*, p. 96.
110. Wagner, *Your Church Can Grow*, pp. 137, 138.
111. Donald McGavran, "The Great Commission," *Reaching All* (Sydney, Australia: World Wide Publications, 1974), pp. 9, 10.
112. Peter Wagner, *Stop the World I Want to Get On*, pp. 108, 109.
113. Ralph Winter, "The King Is Coming," *Reaching All*, p. 28.
114. McGavran and Arn, *Ten Steps for Church Growth*, p. 52.
115. *Ibid.*, pp. 11, 12.
116. Win Arn, "Mass Evangelism: The Bottom Line," *Church Growth: America*, vol. 4, no. 1 (January/February 1978), p. 5.
117. McQuilkin, *Measuring the Church Growth Movement*, p. 74.
118. McGavran, *The Bridges of God*, pp. 107, 108.
119. Harvie M. Conn (ed.), *Theological Perspectives on Church Growth* (Dulk Foundation, 1976), p. 55.
120. Donald McGavran, "Wrong Strategy: The Real Crisis in Missions," *International Review of Missions*, vol. LIV, no. 216 (October 1965), p. 458.
121. McGavran and Arn, *Ten Steps for Church Growth*, p. 114.
122. C. Peter Wagner, "American Church Growth Update, 1974," pp. 38, 39.
123. C. Peter Wagner, *Your Church Can Grow*, p. 77.
124. *Ibid.*, p. 78.
125. McQuilkin, *Measuring the Church Growth Movement*, p. 37.
126. McGavran and Arn, *Ten Steps For Church Growth*, pp. 44, 45.
127. A. R. Tippett, "A Not-So-Secular City," *Christianity Today*, vol. XVII, no. 8 (19 January 1973), pp. 8, 9.

CHAPTER 17, BODY LIFE
1. Lloyd John Ogilvie, *Drumbeat of Love* (Waco, Texas: Word Books, 1976), pp. 60, 63.
2. C. Peter Wagner, *Look Out! The Pentecostals Are Coming*, (Carol Stream, Illinois: Creation House, 1973), p. 79.
3. Ray Stedman, "Church Life," *United Evangelical Action*, April 1967, pp. 27, 28.
4. Roger C. Palms, "Great Churches of Today: Peninsula Bible Church," *Decision*, May 1975, p. 8.
5. Stedman, "*Church Life*," p. 27, 28.
6. Ray Stedman, *Body Life* (Glendale, California: Gospel Light, 1977, revised), p. 170.
7. James C. Hefley, *Unique Evangelical Churches* (Waco, Texas: Word Books, 1977), p. 48.
8. Gene A. Getz, *The Measure of a Church* (Glendale, California: Gospel Light, 1975), p. 154.
9. *Ibid.*, p. 146, 147.
10. Lawrence O. Richards, *Three Churches in Renewal* (Grand Rapids: Zondervan, 1975), p. 8.
11. *Ibid.*, p. 7.
12. *Ibid.*, pp. 8-12.
13. Bob Smith, *When All Else Fails . . . Read the Directions* (Waco, Texas: Word Books, 1974), pp. 128-130.
14. Dan Baumann, *All Originality Makes a Dull Church* (Santa Ana, California: Vision House, 1976), p. 73.
15. Ogilvie, *Drumbeat*, p. 65.
16. Richards, *Three Churches* p. 58, 59.
17. *Ibid.*, p. 42.
18. Hefley, *Unique Evangelical Churches*, p. 34.
19. Ray Stedman, "Should a Pastor Play Pope?" *Moody Monthly*, July/August 1976, p. 42.
20. Gene Getz, *Sharpening the Focus of the Church* (Chicago, Illinois: Moody Press, 1974), p. 121.
21. Ray Stedman, "Biblical Blueprint for a Twentieth Century Church" (Waco, Texas: Timeless Tapes, Word, Inc.).
22. Ray Stedman, "Church Life," p. 29.
23. Smith, *When All Else Fails*, p. 130.
24. Richards, *Three Churches*, p. 38.
25. Palms, "Great Churches," p. 14.
26. Hefley, *Unique Evangelical Churches*, p. 48.
27. Richards, *Three Churches*, p. 64.
28. Hefley, *Unique Evangelical Churches*, p. 29.
29. Stedman, *Body Life* (1972 ed.), pp. 130, 131.
30. *Ibid.*, p. 133.
31. Getz, *Sharpening the Focus of the Church*, p. 114.
32. *Ibid.*
33. Hefley, *Unique Evangelical Churches*, p. 35.
34. Walter McCuistion, "The Magna Carta of Christian Education," A message delivered to the people of Peninsula Bible Church 22 February 1976 at Palo Alto, California; Text—Deuteronomy 6:4-9.
35. Getz, *Sharpening the Focus of the Church*, p. 43.
36. Smith, *When All Else Fails*, p.42.
37. *Ibid.*, p. 103.
38. Getz, *Sharpening the Focus of the Church*, p. 38.
39. Getz, *The Measure of a Church*, p. 114.
40. Hefley, *Unique Evangelical Churches*, p. 49.
41. Smith, *When All Else Fails*, p. 62.
42. Stedman, *Body Life* (1972 ed.), p. 133.
43. Richards, *Three Churches*, p. 56.
44. *Ibid.*, p. 57.
45. McCuistion, "*Magna Carta*," p. 4.
46. Stedman, *Body Life*, (1972 ed.), p. 148.
47. Getz, *Sharpening the Focus of the Church*, pp. 42, 43.
48. Ray Stedman, "The Church in a Modern World," *Moody Monthly*, February 1966, p. 75.
49. Hefley, *Unique Evangelical Churches*, p. 40.

50. Stedman, *Body Life* (1972 ed.), pp. 134, 135.
51. Hefley, *Unique Evanglical Churches*, pp. 39, 40.
52. Smith, *When All Else Fails*, p. 76.

CHAPTER 18, CHARISMATIC RENEWAL

1. Walter J. Hollenweger, *The Pentecostals* (Minneapolis: Augsburg, 1972), p. 29.
2. C. Peter Wagner, *Look Out! The Pentecostals Are Coming* (Carol Stream, Illinois: Creation House, 1973), p. 24.
3. *Ibid.*, p. 61.
4. Donald C. Palmer, *Explosion of People Evangelism* (Chicago, Illinois: Moody Press, 1974), p. 82.
5. Wagner, *Look Out!*, p. 10.
6. Interview with Dr. Rodman Williams, president, Melodyland School of Theology, Anaheim, California, 3 March 1976.
7. *Ibid.*
8. Michael P. Hamilton, *The Charismatic Movement* (Grand Rapids, Michigan: William B. Eerdmans, 1975), p. 7.
9. *Ibid.*, pp. 34, 35.
10. Interview with Rev. Dale VanStennis, Southern California—Arizona District Christ's Ambassadors president, Assemblies of God, 25 March 1976.
11. *Ibid.*
12. Joseph N. Ellis, "The Church That Faith and Works Built," *Christian Life*, vol. 37, no. 6 (October 1975), p. 36.
13. Wagner, *Look Out!*, p. 33.
14. Wagner, *Look Out!*, p. 34.
15. Hollenweger, *The Pentecostals*, p. 357.
16. Henry Lord, "Seven Successful Churches of Southern California," Dissertation, California Graduate School of Theology, 1975, p. 113.
17. Wagner, *Look Out!* pp. 126, 127.
18. *Ibid.*, p. 129.
19. *Ibid.*, p. 131.
20. *Ibid.*, p. 35.
21. *Ibid.*, summary.
22. McGavran, pp. 161, 162.
23. Palmer, *Explosion*, p. 155.
24. Interview with Rev. Dale VanStennis.
25. Lee Lebsack, *10 at the Top: How 10 of America's Largest Assemblies of God Churches Grew* (Stow, Ohio: New Hope Press, 1974), p. 72.
26. *Ibid.*, p. 51.
27. *Ibid.*, p. 110.
28. *Ibid.*, p. 115.
29. *Ibid.*, p. 7.
30. *Ibid.*
31. *Ibid.*, p. 7.
32. *Ibid.*
33. *Ibid.*, p. 62.

CHAPTER 19, EVANGELICAL BIBLE CHURCHES

1. Towns, *America's Fastest Growing Churches* (Nashville, Impact Books, 1973), pp. 168, 169.
2. Gary Inrig, *Life in His Body* (Wheaton, Illinois: Harold Shaw, 1975), pp. 22, 23.
3. Michael R. Tucker, *The Church That Dared to Change* (Wheaton, Illinois: Tyndale House, 1975), p. 11.
4. Tucker, p. 12.
5. *Ibid.*
6. Inrig, p. 43.
7. Dan Baumann, *All Originality Makes a Dull Church* (Santa Ana, California: Vision House, 1976), p. 48.

8. John MacArthur, *The Church: The Body of Christ* (Grand Rapids, Michigan: Zondervan, 1973), pp. 122, 123.
9. Tucker, *The Church That Dared*, p. 14.
10. *Ibid.*
11. Ray Stedman, *Body Life* (Glendale, California: Regal Books, 1972), p. 86.
12. Rev. Joe Aldrich, "Listen To The Music," Address presented to the Southern California-Arizona Ministerium of Grace Brethren Churches at Cypress, California, 12 April 1976.
13. Henry Lord, "Seven Successful Churches of Southern California," Dissertation, California Graduate School of Theology, 1975, pp. 40, 45.
14. Baumann, *All Originality*, p. 45.
15. Tucker, *The Church That Dared*, p. 15.
16. MacArthur, *The Church*, p. 124.
17. Gene A. Getz, *Sharpening the Focus of the Church* (Chicago, Illinois: Moody Press, 1974), pp. 116, 117.
18. David L. Hocking, "Biblical Pattern of Church Government," an unpublished booklet. (Available through First Brethren Church, Long Beach, California)
19. Stedman, *Body Life*, pp. 80, 81.
20. Getz, *Sharpening the Focus*, pp. 116, 117.
21. Robert W. Smith, *When All Else Fails . . . Read the Directions* (Waco, Texas: Word Books, 1974), pp. 86-88.
22. *Ibid.*, p. 119.
23. Gene Getz, *The Measure of a Man* (Glendale, California: Regal Books, 1974), pp. 6, 7.
24. Tucker, *The Church That Dared*, p. 13.
25. Getz, *Sharpening the Focus*, p. 121.
26. Getz, *Sharpening the Focus*, pp. 121, 122.
27. Tucker, *The Church That Dared*, pp. 18, 19.
28. Findley Edge, *The Greening of the Church* (Waco, Texas: Word Books, 1971), p. 40.
29. John MacArthur, "The Marks of a Successful Church." Address presented to the Southern California-Arizona Ministerium at Long Beach, California, 13 October 1975.
30. David Hocking, "The Marks of a Growing Church." Address presented to a Home Missions Pastor's Workshop at Wooster, Ohio, 22 October 1975.

CHAPTER 20, SOUTHERN BAPTISTS

1. Donald A. McGavran and Win Arn, *How to Grow a Church* (Glendale, California: Regal Books, 1973), p. 14.
2. Reprinted from *Our Kind of People* (John Knox Press) by C. Peter Wagner. © Copyright 1979, used by permission.
3. "Sunday School Growth Plan Urges Enrollment of 8.5 Million by '85," *Baptist and Reflector*, Nashville (Newspaper of Tennessee Baptist Convention), 9 January 1980, p. 3.
4. C. Peter Wagner, *Your Church Can Grow* (Glendale, California: Regal Books, 1976), p. 63.
5. *Ibid.*
6. Reprinted from *Where Action Is* (Nashville: Broadman Press) by Andy Anderson. © Copyright 1976, used by permission, p. 37.
7. *Ibid.*, p. 68.
8. Elmer L. Towns, *America's Fastest Growing Churches* (Nashville: Impact Books, 1972), p. 9.
9. Anderson, *Where Action Is*, p. 39.
10. "2,000th Church Constitutes in North Central States," *Baptist and Reflector*, Nashville (Newspaper of Tennessee Baptist Convention), 26 December 1979.
11. Both books are published by Convention Press, Nashville.
12. Interview with Dr. Paul B. Leath, Truett Memorial Baptist Church, Long Beach, California, 2 March 1976.
13. Reprinted from *ACTION: A Reach Out Enrollment Plan for Sunday School* (Sunday School Board of the Southern Baptist Convention, Nashville, Tennessee) by E. S. Anderson. © Copyright 1975, used by permission, p. 6.
14. Anderson, *Where Action Is*, p. 7.

15. Reprinted from *Building a Standard Sunday School* (Nashville: Convention Press) by Arthur Flake. © Copyright 1922, used by permission, pp. 1-135.
16. *Ibid.*, p. 19.
17. *Ibid.*, p. 33.
18. *Ibid.*
19. John T. Sisemore, "Understanding and Applying the Principles of Enlargement," *A Guide to Sunday School Enlargement*, ed. George W. Stuart, p. 36.

CHAPTER 21, MAINLINE DENOMINATIONS

1. Wagner, *Your Church Can Grow* (Glendale, California: Regal Books, 1976), p. 101.
2. Dean M. Kelley, *Why Conservative Churches Are Growing* (New York: Harper and Row, 1972), p. 6.
3. Constant H. Jacquet, Jr., ed., *Yearbook of American and Canadian Churches* (Nashville, Tennessee: Abingdon Press, 1970, 1979).
4. Edward E. Plowman, "Is the United Methodist Church Coming Back to Life?" *Christianity Today*, 30 January 1976, p. 29.
5. General Assembly Mission Council, *Report on Church Membership Trends in Response to the 186th General Assembly (1974) of the United Presbyterian Church in the U.S.A.* (New York: The United Presbyterian Church, 1976), p. 50.
6. Quoted in "Study on Membership Loss and Conservation," *Daily Christian Advocate* (17 April 1972), pp. 81, 82.
7. Kelly, *Conservative Churches*, p. 175.
8. Interview with Rev. Don Thompson, United Methodist Church, Paramount, California, 16 March 1976.
9. Raymond H. Wilson, *Journal of the Southern California-Arizona Annual Conference of the United Methodist Church, One-Hundred Twenty-Fifth Annual Session, Redlands, California, June 13-17, 1975* (Los Angeles: The United Methodist Center, 1975), pp. 42, 43.
10. "Study," p. 82.
11. *Ibid.*
12. *Ibid.*
13. Roy H. Short, *United Methodism in Theory and Practice* (Nashville, Tennessee: Abingdon, 1974), pp. 102, 103.
14. *Ibid.*, pp. 105, 106.
15. Plowman, *Is the United Methodist Church?* p. 29.
16. *Ibid.*
17. M. Wendell Belew, *Churches and How They Grow* (Nashville, Tennessee: Broadman Press, 1971), p. 40.
18. *Ibid.*, p. 61.
19. Belew, *Churches, How They Grow*, p. 98.
20. Staff of *Decision* magazine, "First United Methodist Church, Collingswood, New Jersey," *Great Churches of Today* (Minneapolis, Minnesota: Worldwide Publications, 1970-73), pp. 63, 66, 67.
21. *Ibid.*, p. 67.
22. *Ibid.*, p. 66.
23. General Assembly, p. 51.
24. General Assembly, *Report*, p. 61.
25. Interview with Dr. Ralph M. Grove, First Presbyterian Church, Downey, California, 16 March 1976.
26. John R. Fry, *The Trivialization of the United Presbyterian Church* (New York: Harper and Row, 1975), pp. 5, 6.
27. *Ibid.*, p. 7.
28. *Ibid.*, p. 22.
29. *Ibid.*, p. 45.
30. *Ibid.*, p. 67.
31. *Ibid.*, p. 72.
32. General Assembly, *Report*, p. 76.
33. *Ibid.*, pp. 67, 68.

34. *Ibid.*, p. 69.
35. *Ibid.*, p. 76.
36. *Ibid.*, p. 81.
37. *Ibid.*, p. 95.
38. Roger C. Palms, "Great Churches of Today: First Presbyterian Church, Pittsburgh, Pennsylvania," *Decision* (June 1974), pp. 8, 9.
39. *Ibid.*, p. 9.
40. *Ibid.*

CHAPTER 22, SOUL-WINNING EVANGELISM

1. The Task Force on New Congregations, *Strategy for the Development of New Congregations* (New York: Board of National Missions of The United Presbyterian Church in the United States of America, 1967), p. 4.
2. Elmer L. Towns, *The Ten Largest Sunday Schools and What Makes Them Grow* (Grand Rapids, Michigan: Baker Book House, 1969), p. 118.
3. Harry Covert (ed.), *Faith Aflame*, vol. 1, no. 3 (March 1976), Lynchburg, Virginia: Thomas Road Baptist Church, p. 8.
4. Elmer Towns, *America's Fastest Growing Churches* (Nashville: Impact Books, 1973), p. 158.
5. Melvin Hodges, *A Guide to Church Planting* (Chicago: Moody Press, 1973), p. 58.
6. Paul Benjamin, *The Growing Congregation* (Lincoln, Illinois: Lincoln Christian College Press, 1972), p. 32.
7. *Ibid.*, pp. 66, 67.
8. Donald McGavran, "The Fifth Assembly and Evangelization," *Church Growth Bulletin*, vol. 12, no. 3 (January 1976), p. 500.
9. *Ibid.*
10. Towns, *America's Fastest*, p. 154.
11. Hollis L. Green, *Why Churches Die* (Minneapolis: Bethany Fellowship, 1972), p. 173.
12. *Ibid.*, p. 174.

CHAPTER 23, RESEARCH AND SCIENTIFIC ANALYSIS

1. Wagner, *Your Church Can Grow,* (Glendale, California: Regal Books, 1976), p. 28.
2. *Ibid.*
3. James F. Engel and H. Wilbert Norton, *What's Gone Wrong with the Harvest? A Communication Strategy for the Church and World Evangelism* (Grand Rapids, Michigan: Zondervan, 1975), p. 14.
4. *Ibid.*, p. 152.
5. C. Peter Wagner, *Frontiers of Missionary Strategy* (Chicago, Illinois: Moody Press, 1972), pp. 15, 16.
6. Wagner, *Your Church Can Grow*, pp. 136, 137.
7. Orlando Costas, *The Church and Its Mission: A Shattering Critique from the Third World* (Wheaton, Illinois: Tyndale House, 1974), pp. 128, 129.
8. Wendell Belew, *Churches and How They Grow* (Nashville: Broadman Press, 1971), p. 39.
9. Robert Schuller, *Your Church Has Real Possibilities!* (Glendale, California: Regal Books, 1974), p. 2.
10. Dan Baumann, *All Originality Makes a Dull Church* (Santa Ana, California: Vision House, 1976) p. 23.
11. *Ibid.*, p. 115.
12. McGavran, *Understanding Church Growth*, (Grand Rapids: Eerdmans, 1970) p. 162.
13. Foster H. Shannon, "Predicting Church Growth," *Church Growth: America*, March/April 1976, p. 4.
14. *Ibid.*

CHAPTER 24, PRAYER

1. Melvin L. Hodges, *A Guide to Church Planting* (Chicago: Moody Press, 1973), p. 65.
2. *Ibid.*, p. 68.
3. Gene A. Getz, *Sharpening the Focus of the Church* (Chicago: Moody Press, 1974), p. 64.
4. Hodges, *Guide*, pp. 36, 37.

5. Walter J. Hollenweger, *The Pentecostals* (Minneapolis: Augsburg, 1972), p. 29.
6. Donald C. Palmer, *Explosion of People Evangelism* (Chicago: Moody Press, 1974), p. 135.
7. Lee Lebsack, *10 at the Top: How 10 of America's Largest Assemblies of God Churches Grew* (Stowe, Ohio: New Hope Press, 1974), p. 94.
8. Joseph N. Ellis, "The Church That Faith and Works Built," *Christian Life*, vol. 37, no. 6, October 1975, p. 34.
9. George Edgerly, "Survey of Pastors of 1974's Fast Growing Schools," mimeographed paper, Assemblies of God, Springfield, Missouri, n. d., p. 2.
10. Lebsack, *10 at the Top*, pp. 30-35.
11. Edward F. Murphy, *Spiritual Gifts and the Great Commission* (South Pasadena, California: Mandate Press, 1975), pp. 328, 329.

CHAPTER 25, BIBLE TEACHING AND EDIFICATION
1. Harold L. Fickett, *Hope for Your Church: Ten Principles of Church Growth* (Glendale, California: Regal Books, 1972), p. 11.
2. Hollis L. Green, *Why Churches Die* (Minneapolis: Bethany Fellowship, 1972), p. 55.
3. Elmer L. Towns, *America's Fastest Growing Churches* (Nashville: Impact Books, 1972), p. 183.
4. John R. Rice, *Why Our Churches Do Not Win Souls* (Murfreesboro, Tennessee: Sword of the Lord Publishers, 1966), p. 67.
5. *Ibid.*, p. 41.
6. *Ibid.*, p. 53.
7. Gary Inrig, *Life in His Body* (Wheaton, Illinois: Harold Shaw Publishers, 1975), p. 44.
8. Rice, *Why Our Churches*, pp. 10, 11.
9. *Ibid.*, pp. 12, 13.
10. Gene A. Getz, *Sharpening the Focus of the Church* (Chicago: Moody Press, 1974), p. 22.
11. Melvin L. Hodges, *A Guide to Church Planting* (Chicago: Moody Press, 1973), p. 76.
12. *Ibid.*, p. 77.
13. Donald C. Palmer, *Explosion of People Evangelism* (Chicago: Moody Press, 1974), pp. 75, 76.
14. Michael P. Hamilton, *The Charismatic Movement* (Grand Rapids: William B. Eerdmans Publishing Co., 1975), pp. 36, 37.
15. Juan Carlos Ortiz, "Just Getting 'Fatter' Isn't Growth," *Eternity*, May 1975, pp. 16, 36.
16. Win Arn, Seminar in Church Growth, presented to Southern California-Arizona Grace Brethren Ministerium at Palm Springs, California, January 1976.
17. Donald A. McGavran, *Understanding Church Growth* (Grand Rapids: William B. Eerdmans Publishing Co., 1970), p. 15.
18. *Ibid.*

CHAPTER 26, THE HOLY SPIRIT
1. C. Peter Wagner, *Your Church Can Grow* (Glendale, California: Regal Books, 1976), p. 28.
2. Donald A. McGavran, *Understanding Church Growth* (Grand Rapids: William B. Eerdmans, 1970), pp. 164, 165.
3. *Ibid.*, p. 170.
4. Donald C. Palmer, *Explosion of People Evangelism* (Chicago: Moody Press, 1974), p. 168.
5. *Ibid.*, p. 134.
6. Michael P. Hamilton, *The Charismatic Movement* (Grand Rapids: William B. Eerdmans, 1975), p. 8.
7. Walter J. Hollenweger, *The Pentecostals* (Minneapolis: Augsburg, 1972), p. 33.
8. Hamilton, *The Charismatic Movement*, p. 39.
9. C. Peter Wagner, *Look Out! The Pentecostals Are Coming* (Carol Stream, Illinois: Creation House, 1973), p. 34.
10. Elmer L. Towns, *America's Fastest Growing Churches* (Nashville: Impact Books, 1972), p. 212.
11. *Ibid.*, p. 204.
12. Robert C. Girard, Brethren, *Hang Loose, or What's Happening to My Church?* (Grand Rapids: Zondervan, 1972), p. 29.
13. *Ibid.*, p. 73.

14. Harold R. Cook, *Historic Patterns of Church Growth: A Study of Five Churches* (Chicago: Moody Press, 1971), p. 105.

CHAPTER 27, LAY INVOLVEMENT AND SPIRITUAL GIFTS

1. C. Peter Wagner, *Your Church Can Grow* (Glendale, California: Regal Books, 1976), p. 69.
2. Win Arn, "Let My People Grow," *Eternity*, May 1975, p. 14.
3. *Ibid.*, p. 14.
4. Edward F. Murphy, *Spiritual Gifts and the Great Commission* (South Pasadena, California: Mandate Press, 1975), p. 188.
5. Hollis L. Green, *Why Churches Die* (Minneapolis: Bethany Fellowship, 1972), p. 42.
6. Kenneth O. Gangel, *Leadership for Church Education* (Chicago,: Moody Press, 1970), p. 325.
7. Paul Benjamin, *The Growing Congregation*, (Lincoln, Illinois: Lincoln Christian College Press, 1972), pp. 31, 32.
8. Donald C. Palmer, *Explosion of People Evangelism* (Chicago: Moody Press, 1974), p. 102.
9. *Ibid.*, p. 115.
10. *Ibid.*, pp. 122, 123.
11. Juan Carlos Ortiz, *Call to Discipleship* (Plainfield, New Jersey: Logos International, 1975), p. 26.
12. Elmer L. Towns, *The Ten Largest Sunday Schools and What Makes Them Grow* (Grand Rapids: Baker Book House, 1969), pp. 129, 130.
13. Elmer L. Towns, *America's Fastest Growing Churches* (Nashville: Impact Books, 1972), p. 130.

CHAPTER 28, AGGRESSIVE LEADERSHIP

1. C. Peter Wagner, *Your Church Can Grow* (Glendale, California: Regal Books, 1976), p. 57.
2. Dan Baumann, *All Originality Makes a Dull Church* (Santa Ana, California: Vision House, 1976), p. 35.
3. Harold R. Cook, *Historic Patterns of Church Growth: A Study of Five Churches* (Chicago: Moody Press, 1971), p. 106.
4. Elmer L. Towns, *America's Fastest Growing Churches* (Nashville: Impact Books, 1972), pp. 191, 192.
5. *Ibid.*, p. 184.
6. Robert H. Schuller, *Your Church Has Real Possibilities!* (Glendale, California: Regal Books, 1974), p. 49.
7. *Ibid.*, pp. 10, 11.
8. M. Wendell Belew, *Churches and How They Grow* (Nashville: Broadman Press, 1971), p. 40.
9. Juan Carlos Ortiz, *Call to Discipleship* (Plainfield, New Jersey: Logos International, 1975), p. 14.
10. Michael Green, *Evangelism in the Early Church* (Grand Rapids: William B. Eerdmans, 1970), p. 186.
11. Howard A. Snyder, *The Problem of Wineskins: Church Renewal in a Technological Age* (Downers Grove, Illinois: Inter-Varsity Press, 1975), p. 84.

CHAPTER 29, FAITH AND GOAL-SETTING

1. M. Wendell Belew, *Churches and How They Grow* (Nashville: Broadman Press, 1971), p. 45.
2. Robert H. Schuller, *Your Church Has Real Possibilities!* (Glendale, California: Regal Books, 1974), p. 5.
3. Elmer L. Towns, *Getting a Church Started in the Face of Insurmountable Odds with Limited Resources in Unlikely Circumstances* (Nashville: Impact Books, 1975), p. 203.
4. Elmer L. Towns, *America's Fastest Growing Churches* (Nashville: Impact Books, 1972), p. 203.
5. Elmer Towns, "Nation's Largest 1-Year Anniversary," *Christian Life*, vol. 37, no. 3 (July 1975), p. 40.
6. Harry Covert, ed., *Faith Aflame*, vol. 1, no. 3 (March 1976), p. 8.
7. *Ibid.*, p. 2.
8. Win Arn, "Faith-Goal Power," Christian Life, vol. 37, no. 9 (January 1976), p. 56.

9. Edward R. Dayton, *Tools for Time Management: Christian Perspectives on Managing Priorities* (Grand Rapids: Zondervan, 1974), p. 81.
10. *Ibid.*, p. 80.
11. Towns, *America's Fastest*, p. 212.
12. Henry Lord, "Seven Successful Churches of Southern California," Ph.D. dissertation, California Graduate School of Theology, 1975, p. 116.
13. *Ibid.*, p. 117.

CHAPTER 30, THE SUNDAY SCHOOL
1. Bernard Palmer, *Pattern for a Total Church* (Wheaton, Illinois: Victor Books, 1975), p. 41.
2. Dr. Harold L. Fickett, Jr., *Hope for Your Church* (Glendale, California: Regal Books, 1972), p. 142.
3. Elmer L. Towns, *America's Fastest Growing Churches* (Nashville: Impact Books, 1972), pp. 9, 10.
4. Arthur Flake, *Building a Standard Sunday School* (Nashville: Convention Press, 1922), p. 20.
5. Towns, *America's Fastest*, p. 10.
6. *Ibid.*, p. 8.
7. Jerry Falwell and Elmer Towns, *Church Aflame* (Nashville: Impact Books, 1971), p. 98.
8. Henry Lord, "Seven Successful Churches of Southern California," Ph. D. dissertation, California Graduate School of Theology, 1975, p. 55.
9. *Ibid.*, pp. 70, 71.
10. *Ibid.*, p. 114.
11. *Ibid.*
12. Walter J. Hollenweger, *The Pentecostals* (Minneapolis: Augsburg, 1972), p. 37.
13. *Ibid.*
14. Lee Lebsack, *10 at the Top: How 10 of America's Largest Assemblies of God Churches Grew* (Stowe, Ohio: New Hope Press, 1974), p. 115.
15. C. Peter Wagner, *Your Church Can Grow* (Glendale, California: Regal Books, 1976), pp. 97-104.
16. *Ibid.*, p. 104.

CHAPTER 31, SOCIAL ACTION
1. C. Peter Wagner, *Your Church Can Grow,* (Glendale, California: Regal Books, 1976), p. 149.
2. *Ibid.*
3. Elmer L. Towns, *America's Fastest Growing Churches* (Nashville: Impact Books, 1972), p. 175.
4. M. Wendell Belew, *Churches and How They Grow* (Nashville: Broadman Press, 1971), p. 56.
5. Dan Baumann, *All Originality Makes a Dull Church* (Santa Ana, California: Vision House, 1976), p. 67.
6. Towns, *America's Fastest*, p. 167.
7. Melvin Hodges, *A Guide to Church Planting* (Chicago: Moody Press, 1973), p. 88.

CHAPTER 32, THE BIBLICAL CHURCH IN THE MODERN AGE
1. Howard A. Snyder, *The Problem of Wineskins: Church Renewal in a Technological Age* (Downers Grove, Illinois: Inter-Varsity Press, 1975), p. 22.
2. *Ibid.*, pp. 23, 24.
3. Donald A. McGavran, *Understanding Church Growth* (Grand Rapids: William B. Eerdmans, 1970), p. 216.
4. *Ibid.*, pp. 218-227.
5. *Ibid.*, p. 218.
6. Snyder, *Wineskins*, p. 26.
7. *Ibid.*, pp. 27-33.
8. Edward E. Hindson, *Glory in the Church* (New York/Nashville: Thomas Nelson, 1975), p. 24.
9. Francis Schaeffer, *The Church at the End of the 20th Century* (Downers Grove, Illinois: Inter-Varsity Press, 1970), p. 13.

10. *Ibid.*, p. 13.
11. Snyder, *Wineskins*, p. 180.
12. *Ibid.*, p. 184.
13. Michael R. Tucker, *The Church That Dared to Change* (Wheaton, Illinois: Tyndale House, 1975), pp. 80-90.
14. George Edgerly, "Survey of Pastors of 1974's Fast Growing Schools," Springfield, Missouri: Assemblies of God, n.d., p. 3.
15. Snyder, *Wineskins*, pp. 21, 22.
16. Pat Means, "West Meets East: A Look at a Metaphysical Coup on the Campus," *Worldwide Challenge*, April 1976, pp. 12-14.
17. *Ibid.*, pp. 12-14.
18. Evelyn Christenson, *What Happens When Women Pray* (Wheaton, Illinois: Victor Books, 1975), p. 15.
19. Gary Inrig, *Life in His Body* (Wheaton, Illinois: Harold Shaw, 1975), pp. 10, 11.
20. James F. Engel and H. Wilbert Norton, *What's Gone Wrong with the Harvest? A Communication Strategy for the Church and World Evangelism* (Grand Rapids: Zondervan, 1975), p. 135.
21. *Ibid.*, p. 136.
22. Gene A. Getz, *Sharpening the Focus of the Church* (Chicago: Moody Press, 1974), pp. 15, 16.
23. *Ibid.*, p. 16.
24. *Ibid.*
25. Robert L. Saucy, *The Church in God's Program* (Chicago, Illinois: Moody Press, 1972), p. 58.
26. Inrig, *Life in His Body*, pp. 31, 32.
27. David L. Hocking, "What Is the Church?" Dissertation, California Graduate School of Theology, 1970, p. 19.
28. Snyder, *Wineskins*, p. 190.

CHAPTER 33, PICTURES OF THE CHURCH

1. Earl D. Radmacher, *The Nature of the Church* (Portland, Oregon: Western Baptist Press, 1972) p. 221.
2. Robert L. Saucy, *The Church in God's Program* (Chicago: Moody Press, 1972), p. 26.
3. Howard A. Snyder, *The Problem of Wineskins: Church Structure in a Technological Age* (Downers Grove, Illinois: Inter-Varsity Press, 1975), pp. 130, 131.
4. Saucy, *The Church in God's Program*, p. 32.
5. Gary Inrig, *Life in His Body* (Wheaton, Illinois: Harold Shaw, 1975), pp. 36, 37.
6. Radmacher, *The Nature of the Church*, p. 240.
7. Homer A. Kent, Jr., *Ephesians: The Glory of the Church* (Chicago: Moody Press, 1971), p. 48.
8. Lewis Sperry Chafer, *Systematic Theology*, vol. 4 (Dallas: Dallas Seminary Press, 1948), p. 64.
9. Saucy, *The Church in God's Program*, pp. 33, 34.
10. R. C. H. Lenski, *The Interpretation of St. Paul's First and Second Epistle to the Corinthians* (Columbus, Ohio: The Wartburg Press, 1946), p. 455.
11. James L. Boyer, *For a World Like Ours* (Winona Lake, Indiana: BMH Books, 1971), p. 50.
12. Gene A. Getz, *Sharpening the Focus of the Church* (Chicago: Moody Press, 1974), p. 61.
13. Radmacher, *The Nature of the Church*, p. 246.
14. Saucy, *The Church in God's Program*, p. 45.
15. *Ibid.*, p. 46.
16. Radmacher, *The Nature of the Church*, p. 289.
17. Donald A. McGavran, *Understanding Church Growth* (Grand Rapids: William B. Eerdmans, 1970), p. 41.
18. *Ibid.*, p. 15.
19. Saucy, *The Church in God's Program*, p. 52.
20. C. Peter Wagner, *Your Church Can Grow* (Glendale, California: Regal Books, 1976), p. 101.
21. *Ibid.*, p. 103.
22. *Ibid.*, pp. 104, 105.
23. *Ibid.*

24. Lawrence O. Richards, *A New Face for the Church* (Grand Rapids: Zondervan, 1970), p. 30.
25. Dan Baumann, "Vibrant: Circles of Concern," a pamphlet for visitors (Whittier, California: Whittier Area Baptist Fellowship, n.d.).
26. "Pastoral Care 'Ministers' Shepherd Members," *Community Church News*, vol. 6, no. 16 (April 18, 1976), p. 2.
27. Saucy, *The Church in God's Program*, p. 53.
28. A. R. Tippett, *Church Growth and the Word of God* (Grand Rapids: William B. Eerdmans, 1970), p. 13.
29. *Ibid.*
30. Orlando E. Costas, *The Church and Its Mission: A Shattering Critique from the Third World* (Wheaton, Illinois: Tyndale House, 1974), pp. 93, 94.
31. Edward F. Murphy, *Spiritual Gifts and the Great Commission* (South Pasadena, California: Mandate Press, 1975), pp. 286, 287. (Editor's note: Murphy ignores the singular pastor/messenger of the seven churches in Revelation 2 and 3.)
32. *Ibid.*, p. 303.
33. C. I. Schofield, ed., Schofield Reference Bible, pp. 1136, 1137.
34. Chafer, *Systematic Theology*, pp. 60, 61.
35. W. E. Vine, *An Expository Dictionary of New Testament Words* (London, England: Oliphants, Ltd., 1940), p. 232.
36. Saucy, *The Church in God's Program*, p. 55.
37. Donald Grey Barnhouse, "Chain of Glory," *Eternity*, vol. 2, no. 17 (March 1958), quoted in Radmacher, *The Nature of the Church*, pp. 294, 295.
38. Hollis L. Green, *Why Churches Die* (Minneapolis: Bethany Fellowship, 1972), p. 198.
39. *Ibid.*, pp. 201, 202.
40. Vine, *Expository Dictionary*, p. 9.
41. James F. Engel and H. Wilbert Norton, *What's Gone Wrong with the Harvest? A Communication Strategy for the Church and World Evangelism* (Grand Rapids: Zondervan, 1975), p. 141.
42. McGavran, *Understanding*, pp. 302, 303.
43. Richards, *A New Face*, pp. 21, 22, 29.
44. Inrig, *Life in His Body*, p. 24.

CHAPTER 34, THE PURPOSE OF THE CHURCH

1. George W. Peters, *Saturation Evangelism* (Grand Rapids, Mich.: Zondervan Publishing House, 1970), p. 25.
2. Homer A. Kent, Jr., *Ephesians: The Glory of the Church* (Chicago: Moody Press, 1971), p. 75.
3. Donald J. MacNair, *The Birth, Care, and Feeding of a Local Church* (Washington, D.C.: Canon Press, 1973), p. 6.
4. *Ibid.*
5. Ray Stedman, *Body Life* (Glendale, California: Regal Books, 1972), p. 14.

CHAPTER 35, THE PRIORITY OF THE CHURCH

1. Donald A. McGavran, *Understanding Church Growth* (Grand Rapids: William B. Eerdmans, 1970), p. 51.
2. Robert E. Coleman, *The Master Plan of Evangelism* (Old Tappan, New Jersey: Revell, 1963), pp. 30-33.
3. *Ibid.*, pp. 33, 34.
4. Elmer L. Towns, *America's Fastest Growing Churches* (Nashville: Impact Books, 1972), p. 8.
5. George W. Peters, *Saturation Evangelism* (Grand Rapids: Zondervan, 1970), pp. 32, 33.
6. *Ibid.*, pp. 34, 35.
7. Virgil Gerber, *God's Way to Keep a Church Going and Growing* (Glendale, California: Regal Books, 1973), p. 14.
8. Hollis L. Green *Why Churches Die* (Minneapolis: Bethany Fellowship, 1972), pp. 20, 21.
9. W. E. Vine, *An Expository Dictionary of New Testament Words* (London, England: Oliphants, Ltd., 1940), p. 156.
10. Melvin L. Hodges, *A Guide To Church Planting* (Chicago: Moody Press, 1973), p. 59.

11. C. Peter Wagner, *Your Church Can Grow* (Glendale, California: Regal Books, 1976), pp. 81-83.
12. Peters, *Saturation Evangelism*, p. 41.
13. Charles Kingsley and George Delamarter, *Go!* quoted in Peters, *Saturation Evangelism*, pp. 28, 29.
14. Peters, *Saturation Evangelism*, p. 29.
15. Paul Benjamin, *The Growing Congregation* (Lincoln, Illinois: Lincoln Christian College Press, 1972), p. 15.
16. Francis A. Schaeffer, *The Church at the End of the 20th Century* (Downers Grove, Illinois; Inter-Varisty Press, 1970), pp. 61, 62.
17. Earl D. Radmacher, *The Nature of the Church* (Portland, Oregon: Western Baptist Press, 1972), p. 267.
18. Michael Green, *Evangelism in the Early Church* (Grand Rapids: William B. Eerdmans, 1970), p. 204.
19. *Ibid.*, p. 208.
20. David L. Hocking, "The New Testament Church," class notes presented at the California Graduate School of Theology, Glendale, California, 1973.
21. Michael Green, *Evangelism*, p. 194.
22. C. Peter Wagner, *Look Out! The Pentecostals Are Coming* (Carol Stream, Illinois: Creation House, 1973), pp. 44, 45.
23. *Ibid.*, p. 49.
24. Michael Green, *Evangelism*, p. 48.
25. *Ibid.*, p. 13.
26. Gerhard Kittel, ed., *Theological Dictionary of the New Testament* (Grand Rapids: William B. Eerdmans, 1965), vol. 3, pp. 687, 688.
27. *Ibid.*, p. 703.
28. Dr. Bill Bright, "Today Is Harvest Time," Address presented at First Baptist Church of Downey, California, 19 May 1976.
29. Peters, *Saturation Evangelism*, p. 19.
30. Michael Green, *Evangelism*, p. 70.
31. Gene A Getz, *Sharpening the Focus of the Church* (Chicago: Moody Press, 1974), pp. 34, 35.
32. Hollis Green, *Why Churches Die*, p. 59.
33. McGavran, *Understanding*, p. 40.
34. Wayne Weld and Donald McGavran, *Principles of Church Growth* (South Pasadena, California: William Carey Library, 1974), pp. 1-22, 1-23.
35. Peters, *Saturation Evangelism*, p. 20.
36. Em Griffin, "Winning Over—How to Change People's Minds," *Eternity*, May 1976, p. 28.
37. *Ibid.*
38. Wagner, *Your Church Can Grow*, p. 140.
39. A. R. Tippett, *Church Growth and the Word of God* (Grand Rapids: William B. Eerdmans, 1970), p. 61.
40. *Ibid.*, p. 63.
41. F. F. Bruce, gen. ed., *The New International Commentary on the New Testament* (Grand Rapids: William B. Eerdmans, 1954), "The Book of Acts" by F. F. Bruce, p. 77.
42. Gary Inrig, *Life in His Body* (Wheaton: Illinois: Harold Shaw, 1975), p. 133.
43. David L. Hocking, "What Is the Church?" Dissertation, California Graduate School of Theology, 1970, p. 65.
44. Weld and McGavran, *Principles*, pp. 7-15, 7-16.
45. Craig Skinner, *The Teaching Ministry of the Pulpit* (Grand Rapids: Baker Book House, 1973), p. 84.
46. Edward F. Murphy, "Guidelines for Urban Church Planting," *Crucial Issues in Missions Tomorrow* (Chicago; Moody Press, 1972), ed. Donald McGavran, p. 250.
47. Juan Carlos Ortiz, *Call to Discipleship* (Plainfield, New Jersey: Logos International, 1975), p. 67.
48. John MacArthur, *The Church: The Body of Christ* (Grand Rapids: Zondervan, 1973), p. 168.
49. Skinner, *Teaching Ministry*, pp. 76, 77.
50. Robert L. Saucy, The Church in God's Program (Chicago: Moody Press, 1972), p. 217.

51. Gene Getz, *The Measure of a Church* (Glendale, California: Regal Books, 1975), p. 149.
52. Tippett, *Church Growth*, p. 64.
53. Gerber, *God's Way*, p. 14.
54. *Ibid.*, p. 18.
55. Weld and McGavran, *Principles*, pp. 7-18.
56. Donald McGavran, "Renewal and Church Growth," *Church Growth Bulletin*, vol. 2, no. 1 (September 1965), p. 94.
57. Gerber, *God's Way*, p. 18.
58. *Ibid.*, p. 17.
59. Orlando E. Costas, *The Church and Its Mission: A Shattering Critique from the Third World* (Wheaton, Illinois: Tyndale House, 1974), p. 120.
60. Donald C. Palmer, *Explosion of People Evangelism* (Chicago: Moody Press, 1974), p. 127.
61. Paul Davis, "Church Multiplication," *Church Growth Bulletin*, vol. 2, no. 1 (September 1965), p. 92.
62. James F. Engel and H. Wilbert Norton, *What's Gone Wrong with the Harvest? A Communication Strategy for the Church and World Evangelism* (Grand Rapids: Zondervan, 1975), pp. 143, 144.
63. M. Wendell Belew, *Churches and How They Grow* (Nashville: Broadman Press, 1971), p. 39.
64. Charles L. Chaney, "A New Day for New Churches," *Church Growth Bulletin*, vol. 2, no. 1 (September 1965), pp. 512-516.
65. *Ibid.*, p. 515.
66. *Ibid.*, p. 516.
67. McGavran, *Understanding*, p. 354.
68. *Ibid.*
69. Weld and McGavran, *Principles*, p. 15-2.
70. McGavran, *Understanding*, p. 356.
71. Michael Green, *Evangelism*, p. 261.
72. Roland Allen, *The Spontaneous Expansion of the Church* (Grand Rapids: William B. Eerdmans, 1962), p. 143.
73. Murphy, "Guidelines," p. 257.
74. Palmer, *Explosion*, p. 126.
75. McGavran, *Understanding*, p. 359.
76. Howard A. Snyder, *The Problem of Wineskins: Church Structure in a Technological Age* (Downers Grove, Illinois: Inter Varsity Press, 1975), p. 140.
77. *Ibids.*, pp. 140-142.
78. Elmer Towns, *The Successful Sunday School and Teachers Guidebook* (Carol Stream, Illinois: Creation House, 1976), p. 199.

CHAPTER 38, THE SUNDAY SCHOOL'S FIGHT FOR LIFE

1. All figures, unless otherwise noted, are taken from various editions of *The Yearbook of American and Canadian Churches* (Nashville: Abingdon), ed. Constant Jacquet.
2. The Seventh Day Adventists have consistently averaged 3-5 percent annual growth in their Sabbath schools. Last year they grew from 428,251 to 477,208 (11 percent). Since 1971 SDA Sabbath enrollment has grown from 369,212 (29 percent).
3. George Gallup, "The Unchurched American," *Church Growth: America*, March/April 1979, p. 9.
4. A study by Warren Hartman, *A Study of the Church School in the United Methodist Church* (Nashville: Board of Education, 1972), indicated that "capable and well-trained teachers" were seen as the major factor which contributed to growing Church schools by pastors and regional executives.
5. Lawrence Richards, *A Theology of Christian Education* (Grand Rapids: Zondervan, 1975), p. 56.
6. Reginald M. McDonough, *The Minister of Education as a Growth Agent* (Nashville: Convention Press, 1978), p. 9.
7. Kenneth Van Wyk, "Educate for Church Growth," *Church Growth: America*, March/April 1978, p. 8.

8. Letty M. Russell, *Christian Education and Mission* (Philadelphia: Westminster Press, 1967), p. 38.
9. H. W. Bryne, *Christian Education for the Local Church* (Grand Rapids: Zondervan, 1963), p. 24.
10. Hartman, "Study," p. 20.
11. D. Campbell Wyckoff, *Theory and Design of Christian Education* (Philadelphia: Westminster Press, 1961), p. 22.

CHAPTER 40, WHAT IS A MATURE CHURCH?
1. Alfred Kuen, *I Will Build My Church* (Chicago: Moody Press, 1971), p. 51.
2. Robert Saucy, *The Church in God's Program* (Chicago: Moody Press, 1972), p. 17.
3. Kuen, *I Will Build My Church*, p. 51.

CHAPTER 44, DISCOVERING GROWTH POSSIBILITIES
1. Charles L. Chaney and Ron S. Lewis, *Design for Church Growth* (Nashville: Broadman, 1977).
2. A. V. Washburn, *Outreach for the Unreached* (Nashville: Convention Press, 1960).
3. From the Revised Standard Version of the Bible, copyrighted 1946, 1952, © 1971, 1973. Subsequent quotations are marked RSV.
4. Charles Jefferson, *The Building of a Church* (New York: The Macmillan Co., 1910).
5. John T. Sisemore, *The Ministry of Visitation* (Nashville: Broadman, 1954).

BIBLIOGRAPHY

BOOKS

Allen, Roland. *Missionary Methods: St. Paul's or Ours?* Grand Rapids: William B. Eerdmans, 1962.

Anderson, Andy. *Where Action Is.* Nashville: Broadman Press, 1976.

Anderson, Gerald H., et al. *Mission Trends No. 2: Evangelization.* New York: Paulist Press and Grand Rapids: William B. Eerdmans, 1975.

Baumann, Dan. *All Originality Makes a Dull Church.* Santa Ana, California: Vision House, 1976.

Beebe, Paul. *All About the Bus Ministry.* Murfreesboro, Tennessee: Sword of the Lord, 1970.

Belew, M. Wendell. *Churches and How They Grow.* Nashville: Broadman Press, 1971.

Benjamin, Paul. *The Growing Congregation.* Lincoln, Illinois: Lincoln Christian College Press, 1972.

Boyer, James L. *For a World Like Ours: Studies in 1 Corinthians.* Winona Lake, Indiana: BMH Books, 1971.

Braun, Neil. *Laity Mobilized.* Grand Rapids: William B. Eerdmans, 1971.

Bruce, F. F., gen. ed. *The New International Commentary on the New Testament.* Grand Rapids: William B. Eerdmans, 1954.

Carroll, Jackson W. *Small Churches Are Beautiful.* New York: Harper and Row, 1977.

Chafer, Lewis Sperry. *Systematic Theology, Vol. 4: Ecclesiology—Eschatology.* Dallas: Dallas Seminary Press, 1948.

Chaney, Charles L. and Lewis, Ron S. *Design for Growth.* Nashville: Broadman Press, 1977.

Christenson, Evelyn. *What Happens When Women Pray.* Wheaton, Illinois: Victor Books, 1975.

Coleman, Robert E. *The Master Plan of Evangelism.* Old Tappan, New Jersey: Fleming H. Revell, 1963.

Conn, Harvie M., ed. *Theological Perspectives on Church Growth.* Dulk Foundation, 1976.

Cook, Harold R. *Historic Patterns of Church Growth: A Study of Five Churches.* Chicago: Moody Press, 1971.

Costas, Orlando E. *The Church and Its Mission: A Shattering Critique from the Third World.* Wheaton, Illinois: Tyndale House, 1974.

Dayton, Edward R. *Tools for Time Management: Christian Perspectives on Managing Priorities.* Grand Rapids: Zondervan, 1974.

Dollar, Truman. *How to Carry Out God's Stewardship Plan.* Nashville: Thomas Nelson, 1974.

DuBose, Francis M. *How Churches Grow in an Urban World.* Nashville: Broadman Press, 1978.

Edge, Findley. *The Greening of the Church.* Waco, Texas: Word Books, 1971.

Engel, James F. and Norton, H. Wilbert. *What's Gone Wrong with the Harvest? A Communication Strategy for the Church and World Evangelism.* Grand Rapids: Zondervan, 1975.

Engstrom, Ted. W. *What in the World Is God Doing?* Waco, Texas: Word Books, 1978.

Entzminger, Louis. *How to Organize and Administer a Great Sunday School.* Fort Worth, Texas: The Manning Company, 1949.

Falwell, Jerry and Towns, Elmer. *Capturing a Town for Christ.* Old Tappan, New Jersey: Revell, 1973.

——. *Church Aflame.* Nashville: Impact Books, 1971.

Fickett, Harold L. *Hope for Your Church: Ten Principles of Church Growth.* Glendale, California: Regal Books, 1972.

Fife, Eric S. and Glasser, Arthur F. *Missions in Crisis: Rethinking Missionary Strategy.* Downers Grove, Illinois: Inter-Varsity Press, 1961.

Flake, Arthur. *Building a Standard Sunday School.* Nashville: Convention Press, 1922.

Fry, John R. *The Trivialization of the United Presbyterian Church.* New York: Harper and Row, 1975.

Gangel, Kenneth O. *Competent to Lead.* Chicago: Moody Press, 1974.

Gentry, Gardiner. *Bus Them In.* Nashville: Church Growth Publications, 1973.

Gerber, Virgil. *God's Way to Keep a Church Going and Growing.* Glendale, California: Regal Books, 1973.

Getz, Gene A. *Sharpening the Focus of the Church.* Chicago: Moody Press, 1974.

——. *The Measure of a Church.* Glendale, California: Regal Books, 1975.

Girard, Robert C. *Brethren, Hang Loose, or What's Happening to My Church?* Grand Rapids: Zondervan, 1972.

Green, Hollis, L. *Why Churches Die.* Minneapolis: Bethany Fellowship, 1972.

Green, Michael. *Evangelism in the Early Church.* Grand Rapids: William B. Eerdmans, 1970.

Hamilton, Michael P. *The Charismatic Movement.* Grand Rapids: William B. Eerdmans, 1975.

Hefley, James C. *Unique Evangelical Churches.* Waco, Texas: Word Books, 1977.

Hindson, Edward E. *Glory in the Church.* New York/Nashville: Thomas Nelson, 1975.

Hocking, David L. *World's Greatest Church.* Long Beach, California: Sounds of Grace, 1976.

Hodges, Melvin L. *Growing Young Churches.* Chicago: Moody Press, 1920.

——. *A Guide to Church Planting.* Chicago: Moody Press, 1973.

Hollenweger, Walter J. *The Pentecostals.* Minneapolis: Augsburg, 1972.

Hyles, Jack. *How to Rear Children.* Hammond, Indiana: Hyles-Anderson, 1972.

——. *They Hyles Church Manual.* Murfreesboro: Tennessee: Sword of the Lord, 1968.

——. *The Hyles Sunday School Manual.* Murfreesboro, Tennessee: Sword of the Lord, 1969.

——. *Let's Baptize More Converts.* Murfreesboro, Tennessee: Sword of the Lord, 1967.

——. *Let's Build an Evangelistic Church.* Murfreesboro, Tennessee: Sword of the Lord, 1962.

——. *Let's Go Soul Winning.* Murfreesboro, Tennessee: Sword of the Lord, 1962.

Inrig, Gary. *Life in His Body.* Wheaton, Illinois: Harold Shaw, 1975.

Jacquet, Constant H., Jr., ed. *Yearbook of American and Canadian Churches.* Nashville: Abingdon Press, 1972-1975.

Kelly, Dean M. *Why Conservative Churches Are Growing: A Study in Sociology of Religion.* New York: Harper and Row, 1972.

Kent, Homer A., Jr. *Ephesians: The Glory of the Church.* Chicago: Moody Press, 1971.

Kittel, Gerhard, ed. *Theological Dictionary of the New Testament, Volume 3.* Grand Rapids: William B. Eerdmans, 1965.

Lawson, E. LeRoy and Yamamori, Tetsunao. *Church Growth: Everybody's Business.* Cincinnati: New Life Books, n.d.

Lebsack, Lee. *10 at the Top: How 10 of America's Largest Assemblies of God Churches Grew.* Stowe, Ohio: New Hope Press, 1974.

Lenski, R. C. H. *The Interpretation of St. Paul's First and Second Epistle to the Corinthians.* Columbus, Ohio: The Wartburg Press, 1946.

Lindsell, Harold. *The Battle for the Bible.* Grand Rapids: Zondervan, 1976.

John MacArthur. *The Church: The Body of Christ.* Grand Rapids: Zondervan, 1973.

McGavran, Donald A. *The Bridges of God.* New York: Friendship Press, 1955.

——, ed. *Church Growth and Christian Mission.* New York: Harper and Row, 1965.

——, ed. *Eye of the Storm: The Great Debate in Mission.* Waco, Texas: Word Books, 1972.

——. "The Great Commission," *Reaching All.* Sydney, Australia: World Wide Publications, 1974.

——. *How Churches Grow.* London, England: World Dominion Press, 1959.

——. *Ten Steps for Church Growth.* San Francisco: Harper and Row, 1977.

——. *Understanding Church Growth.* Grand Rapids: William B. Eerdmans, 1970.

McGavran, Donald A. and Arn, Winfield C. *How to Grow a Church.* Glendale, California: Regal Books: 1974.

Mackie, Steven G., ed. *Can Churches Be Compared?* Geneva: World Council of Churches, 1970.

Malone, Tom. *The Sunday School Reaching Multitudes.* Murfreesboro, Tennessee: Sword of the Lord, 1973.

MacNair, Donald J. *The Birth, Care, and Feeding of a Local Church.* Washington, D. C.: Canon Press, 1973.

McQuilken, J. Robertson. *Measuring the Church Growth Movement.* Chicago: Moody Press, 1973.

Murphy, Edward F. *Spiritual Gifts and the Great Commission.* South Pasadena, California: Mandate Press, 1975.

Ogilivie, Lloyd John. *Drumbeat of Love.* Waco, Texas: Word Books, 1976.

Olson, Gilbert W. *Church Growth in Sierra Leone.* Grand Rapids: William B. Eerdmans, 1969.

Ortiz, Juan Carlos. *Call to Discipleship.* Plainfield, New Jersey: Logos, 1975.

Packer J. I. *Fundamentalism and the Word of God.* Grand Rapids: William B. Eerdmans, 1958.

Palmer, Bernard. *Pattern for a Total Church.* Wheaton, Illinois: Victor Books, 1975.

Palmer, Donald C. *Explosion of People Evangelism.* Chicago: Moody Press, 1974.

Peters, George W. *Saturation Evangelism.* Grand Rapids: Zondervan, 1970.

Radmacher, Earl D. *The Nature of the Church.* Portland, Oregon: Western Baptist Press, 1972.

Richards, Lawrence O. *A New Face for the Church.* Grand Rapids: Zondervan, 1970.

——. *Three Churches in Renewal.* Grand Rapids: Zondervan.

Rice, John R. *Come Out or Stay In.* Nashville: Thomas Nelson, 1974.

——. *God's Work: How to Do It.* Murfreesboro, Tennessee: Sword of the Lord, 1971.

——. *Why Our Churches Do Not Win Souls.* Murfreesboro, Tennessee: Sword of the Lord, 1966.

Russell, C. Allyn. *Voices of American Fundamentalism.* Philadelphia: The Westminster Press, 1976.

Saucy, Robert L. *The Church in God's Program.* Chicago: Moody Press, 1972.

Schaeffer, Francis A. *The Church at the End of the 20th Century.* Downers Grove, Illinois: Inter-Varsity Press, 1970.

Schuller, Robert H. *Your Church Has Real Possibilities.* Glendale, California: Regal Books, 1974.

Short, Roy H. *United Methodism in Theory and Practice.* Nashville: Abingdon Press, 1974.

Skinner, Craig. *The Teaching Ministry of the Pulpit: Its History, Theology, Psychology, and Practice for Today.* Grand Rapids: Baker Book House, 1973.

Smith, Ebbie C. *A Manual for Church Growth Surveys.* South Pasadena: William Carey Library 1976.

Smith, Robert W. *When All Else Fails . . . Read the Directions.* Waco, Texas: Word Books, 1974.

Snyder, Howard A. *The Problem of Wineskins: Church Structure in a Technological Age.* Downers Grove, Illinois: Inter-Varsity Press, 1975.

Stedman, Ray C. *Body Life.* Glendale, California: Regal Books, 1972.

Stevick, Daniel B. *Beyond Fundamentalism.* Richmond, Virginia: John Knox Press, 1964.

Stuart, George W., ed. *A Guide to Sunday School Enlargement.* Nashville: Convention Press, 1968.

Task Force on New Congregations. *Strategy for the Development of New Congregations.* New York: Board of National Missions of the United Presbyterian Church in the U.S.A. 1967.

Tippett, Alan R. *Church Growth and the Word of God.* Grand Rapids: William B. Eerdmans, 1970.

Towns, Elmer. *America's Fastest Growing Churches.* Nashville: Impact Books, 1972.

——. *Getting a Church Started in the Face of Insurmountable Odds with Limited Resources in Unlikely Circumstances.* Nashville: Impact Books, 1975.

——. *Great Soul-Winning Churches.* Murfreesboro, Tennessee: Sword of the Lord, 1973.

——. *Is the Day of the Denomination Dead?* Nashville: Thomas Nelson, 1973.

——. *The Successful Sunday School and Teachers Guidebook.* Carol Stream, Illinois: Creation House, 1976.

——. *The Ten Largest Sunday Schools.* Grand Rapids: Baker Book House, 1969.

——. *World's Largest Sunday Schools.* Nashville: Thomas Nelson, 1974.

Tucker, Michael R. *The Church That Dared to Change.* Wheaton, Illinois: Tyndale House, 1975.

Vine, W. E. *An Expository Dictionary of New Testament Words.* London, England: Oliphants, Ltd., 1940.

Vineyard, Jim and Falwell, Jerry. *Winning Souls through Buses.* Nashville: Impact Books, 1972.

Wagner, C. Peter, ed. *Church/Mission Tensions Today.* Chicago: Moody Press, 1972.

——. *Frontiers of Missionary Strategy.* Chicago: Moody Press, 1972.

——. *Look Out! The Pentecostals Are Coming.* Carol Stream, Illinois: Creation House, 1973.

——. *Our Kind of People.* Atlanta: John Knox Press, 1979.

——. *Stop the World I Want to Get On.* Glendale, California: Regal Books, 1974.

——. *Your Church Can Grow.* Glendale, California: Regal Books, 1976.

Wakatama, Pius. *Independence for the Third World Church.* Downers Grove, Illinois: Inter-Varsity Press, 1976.

Weld, Wayne and McGavran, Donald. *Principles of Church Growth.* South Pasadena, California: William Carey Library, 1974.

Werning, Waldo J. *Vision and Strategy for Church Growth.* Chicago: Moody Press, 1977.

Winter, Ralph. *The 25 Unbelievable Years: 1945-1969.* South Pasadena, California: William Carey Library, 1970.

——. *The Grounds for a New Thrust in World Missions*. South Pasadena, California: William Carey Library, 1977.

Yamamori, Tesunao, and Tabor, Charles R., eds. *Christopaganism or Indigenous Christianity?* South Pasadena, California: William Carey Library, 1975.

PERIODICALS

Abedego, Benjamin A. "Church Growth in East Java." *International Review of Missions*, vol. LXII, no. 251 (July 1974), p. 342.

Arn, Win. "Faith-Goal Power." *Christian Life*, vol. 37, no. 9 (January 1976), pp. 56-58.

——. "Let My People Grow!" *Eternity*, vol. 26, no. 5 (May 1975), pp. 14, 58.

——. "Mass Evangelism: The Bottom Line." *Church Growth: America*, vol. 4, no. 1 (January/February 1978), p. 5.

Arn, W., Wagner, C. P., and Montgomery, James H. "Church Growth Flourishes in America." *Church Growth Bulletin*, vol. XIII, no. 2 (November 1976), p. 68.

"Babies and the 'New Birth' Rate." *Christianity Today*, vol. X, no. 15 (29 April 1966).

Barrett, David B. "AD 2000; 350 Million Christians in Africa." *International Review of Missions*, vol. LIX, no. 233 (January 1970), pp. 49, 50.

Baumann, Dan. "Body Life—Two Sets of Shoulders." *Eternity*, vol. 28, no. 3 (March 1977), pp. 80, 83, 84.

——. "Dallas Group Covers Three Vital Areas." *Eternity*, vol. 28, no. 2 (February 1977), pp. 57, 58.

Branner, John K. "McGavran Speaks on Roland Allen." *Evangelical Missions Quarterly*, vol. 8, no. 3 (Spring 1972), pp. 170-173.

Chaney, Charles L. "A New Day for New Churches." *Church Growth Bulletin*, vol. 12, no. 4 (March 1976), pp. 512-516.

"Churches Leaving the SBC." *The Sword of the Lord*, vol. XL, no. 26 (28 June 1974), p. 4.

Coote, Robert T. "Church Growth: Shot in the Arm for Evangelism." *Evangelical Newsletter*, vol. 2, no. 14 (9 May 1975), p. 4.

Coote, Robert T., ed. "Is 'Church Growth' on the Right Track?" *Eternity*, vol. 26, no. 6 (June 1975).

Copeland, E. Luther. "Church Growth in Acts." *Missiology*, vol. 4, no. 1 (January 1976).

Covert, Harry, ed. *Faith Aflame*, vol. 1, no. 3 (March 1976), p. 8.

Davis, Paul. "Church Multiplication." *Church Growth Bulletin*, vol. 2, no. 1 (September 1965), pp. 92, 93.

Ellis, Joseph N. "The Church That Faith and Works Built." *Christian Life*, vol. 37, no. 6 (October 1975), pp. 34, 36.

"Equipping the Saints for the Work of the Ministry." *Church Growth: America*, vol. 4, no. 1 (September/October 1978), p. 6.

Gill, Donald H. "Apostle of Church Growth." *World Vision*, vol. 12, no. 7 (September 1968), p. 11.

Glasser, Arthur F. "Timeless Lessons from the Western Missionary Penetration of China." *Missiology*, vol. 1, no. 4 (October 1973), pp. 448-462.

Gouzee, C. "Counterpoint." *International Review of Missions*, vol. LVII, no. 227 (July 1968).

Greenway, Roger S. "Mission to an Urban World." *Church Growth Bulletin*, vol. XII, no. 1 (September 1975), p. 475.

Griffin, Em. "Winning Over—How to Change People's Minds." *Eternity* (May 1976), pp. 28-34.

Horn, Pat. "The New Middle-Class Fundamentalism." *Psychology Today*, vol. 10, no. 4 (September 1976), pp. 24, 25.

Jones, Medford. "American Church Growth Explored." *Church Growth Bulletin*, vol. VI, no. 2 (November 1969), pp. 30, 31.

Jones, Rufus. "Where 'Church Growth' Fails the Gospel." Eternity, vol. 26, no. 6 (June 1975).

Kessler, J. B. A., Jr. "Hindrances to Church Growth." *International Review of Missions*, vol. LVII, no. 227 (July 1968).

Kraft, Charles H. "North America's Cultural Challenge." *Christianity Today*, vol. XVII, no. 8 (19 January 1973), p. 6.

"Local Church Reaches 100,000 Membership." *Global Church Growth Bulletin*, vol. XVII, no. 1 (January/February 1980), p. 9.

Martin, Marie-Louise. "Does the World Need Fantastically Growing Churches?" *International Review of Missions,* vol. LVII, no. 227.

Marsden, George. "Defining Fundamentalism." *Christian Scholar's Review,* vol. 1, no. 2 (Winter 1971), p. 141.

McGavran, Donald A. "Barred Populations and Missionaries." *International Review of Missions,* January 1975.

——. "Church Growth Strategy Continued." *International Review of Missions,* vol. LVII, no. 227.

——. "The Coming Era of Advance." *Church Growth Bulletin,* vol. 12, no. 5 (May 1976), pp. 523, 524.

——. "The Dividends We Seek." *Christianity Today,* vol. XVII, no. 8 (19 January 1973).

——. "Focus and Reflection." *In Focus,* vol. 1, no. 10 (Waco; Word, Inc., 1976), p. 2.

——. "Loose the Churches. Let Them Go!" *Missiology,* vol. 1, no. 2 (April 1973), p. 91.

——. "New Methods for a New Age in Missions." *International Review of Missions* (October 1955), p. 402.

——. "Renewal and Church Growth." *Church Growth Bulletin,* vol. 2, no. 1 (September 1965), pp. 93-95.

——. "Why Neglect Gospel-Ready Masses?" *Christianity Today,* vol. 10, no. 5 (29 April 1966), pp. 17-19.

——. "World Evangelization at the Mercy of Church-Mission 'Disease.' " *Evangelical Missions Quarterly,* vol. 13, no. 4 (October 1977).

——. "Wrong Strategy: The Real Crisis in Missions." *International Review of Missions,* vol. LIV, no. 216 (October 1965), p. 458.

McQuilken, J. Robertson. "Making the Numbers Count." *Moody Monthly,* vol. 77, no. 10 (June 1977), p. 30.

McWilliams, Carey. "The New Fundamentalists." *The Nation,* vol. 222, no. 22 (5 June 1976), pp. 686, 687.

Means, Pat. "West Meets East: A Look at a Metaphysical Coup on the Campus." *Worldwide Challenge,* (April 1976), pp. 12-15.

Montgomery, James H. "Resistant, Neglected or Turned Off?" *Church Growth Bul. n,* vol. XV, no. 1 (September 1978), p. 217.

Ortiz, Juan Carlos. "Just Getting 'Fatter' Isn't Growth." *Eternity,* (May 1975), pp. 15, 16, 27, 28, 30, 33, 36.

Palms, Roger C. "Great Churches of Today: First Presbyterian Church, Pittsburgh, Pennsylvania." *Decision,* (June 1974), pp. 8, 9.

——. "Great Churches of Today: Peninsula Bible Church." *Decision,* vol. 16, no. 5 (May 1975), pp. 8, 9, 14.

Plowman, Edward E. "Is the United Methodist Church Coming Back to Life?" *Christianity Today,* (30 January 1976), pp. 29-31.

Schuller, Robert. "Pastoral Care 'Ministers' Shepherd Members." *Community Church News,* vol. 6, no. 16 (18 April 1976), p. 2.

Seamands, John T. "What McGavran's Church Growth Thesis Means." *Evangelical Missions Quarterly,* vol. 3, no. 1 (Fall 1966).

Shannon, Foster H. "Predicting Church Growth." *Church Growth: America* (March/April 1976), pp. 4-6.

Stedman, Ray. "Church Life." *United Evangelical Action,* vol. 26, no. 2 (April 1967), pp. 27-29.

——. "Should a Pastor Play Pope? *Moody Monthly,* vol. 76, no. 11 (July/August 1976) pp. 41, 42, 44.

——. "The Church In a Modern World." *Moody Monthly,* vol. 66, no. 6 (February 1966), pp. 70-72, 75, 76.

Stetz, John. "Biggest Little Church in the World," *Church Growth Bulletin,* vol. XIII, no. 1 (September 1976), pp. 78-83.

"Study on Membership Loss Conservation." *Daily Christian Advocate* (7 April 1972), pp. 81-83.

"Sunday School Growth Plan Urges Enrollment of 8.5 Million By '85." *Baptist and Reflector* (9 January 1980), p. 3.

"Sunday School Newsmakers of the Decade." *Christian Life,* vol. 39, no. 6 (October 1977), p. 33.

Thomas, Wilburn T. "Growth: A Test of the Church's Faithfulness." *International Review of Missions,* vol. LII, no. 208 (October 1963).

Tippett, A. R. "A Not-So-Secular City." *Christianity Today*, vol. XVII, no. 8 (19 January 1973), pp. 8, 9.

——. "Anthropology and Post-Colonial Mission Through a China Filter." *Missiology*, vol. 1, no. 4 (October 1973), p. 470.

——. "Conversion As a Dynamic Process in Christian Mission." *Missiology*, vol. 5, no. 2 (April 1977).

Towns, Elmer." America's Largest Sunday Schools Are Growing." *Christian Life*, vol. 32, no. 4 (August 1970), p. 16.

——. "Nation's Largest 1-Year Anniversary." *Christian Life*, vol. 37, no. 3 (July 1975), p. 40.

——. "The Small, Personal Sunday School." *Christian Life*, vol. 32, no. 12 (April 1971), p. 48.

——. "Sunday Schools in the U.S. — The 100 Largest '76." *Christian Life*, vol. 38, no. 6 (October 1976), pp. 38-45.

——. "Trends Among Fundamentalists." *Christian Today*, vol. 17, no. 20 (6 July 1973), p. 12.

——. "Trends in Sunday School Growth." *Christian Life*, vol. 38, no. 6 (October 1976), p. 37.

——. "What Do We Communicate?" *Christian Life*, vol. 30, no. 12 (May 1969), p. 33.

"2,000th Church Constitutes in North Central States." *Baptist and Reflector*, 26 December 1979.

Wagner, C. Peter. "American Church Growth Update 1974." *United Evangelical Action*, vol. 33, no. 1 (Spring 1974), pp. 15, 16, 36-40.

——. "Bibliography: My Top Twenty Books on Church Growth," *Action* (Spring 1975).

——. " 'Church Growth': More Than A Man, A Magazine, A School, A Book." *Christianity Today*, vol. 18, no. 5 (7 December 1973), pp. 11-14.

——. "How to Diagnose the Health of Your Church." *Christianity Today*, vol. XVII, no. 8 (19 January 1973), pp. 24, 25.

——. "Mission and Hope: Some Implications of the Theology of Jurgen Moltmann." *Missiology*, vol. 2, no. 4 (19 October 1974) pp. 462-473.

——. "What Makes Churches Grow?" *Eternity*, vol. 25, no. 6 (June 1974), p. 17.

——. "World Baptists: 3,176,954 New Members and Standing Still!" *Church Growth Bulletin*, vol. X, no. 4 (March 1974), pp. 401-403.

"Why Pentecostal Churches Are Growing Faster in Italy." *Evangelical Missions Quarterly*, vol. 8, no. 3 (Spring 1972).

Wills, Garry. "What Religious Revival?" *Psychology Today*, vol. 11, no. 11 (April 1978), p. 80.

Winter, Ralph. "Existing Churches: Ends or Means? *Christianity Today*, vol. XVII, no. 8 (19 January 1973).

——. "Quality or Quantity?" *Evangelical Missions Quarterly*, vol. 8, no. 4 (Summer 1972).

——. "The New Missions and the Mission of the Church." *International Review of Missions*, vol. LX, no. 237 (January 1971).

"World's Largest Church Grows Through House Units." *Church Growth Bulletin*, vol. XIV, no. 5 (May 1978), p. 195.

BIBLES
Scofield, C. I. *The Holy Bible*. New York: Oxford University Press, 1909.

CLASS NOTES
Hocking, David L. "The New Testament Church." Class notes at the California Graduate School of Theology, Glendale, California, February 1973.

DISSERTATIONS AND PAPERS
Hocking, David L. "Biblical Pattern of Church Government." Long Beach, California, n.d.

——. "What Is the Church?" D. Min. dissertation, California Graduate School of Theology, 1970.

Lord, Henry. "Seven Successful Churches of Southern California." Ph.D. dissertation, California Graduate School of Theology, 1975.

ORAL ADDRESSES AND SEMINARS
Aldrich, Joe. "Listen to the Music." Address at the Southern California-Arizona Ministerium of Grace Brethren Churches.

Arn, Win. "Seminar in Church Growth." Seminar at Southern California-Arizona Grace Brethren Ministerium, Palm Springs, January 1976.

Bright, Bill. "Today Is Harvest Time." Address at the First Baptist Church of Downey, California, 19 May 1976.

Hocking, David L. "The Marks of a Growing Church." Address at a Home Missions Pastor's Workship, Wooster, Ohio, 22 October 1975.

MacArthur, John. "The Marks of a Successful Church." Address at the Southern California-Arizona Ministerium, Long Beach, California, 13 October 1975.

SERMONS

McCuistion, Walter. "The Magna Carta of Christian Education." A message delivered to the people of Peninsula Bible Church, Palo Alto, California, 22 February 1976. Text: Deuteronomy 6:4-9.

SPECIAL PUBLICATIONS

Anderson, E. S. "ACTION: A Reach Out Enrollment Plan for Sunday School." Nashville: Sunday School Board of the Southern Baptist Convention, 1975.

Edgerly, George. "Survey of Pastors of 1974's Fast Growing Schools." Springfield, Missouri: Assemblies of God, n.d., mimeograph.

General Assembly Mission Council. "Report on Church Membership Trends in Response to the 186th General Assembly (1974) of the United Presbyterian Church in the U.S.A. New York: The United Presbyterian Church, 1976.

Wilson, Raymond H. "Journal of the Southern California-Arizona Annual Conference of the United Methodist Church, One Hundred and Twenty-Fifth Annual Session, Redlands, California, 13-17 June 1975." Los Angeles: The United Methodist Center, 1975.

UNPUBLISHED SOURCES

Grove, Ralph M. First Presbyterian Church, Downey California. Interview, 16 March 1976.

Leath, Paul B. Truett Memorial Baptist Church, Long Beach, California. Interview, 2 March 1976.

Thompson, Don. United Methodist Church, Paramount, California. Interview, 16 March 1976.

VanStennis, Dale. Southern California-Arizona District Christ's Ambassadors, Assemblies of God, Long Beach, California. Interview, 31 March 1976.

Williams, Rodman. Melodyland School of Theology, Anaheim, California. Interview, 3 March 1976.

ACKNOWLEDGMENTS

The authors would like to thank all of the denominational executives and the independent congregations without denominational affiliation who have made lists and other information available for use in this book. Also, thanks is given to those churches which provided information but for reasons of size were not listed.

A trend may have been set in the process of researching the statistical material that went into the making of *The Complete Book of Church Growth*, since many black church congregations were most cooperative in providing information to us. As a result, a number of black churches are listed in a comprehensive American church profile for the first time in any publication. We welcome hearing from other black church groups.

We, the authors, are concerned to be accurate and reliable in our research. We invite any corrections, updates, or additional information which might come to readers' attention. This may be helpful in subsequent editions of this book or in other future publications concerning church growth. Send such information to Dr. Elmer Towns, Box 1111, Lynchburg, VA 24506.

The authors wish to credit the following publications and publishers for information that has proven essential in the writing of this book. Special thanks is given to Gospel Light/Regal for its cooperation in allowing us to quote extensively from a number of its books, and to *Christian Life* magazine and *Church Growth: America*, the publication of the Institute of American Church Growth, Pasadena, CA.

Material quoted from YOUR CHURCH CAN GROW (Regal book) by C. Peter Wagner, © Copyright 1976 by Peter Wagner, published by Gospel Light Publications, Glendale, CA 91209, is used by permission.

Material quoted from HOW TO GROW A CHURCH (Regal book) by Donald A. McGavran and Win Arn, © Copyright 1974, published by Gospel Light Publications, Glendale, CA 91209, is used by permission.

Material quoted from GOD'S WAY TO KEEP A CHURCH GOING AND GROWING (Regal book) by Virgil Gerber, © Copyright 1973, published by Gospel Light Publications, Glendale, CA 91209, is used by permission.

Material quoted from BODY LIFE (Regal book) by Ray Stedman, © Copyright 1972, published by Gospel Light Publications, Glendale, CA 91209, is used by permission.

Material quoted from THE MEASURE OF A CHURCH (Regal book) by Gene A. Getz, © Copyright 1975, published by Gospel Light Publications, Glendale, CA 91209, is used by permission.

Material quoted from A GUIDE TO CHURCH PLANTING by Hodges, Copyright 1973, published by Moody Press, Moody Bible Institute of Chicago, is used by permission.

Material quoted from EXPLOSION OF PEOPLE EVANGELISM by Palmer, Copyright 1974, published by Moody Press, Moody Bible Institute of Chicago, is used by permission.

Material quoted from SHARPENING THE FOCUS OF THE CHURCH by Getz, Copyright 1974, published by Moody Press, Moody Bible Institute of Chicago, is used by permission.

Material quoted from THE CHURCH IN GOD'S PROGRAM by Robert Saucy, Copyright 1972, published by Moody Press, Moody Bible Institute of Chicago, is used by permission.

Material quoted from A GUIDE TO SUNDAY SCHOOL ENLARGEMENT by George Stuart (Nashville: Broadman Press, 1968), p. 36, all rights reserved, is used by permission.

Material quoted from WHERE ACTION IS by Andy Anderson (Nashville: Broadman Press, 1976), pp. 37, 68, all rights reserved, is used by permission.

Material quoted from ACTION: A REACH OUT ENROLLMENT PLAN FOR SUNDAY SCHOOL by Andy Anderson (Nashville: The Sunday School Board of the Southern Baptist Convention, 1975), pp. 6, 7, all rights reserved, is used by permission.

Material quoted from BUILDING A STANDARD SUNDAY SCHOOL by Arthur Flake (Nashville: The Sunday School Board of the Southern Baptist Convention, 1934), p. 19, all rights reserved, is used by permission.

Material quoted from SATURATION EVANGELISM by George W. Peters, Copyright © 1970 by Zondervan Publishing House, is used by permission.

Material quoted from UNDERSTANDING CHURCH GROWTH by Donald McGavran, published by William B. Eerdmans Publishing Company, is used by permission.

Material quoted from AMERICA'S FASTEST GROWING CHURCHES by Elmer Towns, Copyright © 1972 by Impact Books, a division of the Benson Company, Nashville, all rights reserved, is printed by permission.

Material quoted from LOOK OUT! THE PENTECOSTALS ARE COMING by C. Peter Wagner, Copyright © 1973, published by Creation House Publishers, Carol Stream, IL 60187, is used by permission.

Material quoted from WHY CHURCHES DIE by Hollis Green, published and copyrighted 1972, Bethany Fellowship, Inc., Minneapolis, MN 55438, is used by permission.

Material quoted from WHEN ALL ELSE FAILS . . . READ THE DIRECTIONS by Robert W. Smith, Copyright © 1974, published by Word Books, Waco, TX 78703, is used by permission.

Material quoted from CALL TO DISCIPLESHIP By Juan Carlos Ortiz with Jamie Buckingham, Copyright © 1975 by Logos International, Inc., published by Logos International Fellowship, Inc., Plainfield, NJ 07060, is used by permission.

PRAY with us that this volume may contribute to further church growth.

— *THE AUTHORS*

71927